NEW JERSEY

SETTING THE PACE FOR THE TWENTY-FIRST CENTURY

II NEW JERSEY: SETTING THE PACE FOR THE TWENTY-FIRST CENTURY

NEW JERSEY

SETTING THE PACE FOR THE TWENTY-FIRST CENTURY

By Stephen Barr

CHERBO PUBLISHING GROUP, INC.
ENCINO, CALIFORNIA

DEDICATION

To Rebecca and Sam

ACKNOWLEDGMENTS

The publisher would like to thank Lisa Kruse and Karen Wolfe of the New Jersey Commerce and Economic Growth Commission, Rebecca Perkins of the HealthCare Institute of New Jersey, and Douglas Tarr of the Edison National Historic Site for their assistance in the making of this publication.

Cherbo Publishing Group, Inc.

President **Jack C. Cherbo**
Executive Vice President **Elaine Hoffman**
Editorial Director **Christina M. Beausang**
Manuscript Editor **Maria A. Collis**
Profiles Editor **J. Kelley Younger**
Essay Editor **Tina G. Rubin**
Contributing Editors **Gina K. Thornburg, Margaret Martin, and Linda Chase**

Senior Designer **Mika Toyoura**
Contributing Designer **Mary Cameron**
Photo Editor **Catherine A. Vandenberg**
Sales Administrator **Joan K. Baker**
Production Coordinator **Ellen T. Kettenbeil**
Administrative Coordinator **Jahnna Biddle**
Eastern Regional Manager **Marcia Weiss**
Eastern Development Director **Glen Edwards**

Cherbo Publishing Group, Inc., Encino, CA 91316
© 1998 by Cherbo Publishing Group, Inc.
All rights reserved. Published 1998
Printed in the United States of America

Visit CPG's Web site at www.cherbo-publishing.com

Library of Congress Cataloging-in-Publication Data
Barr, Stephen
  A pictorial guide highlighting 20th-century New Jersey lifestyle and economic history. 1. New Jersey. 2. Economic history—New Jersey. 3. Lifestyle—New Jersey.
    98-71768
    ISBN 1-882933-22-2

Disclaimer The information in this publication is the most recent available and has been carefully researched to ensure accuracy. Cherbo Publishing Group, Inc., cannot and does not guarantee either the correctness of all the information furnished it or the complete absence of errors and omissions.

INDEX OF CORPORATE AND ORGANIZATIONAL PROFILES

THE FOLLOWING COMPANIES AND ORGANIZATIONS HAVE MADE
A VALUABLE COMMITMENT TO THE QUALITY OF THIS PUBLICATION.
CHERBO PUBLISHING GROUP GRATEFULLY ACKNOWLEDGES THEIR PARTICIPATION
IN *NEW JERSEY: SETTING THE PACE FOR THE TWENTY-FIRST CENTURY*.

BASF Corporation, 280

Bederson & Company, 194

Benjamin Moore & Co., 290

Bergen Community College, 312

Bristol-Myers Squibb Company, 168

Brookdale Community College, 310

College of New Jersey, The, 320

Columbia Savings Bank, 252

Continental Airlines, 96

Cooper Health System, The, 142

Covance, 178

CUH2A, Inc., 216

Cytec Industries Inc., 278

Deloitte & Touche LLP, 196

Dendrite International, Inc., 72

DiCara Malasits and Rosenberg Architects, 212

DRS Technologies, Inc., 75

Dun & Bradstreet Corporation, The, 254

Edwards and Kelcey, Inc., 218

Elizabethtown Water Company, 108

Fairleigh Dickinson University, 316

First Union National Bank, 258

Franciscan Health System of New Jersey, 144

Gibbons, Del Deo, Dolan, Griffinger & Vecchione, 206

Giordano, Halleran & Ciesla, P.C., 204

GPU Energy, 100

Greenbaum, Rowe, Smith, Ravin, Davis & Himmel LLP, 208

Hackensack University Medical Center, 130

Hoffmann–La Roche, 171

Howmedica, 172

Ingersoll-Rand Company, 282

Insignia/ESG, 238

Interpool, Inc., 94

J. H. Cohn LLP, 198

J. M. Huber Corporation, 286

Johnson & Johnson, 176

KPMG Peat Marwick LLP, 192

Langston Corporation, 284

Lucent Technologies, 70

Merrill Lynch & Co., Inc., 256

Michael Graves, Architect, 214

Montclair State University, 318

Neuman Distributors, Inc., 162

Newark Group, The, 288

New Jersey–American Water Company, 104

New Jersey Business & Industry Association, 294

New Jersey City University, 326

New Jersey Devils, 344

New Jersey Institute of Technology, 331

New Jersey Nets, The, 346

New Jersey Technology Council, 76

Novartis Pharmaceuticals Corporation, 174

NUI Corporation, 110

Nycomed Amersham Imaging, 164

Pharmacia & Upjohn, 180

PricewaterhouseCoopers, 200

Public Service Electric & Gas Company, 102

Reckitt & Colman Inc., 292

Ricoh Corporation, 272

Rider University, 330

Robert Wood Johnson University Hospital, 134

Rowan University, 322

Rutgers, The State University of New Jersey, 328

Saint Barnabas Health Care System, 138

St. Peter's University Hospital & Health System, 126

Sarnoff Corporation, 74

Seton Hall University, 314

Silver Line Building Products, 276

Sitar Company • Oncor International, 236

Solaris Health System, 140

South Jersey Industries, Inc., 106

Stevens Institute of Technology, 329

Summit Bank, 248

Thomas Edison State College, 332

Toys "R" Us, 224

United National Bank, 250

United Parcel Service, 222

University of Medicine and Dentistry of New Jersey, 324

Valley Health System, 146

West Jersey Health System, 148

CONTENTS

INTRODUCTION x

PART ONE SOMETHING FOR EVERYONE 2

CHAPTER ONE A Many-Colored Quilt 4
New Jersey's prime location and natural riches have nurtured a dazzling array of thinkers, doers, and builders.

CHAPTER TWO From Revolution to Rock 'n' Roll 10
One of the original thirteen colonies, New Jersey has been a wellspring of excitement and invention since before the country was born.

CHAPTER THREE Beauty in Contrast 14
Despite its reputation as a hive of industry, nearly half of the Garden State remains pristine wilderness.

CHAPTER FOUR A Garden of Many Delights 20
From the Meadowlands Sports Complex to Atlantic City's casinos; from pine-scented mountain air to salty beach breezes, New Jersey has it all.

PART TWO A PLACE FOR EVERYTHING 26

CHAPTER FIVE The Northwest 28
Almost untouched by industry, the Skylands' endless pine forests and glacial lakes invite hiking, biking, and year-round water sports.

CHAPTER SIX Western Counties 32
A land of history, rolling hills, and luxurious estates, this region also is the chosen home of many Fortune 500 companies.

CHAPTER SEVEN New York Metropolitan Region 36
Gleaming offices, stylish suburbs, some of the best shopping in the country, and more await just across the border from Manhattan.

CHAPTER EIGHT Central New Jersey 42
This region could be called the "brain center," with prestigious educational institutions and computer and biotechnology firms turning out innovations every day.

CHAPTER NINE Delaware River Region 48
A train hop from Philadelphia, this area boasts a rich harvest of tomatoes, cranberries, and other produce. The mysterious Pine Barrens are here, too.

CHAPTER TEN Jersey Shore 52
From Sandy Hook to Atlantic City, from Wildwood to Cape May; each shore community offers a unique collection of seaside delights.

PART THREE CREATING THE FUTURE 58

CHAPTER ELEVEN High Technology 60
TECHNOLOGY AND TELECOMMUNICATIONS
Big hitters such as AT&T and Sony have made New Jersey famous, but the state supports the growth of smaller companies as well.

CHAPTER TWELVE Getting the Word Out 78
MEDIA
Cable is bringing more local news to television, radio has a new "voice," and every media source has gone on-line. But New Jerseyans still value the printed word.

© Frank Saragnese/FPG International

CHAPTER THIRTEEN POWER AND MOTION   **84**
TRANSPORTATION AND UTILITIES
New Jersey operates some of the busiest ports in the country, and the state's mass transit system is stellar.

CHAPTER FOURTEEN PEOPLE HELPING PEOPLE   **112**
HEALTH CARE
New Jersey's competitive health care environment results in state-of-the-art medical facilities and top-quality medicine.

CHAPTER FIFTEEN MODERN MEDICINE'S TOOLS   **150**
PHARMACEUTICALS, MEDICAL DEVICES, AND BIOTECHNOLOGY
The "Medicine Chest of the World" is also home to some of the world's leading biotechnology venture capitalists.

CHAPTER SIXTEEN SERVICES THAT SUCCEED   **182**
PROFESSIONALS, BUSINESS SERVICES, AND RETAIL
New Jersey attorneys, accountants, architects, marketing professionals, retail, and outsourcing services are among the best—and busiest—in the country.

CHAPTER SEVENTEEN LOCATION, LOCATION, LOCATION   **226**
REAL ESTATE, DEVELOPMENT, AND CONSTRUCTION
New Jersey's superb geographic location, excellent infrastructure, and innovative builders draw more new companies than ever. And there's still plenty of room for families.

CHAPTER EIGHTEEN MONEY MATTERS   **240**
FINANCIAL SERVICES AND INSURANCE
New Jersey's newly formed Department of Banking and Insurance promises better service and more choices in this fast-changing industry.

CHAPTER NINETEEN MADE IN NEW JERSEY   **260**
MANUFACTURING, DISTRIBUTION, AND WAREHOUSING
New Jersey innovators keep the state at the forefront of manufacturing, and keep New Jersey products in homes around the world.

CHAPTER TWENTY LEADING IN EDUCATION   **296**
EDUCATION
Most New Jersey high school graduates stay in-state for college. With the wealth and variety of learning opportunities here, it's no wonder.

CHAPTER TWENTY-ONE NEW JERSEY FUN   **334**
ARTS, RECREATION, HOSPITALITY, SPORTS, AND TOURISM
From the Skylands to Atlantic City, New Jersey offers its 170 million annual visitors a smorgasbord of travel delights.

FIRSTS AND INNOVATIONS FROM THE GARDEN STATE   **348**

HISTORICAL HIGHLIGHTS   **350**

PART FOUR TOWARD THE NEW MILLENNIUM   **352**
New Jersey's twentieth-century advancements and its future possibilities are highlighted in essays from state leaders in important business sectors.

BIBLIOGRAPHY   **369**

GENERAL INDEX   **372**

ESSAY CONTRIBUTORS

The following individuals have made important contributions to this publication by writing essays on their particular sectors of business in New Jersey.

CHEMICALS — Page 354
Peter Oakley, Chairman and Chief Executive Officer, BASF Corporation

EDUCATION — Page 356
Dr. Lawrence A. Nespoli, President, New Jersey Council of County Colleges

HIGHER EDUCATION — Page 358
Dr. J. Barton Luedeke, President, Rider University

PHARMACEUTICALS — Page 360
Patrick J. Zenner, President and Chief Executive Officer, Hoffmann–La Roche Inc.

PROFESSIONALS — Page 362
Edward P. Bond, C.P.A., C.F.E., C.I.R.A., Bederson & Company LLP

SHIPPING — Page 364
Martin Tuchman, Chairman and Chief Executive Officer, Interpool, Inc.

TECHNOLOGY — Page 366
Saul K. Fenster, President, New Jersey Institute of Technology

Drumthwacket
Princeton, New Jersey
08540

Dear Reader:

I am delighted to introduce you to *New Jersey: Setting the Pace for the Twenty-first Century*.

New Jersey takes great pride in its rich heritage and in the many pioneering accomplishments of its citizens throughout centuries of tremendous change and challenge. From its prominent role in the Revolutionary War and the Industrial Revolution to today's energetic leadership in business and industry, the Garden State has remained at the forefront of American history. Our state is the source of many important scientific and industrial innovations that have transformed the way we live. New Jersey is where Thomas Edison invented the light bulb, the phonograph, and the motion picture camera; where Selman Waksman developed streptomycin, the antibiotic used to combat tuberculosis; and where Campbell's canned its first condensed soup.

As you turn the pages and learn about the inventiveness and entrepreneurial spirit that have helped shape the Garden State's history and vibrant economy, you will see why we will be striding into the new millennium with great confidence and excitement. Discover for yourself why we tell anyone looking for a bright future, "New Jersey & You . . . Perfect Together."

Sincerely yours,

Christine Todd Whitman

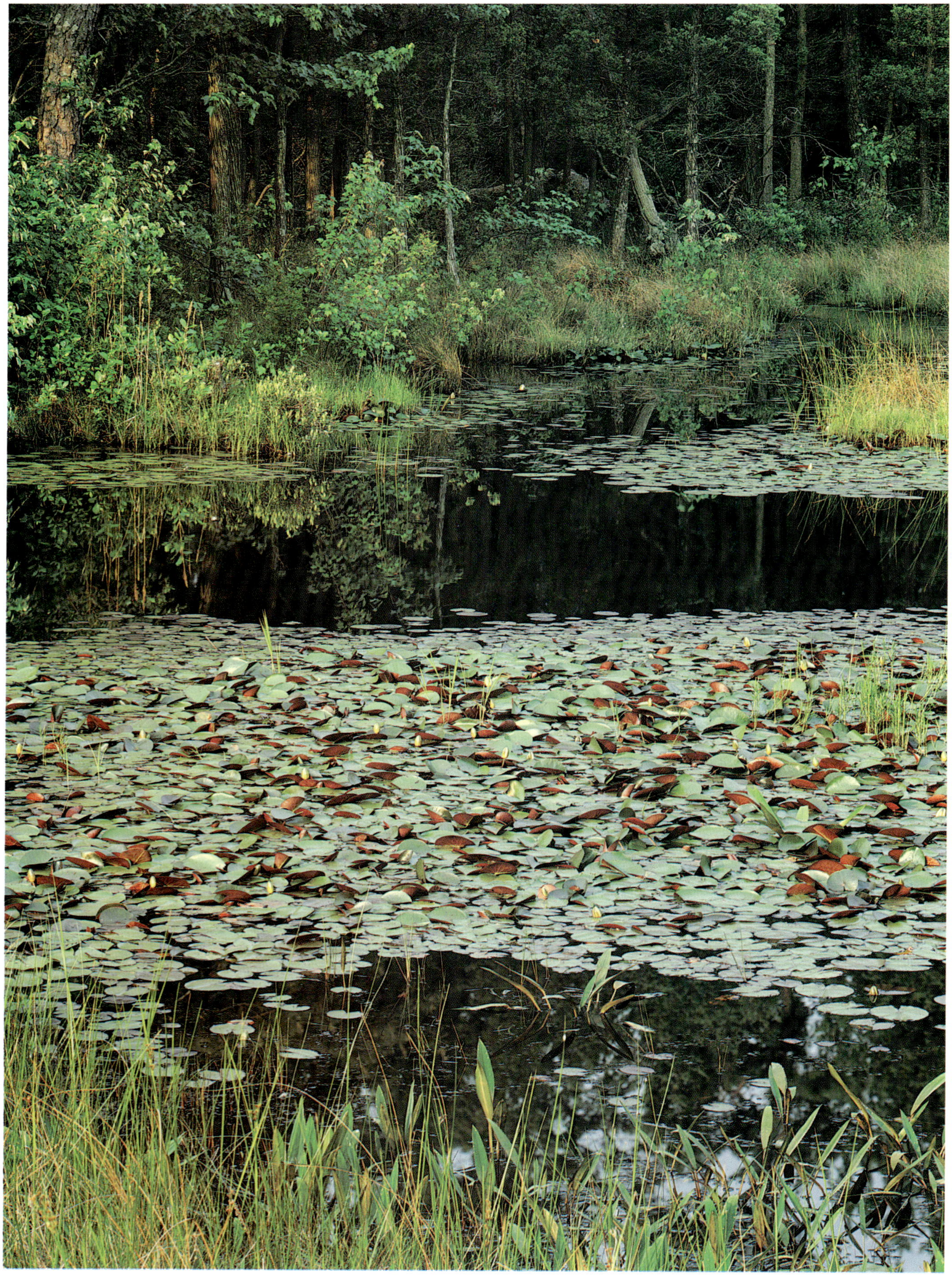

INTRODUCTION

Since the first Native Americans walked through its tranquil forests, New Jersey's beauty and mystery have been a source of wonder. New Jersey today is a collage of quaint towns that preserve the spirit of colonial times; seashore resorts that are among the nation's oldest summertime playgrounds; stretches of rolling hill country where crystal lakes and clear-running trout streams are bountiful; and the mysterious Pine Barrens, an ecological wonderland of over two thousand square miles of dense, dark forests and murky bogs as unblemished as any spot in the United States.

Complementing New Jersey's scenic beauty is a rich legacy of innovation and economic vitality. New Jerseyans played significant roles in the development of steamboats, railroads, submarines, and the telegraph. Here Thomas Edison patented the light bulb, the phonograph, and the motion picture camera; the scientists at Bell Laboratories made the world's first transistor; and Albert Einstein unraveled the mysteries of the universe.

Once the nation's industrial leader, New Jersey is in the midst of transition from heavy manufacturing to a broader mix of technology-based production and service industries. New Jersey has the largest concentration of global pharmaceutical companies anywhere, and can justifiably claim the title "Medicine Chest of the World." With the eighth-largest economy in the United States and four million highly skilled, highly educated workers, the state's diverse economic base offers both vigor and stability. New Jersey's citizens boast the second-highest per capita income in the nation.

New Jersey has tried to keep the secret of its enviable lifestyle. But it is hard to overlook success. As the new millennium approaches, new technologies and services put the Garden State in the public eye practically every day. And that's only fitting for a state that has and always will be a pacesetter.

The Wading River begins as one of many streams winding through Wharton State Forest on its way to the Atlantic Ocean. Here, the river's west branch offers wordless testimony to the grace and secrecy of the Pine Barrens. © David Muench/Tony Stone Images

SOMETHING FOR EVERYONE

PART ONE

From the rolling hills and deep forests of Sussex County at the northernmost point to the quaint Victorian mansions of Cape May County at the southernmost point, every corner of New Jersey has a distinctive character. What makes one fall in love with New Jersey is the special bond that forms between people and their hometowns. Each New Jersey town has just over thirteen thousand residents on average and can claim its own school system, shopping district, and recreational activities. The unique traits of each lend themselves to a close-knit community and a passionate sense of place.

At the dawn of the twenty-first century, New Jersey is a leading center for health care, pharmaceuticals, and high technology. It has the nation's third-largest concentration of corporate and division headquarters and the highest concentration of office space. Twenty-three of the Fortune 500 call the Garden State home.

There is no prototypical spot where you could say, "This is New Jersey." Rather, New Jersey is a vibrant quilt of people and geography, each piece invigorating the whole.

Footprints are the only evidence of visitors to this lonely stretch of dunes in Island Beach State Park. © Bob Krist

INTRODUCTION 3

A MANY-COLORED QUILT

4   SOMETHING FOR EVERYONE

CHAPTER ONE

WHEN NEW JERSEY WAS FOUNDED AS AN ENGLISH COLONY IN 1664 IT HAD A SMALL NATIVE AMERICAN POPULATION OF ABOUT SIX THOUSAND LENNI LENAPE. FROM COLONIAL TIMES ON, THE STATE DREW A VARIED MIX OF SETTLERS AND BECAME HOME TO WAVES OF BRITISH, DUTCH, FRENCH, IRISH, POLISH, ITALIAN, AND GERMAN IMMIGRANTS. AS A RESULT, THE PEOPLE OF NEW JERSEY MIRROR THE NATION.

The ninth-largest state in population, New Jersey passed the eight-million mark for the first time in 1997. Like much of the Northeast region of the United States, the state's population growth slowed in the 1990s, to about half the national growth rate. Of New Jersey's twenty-one counties, the five most densely populated—Bergen, Essex, Hudson, Passaic, and Union—are nestled in the northeastern portion of the state, while the five most sparsely populated—Cape May, Cumberland, Salem, Sussex, and Warren—are spread across the northwestern portion of the state and the south.

Historically, New Jersey has been a major gateway for immigrants from other countries. And thanks to the ongoing influx of immigrants, largely from Eastern Europe and Asia, New Jersey's total population is expected to increase another 1.6 million people by the year 2025. With the most diverse foreign-born population in the nation, the state enjoys a rich cultural mixture of ethnic, racial, and national groups. This diversity can be found at ethnic festivals among the Portuguese in the Ironbound section of Newark, the Cubans in Hudson County, and the Indians in Edison.

What all New Jerseyans share is a commitment to education, a clean environment, and safe communities. The state spends more per pupil than any other state to educate its 1.3 million public school students—about $9,967 on average. And educational achievement is consistently close to the top in national norms. New Jersey high schools offer more college-level courses than any other state, and the state's fifty-five schools of higher education include Princeton University, an Ivy League institution, and Rutgers University, one of the nation's top state universities. Both were founded in colonial times and are among the country's oldest colleges.

OPPOSITE: *A member of the Powhatan tribe, one of over fifty North and South American tribes represented at the American Indian Arts Festival on the Rankokus Reservation in Westampton.* © Kelly/Mooney. ABOVE: *Portugal Day, part of Newark's annual Ironbound celebration.* © Carol Kitman

A MANY-COLORED QUILT 5

New Jersey's high population density and its concentration of industry are two factors that make environmental protection of paramount concern. For several decades now, strict control over auto emissions, sewage treatment, water supply, and household and industrial waste disposal have put the state at the forefront nationally. And the benefits are evident. In 1995 the state recorded only one hour of unhealthy levels of carbon monoxide compared to 864 hours in 1975. Beach closings due to unhealthy water dropped from a peak of 803 in 1988 to just four in 1995. And as a major recipient of clean-up money from the federal Superfund, New Jersey's industrial sites are "greener" than at any time in recent history.

Like most of the nation, New Jersey saw its crime rate decline year after year in the late 1990s. But the Garden State became even safer than many other states.

Members of a Sikh temple attend services in Glen Rock. New Jerseyans practice many faiths. While 85 percent are registered Christians, the state ranks second nationally in its percentage of Hindu, Jewish, and Muslim residents. © Carol Kitman

New Jersey's largest cities experienced decreases that were three times the national average and twice the regional average. At the same time, the state legislature enacted major new crime policies, including mandatory minimum sentences for repeat offenders and those using firearms, longer sentences for offenses such as drug sales, and a boot camp for juvenile offenders. New Jersey is also the home of Megan's Law, which calls for community notification if repeat sex offenders live in your town. A similar federal law was based on the one passed in New Jersey.

6 SOMETHING FOR EVERYONE

ABOVE: *More than forty ethnic festivals take place in New Jersey each year, from the Caribbean Dance Party in Somerset and Saint Ann's Italian Festival in Hoboken to Oktoberfest on Point Pleasant Beach. Shown here is a performer in Spanish dress at the New Jersey Ethnic Festival in Liberty State Park. © Kelly/Mooney.* BELOW: *The Ralston General Store in Morris County stands in mute tribute to the people who lived and worked in New Jersey in the early part of the twentieth century. © Scott Barrow*

ABOVE: *Preparing to re-enact a Revolutionary War skirmish in South Jersey.* © Carol Kitman. BELOW LEFT: *Children from Newark and Portugal join Harlem's Batoto Yetu African dance troupe in a performance for the New Jersey Performing Arts Center's first annual World Festival.* Courtesy, Batoto Yetu and the New Jersey Performing Arts Center. BELOW RIGHT: *Teenagers mug for the camera during a day of fun on one of New Jersey's many beaches.* © Scott Barrow. OPPOSITE: *The Festival of India in Middlesex County.* © Kelly/Mooney

8 SOMETHING FOR EVERYONE

A MANY-COLORED QUILT 9

FROM REVOLUTION
TO ROCK 'N' ROLL

10 SOMETHING FOR EVERYONE

CHAPTER TWO

One of the thirteen original colonies, New Jersey earned its nickname, "The Garden State," in pre-Revolutionary War times. America's first stagecoach line crossed the state, linking New York and Philadelphia, and New Jersey farmers prospered by supplying goods and products to those two growing cities. In his oft-quoted observation, Benjamin Franklin referred to the state as "a barrel tapped at both ends."

During the War of Independence George Washington won three of his most important battles in New Jersey at Trenton, Princeton, and Monmouth. In all, a third of the war's campaigns were fought within the state's borders, and Washington spent two winters in Morristown. After the end of the war in 1781, two New Jersey cities, first Princeton and then Trenton, served briefly as the nation's capital. In 1787 the state was the third to ratify the U.S. Constitution.

By the early twentieth century, the opening of bridges and tunnels across the Hudson and Delaware Rivers transformed the rural towns near New York and Philadelphia into suburban communities. At the same time, thanks to the state's transportation infrastructure and its proximity to major cities and ports, a growing number of businesses recognized the benefits of expanding in New Jersey. In the boom years after World War II, New Jersey's population grew from four to six million, a growth rate second only to that of California. What that period produced was a balanced mix of industries and a robust economy that is the eighth largest in the country.

Five signers of the Declaration of Independence were from New Jersey. President Grover Cleveland was born in the state, in Caldwell, while Woodrow Wilson was the president of Princeton University and then New Jersey governor before he went on to reside in the White House in 1913. Other famous people from New Jersey include

OPPOSITE: *More than one hundred Revolutionary War battles were fought on New Jersey soil. Shown here is an engraving from an original painting by J. Trumbull of the 1777 Battle of Princeton. © UPI/Corbis-Bettmann.* ABOVE: *Traffic headed for Jersey City converges at the Manhattan entrance to the Holland Tunnel in the 1930s. © Archive Photos*

FROM REVOLUTION TO ROCK 'N' ROLL   11

Frank Sinatra (Hoboken), Aaron Burr (Newark), James Fenimore Cooper (Burlington), Whitney Houston (Newark), and Jack Nicholson (Neptune). The beach town of Asbury Park launched the career of rock superstar Bruce Springsteen, who was born in Freehold and, after several years of living in California, moved back to the state to raise his children.

ABOVE: *Wick House, in Jockey Hollow, was occupied by one of Washington's major generals during the winter of 1779–1780. This restored farmhouse, part of Morristown National Historical Park in Morris County, re-creates daily life during the Revolutionary War period. © Kelly/Mooney.* BELOW: *Countryside still surrounds the town of Milford, whose nearest neighbor lies across the Delaware River in Pennsylvania. © J. Pickerell/FPG International*

Opposite: *Trenton Bridge's neon sign blazes proudly over the Delaware River. © Scott Barrow.* Above: *The New Wave Mall at Princeton's Forrestal Village, part of the 1,750-acre Princeton Forrestal Center, a retail and corporate park developed by Princeton University. © Bob Krist.* Below: *One of the country's best examples of colonial army barracks, the Old Barracks in Trenton recently underwent major renovations. Its museum features period-costumed guides, restored environments, and relics of the Revolutionary War. © Scott Barrow*

CENTRAL NEW JERSEY 45

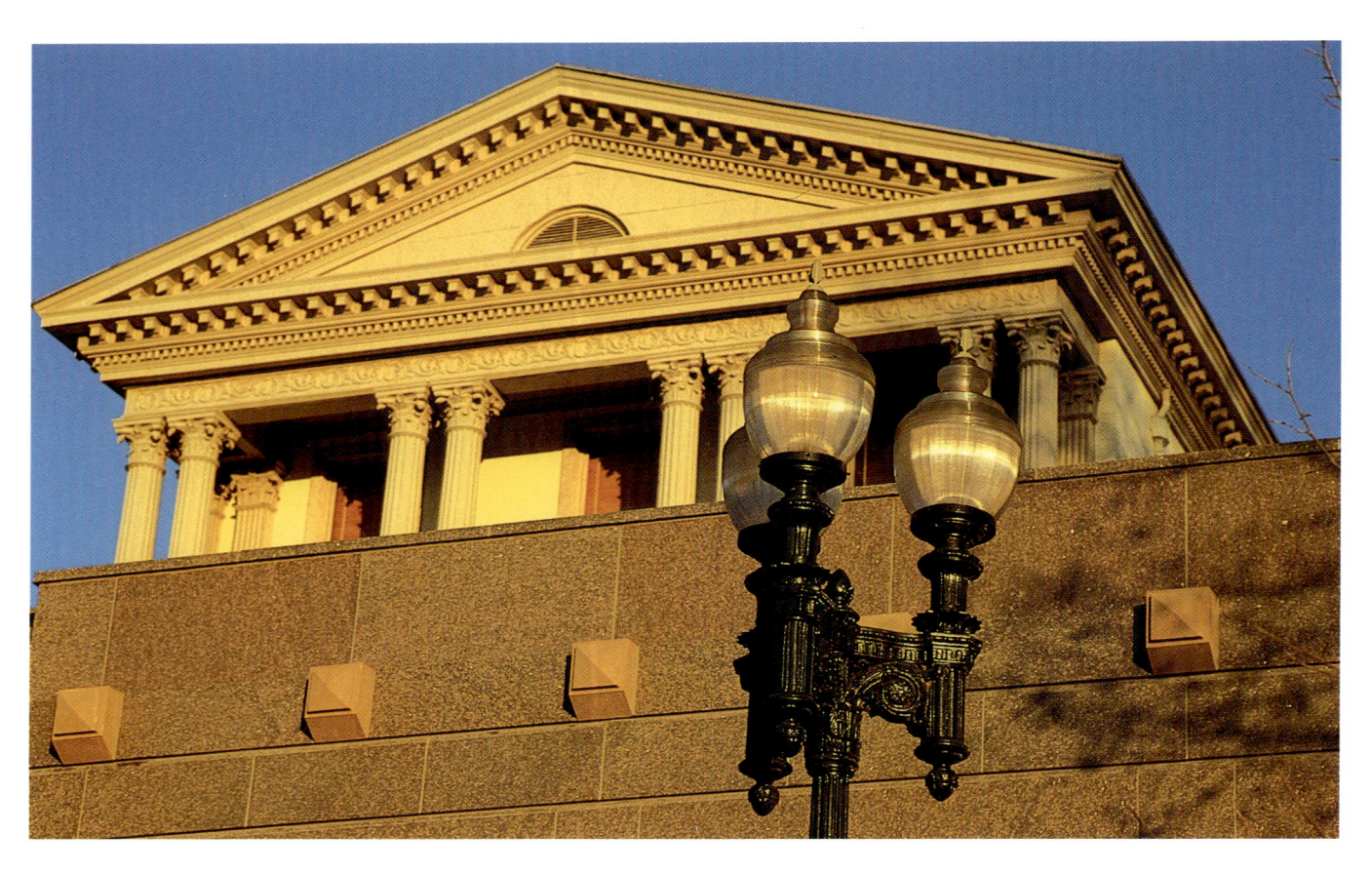

ABOVE: *Originally completed in 1792, the State House has been renovated several times and is now part of an extensive government complex that presides over Garden State politics from the Trenton riverfront. Trenton, itself, is one of the nation's fastest-growing business and industrial centers. © Jeffrey Sylvester/FPG International.* BELOW: *The Rutgers University crew team trains on the Raritan River. © Rutgers/Nick Romanenko.* OPPOSITE: *Princeton's chapel looms in classic Gothic style. © Michael Philip Manheim/International Stock*

46 A PLACE FOR EVERYTHING

CENTRAL NEW JERSEY 47

CHAPTER NINE
DELAWARE RIVER
THE HEART OF NEW JERSEY

At the southern end of New Jersey, Philadelphia exerts the same kind of influence as New York does in the north. As in the northern reaches of the state, this is an area of suburbs and commuter rail lines. Cherry Hill wasn't even on the map before 1950, but experienced rapid growth in the postwar years and won acclaim as home of one of the nation's first enclosed malls. What makes this region different from the New York metropolitan region is that, as you move further inland, you'll find the four New Jersey counties where agriculture remains a major industry. There you also will find the mysterious, undeveloped Pine Barrens.

Directly across the Delaware River from the City of Brotherly Love sits Camden, where the poet Walt Whitman spent his last days. This period was among his happiest and most productive, as he revised *Leaves of Grass,* his most famous work, and saw a transformation of public opinion in his favor before he died in 1892. Camden has been world headquarters of the Campbell's Soup Company since 1869, when the company's founder first put tomatoes in cans. New attractions, such as the New Jersey State Aquarium and the Blockbuster/Sony Music Entertainment Center, have drawn crowds to this urban area.

Most of the Garden State's vegetable farms and fruit orchards are found in Burlington, Gloucester, Salem, and Cumberland Counties. Well over half of all world-famous Jersey tomatoes are picked here, and nearly all of the state's asparagus. One of the most stunningly colorful scenes imaginable plays out each fall at harvest time in towns such as Chatsworth, where acre upon acre of shallow bogs turn into a crimson sea of cranberries. More than forty thousand holly trees are harvested annually in Millville, which calls itself "America's Holly City."

At the heart of South Jersey lies the massive Pine Barrens, 1.1 million acres of pine, cedar, and oak forests. One of the most beautiful areas of New Jersey, and one

PINE BARRENS

Many southern New Jersey residents work across the river in Philadelphia. Here, among the skyscrapers, the bronze figure of William Penn surveys the bejeweled night from his perch atop the City Hall clock tower. © Roberto Arakaki/International Stock

48   A PLACE FOR EVERYTHING

of the least known, it was designated the nation's first National Reserve in 1977. The Pine Barrens' deep sand holds a seventeen-trillion-gallon aquifer of glacially pure water. Botanists come from all over the world to study the rare plants that grow here, bird lovers tramp among its wide marshes and countless streams and rivers, and archaeologists seek out its many crumbling ghost towns. This wilderness area has long been the source of legend, such as that of the Jersey Devil, a friendly creature, part horse, part kangaroo, and part bat. True or not, such legends add to the mysterious beauty of the Pine Barrens.

LEFT: *A Roadstown bean farmer pauses to smile at his visitor.* BELOW: *Workers in a Chatsworth bog use hand-guided machines to whip ripe cranberries loose from their branches. The berries then float to the surface. Both photos © Scott Barrow*

ABOVE: *Across the river from Philadelphia, Camden's New Jersey State Aquarium features a 760,000-gallon open ocean tank and more. © Andre Jenny/International Stock.* BELOW: *Homes in the city of Bridgeton, New Jersey's largest historic district, with over 2,200 registered landmarks. © Scott Barrow.* OPPOSITE: *Hiking through scrub oak at dawn in the Pine Barrens. © Jamey Stillings/Tony Stone Images*

50   A PLACE FOR EVERYTHING

DELAWARE RIVER 51

CHAPTER TEN
JERSEY SHORE
THE JEWEL OF NEW JERSEY

All roads in New Jersey lead to the Jersey Shore. And what makes that 127-mile expanse of sandy beaches along the Atlantic Ocean so distinctive is that up and down the oceanfront and for miles inland, you'll find that no town is quite the same as the one right next door.

The Jersey Shore begins at the Sandy Hook National Seashore at the mouth of New York harbor, within sight of the concrete canyons of Manhattan. First lit in 1764, the Sandy Hook Light is the oldest operating lighthouse in the country. The nearby town of Long Branch was the summer home of seven presidents, including Ulysses S. Grant and Woodrow Wilson. And just a few miles inland from the ocean, along the Shrewsbury, Navesink, and Manasquan Rivers, live some of New Jersey's wealthiest citizens. Towns such as Rumson and Colts Neck are known for their elegant estates and massive farms where race horses are bred.

The shore extends southward to the tip of Cape May, which is full of quaint Victorian houses. Many of these are now used as restaurants and bed-and-breakfast inns, which makes the town a popular destination for romantic getaways. Barnegat Light, known to millions of summer visitors as "Old Barney," is one of the best-known landmarks along the shore. Boating and fishing in the ocean and the nearby back bays are the most popular forms of recreation—after swimming in the pounding surf, of course.

Tourism is New Jersey's number-two industry, and vacationers can find a beach to fit everyone's taste, from the carnival-style boardwalks and amusement piers of Wildwood to the pristine beauty of Island Beach State Park. The towns run the gamut from the religious retreat of Ocean City, which was founded in 1879 as a temperance-minded Christian summer resort and is still dry, to the gambling mecca of Atlantic City. The latter resort introduced the boardwalk in 1870 and the Miss America Pageant in 1921. More recently, the advent of casinos has helped turn Atlantic City into a year-round destination that draws more visitors than any other resort in the United States.

The Jersey Shore also attracts performing artists. Holmdel's PNC Bank Arts Center's open-air theater hosts heritage festivals and a concert series that draws talents such as James Taylor and Bill Cosby. Point Pleasant Beach showcases a different artist weekly during its summer Festival of the Sea. The Cape May Music Festival is for those who enjoy chamber and symphonic concerts. Cape May is also the South Jersey home of the New Jersey Ballet.

52 A PLACE FOR EVERYTHING

ABOVE: *A lifeboat stands at the ready in Cape May, America's oldest seashore resort. In the background are several examples of the area's renowned Victorian architecture, lined up just a few hundred feet from the water.* BELOW: *Belmar's wide beaches teem with summer events, including kite festivals, lifeguard tournaments, volleyball championships, and the annual New Jersey Seafood Festival. Here, a little girl considers her entry to the Belmar Sand Castle Contest. Both photos © Scott Barrow*

ABOVE: *The family resort of Ocean Grove was founded in 1869 as a Methodist camp meeting ground and still has many structures from that period, such as the Queen Anne cottages pictured here.* © Scott Barrow. BELOW: *Long Beach Island lies six miles offshore of Ocean County. Barnegat Light Township was founded by Nordic fishermen in the 1700s. Artists come for the view from the top of the lighthouse and often stay.* © Bob Krist. OPPOSITE: *Long Beach Island's shore still turns up an occasional gold or silver coin from an old shipwreck.* © Kelly/Mooney

54   A PLACE FOR EVERYTHING

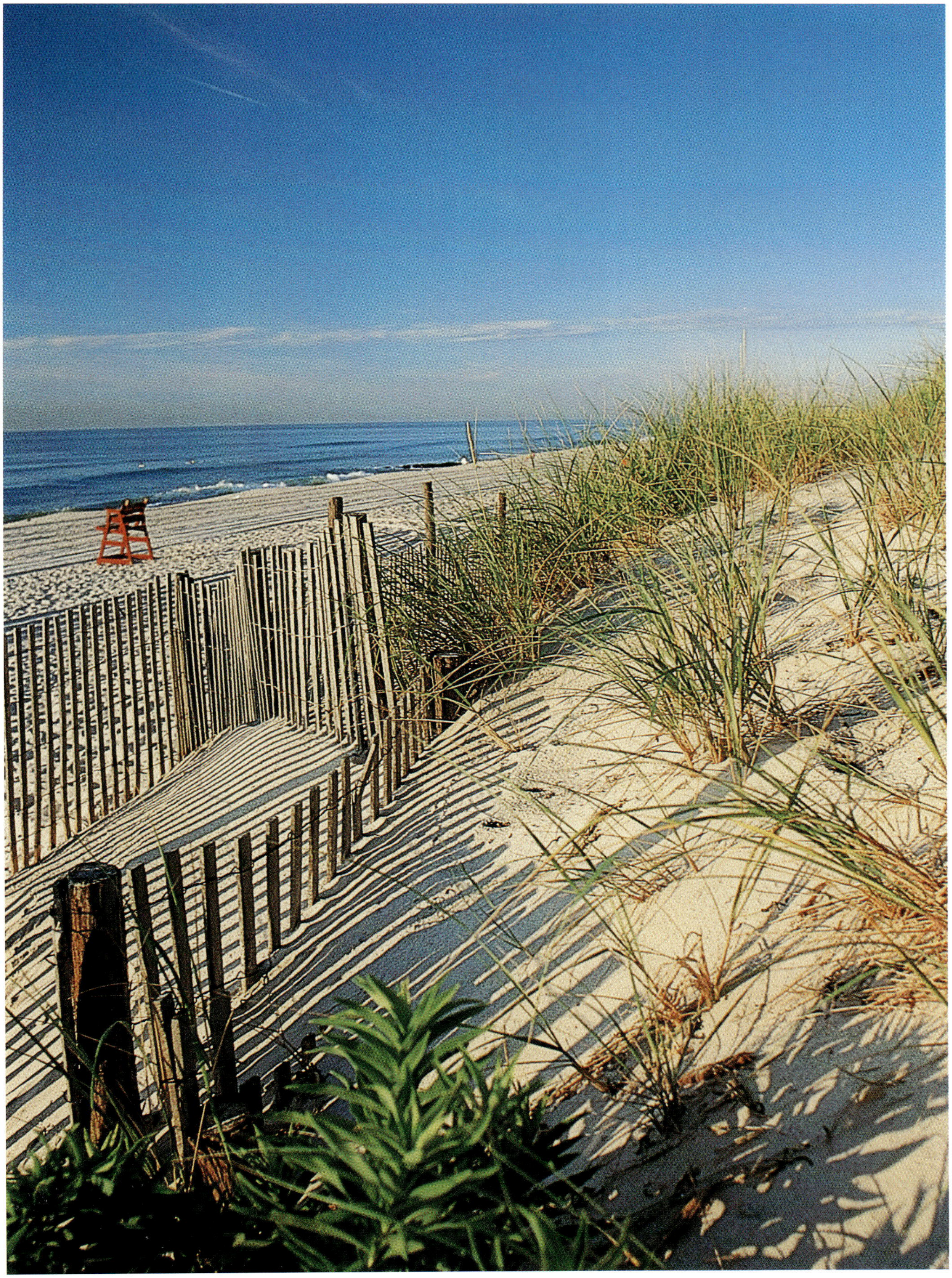

ABOVE: *Welcome to Atlantic City's Taj Mahal. Big-name performers, lush productions, and, of course, world-class gambling are found in casino-hotels such as this one. Also along the famous boardwalk are rides, shops, and vendors selling saltwater taffy.* © Bob Krist.
BELOW: *The Kohr brothers have sold their creamy confection in Seaside Heights for more than eighty years.* © Kelly/Mooney

ABOVE: *Island Beach State Park has more than three thousand acres of beaches and nature walks. Here, a young boy casts his line into the surf. © Bob Krist.* BELOW: *One of Seaside Heights' two amusement piers, where you can find an antique carousel, arcades, food, fishing, and the only beach skyride in New Jersey. This resort lies between the Atlantic Ocean and Barnegat Bay. © Scott Barrow*

CREATING THE FUTURE

PART THREE

The wealth and economic strength that we enjoy today in the United States has its roots in New Jersey.

In early America, the Garden State was one of the country's first industrial centers, known as the "Workshop of the Nation." In the nineteenth century the state was a hotbed of innovation, where people such as Samuel Morse and Thomas Edison came up with inventions that would revolutionize the world as we knew it. And in the twentieth century New Jersey grew as a transportation hub and as a giant in chemical manufacturing and pharmaceuticals, among other key industries.

Today New Jersey maintains a rich and diverse economic base, reflecting a fine balance between traditional manufacturing businesses and a broad mix of technology-based production and service companies. Out of a total labor force of four million, manufacturing accounts for the most jobs (477,000), followed by health services (332,800), business services (309,800), and wholesale trade (280,700). It's no wonder that New Jerseyans enjoy the second-highest standard of living in the country.

As the twenty-first century dawns, those intertwined roots of industrial vitality, innovation, and diversity that first took hold in New Jersey continue to spread. The state is home to the nation's third-largest concentration of corporate and division headquarters and the highest concentration of office space. Garden State entrepreneurs are among the nation's leaders in such areas as biotechnology, telecommunications, and electronics. The state is a place where its highly educated, highly skilled workers can do more than earn a good living. They can make a contribution to the future of America, as New Jerseyans always have.

OPPOSITE: *Newark's Riverfront Plaza is a symbol of this great city's renaissance as a financial and cultural center. The last decade of the twentieth century has seen major investments in Newark's downtown area, and the resulting increased vitality and quality of life. As the new millennium begins, Newark is poised to be a leader in New Jersey's ongoing tradition of success.* © Frank Saragnese/FPG International

HIGH TECHNOLOGY

60 CREATING THE FUTURE

CHAPTER ELEVEN

Some of the greatest technological innovations of the twentieth century—from the light bulb and the phonograph to the transistor and the semiconductor—were developed in New Jersey, and some of the greatest advances of the twenty-first century promise to come from the Garden State, too. New Jersey maintains a reputation as a worldwide hub for the high-technology industry.

While the state lost defense electronics and high-tech manufacturing jobs in the recession of the early 1990s, it had re-established itself by the millennium's close through rapid growth in telecommunications and several other computer-related fields.

Today New Jersey is home to more than seventeen thousand high-tech businesses with approximately 460,000 employees generating $23.1 billion in wages a year, according to a 1997 study by the state Department of Commerce and the National Science Foundation. The high-tech jobs in New Jersey pay an average annual salary of $55,970, second only to Washington State, according to the American Electronics Association.

The state offers students strong technical training at several major universities, including New Jersey Institute of Technology, which *Yahoo! Internet Life* labeled the second most "wired" college in the country. Graduates find the job market in New Jersey abundant with opportunities. The state ranks seventh in the number of high-tech jobs and fourth in the number of high-tech companies nationally.

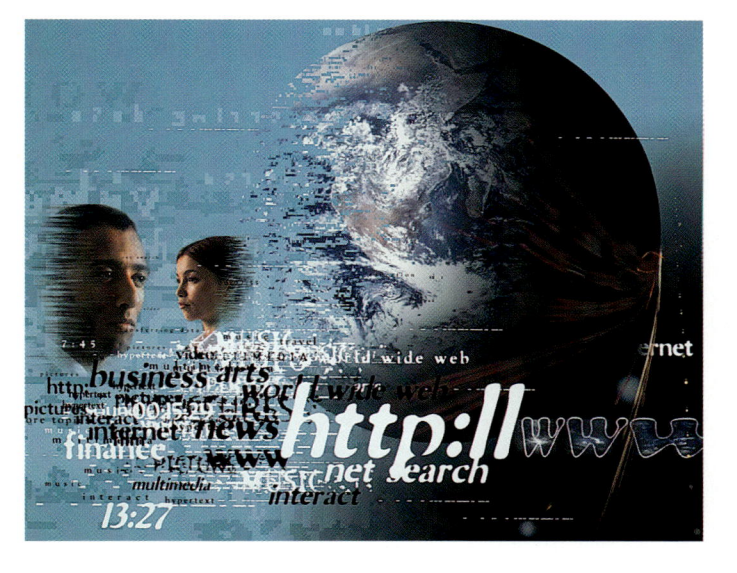

Fostering Growth in Technology

Industry growth has come in part thanks to the work of the New Jersey Commission on Science and Technology, which was established in 1985 as part of the state Department of Commerce and has since been a strong supporter of high technology research and development. The commission has encouraged the emergence of high-tech businesses and technology transfer, promoted academic research in high

Opposite: This replica of the first light bulb commemorates a new dawn in the technological history of the world. Thomas Edison worked long and hard to develop a filament that would stay lit. On the evening of 19 October 1879, he turned on the current, and his filament of cotton thread proved a glowing success. That New Year's Eve, three thousand visitors traveled to Edison's rural Menlo Park laboratory to view the new light source. © U.S. Department of the Interior, National Park Service, Edison National Historic Site. Above: New Jersey businesses and educational institutions have been quick to embrace the expansive resources of the World Wide Web. © Uniphoto, Inc.

HIGH TECHNOLOGY 61

IN DECEMBER 1877 THOMAS EDISON FIRST DEMONSTRATED HIS NEW INVENTION, THE PHONOGRAPH, BY TURNING THE CRANK ON A MACHINE AFFIXED WITH TINFOIL WRAPPED AROUND A DRUM AND SHOUTING "MARY HAD A LITTLE LAMB." TO THE AMAZEMENT OF LAB ASSISTANTS, THE DRUM WAS REWOUND, CRANKED AGAIN, AND OUT CAME THE SOUND OF EDISON'S HIGH-PITCHED VOICE.

technology, explored new fields of technology, and emphasized the preparation of a technology-literate workforce in the state.

So far, the commission has helped bring in more than $31 million in new federal dollars to New Jersey universities, more than $32 million in federal grants to small firms, and more than $15 million in private-sector support for its programs. More than one thousand New Jersey companies have benefited from the commission's broad spectrum of programs.

The commission recently supported the formation of a National Science Foundation Industry/University Cooperative Research Center, which includes the New Jersey Center for Multimedia Research, the New Jersey Institute of Technology, and Princeton University. This collaboration harnesses university and industrial resources to create a New Jersey–based magnet for multimedia companies and high-technology talent.

But perhaps the Commission on Science and Technology's most significant contribution to high-technology development was $4 million toward the construction of the Technology Centre of New Jersey. Located on Route 1 in North Brunswick, the center has 750,000 square feet of research and development space. Its mission is to offer technology-based enterprises affordable space for research and development work on new products and services. Modules as small as six thousand square feet are available to support young, growing

The control room of the Basking Ridge headquarters of AT&T features the high technology of the nation's premier long-distance telephone carrier. AT&T has expanded its product line into wireless communications and Internet technology. © Bob Krist

62 CREATING THE FUTURE

IN 1940 BELL LABORATORIES SCIENTIST RUSSELL OHL FOUND THAT A PIECE OF SILICON COULD PRODUCE ELECTRICAL ENERGY WHEN PLACED UNDER LIGHT. THAT EVENTUALLY LED TO THE 1948 DISCOVERY OF THE TRANSISTOR, THE MOST IMPORTANT COMPONENT PART OF TODAY'S RADIOS, TELEVISIONS, COMPUTERS, AND ALL SORTS OF ELECTRONIC GADGETS AND GIZMOS.

© PhotoDisc, Inc.

companies within a multitenanted building. The initial sixty-thousand-square-foot lab and production facility was targeted at biotechnology and microelectronic companies. Another twenty thousand square feet was allotted for office and conference space.

Some of the recent growth in New Jersey's high-tech industry also comes thanks to Governor Christie Whitman's Business Employment Incentive Program, an economic development initiative through which companies that create jobs are eligible for grants equal to up to 80 percent of the income taxes paid by newly hired employees for up to ten years. To qualify, a company must create a minimum of twenty-five jobs in urban areas or seventy-five jobs elsewhere in the state. So far, at least 120 companies have participated, leading to the creation of over thirty thousand new jobs.

THE FUTURE OF TELECOMMUNICATIONS

The high-tech business community in New Jersey includes a mixture of both established corporations and start-up firms, with all focused on developing technology for the future. Products are being developed for telecommunications, software and computer services, biological technology, digital convergence, broadcast and entertainment technology, and consumer electronics.

Certainly the oldest and most widely recognized technology company in the state is AT&T, based in Basking Ridge. Best known as Ma Bell, the world's premier long-distance telephone carrier, AT&T has rapidly

Chubb Computer Services is a tenant of the Technology Centre of New Jersey, developed by the New Jersey Economic Development Authority to provide affordable R&D space to high-tech businesses. Courtesy, New Jersey Economic Development Authority

developed capabilities in the realm of wireless communications, local telephone service, and Internet access. The company has introduced a flat-rate, unlimited access Internet product for consumers and businesses, and a security service for making secure purchases over the World Wide Web. Its development of high-speed wireless technology that will carry digital communications directly to the home will help AT&T compete for local telephone service. The acquisition of Tele-Communications, Inc., should enhance AT&T's position in the emerging field of cable modems, while its strategic partnership with British Telecom should hasten global expansion.

In 1996 AT&T split into three separate companies. One of those spin-offs, Lucent Technologies, located in

NEW JERSEY BEATS NEW YORK

IN 1997 TWENTY-FIVE NEW JERSEY FIRMS WERE AMONG THE "TECHNOLOGY FAST 500" OF THE COUNTRY'S FASTEST-GROWING TECHNOLOGY COMPANIES. WITH 5 PERCENT OF THE LIST, THE GARDEN STATE PLACED AHEAD OF NEW YORK AS A HIGH TECHNOLOGY HUB.

HIGH TECHNOLOGY 63

HELLO, OUT THERE

PROJECT SCORE, THE FIRST COMMUNICATIONS SATELLITE THAT COULD BEAM MESSAGES AROUND THE WORLD, WAS DEVELOPED BY THE SIGNAL CORPS LABORATORIES AT FORT MONMOUTH. LAUNCHED INTO ORBIT ON 18 DECEMBER 1958, SCORE (SIGNAL COMMUNICATIONS VIA ORBITING RELAY EXPERIMENT) BROADCAST PRESIDENT EISENHOWER'S CHRISTMAS GREETING, PROVING THAT VOICE AND CODE SIGNALS COULD BE RELAYED OVER VAST DISTANCES.

Murray Hill, combines the systems and technology equipment units that were formerly part of Bell Labs, AT&T's world-renowned research and development arm. Lucent, which retains 17,300 employees in New Jersey and 121,000 employees worldwide, creates and distributes commercial communications technology from microchips to whole networks.

In Lucent's brief existence, this $21-billion "start-up" has quickly become a world leader in switching systems, transmission systems, wireless networks, and networking software; as well as power supply systems, video conferencing, integrated circuits, and standard cell and structured cabling systems. It owns top market-share in the nation for business communication systems, voice processing systems, call centers, telephone answering systems, and corded and cordless phones. Lucent has more recently set its sights on aggressive acquisitions and the development of multimedia products.

The telecommunications world is rapidly changing with the growth of wireless and Internet capabilities, and New Jersey start-ups hope to be at the forefront one day. RAM Mobile Data in Woodbridge has launched an innovative paging service that lets users send e-mail or faxes and even access the Internet. Likewise, the state is home to at least six companies involved in Internet telephony, which promise telephone service through the Internet at a fraction of the cost of traditional phone calls. Not surprisingly, telecommunications giants such as AT&T have made investments in this technology.

ELECTRONICS FOR EVERYONE

It is entirely appropriate that New Jersey, where Thomas Edison came up with his revolutionary inventions, is home to companies that will change the face of consumer electronics in the new century. The state is the base of operations for numerous well-known electronics companies, including Panasonic, Casio, and Sony Electronics.

Based in Park Ridge, Sony is the first company to bring the convergence of audio, video, computing, and communications to consumer electronics. Its Video Audio Integration product allows consumers to expand the use of computers in the home so that computers become the nucleus of a complete communication system capable of plugging users into the world. Other Sony products include Internet TV, notebook PCs, and the digital television receiver, capable of receiving high-definition broadcasts.

Though Sarnoff Corporation in Princeton does not possess the same degree of name recognition as

Using the company's own state-of-the-art IR camera, a senior engineer from Sensors Unlimited, Inc., of Princeton examines a semiconductor wafer. The camera makes it possible to see through the wafer for mask-alignment purposes. Courtesy, Sensors Unlimited

KEEPING THE BEAT

IN 1972, WORKING WITH DOCTORS FROM FORT MONMOUTH'S PATTERSON ARMY HOSPITAL, U.S. ARMY ELECTRONICS COMMAND SCIENTISTS DEVELOPED A LIFE-SAVING COMBINATION OF A DEFIBRILLATOR AND PACEMAKER THAT COULD BE IMPLANTED IN THE HUMAN BODY. NOT ONLY DID THE DEVICE REGULATE HEARTBEAT, IT COULD ALSO DETECT THE START OF FIBRILLATION—WILD AND DISCORDANT TREMORS OF THE HEART'S MUSCLE FIBERS—AND BRIEFLY STOP THE HEART TO ALLOW A NORMAL BEAT TO RESUME.

HIGH-TECH "UPSTARTS"

Pick almost any aspect of the high-tech world, and you'll find innovative New Jersey start-ups hard at work and showing amazing promise. Since its founding in 1997, Tellium, Inc., in Edison, has designed optical fiber communications products that can transmit information at high speeds on the World Wide Web for a customer base that includes major long-distance carriers and regional telephone service providers. Also relatively new is Sapient Corporation, in Jersey City, which

Amid computer components and circuit boards, a technician tests a system's operations. © Mark Bolster/International Stock

Sony, the research laboratory has been at the forefront of high-tech development for over fifty years. Once the research and development arm of RCA, and largely responsible for development of the nation's first televisions, Sarnoff today generates products for clients in telecommunications, digital convergence, and PCs; biomedical technology; broadcast and entertainment technology; and consumer electronics. One of Sarnoff's most recent innovations—an image sensor based on complementary metal oxide semiconductor technology—could make the digital camera as inexpensive as a computer mouse.

created the first browser-based on-line banking applications for small business clients and helped Bell Atlantic build the infrastructure for its nationwide Yellow Pages. A Sarnoff spin-off, Sensar, Inc., of Moorestown, is one of many firms making breakthroughs in electronic banking applications.

THE SILICON VALLEY OF THE EAST

New Jersey's software industry is composed of as many as four thousand firms and employs, according to one report, more than sixty-six thousand computer programmers. The Garden State has not been recoined as a software

IN 1838, IN A SECRET LABORATORY ON A COUNTRY ESTATE IN SPEEDWELL, SAMUEL F. B. MORSE AND ALFRED VAIL PERFECTED THEIR ELECTROMAGNETIC TELEGRAPH. THEY FIRST PUBLICLY DEMONSTRATED IT BY SENDING MESSAGES BACK AND FORTH OVER TWO MILES OF WIRE.

productivity of large sales organizations, including the pharmaceutical market in New Jersey.

All this goes to prove that when it comes to the full range of high-tech fields, New Jersey is wired and moving forward at warp speed.

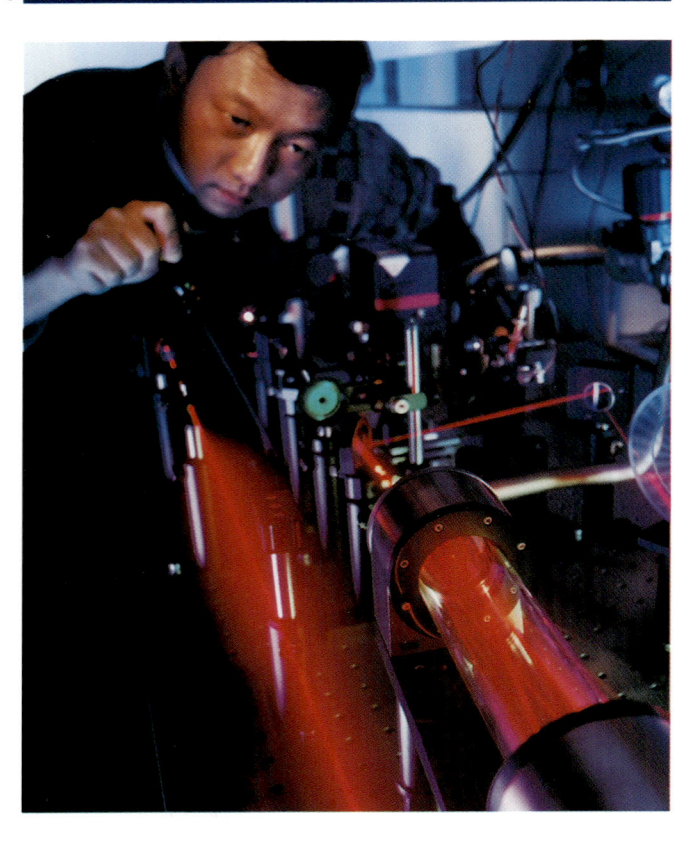

Sarnoff Corporation's laser application laboratory (LEFT) and high-definition television (RIGHT) are just two results of the company's innovations. Courtesy, Sarnoff Corporation. OPPOSITE: *A technician monitors the flow and function of an optical waveguide and laser equipment. © Michael Rosenfeld/Tony Stone Images*

innovator the way California's Silicon Valley or Boston's Route 128 corridor have, though many believe it should be.

Mountain Lakes–based Computer Horizons, one of the largest software companies in New Jersey, with over one thousand employees, is a leader in fixing the Year 2000 computer glitch for clients such as AT&T, Prudential, and Chubb Corporation. In 1998, it purchased Princeton Softech, which helps large companies manage data more efficiently. Now publicly traded, Voxware of Princeton licenses digital signal processing software to companies with products that require voice and audio capabilities. Another new company, Dendrite International, in Morristown, has provided software, services, and information that enhance the efficiency and

WHEN ELECTRONICS RESEARCHER C. HARRY KNOWLES STARTED HIS OWN COMPANY IN BLACKWOOD IN 1968, HE KNEW NOTHING ABOUT LASERS EXCEPT WHAT HE HAD READ IN AN ARTICLE IN POPULAR ELECTRONICS. SEVEN YEARS LATER HE INVENTED THE BAR CODE SCANNER, NOW AN EVERYDAY FIXTURE IN THE RETAIL WORLD. HE FINANCED HIS INVENTION PARTLY BY SELLING A HOME-USE "LASER KIT" FOR $79.95, ADVERTISING IT IN—YOU GUESSED IT—POPULAR ELECTRONICS.

66 CREATING THE FUTURE

HIGH TECHNOLOGY 67

TotalTel is a rapidly expanding telecommunications company based in Little Falls, New Jersey. Courtesy, TotalTel

68 CREATING THE FUTURE

TECHNOLOGY AND TELECOMMUNICATIONS

LUCENT TECHNOLOGIES

FOR THE NEW MILLENNIUM LUCENT TECHNOLOGIES BUILDS ON ITS RECORD INNOVATION AND ACHIEVEMENT TO CREATE GLOBAL INTEGRATED DATA NETWORKING SOLUTIONS WITH EVEN GREATER SPEED, ACCESS, AND BANDWIDTH, AND LOWER COST

Lucent Technologies, headquartered in Murray Hill, New Jersey, is a leader in a global communications industry that will soon reach 500 billion United States dollars per year. Lucent is a young $30 billion company with Fortune 500 credentials. Its roots go back to the nineteenth century and its vision extends through the twenty-first and beyond.

Lucent's 135,000 employees in more than ninety countries work to help the company's customers shape today's rapidly evolving communications environment to meet their needs. Bell Labs, its research and development unit, has been the source of profound technological innovations that have helped shape this world.

Connections forged by Lucent's innovations—in voice and data, wired and wireless communications—are transforming the way people everywhere live, work, and learn.

Lucent's business has been to invent and build the technology that defines communication since the days of the telegraph, first as Western Electric and later as part of AT&T. AT&T spun the entity off into a totally separate company in 1996. Lucent's predecessors built the telephones and networks that let people talk to each other in this century. Now, as Lucent, the company is at the center of the networking revolution that will drive the world's business and societies during the next century.

Lucent helps companies connect with their customers, employees, and business partners—not simply with telephone lines but via the networks within networks that are evolving today. Lucent has shaped its business into a portfolio of agile companies to tightly focus on customers and the fastest-growing markets, streamlining the creation

As many as 600 digital switches and transmission facilities can be managed from the hub of the Lucent Technologies Network Reliability Center in Aurora, Colorado.

and delivery of the services and technology solutions they need.

Of the top 500 United States–based businesses, 70 percent rely on Lucent's network services. And its business communications systems give world enterprises of all sizes comprehensive solutions that make use of the newest advances in technologies, such as the Internet, call centers, and messaging.

Lucent also helps service providers create and run the networks that connect nearly everyone with increasingly rich communications options. Major service providers in more than fifty countries depend on Lucent's notable reliability for the wired and wireless systems and software that power their networks, bringing modern communications to every corner of the planet.

A communications revolution is taking place, a digital transformation that blends voice, data, and video into a seamlessly networked flow of information over public and private networks. Internet Protocol (IP)–based data-networking products hold the promise of faster speeds, greater access, more bandwidth, and lower costs. Lucent also is bringing to data networks the quality of service it invented for the voice network. Lucent has placed revolutionary new ideas coupled with 126 years of networking experience at its customers' service. Lucent helps businesses make the choices

Richard A. McGinn, Lucent Technologies chairman and chief executive officer, says, "We're a young company with a unique heritage, well-positioned to lead the communications networking revolution that is under way."

Employees celebrate Lucent's first day as an independent company on 1 October 1996.

that are right for them—from a ground-up network to a measured evolution from any installed network base.

"Lucent understands better than anyone the way data and voice communications must work together to give customers new networks with expanded features, reduced cost, and absolute quality," says company chairman, Richard McGinn. "We are leaders in the technologies, applications, services, and support that must come together to build the ultra-reliable all-media networks needed to revolutionize communications. Wireless systems, messaging systems, call centers, optical networking, semiconductors, data networking, and communications software are all Lucent strengths."

Lucent's customers span the globe, and the company derives a quarter of its revenues from international markets, including both large customers, such as national governments and major multinational corporations, and small enterprises, such as companies that may be purchasing their first business-telephone system. This is only a beginning, according to Lucent. The company sees much of its future growth occurring as demand outside the United States increases, fueled by deregulation, the expanding connections of a globalizing economy, and the pressing needs of developing nations to create modern communications systems.

When conducting research and development, Lucent's international Bell Labs works to gain a native knowledge of unique local needs, whatever the scale of the project. It may be creating

Laser 2000, a state-of-the-art laser-chip packaging platform, reduces costs and increases productivity at Lucent's Microelectronics Group facility in Breinigsville, Pennsylvania.

small-business solutions for customers in Poland and Mexico, or pursuing major new technologies, as in its leading work on passive optical networking in its expanded Japan center. In every case, Lucent uses the connections that its customers in each country say make sense—from direct sales organizations and regional "centers of excellence" to joint ventures, alliances, and partnerships. In a global economy, local understanding is the key to solutions that have lasting value.

"At Lucent we're committed to building, worldwide, a fast track between brilliant ideas and new innovative products that provide customer solutions," McGinn says.

INNOVATION DEFINES LUCENT

Lucent Technologies has produced eleven Nobel laureates (including winners of the 1998 Physics Prize) and has more than 25,000 active patents worldwide. "We're continuing to advance the technologies and come up with the breakthroughs that will keep us at the center of the revolution in networking," chairman McGinn says.

"Bell Labs researchers and developers around the world are reinventing the industry. They earn more than three patents every working day, creating technological breakthroughs and teaming with Lucent colleagues around the world to turn concepts into products in record time," says McGinn. Highlights of the company's innovations over more than a century include:

- Telephone invented by Alexander Graham Bell (1876)
- The transistor (1947)
- The solar cell (1954)
- The laser (1958)
- Telstar communications satellite (1962)
- UNIX® (1969)
- First single-chip digital signal processor (1979)
- Digital Cellular telephony (1988)
- HDTV (1989)
- Data mining and data visualization algorithms (1995)
- SCALPEL™ electron-beam lithography system (1996)
- World's smallest practical transistor (1997)
- Second-generation ATM switching chips (1997)
- First high-resolution map of cosmic dark matter (1997)
- World's first all-plastic transistor (1998)
- World's widest-bandwidth optical amplifier (1998)
- New Internet Protocol (IP) router (1998)
- Optical-fiber capacity expanded by 50 percent with AllWave™ (1998)

DENDRITE INTERNATIONAL, INC.

FOCUSING ON SOLUTIONS FOR PHARMACEUTICAL AND CONSUMER PRODUCT GROUP SALES FORCES, DENDRITE INTERNATIONAL, INC., PROVIDES HIGH-VALUE, HIGH-IMPACT SERVICES AND SUPPORT TO THE GLOBAL COMMUNITY

"The strong economy, an outstanding workforce, and a thriving pharmaceutical industry are what have made us succeed," says Dendrite International president and chief executive officer, John Bailye, who established the company in 1986 to develop computer programs for health care organizations. Bailye has overseen Dendrite's growth in sales from $250,000 in 1986 to $78 million in 1997.

"Our success in New Jersey is based on our tradition of growing in concert with the state's flourishing pharmaceutical research community," he continues. "Dendrite is a quintessential American success story located right here in New Jersey."

The company moved its headquarters to Warren, in Somerset County, one year after opening its doors in Sydney, Australia. Dendrite was one of New Jersey's first high-tech companies, and experienced tremendous growth in a short period of time. It became a leader in Sales Force Automation (SFA) in the pharmaceutical industry, and is one of the largest companies in its field. The company exceeded its year 2000 sales goal two years early.

John E. Bailye is president and chief executive officer of Dendrite International.

Dendrite International, Inc.'s global headquarters, above, is located in Morristown. The company employs more than 750 people worldwide, with more than 500 based in New Jersey.

Dendrite's high-end, high-value, high-impact services to the drug industry allow the industry's sales organizations to adapt to and manage change. The company serves its clients by integrating solutions to problems affecting sales efforts. Dendrite has changed with the marketplace and adapted new solutions to meet client demands. For example, rather than viewing the advent of managed care as a problem, as many in the industry did, Dendrite saw it as a new marketing challenge and developed solutions that would enable its clients to remain profitable.

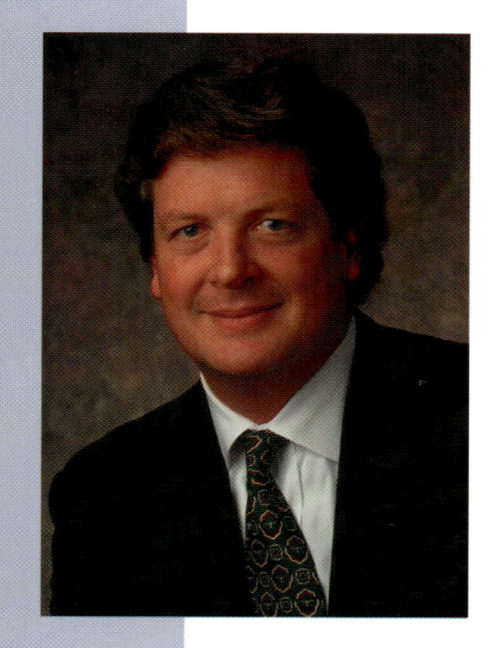

Approximately 40,000 sales representatives and their managers in more than 150 major corporations in seventeen countries rely on Dendrite for a uniquely tailored combination of tools, information, and skills to help them adapt to change and improve their sales. Dendrite uses its highly specialized industry knowledge to develop modular software products that enhance sales force effectiveness by leveraging massive amounts of data to create usable information, direct sales activities, and facilitate enterprisewide communication. The products, combined with specifically tailored coaching and support services, focus sales representatives on improving their performance. With a global infrastructure as its foundation, Dendrite's commitment to unparalleled service has been the hallmark of its business.

The company's focus on outcomes has allowed it to become a leading provider of application software and professional services on a worldwide basis. Dendrite's revolutionary approaches to laptop computing link entire sales operations all over the world for pharmaceutical customers such as Pfizer, Eli Lilly, and Johnson & Johnson, and consumer product customers including L'Oreal, Bacardi/Martini, and Ralston Purina.

Dendrite has two major divisions: Healthcare, which is the largest supplier of sales force–effectiveness solutions to the global pharmaceutical industry; and Consumer Business, which serves the over-the-counter drug, cosmetics, and consumer packaged-goods industries worldwide.

Headquartered in Morristown, New Jersey, Dendrite employs more than 750 people in fourteen offices around the world. The company has more than 500 employees in New Jersey.

"The collective work of our staff has produced record results, strong new business, and expanding partnerships with ongoing customers. We help drug companies sell products better by providing support services. Other companies just sell product. We provide high-knowledge support services that make a difference in how companies work. We become part of our clients' strategic sales plans," says Bailye.

Dendrite has played an important behind-the-scenes role, as well, in supporting entrepreneurial companies. It sponsors the New Jersey Business Awards and the New Jersey Fast 50 and is a founding member of the New Jersey Technology Council.

Dendrite also supports numerous community and charitable organizations. The company is especially active in local community

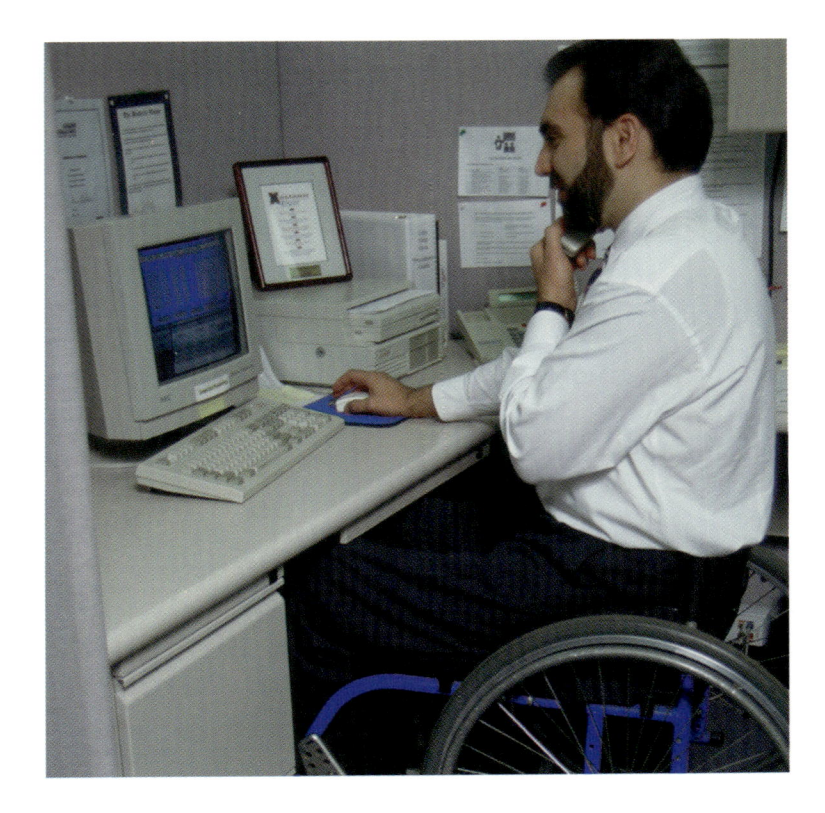

One of Dendrite's customer team Quality Assurance (QA) managers, Al DiFonzo, inspects a product before it is sent to the client. Each Dendrite client has its own QA team, and all software passes through a team for quality assurance before being sent out.

education, training, and hiring initiatives. CEO Bailye sits on the board of overseers for the New Jersey Institute of Technology, is a trustee at Bloomfield College, and is on the corporate advisory board of the New Jersey Scholars, Educators, Excellence, Dedication, Success (SEEDS) education initiative. SEEDS is a privately funded nonprofit organization committed to developing effective future leaders through education and work with inner-city school children.

Dendrite has endowed both Bloomfield College and the New Jersey Institute of Technology with scholarships and actively provides employment opportunities to students of both institutions. Dendrite also makes substantial financial and computing equipment donations to local educational organizations.

"The high quality of New Jersey's broad-based, sophisticated workforce keeps us in New Jersey. We see our support of New Jersey education and entrepreneurial companies as an investment in our future," says Bailye.

At left, members of the Dendrite International technical support staff check information in the company's data center.

TECHNOLOGY AND TELECOMMUNICATIONS

SARNOFF CORPORATION

ADDING BIOMEDICAL AND HEALTH CARE ADVANCES TO ITS PORTFOLIO OF GROUNDBREAKING RESEARCH IN VIDEO, HIGH-PERFORMANCE COMPUTING, AND SOLID-STATE TECHNOLOGY, SARNOFF CONTINUES TO DEVELOP INNOVATIVE TECHNOLOGY TO CHANGE THE WORLD

Sarnoff Corporation is a world leader in the creation, application, and commercialization of innovations in electronics, information technology, and the biomedical and health care fields.

The company works with multinational corporations, government agencies, research universities, and leading high-tech organizations to move its technologies into the marketplace. Its partners, clients, and investors include Motorola, Perkin Elmer, Thomson, Toshiba, SmithKline Beecham, and government organizations such as the National Imagery and Mapping Agency (NIMA) and the Defense Advanced Research Projects Agency (DARPA).

Over the past ten years Sarnoff has transformed itself from a contract research lab into a product development, high-tech start-up engine. It develops new technology through research funded by commercial and governmental clients. It also licenses the use of Sarnoff innovations to other companies. In 1992 it embarked on a strategy to commercialize its technology by starting new venture companies. Eleven such companies are now in various stages of development.

Sarnoff is a world leader in producing new technology to acquire, process, communicate, display, and make use of electronic images. Its pioneering work helped create today's television system, and the company invented all-electronic color TV. Today, as a leader in the development of digital and high-definition television (HDTV), Sarnoff is once again transforming this vital medium.

Other Sarnoff video innovations include server technology for video-on-demand, an exciting new way to order and view movies over a cable system, and new imaging devices for visible and infrared light. A new image sensor, based on the Complementary Metal Oxide Semiconductor (CMOS) technology pioneered here, could result in high-quality video cameras at the price of a computer mouse.

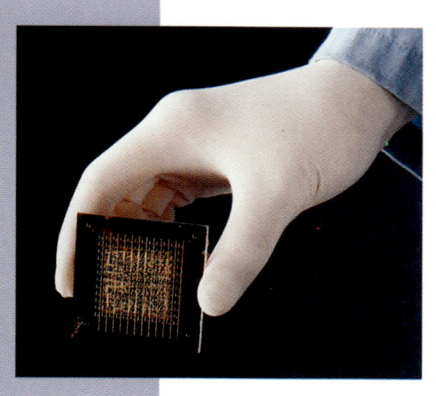

Sarnoff's breadth positions it as a major player in the rapid convergence of video, computing, communications, and display technologies. This trend promises to create additional global markets for wireless services, video processing, optoelectronics, and other vision technologies—all Sarnoff specialties.

The company is also doing significant work in biomedical and health care systems. Three of Sarnoff's venture companies address this market:
- Orchid Biocomputer is developing a lab-on-a-chip that uses microscopic devices to run thousands of combinatorial experiments at once.
- Delsys Pharmaceutical is improving the quality, safety, and speed of pharmaceutical tablet manufacturing and drug delivery using electrostatic-dry-powder-handling technology.
- Songbird Medical is developing the world's first disposable hearing aid.

Other Sarnoff venture companies target the markets for anticounterfeiting measures, radio ID tags, and consumer graphics software for the PC. Sarnoff's first start-up, Sensar, is a leader in biometrics for security purposes via iris recognition.

Originally established in 1942 as RCA Laboratories and renamed in 1951 for David Sarnoff, its founder, Sarnoff Corporation became a subsidiary of SRI International in 1987.

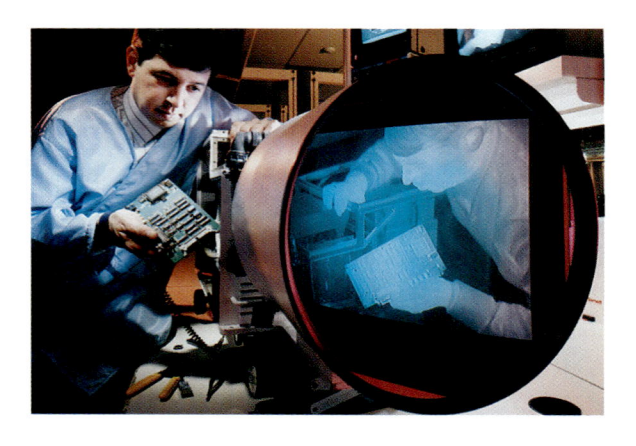

Miniaturized versions of this infrared camera will allow users to see in the dark via night vision for security, surveillance, and other purposes.

This computer chip is also a miniature biochemistry "lab." Now being developed by Sarnoff venture company Orchid Biocomputer, it uses Sarnoff microfluidics technology to dramatically improve the speed and cost of pharmaceutical research and diagnostic applications. © Don Connors, Princeton, New Jersey

DRS TECHNOLOGIES, INC.

Award-winning DRS Technologies, Inc., produces advanced electronic systems primarily for the processing, display, and storage of data for government and commercial niche markets worldwide

According to chairman of the board, president, and chief executive officer Mark S. Newman, the mission of DRS Technologies, Inc., is to become a mid-tier technology leader in worldwide defense and commercial niche markets. "DRS is committed to growth by strategically leveraging existing business areas, partnering with industry leaders on high-priority programs, and acquiring companies that are synergistic with our core strengths," Newman says.

Founded in 1968 in Mount Vernon, New York, DRS originally produced electronic signal processing and high-density recording systems for use in the United States antisubmarine warfare program. Today the company develops and manufactures leading-edge systems, including combat display workstations and electronic sensor, mission recording, digital imaging, electro-optical, ship communications, and flight safety systems for United States and international military forces. In 1998 DRS was named one of the fastest-growing technology companies in New Jersey by the New Jersey Technology Council, one of the fastest-growing companies on the American Stock Exchange by *Equities* magazine, and one of the best-managed small aerospace companies by *Aviation Week & Space Technology*.

In the early years DRS pioneered passive sonar submarine detection for the United States Navy's surface ships by introducing into the fleet narrowband signal processing systems. These systems tracked nuclear-powered submarines that previously had evaded detection. Similar systems were installed on aircraft carriers, helicopters, and fixed-wing aircraft.

Since 1981, when DRS became publicly held, the company has vigorously enhanced its growth strategy through acquisitions that have contributed to its diversification. Its core technology base now includes an array of advanced defense electronics products, in addition to precision magnetic test heads for the commercial airline, banking, computer disk drive, security, transportation, retail sales, and television/radio broadcast industries.

DRS Technologies primarily serves global high-technology requirements of armed forces (as symbolized in the rendering above) including the United States Army, Navy, Air Force, and Marine Corps, as well as allied international military forces.

DRS Technologies produces military information processing and display workstations using commercial technology for the AN/UYQ-70 Advanced Display Systems program, as shown at left.

In 1998 the United States Navy selected the Lockheed Martin–DRS Technologies–Raytheon team for the recompetition of a major milestone contract award for the AN/UYQ-70 Advanced Display Systems program, which solidifies DRS's core electronic systems business base for the next several years. The Navy considers the UYQ-70 systems fundamental to modernizing its ship, submarine, and aircraft fleets. These systems, manufactured by DRS, operate on AEGIS surface ships and E-2C surveillance aircraft and are slated for the NSSN New Attack Submarine. Pivotal to winning this contract was the team's on-time performance and the high quality of the systems—hallmarks of DRS.

Newman's goal is to triple DRS sales in the next three to five years. "We focus our resources on innovation, quality, cost-effectiveness, and superior value for our customers," he says. "Our plans include an aggressive strategy to globalize our market reach, partner with industry leaders on high-priority defense programs, and further penetrate commercial markets. DRS Technologies is well positioned as a vibrant, emerging technology leader."

NEW JERSEY TECHNOLOGY COUNCIL

BY PROVIDING TECHNOLOGY LEADERS A FERTILE ENVIRONMENT FOR THE EXCHANGE OF IDEAS, THE NEW JERSEY TECHNOLOGY COUNCIL SUSTAINS THE GROWTH AND DEVELOPMENT OF THIS BURGEONING INDUSTRY

One of the ingredients in success is the ability to network. Over the last fifty years, as New Jersey's technology industry burgeoned in the state, technology company executives found themselves isolated and in need of a way to share ideas, experiences, and strategies with like-minded individuals. To instill a sense of community within the industry, the New Jersey Technology Council (NJTC) was formed by Maxine Ballen, president; and John Martinson, chairman; with the support of the council's charter members: Aon Risk Services; Arthur Anderson, LLP; Buchanan Ingersoll; Dendrite International; Edison Venture Fund; New Jersey Commission on Science and Technology; and PNC Bank.

Cultivating technology in the Garden State is NJTC's goal. By directly fostering positive relationships among companies, the NJTC offers technology leaders a fertile environment for sharing ideas, exchanging news, and simply meeting one another. The council also provides recognition, networking, information, and services for technology businesses.

Membership in NJTC is open to technology-oriented companies and technology supporters. Members leverage their experience with other leaders in the industry and build on their knowledge to create new growth opportunities for their businesses and for the state.

NJTC members typically fall into these categories: technology, technology support, and nonprofit members. Technology members are companies involved in the research, development, manufacture, supply, or sales of high-technology products, services, materials, or components. Technology support members are professional service firms and other vendors serving technology companies. Nonprofit members are organizations supporting the technology community, such as business associations, economic development agencies, and entrepreneurial support groups.

By collectively representing technology-intensive industries and the institutions and service companies that support them, the NJTC can recognize and promote technology leaders; provide access to financing sources; collect and disseminate valuable information; and support public policy with sustained growth and development of technology-intensive industries.

Firms that join the council receive reduced admission to all regularly scheduled roundtables, panel discussions, and networking events for executives and staff; a subscription to the council's bimonthly newspaper, *TechNews;* a membership directory with promotional listings; marketing, advertising, and sponsorship opportunities; and timely legislative alerts.

General membership activities and programs include the annual awards gala; financing programs including the New Jersey Venture Fair, the New Jersey Technology Transfer Conference, the Public Company Showcase, and the New Jersey Capital Conference.

An interactive robot named "Frankie" is just one of the unique products that have debuted at the council's annual Venture Fair, an exposition that brings emerging companies together with funding sources.

Joseph Karas, president of AT&T in New Jersey, accepts the award for Master Technology Company of the Year at the 1996 Inaugural NJTC Awards Gala.

76   CREATING THE FUTURE

Courtesy, New Jersey Economic Development Authority

TECHNOLOGY AND TELECOMMUNICATIONS 77

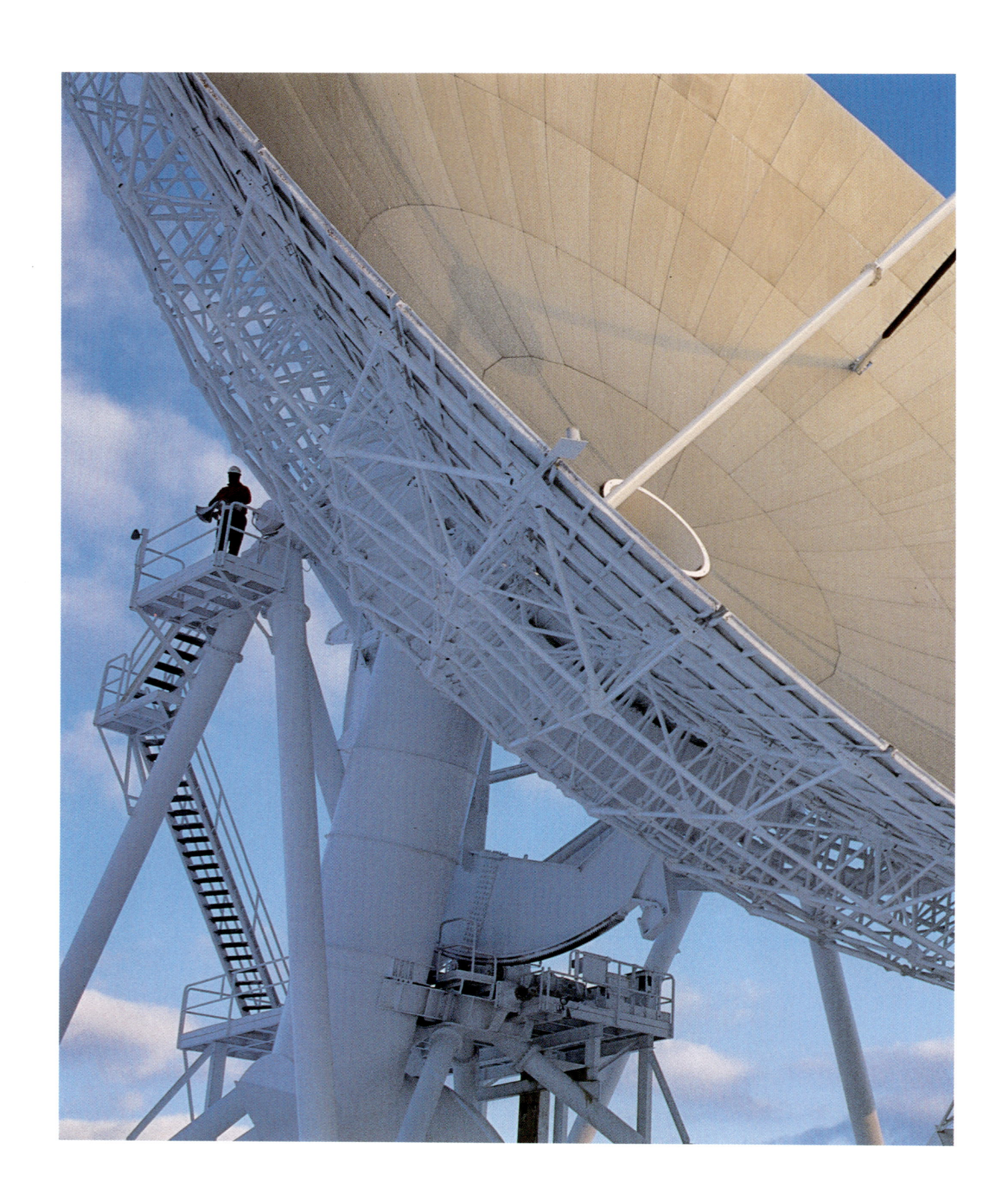

GETTING THE WORD OUT

78 CREATING THE FUTURE

CHAPTER TWELVE

Sandwiched between New York and Philadelphia, two of the nation's largest media markets, New Jersey has long been one of the most unusual environments for print, radio, and television found anywhere in the country. Electronic media have been dominated by stations that are based out of state. As a result, New Jerseyans are avid readers of regional and local newspapers that cover events and issues directly affecting their lives. Despite declining newspaper readership nationally, the Garden State can boast of more newspapers per square mile than any other state.

That situation is changing as the twenty-first century dawns. The advent of New Jersey–based cable news operations has brought a more local look to television news coverage, and the merger of several newspaper operations under a single corporate umbrella has changed the competitive landscape among newspapers. Meanwhile, the emergence in the 1990s of New Jersey 101.5, a truly statewide radio station, has given the state its first unified media voice.

The Power of Print

Despite the presence of such newspaper powerhouses as the *New York Times* and the *Philadelphia Inquirer*, New Jersey supports twenty-one daily newspapers of its own—a surprisingly large number given the state's small size.

Largely because there are no network television stations based in the state, smaller newspapers that serve local readers with local news have been able to survive.

Among New Jersey newspapers, the Newark *Star-Ledger* outstrips all the others in terms of size. Sold in sixteen of the state's twenty-one counties, its circulation—425,000 daily and 650,000 on Sunday—makes it one of the fifteen largest newspapers in the country. Owned by Newhouse Publications, the *Star-Ledger* maintains nine local bureaus, as well as a Washington, D.C., office, and is avidly read by politicians and power brokers for its coverage of state government. (Newhouse also owns the Jersey City–based *Jersey Journal* and the *Times* of Trenton.)

Opposite: *Satellite dishes are an indispensable part of the vast information and entertainment net blanketing the planet. As cable television programming and the networks that promote it expand, New Jersey has kept abreast of the latest developments. Cable companies in the state have recently developed many interesting programs centered on New Jersey topics.* © Mark Bolster/International
Above: *Like all good salesmen, newspaper delivery boy Jimmy Whalen makes sure he knows his product. Scanning an edition of the* Elizabeth Daily Journal *before he covers his route, Jimmy plied his trade in 1953.* © UPI/Corbis-Bettmann

GETTING THE WORD OUT 79

Martian Sighting

The news that Martians had landed in Grovers Mill, New Jersey, filled the radio airwaves on the night of 30 October 1938. Stirring panic at first, the landmark broadcast stirred controversy after the public learned that they had been listening to Orson Welles's Mercury Theater presentation of H. G. Wells's novel *The War of the Worlds*.

Though much smaller than the *Star-Ledger,* two other dailies—the *Record* of Hackensack and the *Asbury Park Press*—are among the most respected regional newspapers in the country. The *Record,* with a circulation of 160,000, serves Bergen and Passaic counties in North Jersey; while the *Press,* with a circulation of 162,000, serves Monmouth and Ocean counties along the Jersey Shore. Both papers are recognized annually for their aggressive, enterprising reporting on pressing public concerns. The *Record* consistently gets accolades for its work on environmental and good-government issues. In 1998 the editorial cartoonist for the *Press,* Steve Breen, was the first New Jersey journalist in twenty-seven years to win a Pulitzer Prize, the newspaper industry's top award.

The *Asbury Park Press* was one of several New Jersey newspapers bought by Gannett Company in 1997 and 1998 in a series of deals that have altered the newspaper landscape in the state. Gannett, the nation's largest newspaper chain, now owns six Garden State properties, including the Camden *Courier Post,* the Morristown *Daily Record* and the Bridgewater *Courier News.* While maintaining the identity of the individual newspapers, Gannett's moves are expected to make the papers even more attractive to advertisers.

A workman makes sure that all flows smoothly through a printing press. © Telegraph Colour Library/FPG International

> ## HELLO, DAILY
>
> IN MARCH 1832 THE NEWARK *DAILY ADVERTISER* DEBUTED AS NEW JERSEY'S FIRST DAILY NEWSPAPER. AT THE TIME, AT LEAST TWENTY-FIVE OTHER NEWSPAPERS CIRCULATED IN THE STATE ON A LESS FREQUENT BASIS.

The *Trentonian* is unique among New Jersey dailies. A tabloid with about sixty-eight thousand readers, the newspaper is renowned for its screaming headlines about murders and sex scandals. The *Press* of Atlantic City, with a circulation of seventy-four thousand, is the dominant paper along the shore in South Jersey, while five smaller papers remain strong in the state's less populated southern counties. The *Burlington County Times* is the largest of the group with a circulation of just forty thousand.

In addition, there are over three hundred weekly papers that serve communities across New Jersey. Many are owned by large media conglomerates. One of the largest, North Jersey Newspapers Company, owns forty-eight publications throughout the state, while Worrall Community Newspapers owns twenty-two, largely in Essex and Union counties. The Princeton Packet also is a formidable publishing company, owning fifteen local newspapers. *Business News New Jersey* covers statewide business issues on a weekly basis.

Other New Jersey–based news providers serve a national audience, including two daily business news services from Dow Jones, publisher of the *Wall Street Journal*. The *Dow Jones Capital Markets and News Service* covers breaking news on publicly traded companies and financial markets, while the *Dow Jones Professional Investor Report* furnishes reports to investment organizations.

Murray Hill–based Dun & Bradstreet also specializes in providing news for investors, packaging financial profiles and, through its affiliate Moody's Investors Service, publishing credit ratings on corporate and public finance securities. Similarly, *Bloomberg News Service* publishes daily financial and business advice to both professional and personal investors. With its New Jersey operations based in Montgomery, Bloomberg also publishes two business-related magazines: *Bloomberg Personal,* which provides monthly financial advice to 160,000 personal investors; and *Bloomberg Magazine,* with monthly advice to 85,000 readers on investment management issues.

New Jersey is also home to a number of medical publishers, including Medical Economics. The Montvale-based company publishes a number of magazines for health care professionals. Its leading title, *Medical Economics Magazine,* is read by 174,000 physicians in office-based practices. The bimonthly magazine *Drug Topics* goes to 100,400 pharmacists. Another medical publisher, Slack, offers more than twenty-five magazines and journals for health care professionals.

New Jersey is also big in technology and science publishing. The Institute for Electrical and Electronics Engineers in Piscataway publishes a wide range of journals, magazines, books, and multimedia tools for engineering professionals. And Penton Publishers puts out the biweekly *Electronic Design,* a magazine for engineering professionals with a circulation of 165,000.

Two popular national women's magazines are published in Englewood by Bauer Publishing Company. *Woman's World* publishes weekly for middle-class women ages eighteen to forty-nine years old and has a circulation of 1.4 million. *First for Women* is published every three weeks for women ages twenty to forty years old. Its circulation is 1.2 million.

Magazines geared to a state audience include *New Jersey Monthly,* which offers feature stories on people, places, and trends in the Garden State to one hundred thousand readers. *Savvy Living,* with a circulation of fifty thousand, has local lifestyle and entertainment information, while *Atlantic City Magazine,* also with fifty thousand readers, is geared to casino coverage. *New Jersey Reporter,* published by the nonprofit Center for the

> ## GOOD-BYE, HOLLYWOOD
>
> IN 1997 METROMEDIA COMPANY OF EAST RUTHERFORD SOLD ITS ENTERTAINMENT ASSETS, INCLUDING MOVIE STUDIOS AND FILM LIBRARIES, TO FOCUS ON ITS COMMUNICATIONS BUSINESSES IN EMERGING MARKETS. CONTROLLED BY BILLIONAIRE JOHN KLUGE, THE COMPANY PROVIDES MODERN TELECOMMUNICATIONS AND INFORMATION SERVICES TO EASTERN EUROPE, THE REPUBLICS OF THE FORMER SOVIET UNION, CENTRAL ASIA, AND CHINA. ITS MEDIA VENTURES ALSO INCLUDE NINE WIRELESS CABLE-TV SYSTEMS, FOURTEEN RADIO STATIONS, ELEVEN PAGING SYSTEMS, TWO MOBILE PHONE SYSTEMS, FIVE TRUNKED MOBILE RADIO SYSTEMS, AND AN INTERNATIONAL TOLL-CALLING SERVICE.

Analysis of Public Issues, has a small readership of just two thousand, but is widely read by state decision-makers.

Hot off the press, these galleys must be carefully checked by printers, editors, and art directors before the final pages are made up. © Charlie Westerman/International Stock

BROADCAST MEDIA

Without a doubt, the "Voice of the Garden State" among media outlets is the Trenton-based radio station WKXW-FM. Widely known as New Jersey 101.5, the station pumps fifty thousand watts across the airwaves and can be heard across most of the state. With its talk-radio format, its outspoken hosts and its loyal listeners, New Jersey 101.5 is the place to go for commentary and opinion on the political and social issues that are in the news.

New Jersey 101.5 hit the airwaves in 1990, just before then-Governor Jim Florio raised taxes a record amount. Outraged listeners flooded the station with calls that prompted rallies on the steps of the State House in Trenton, and their ire helped define the political world in New Jersey for the next several years. More recently, afternoon hosts Jeff Deminski and Bill Doyle brought the issue of auto insurance costs to the fore, and their public conversation on the topic had a direct influence on the outcome of the 1997 governor's race.

As for television coverage of New Jersey, viewers historically have relied largely on New Jersey Network, the state's public television network, with transmitter sites in Trenton, Montclair, and Camden. NJN specializes in arts and culture programming, and produces both a nightly New Jersey–centered newscast and weekly public affairs shows. Secaucus-based WWOR TV Channel 9 offers a diverse broadcasting alternative to the major networks, with locally produced programs such as *Hispanic Horizons, Viewpoint, Black Experience,* and *Garden State Matters.* In 1997 and 1998 the station won Emmys for outstanding single newscast in the New York metropolitan region. Additionally, the Spanish-language network Telemundo is based in Teterboro. Telemundo produces two Spanish-language newscasts daily for seventeen markets in the United States. It is one of only two Hispanic networks in the nation.

THE FIRST ALL-ELECTRONIC COLOR TELEVISION WAS DEVELOPED IN 1946 AT PRINCETON-BASED SARNOFF CORPORATION, AN ORGANIZATION THAT HAS SINCE BEEN RESPONSIBLE FOR DEVELOPING LIQUID CRYSTAL DISPLAY (LCD) TECHNOLOGY, SOLID-STATE BROADCAST TV CAMERAS, AND ADVANCED DIGITAL HIGH-DEFINITION TELEVISION (HDTV).

© Sarnoff Corporation

82 CREATING THE FUTURE

The historic RCA factory building, with its widely recognizable emblem, is a familiar landmark in Camden. © Jeffrey Sylvester/FPG International

IN 1996, JUST SIX MONTHS AFTER IT WAS LAUNCHED, *NEW JERSEY ONLINE* WAS CITED AS THE "BEST ON-LINE NEWSPAPER" IN THE UNITED STATES BY THE NEWSPAPER ASSOCIATION OF AMERICA.

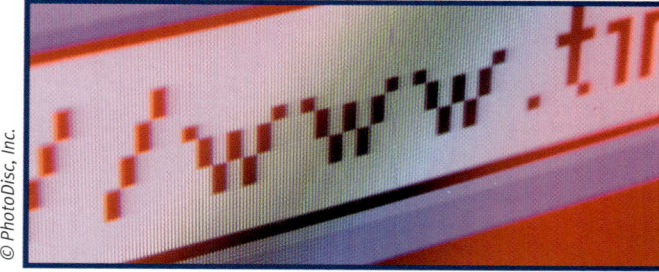

In the late 1990s the New Jersey television scene began to shift with the rise of cable television networks. Though there are thirty-nine cable companies in the state, a flurry of mergers has given several access to a large number of statewide viewers: Cablevision now reaches over one million New Jersey homes, while Comcast has over five hundred thousand subscribers. And because of their size, both companies have started to develop New Jersey–oriented programming on their cable networks the likes of which New Jersey television viewers have never seen before.

In 1996 Cablevision joined with the *Star-Ledger* to launch a twenty-four-hour cable news service, News 12 New Jersey, which provides comprehensive coverage of New Jersey news and public affairs. In a similar vein, Comcast started the Comcast Network Channel in 1997 with an emphasis on local sports programming and call-in talk shows. The Cable Television Network of New Jersey, which is owned by the New Jersey Cable Industry, provides twenty-four-hour programming on state topics as part of the basic cable package to 1.7 million cable subscribers.

In the future, the World Wide Web promises to add a new media voice to the Garden State. Every major newspaper, magazine, radio station, and television operator in the state has an on-line presence. Sites such as *New Jersey Online* and IN Jersey offer Internet users a central place to go for Garden State news, sports, entertainment listings, and recreation ideas. No one knows how big these Internet operations will become in the new century, but there's no question that New Jersey media businesses are primed to be as successful in the twenty-first century as they have been in the twentieth.

POWER AND MOTION

84 CREATING THE FUTURE

CHAPTER THIRTEEN

NEW JERSEY'S TRANSPORTATION AND UTILITY INDUSTRIES ARE BOTH IN THE PROCESS OF INCREASING THEIR EFFICIENCY TO CONSUMERS—BUT WITHOUT INCREASING THEIR COSTS. COMMUTERS AND BUSINESSES HAVE BEGUN TO BENEFIT FROM INCREASED TRANSPORTATION OPTIONS, AND ENERGY CUSTOMERS CAN LOOK FORWARD TO REDUCED ENERGY COSTS AS A RESULT OF ONGOING DEREGULATION AND INDUSTRY INNOVATION.

PEOPLE ON THE MOVE

New Jersey Transit, whose nine thousand employees provide bus, rail, and light rail services to 321,000 passengers daily, earned an Outstanding Achievement award from the American Public Transit Association in 1994, 1996, and 1998. More than 13,300 trips are made a day on its 598 trains and 1,900 buses throughout the state and to New York and Philadelphia, covering 5,325 square miles in all. The system comprises 12 rail lines and 178 bus routes.

Ridership on NJ Transit has increased in recent years thanks to new services and a focus on quality of service, on-time performance, safety, and cleanliness. NJ Transit provides an astounding 188 billion passenger trips a year. The agency, founded in 1983, is the third-largest provider of bus and commuter rail service in the country after Chicago and New York, respectively. Best of all for riders on New Jersey's trains and buses, there were no fare hikes for the bulk of the past decade, including none for seven consecutive years from 1991 to 1998. By privatizing special services, the agency has actually reduced its dependency on state subsidies by about $70 million since 1991. Recently, the agency added the popular Midtown Direct line, which lets riders on the Morris and Essex line take the train directly into midtown Manhattan.

The Hudson-Bergen Light-Rail system is planned to provide service by 2002 for commuters from Bayonne to the Vince Lombardi Park-and-Ride lot just off the New Jersey Turnpike in Ridgefield. The twenty-mile-long line is expected to carry fifty thousand Northern New Jersey commuters daily. Also due for 2002, the $450-million Secaucus Transfer station will give people living in Bergen and Passaic Counties quick

OPPOSITE: *Tanker cars wait in a rail yard in Port Elizabeth, one of the two significant shipping points for freight coming into the Port of New York and New Jersey, the third-largest port in the United States. © Scott Barrow.* ABOVE: *Who needs a car when the commuter rail system is this good? On a sunny morning, commuters wait for one of the many trains that are part of the New Jersey Transit Passenger Rail System. The rail and light-rail services join bus lines to move 321,000 passengers every day. © Ken Levinson/International Stock*

POWER AND MOTION 85

CHIEF ENGINEER CLIFFORD M. HOLLAND DID NOT LIVE TO SEE THE FRUITS OF HIS EFFORT COMPLETED, BUT THE TUNNEL BETWEEN NEW JERSEY AND NEW YORK THAT OPENED IN 1927 AND BEARS HIS NAME IS KNOWN FAR AND WIDE FOR ITS INNOVATIVE ENGINEERING. THE HOLLAND TUNNEL IS ALSO KNOWN FOR ACCOMMODATING OVER SIXTEEN MILLION VEHICLES A YEAR.

© UPI/Corbis-Bettmann

and easy access to Manhattan. Currently, commuters have to travel to Hoboken and switch to PATH trains if they want to go to Manhattan. The Secaucus Transfer station will connect both to NJ Transit's Northeast Corridor line, which runs between Trenton and New York, and to the Main-Bergen and Pascack Valley lines.

The PATH (Port Authority Trans-Hudson Corporation) system, the fourteen-mile rail link between New Jersey and New York, is undergoing a $200-million renovation. Train cars and signal systems are being overhauled, among other improvements. Beginning in 1908 as the Hudson and Manhattan Railroad, the PATH is now operated by the Port Authority of New York and New Jersey. Annual ridership is up to 60 million passengers and no increase is scheduled for the one-dollar fare.

New Jersey also is served by three airports, all of which receive both international and domestic flights. The largest and busiest is the Newark International Airport, which employs eighteen thousand people and contributes $10 billion to the New Jersey and New York metropolitan region's economy. The airport is among the fastest growing in the nation and currently serves over thirty million travelers and has over 450,000 flights annually. It is a hub for Continental Airlines.

Recent renovations have secured Newark Airport's place among top airports in the country. A smooth, new monorail system transports travelers from and to their cars, making that stressful time somewhat less so. Monorail trains come every two to three minutes and, once you have trundled in with your bags, you are just minutes from the airport terminals.

This early photograph of the intersections of Highways 4 and 17 shows an engineering design new for its time: the cloverleaf. New Jersey was one of a few states that pioneered the building of innovative high-speed roadways. © Corbis-Bettmann

86 CREATING THE FUTURE

NJ Transit is working with Newark Airport on a new 8.8-mile Newark–Elizabeth Rail Link that will join the state's Northeast Corridor commuter line and the Newark subway system to the airport monorail. Expected to be fully operational by the year 2000, the new $250-million system will make the airport accessible by rail

The Newark Airport monorail affords an unobstructed view of the airfield. The monorail soon will be linked to the Newark subway and the Northeast Corridor commuter line. © Scott Barrow

BRIDGES UNCOVERED

ALL TWENTY-ONE NEW JERSEY COUNTIES ONCE HAD AT LEAST ONE COVERED BRIDGE SPANNING A PUBLIC HIGHWAY. TODAY THE ONLY QUAINT REMINDER OF YESTERYEAR IS THE GREAT SERGEANT'S BRIDGE IN SERGEANTSVILLE, HUNTERDON COUNTY. THE SINGLE-LANE BRIDGE WAS BUILT IN 1872 AND SPANS THE WICKECHEOKE CREEK.

POWER AND MOTION

HERE COME THE BUSES

IN 1934 ENGINEERS AT PUBLIC SERVICE COORDINATED TRANSPORT, WHICH DOMINATED NEW JERSEY PUBLIC TRANSPORTATION AT THE TIME, DESIGNED THE WORLD'S FIRST DIESEL-ELECTRIC BUS. BY 1937, THE COMPANY HAD THE FIRST DIESEL-ELECTRIC BUS FLEET, WITH TWENTY-SEVEN VEHICLES.

from New York City, as well as Union, Middlesex, Monmouth, Ocean, Mercer, and Somerset Counties. Air travelers will soon be able to bypass cars and busses completely, enjoying a virtually seamless journey to the airport gate by rail.

Teterboro Airport in Bergen County serves a smaller clientele—primarily the corporate business traveler—seeking high-quality transportation service with minimal hassle. Located just seven miles outside of Manhattan, the airport accommodates smaller jets and is easily accessed by New York and New Jersey residents alike. Further south, the Trenton-Mercer Airport serves corporate clients and also is the hub for Eastwind Airlines, which flies to Boston, MA; Orlando, FL; Rochester, NY; and Greensboro, NC. Located five miles north of Trenton in Ewing Township, the airport is used by executives and travelers from Philadelphia and central New Jersey.

MOVING THE GOODS

New Jersey is not just well-equipped for air and land transportation. It also plays a prominent role in shipping cargo. The Port of New York and New Jersey is the third-largest port in the United States, with most of the shipping taking place on the New Jersey side of the Hudson River, in the ports of Newark and Elizabeth.

The harbor serves as a valuable hub in the region's economy, bringing $29 billion annually to the local economy. Approximately 180,000 employees earning $6.2 billion in regional wages work in the shipping industry here. Ten percent of all shipments in and out of the United States come through New Jersey, including more than one million twenty-foot cargo containers; four hundred thousand autos; thirty-two million tons of bulk cargo; and thirty billion gallons of petroleum products. About four hundred thousand passengers on 226 cruise ships come through the port, as well.

Only the ports in Los Angeles and in Long Beach, California, do more business than New York/New Jersey ports. And that may not be true for long. The Port Authority of New York and New Jersey, which maintains and manages the area's ports, estimates that port activity will increase from 1.3 million containers shipped in 1996, to 3.1 million in 2015, to 6.5 million in 2040.

The New York/New Jersey port is made up of a 423-mile network of port berths, channels, and bays. But rising

These numerous cargo containers along the Hudson River attest to the huge volume of traffic moving through Port Newark, a vital hub for the shipping of goods nationwide. © Bob Krist

88 CREATING THE FUTURE

shoals of silt threatened to shut down these waterways in the 1990s. Many of these channels have a natural depth of only nineteen feet, and many supersized ships require as much as forty-two feet of draft. As the decade drew to a close, the state was moving aggressively with extensive dredging plans to ensure access to the harbor by all ships.

Half of the 1.3 million cargo containers that pass through the New York/New Jersey port each year are handled by Maher Terminals. The channels at Maher Terminals have been deepened to forty-five feet to accommodate the new, bigger ships. The ships can carry about twenty-five hundred containers compared to older ships which carry about fifteen hundred containers. The renewed dredging effort has been hailed for successfully balancing commercial and environmental interests.

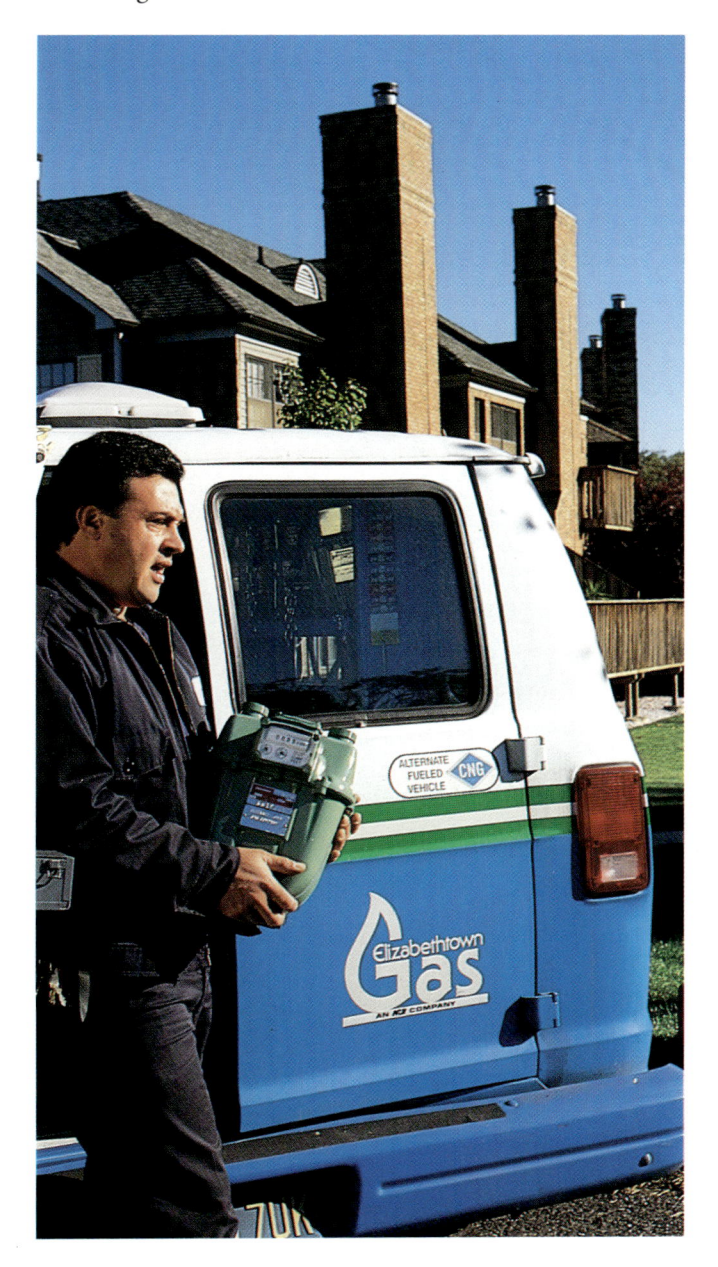

IN 1927 THE CITY OF NEWARK SET ASIDE SIXTY-EIGHT ACRES FOR THE FIRST MAJOR AIRPORT IN THE NEW YORK METROPOLITAN REGION. TODAY NEWARK INTERNATIONAL AIRPORT COVERS SOME TWENTY-THREE HUNDRED ACRES AND IS ONE OF THE FASTEST GROWING AIRPORTS IN THE WORLD.

THE FUTURE OF POWER

New Jersey's stringent air pollution policies have forced electric utilities to generate cleaner emissions, and that has had an influence on electricity costs. But in the new century, energy customers will get a break thanks to a plan developed by the New Jersey Board of Public Utilities to deregulate the energy utilities. Under the plan, 10 percent of New Jersey consumers began selecting their electric energy supplier in October 1998, and all will be given the chance to do so by July 2000.

The state's $7-billion electric power industry has been regulated since 1911. Of the four electric companies that have served New Jersey, Public Service Electric and Gas (PSE&G) is the largest. Perhaps the most famous of the $17-billion company's 2.2 million customers is the Statue of Liberty, which PSE&G has lit for ninety years. PSE&G ranks as the fourth-largest gas and electric utility in the country and is the largest electric company east of Michigan and the Mississippi River. About 70 percent of the New Jersey population currently uses the company for its energy needs.

Joining PSE&G in deregulation are the state's three other electricity suppliers: GPU (formerly Jersey Central Power and Light); Conectiv, formed by a merger between Atlantic Electric and Delmarva Power and Light, and now headquartered in Wilmington, Delaware; and Orange and Rockland Utilities, which was purchased by Consolidated Edison, Inc., of New York in 1998. All are promising lower rates for customers. With the onset of deregulation, these four major energy providers will face

A service technician prepares to install a meter in a new townhouse development. Currently serving 240,000 customers, Elizabethtown Gas is one of three principal suppliers of natural gas in New Jersey. © Bob Sacha/Courtesy, Elizabethtown Gas

POWER AND MOTION 89

ABOVE: *This PATH station in Hoboken provides direct service to Manhattan. Over eleven hundred PATH trains run every day, twenty-four hours a day, all year. During rush hour, a train pulls into the station every three to six minutes.* © Scott Barrow. BELOW LEFT: *These bales of tin await their journey to a recycling center.* © Bill Heinsohm/Tony Stone Images. BELOW RIGHT: *Harnessed for hydroelectric power, the Passaic Falls at Paterson was called* Totowa *by the Lenni Lenape, meaning "heavy, falling weight of waters."* © Scott Thode/International Stock

90   CREATING THE FUTURE

competition from fifty to one hundred firms, many from out of state, that are expected to go after a piece of New Jersey's electricity market.

In contrast, the gas and water utilities face a far less competitive landscape. Although the natural gas market is open to new entrants, it is served largely by three long-time companies: New Jersey Natural Gas with 360,000 customers; South Jersey Gas with 257,000 customers; and Elizabethtown Gas (NUI) with 240,000 customers. However, market forces and government intervention are expected to spur consolidation among water companies in the new century. And New Jersey, which is home to American Water Works and United Water Resources, two of the country's largest investor-owned water utilities, will be at the center of this transformation.

The increasing options in the state's transportation and utilities industries are helping to improve conditions for all people living, working, and conducting business in New Jersey.

... WAITING TO HAPPEN

IN 1903 A NEWARK TROLLEY CAR FULL OF HIGH SCHOOL STUDENTS COLLIDED WITH A TRAIN. WHILE INVESTIGATING THE CRASH, STATE ATTORNEY GENERAL THOMAS MCCARTER DISCOVERED THE UNDERLYING FINANCIAL WEAKNESS OF THE TROLLEY COMPANY AND MANY OF NEW JERSEY'S OTHER TRANSPORTATION, GAS, AND ELECTRIC COMPANIES. MCCARTER RESIGNED HIS GOVERNMENT OFFICE TO BUY AND CONSOLIDATE THESE COMPANIES INTO THE PUBLIC SERVICE CORPORATION. PUBLIC SERVICE ENTERPRISE GROUP REMAINS NEW JERSEY'S DOMINANT ELECTRIC UTILITY. THE COMPANY'S TRANSPORTATION ARM WAS SOLD TO THE STATE IN 1980 TO FORM NEW JERSEY TRANSIT.

Passing through Manasquan, a rapid-transit train crosses the Manasquan River, the starting point of the vital Intracoastal Waterway, which stretches all the way to Florida. © Scott Barrow

POWER AND MOTION

© Scott Barrow

92   CREATING THE FUTURE

TRANSPORTATION

INTERPOOL, INC.

ONE OF THE WORLD'S LARGEST LESSORS OF SHIPPING CONTAINERS AND CHASSIS, INTERPOOL, INC., PROVIDES EQUIPMENT MANAGING, LEASING, AND FINANCING, SUPPORTING NEW JERSEY'S TRADE AND COMMERCE AROUND THE GLOBE

When Thomas Edison invented the light bulb, it quickly gained acceptance by the world and immediately revolutionized lighting—the new invention's size, shape, and function became the lighting industry standard. In the container industry a similar revolution occurred. With the simple design in the mid-1960s of the so-called Twenty-foot Equivalent Unit (TEU), or "intermodal container," the seagoing container—with standardized fittings and accessories, dimensions, and internal cubic size—was immediately accepted and revolutionized the shipping industry. The new industry standard, called "containerization," allowed shippers to deter pilferage and overcome the expense of separately handling thousands of small items. Shippers also were able to decrease the time needed for loading and unloading vessels in port. The new practice of shipping by container spawned thousands of trucking, inspection, maintenance, freight-forwarding, and other transport- and shipping-related companies worldwide.

Interpool, Inc., was one of the many companies that was formed as a direct result of containerization. The international intermodal container and chassis lessor was founded by Martin Tuchman, one of the original designers of the standard cargo container, in 1968. Today Interpool's economic strength, stability, and fleet size rank it as one of the top three intermodal container leasing companies.

Based in Princeton, New Jersey, Interpool has developed a client base of more than 200 customers, including the twenty largest international container shipping lines in the world. With a container fleet exceeding 700,000 TEUs and a domestic chassis fleet exceeding 71,000 units, Interpool has the capability of providing a "one-stop shop" for all equipment managing, leasing, and financing.

Furthermore, Interpool records an unprecedented 99 percent utilization rate for both its container and chassis divisions.

Martin Tuchman, chairman and chief executive officer of Interpool, Inc., founded the intermodal container and chassis lessor in 1968.

A typical container ship, such as the one shown above, carries thousands of containers above deck as well as below.

In just thirty years Interpool has become the world's third largest lessor of containers and second largest lessor of chassis.

In an industry where products infrequently undergo structural changes, Interpool's long-standing success is credited to its ability to offer customers attractive, flexible leasing options and superior customer service, coupled with an experienced and innovative executive board. Interpool is able to create pioneering programs that are beneficial to its customers, its vendors, and even New Jersey's local communities.

Interpool's chassis division, Trac Lease, is an industry leader. Trac Lease stresses the importance

More than $1 trillion worth of world trade products are transported by containers such as these every year.

94 CREATING THE FUTURE

of safety and quality and has implemented chassis standards for itself that are tougher than those of most other lessors. Since its inception, Trac Lease has preferred to purchase, maintain, and refurbish its chassis within the Garden State, and since its business has tripled during the past eight years, the company has helped foster many business opportunities throughout New Jersey.

One of Interpool's most recent achievements was the installation of its proprietary weight indicator, which is attached directly to the chassis. The weight indicator was designed by Martin Tuchman back in 1969 and updated in 1998. Historically, truckers have driven in to weigh stations alongside highways to verify the weight of their truck's cargo. With the introduction of the axle weight indicator, truckers, authorities, and shippers can record container payloads simply by looking at the chassis scales. This invention allows for a reduction in the number of fines for overloading equipment and provides shippers with more accurate weight readings on cargo, yielding quicker and more efficient transport of cargo and enabling safer carriage of cargo over the nation's highways.

Through research and development of the axle scale, Interpool has built a relationship with a reputable and long-standing New Jersey institution, New Jersey Institute of Technology (NJIT). Currently Interpool is working closely with NJIT in producing measuring devices to exacting engineering standards.

This Interpool chassis pool at a port facility is accepting containers from a vessel by means of an overhead crane.

Interpool also holds a competition for high school students to design safer and more efficient shipping and transport equipment. In the past two years more than 800 students have entered designs in this competition. NJIT tests the new designs and gives Interpool scholarships to students who submit outstanding entries.

Within its industry, Interpool has pioneered many distinguished programs, such as the Shipper's Pool and Contrailer. Developed in the 1970s, these programs offer shippers and customers more cost-effective solutions for storing, transporting, and repositioning containers. In an effort to provide shippers with efficient alternatives in chassis management, maintenance, storage, and repair, Interpool introduced the PoolStat program. Originally developed and now located in Princeton, New Jersey, PoolStat now manages more than thirty chassis pools nationwide.

Interpool prides itself on its well-trained, experienced staff, its hands-on management, and its ability to adapt to present times. To illustrate management's dedication to Interpool employees, Martin Tuchman created a professionally staffed in-house day care center and a fully equipped fitness center in its Princeton office. Tuchman also has handpicked several recent New Jersey college graduates and placed them in management-training positions throughout Interpool's global offices.

Since its founding more than thirty years ago by a small group of engineers, Interpool, Inc., has become an integral part of New Jersey trade and commerce, and integral to its global industry.

LEFT AND ABOVE: *These "double-stack" trains carry containers to inland locations.*

TRANSPORTATION 95

CONTINENTAL AIRLINES

RECOGNIZED IN INDEPENDENT STUDIES AS AN INDUSTRY LEADER, CONTINENTAL AIRLINES CONTINUALLY STRIVES TO IMPROVE UPON ITS CURRENT SUCCESSES, AND INCREASE ITS GLOBAL SYSTEM OF ROUTES AND DESTINATIONS

The roots of Continental Airlines reach back to 1934 and an airline known as Varney Speed Lines, which flew between El Paso, Texas, and Pueblo, Colorado. Today Continental Airlines is the fifth largest United States airline, serving approximately forty million passengers per year worldwide. Continental offers more than 2,000 departures daily to 122 domestic and 70 international destinations.

After facing major financial challenges in 1995, Continental implemented its Go Forward Plan program, which launched the airline from its 1995 $175 million market value to its present $4 billion market value, and made Continental a two-time J. D. Power and Associates Award winner. The credo of the program is: What gets measured and rewarded gets done. The four cornerstones of the program are Fly to Win, Fund the Future, Make Reliability a Reality, and Working Together. "These goals are practical, measurable, flexible, and, most importantly, make sense to our coworkers," says Continental chairman of the board and CEO, Gordon Bethune.

"Tremendous results occur when 40,000 people focus on the same objectives," he says. "Like a championship football team, everyone is in our huddle before every play. We communicate constantly. We are proud coaches as we watch our team work together to successfully execute the game plan time after time."

The Go Forward Plan program has succeeded by focusing on the values by

The Go Forward Plan has resulted in fewer workers' compensation claims, reduced sick leave, and a dramatic increase in the sale of company logo merchandise to employees.

Continental Airlines has succeeded by focusing on the values that produce the greatest amount of customer satisfaction, including the best on-time arrivals record and baggage handling, the fewest involuntary denied boardings, and the fewest complaints.

which the customers of Continental measure its effectiveness, including on-time arrivals; baggage handling; fewest complaints received; and fewest customers who were involuntarily denied boarding. The statistics are gathered by the United States Department of Transportation.

As part of its plan, all Continental's aircraft were deployed to its franchise hubs, which are in Houston, New York/Newark, Cleveland, and Guam. A profitable core schedule was determined. Serving as the hub carrier in these four markets has increased the amount and predictability of Continental's profits. Workers' compensation claims are down 51 percent; sick leave is down 29 percent; and sales of merchandise with the Continental logo at its company store are up by 400 percent.

In May 1997 customers surveyed by J. D. Power and Associates and *Frequent Flyer* magazine voted and awarded Continental Airlines, for an unprecedented second straight year, the coveted J. D. Power and Associates Award for customer satisfaction for flights 500 miles or more. In 1996 Continental had been the first company in any industry to go from the lowest to the highest in the J. D. Power rankings. All United States airlines compete vigorously for this award because most

96 CREATING THE FUTURE

customers, particularly connecting passengers, have many choices as to which airline they will fly.

While continuing to provide superior customer service, Continental has reaped accolades from its customers and industry observers. In January 1997 *Air Transport World,* the airline industry's leading publication, evaluated the world's 300-plus air carriers and named Continental "Airline of the Year." In March 1997 the *Wall Street Journal's Smart Money* magazine picked Continental's BusinessFirst service as the best transatlantic business-class service of any United States airline, calling Continental the "Cinderella of the Skies." In January 1998 the industry-leading OnePass frequent flyer program dominated *Inside Flyer* magazine's prestigious Freddie Awards. The Freddie Awards are voted on by frequent flyers, and OnePass captured six of the nine awards, including Program of the Year and Best Elite-Level Program. In March 1998 *Fortune* magazine named Continental the most improved company of the 1990s on its annual Most Admired Companies list.

As it continues to improve all aspects of its airline, Continental plans to have one of the youngest aircraft fleets in the industry by the year 2000. Shown below is a DC-10.

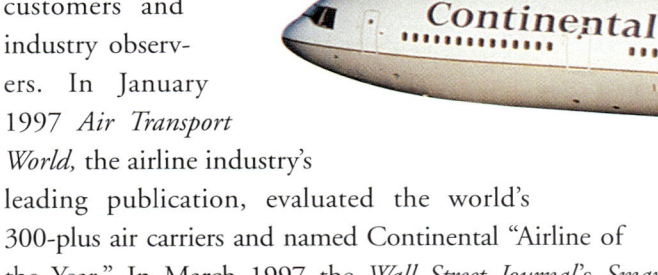

In 1998 Continental began an innovative alliance with Northwest Airlines that will benefit customers for years to come. By aligning with Northwest and its joint alliance partners, Continental can provide customers with the largest seamless network in the world, spanning Asia; Europe; and North, Central, and South America. Customers will earn OnePass miles anywhere in the world; businesses can expect volume discounts for using the combined network; and the airline's travel agent partners will be able to sell a network that rivals any of its competitors.

Continental continues to strengthen its route network from its Newark, Houston, and Cleveland hubs. While growing its domestic route system, the airline also inaugurated service to thirteen new international destinations in 1998. In addition, Continental inaugurated United States mainland–to–Japan service with nonstop flights from both Newark and Houston to Tokyo.

In 1998 the National Airline Quality Rating study ranked Continental Airlines as the Most Improved Airline for the second year in a row. The annual study compares the service quality of the ten major United States airlines, based on factors such as baggage handling, customer service, and frequent-flyer programs, among others.

"We're always proud to be recognized as an industry leader in independent studies," said Greg Brenneman, Continental's president and chief operating officer. "The Airline Quality Rating study's results are consistent with many other assessments performed by the industry and by customers. We're continuously working to improve our product, and this study is proof that our efforts are paying off."

Superior customer service at every step of the travel experience has won accolades for Continental both from its customers and from industry observers.

TRANSPORTATION 97

© Kelly/Mooney

98   CREATING THE FUTURE

UTILITIES

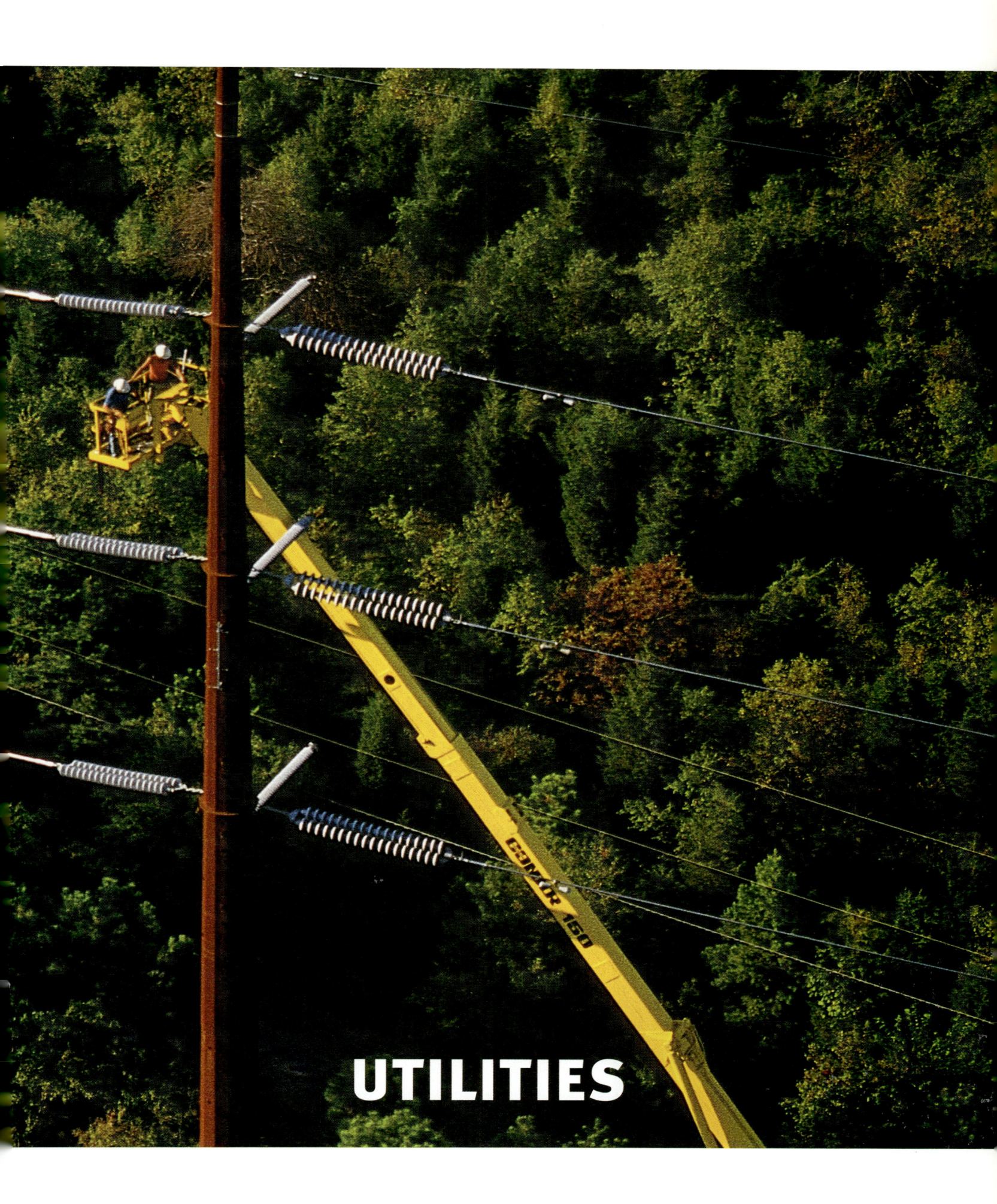

GPU ENERGY

IN THE NEW ERA OF DEREGULATION, GPU ENERGY BUILDS ON ITS FOUNDATION OF SUCCESS BY HELPING BUSINESSES WITH DEVELOPMENT AND PROVIDING HIGH-QUALITY, COST-EFFECTIVE CUSTOMER SERVICE

Building on its reputation as a customer-driven deliverer of electricity, GPU Energy works to create opportunities for new and existing businesses in New Jersey.

To maintain its leadership position in the transmission and distribution of electricity, GPU Energy management has taken steps to operate more efficiently and be more responsive to customers.

"Over the past decade we have made significant efforts to reduce costs to benefit our customers and to achieve a higher level of overall customer satisfaction," says Dennis Baldassari, president and chief operating officer of GPU Energy. "GPU Energy's record of customer service will be what makes the company successful as our industry becomes more competitive."

GPU Energy's mission includes providing developmental opportunities for existing and potential businesses in the state. The company's Business Development staff and other experts assess customers' office, manufacturing, and warehousing needs and help customers deal with financing issues, technical and training needs, and government regulations. Businesses, in turn, are able to review available commercial and industrial sites through a computerized list maintained by the company.

GPU Energy has working partnerships with municipal and state governments, real estate brokers, and development professionals. Most recently the company has cooperated in projects with companies such as Barnes and Noble, Blinds To Go, and Anadigics.

"We have all the ingredients to serve business and industry: an experienced business development

Bringing power to businesses and residences, GPU Energy is poised to be a leader in providing customer-driven energy services. © Tim Tannous/GPU Energy

As a responsible corporate citizen, GPU Energy supports the volunteer activities of its employees that help strengthen the communities across its service territory.

100 CREATING THE FUTURE

team, a strong international presence, and a service area with available skilled labor that spans two states in the mid-Atlantic region—the heart of the United States marketplace," says Rebecca Wingenroth, GPU Energy director of business development.

GPU Energy has a tradition of supporting the communities it serves as a deliverer of electricity. In addition to supporting charitable organizations, GPU Energy employees volunteer their time for community activities.

GPU Energy is the trade name for the group of subsidiaries of GPU, Inc., a Fortune 500 company. The company provides electric services to two million customers in New Jersey and Pennsylvania. GPU, Inc., recorded operating revenues of $4.1 billion in 1997. In addition, the GPU International Group has ownership and interests in the electricity distribution and supply business in England and Australia and in generating facilities in six foreign countries.

GPU Energy's competitive position in the industry has been championed through the business strategy of GPU, Inc., to make the transmission and distribution of electricity the core business of the corporation.

When Blinds To Go was looking for a manufacturing location to serve the United States market, GPU Energy's business development professionals helped the company find this Lakewood, New Jersey, location.

"We are seeing a period of unprecedented change for both the industry and GPU," says Fred D. Hafer, chairman, president, and chief executive officer of GPU, Inc. "Our industry is entering a new era—one that will see competition among electric suppliers, and the emergence of new products and services for customers. GPU, too, is embarking on a new era, and our ability to develop and pursue an appropriate strategy for this journey is critical to our future success. We are building on a solid foundation of success.

"We will continue that success as we face a new, exciting future," Hafer says. "Our future is bright. GPU Energy will keep functioning as a key element of the GPU, Inc., strategy for success in the new electric utility frontier. The changes taking place in our industry will benefit the citizens of New Jersey. We are excited to do business and have our corporate headquarters in the Garden State."

An experienced and skilled workforce supports GPU Energy's core business of transmitting and distributing electricity to more than two million customers in New Jersey and Pennsylvania.

UTILITIES 101

PUBLIC SERVICE ELECTRIC & GAS COMPANY

AS NEW JERSEY'S OLDEST AND LARGEST GAS AND ELECTRIC UTILITY FIRM, PUBLIC SERVICE ELECTRIC & GAS COMPANY IS COMMITTED TO DELIVERING THE FINEST SERVICE AND A WEALTH OF COMMUNITY SUPPORT

Public Service Electric & Gas Company (PSE&G) has been a leading corporate citizen in New Jersey for more than ninety years. The company was formed in 1903 with the amalgamation of more than 500 gas, electric, and transportation companies in New Jersey. Early in its existence, PSE&G ran trolley and bus lines, and even ran an elevator for moving horse-drawn wagons up the cliffs of the Palisades. It also sold appliances and started amusement parks—always at the end of a trolley or a bus line.

Though it is no longer in the transportation business, PSE&G has grown into one of the largest combined gas and electric companies in the nation. Its 10,500 employees serve 2.2 million customers, in a 2,600-square-mile service territory that includes all of New Jersey's six largest cities.

PSE&G is the largest subsidiary of Public Service Enterprise Group (PSEG), a publicly traded (NYSE:PEG) Fortune 500 company. In January 1997 PSEG launched PSEG Energy Technologies, which provides energy, energy services, and integrated energy-management services in the eastern region of the United States.

PSEG's international power company, PSEG Global, is one of the fastest-growing independent power companies in the world. In 1997 it increased its generation and distribution assets by more than 400 percent, to nearly $1.2 billion, positioning the company to capitalize on growing energy demands in developing economies. By the end of 1997 PSEG Global had twenty-eight projects located in countries around the world.

While new businesses are growing, PSE&G remains PSEG's core business, and the company's commitment to New Jersey grows ever stronger. As the state's oldest and largest gas and electric utility, PSE&G has a long-term vested interest in ensuring that New Jersey remains a good place to live, work, and do business.

PSE&G has one of the oldest Area Development Departments of any utility, and today this department continues to be one of the most active and innovative groups in the company. One example of its spirit of innovation is a recently created $30 million New Millennium Economic Development Fund, designed to help attract new businesses to New Jersey and to encourage the growth of the state's existing businesses.

As the energy provider to New Jersey's main urban centers, PSE&G has a long history of community involvement and commitment to New Jersey's cities. In 1997 PSE&G took a new approach on behalf of the urban communities it

The headquarters, above, of Public Service Electric & Gas Company is in Newark, New Jersey's largest city.

The city of New Brunswick, at left, is an example of major New Jersey cities that have been revitalized through the efforts of PSE&G working in concert with local economic development organizations.

102 CREATING THE FUTURE

serves and launched the PSE&G Urban Initiatives, a holistic approach to bringing about fundamental change in urban neighborhoods. The pilot program, in Newark's South Ward, focused on economic development, educational and housing programs, improvements in the delivery of social-service programs, and support for local small businesses. For this effort, PSE&G was one of five companies in the nation recognized at a Ron Brown Awards ceremony at the White House.

PSE&G's community commitment also extends to the environment. As New Jersey is the most densely populated state in the nation, its residents are especially concerned about clean air and water and open-space preservation. PSE&G shares these concerns. PSE&G is one of just two utility companies in the nation to voluntarily comply with the president's initiative to reduce greenhouse gas emissions. PSE&G also has undertaken a comprehensive program to reduce smog-causing emissions from its plants by at least 80 percent by the year 2000, a goal that it is well on its way to achieving. PSE&G also currently recycles more than 90 percent of its nonhazardous waste. Since 1991 it has reduced the amount of hazardous waste generated by 67 percent. Finally, PSE&G has undertaken the largest wetlands preservation program in the United States, restoring and preserving more than thirty-two square miles of wetlands in southern New Jersey.

Throughout its ninety-year history, PSE&G has always felt that corporations have an obligation to be active in the

The PSE&G Area Development Department was instrumental in the decision by Audi and Volkswagen to locate a distribution center in South Brunswick, in central New Jersey, to serve the entire northeast and middle Atlantic regions.

communities they serve. The company fosters a corporate culture that encourages its employees to be volunteers in their home communities. The company leads by example. PSE&G contributes $4 million per year to local nonprofit groups and contributes vans, computers, and training to schools and community-based groups, as well. For example, PSE&G has agreed to donate more than $1 million in used computer equipment to New Jersey schools over the next three years and has found partners to provide teachers and parents with computer training.

PSE&G has witnessed many changes over the decades, and in each case has risen to meet the challenge and better serve the people of New Jersey. In the near future a new challenge will arise as most energy markets are deregulated and open to competition. PSE&G is primed and ready for competition. It is convinced that the skills and commitment of its employees will allow it to identify and seize new opportunities offered by deregulation, and that it will remain a strong and vibrant corporate citizen of New Jersey.

While it is clear that the next several years will bring continuing changes to the utility industry, both in the state of New Jersey and throughout the country, PSE&G is determined to provide its customers with the same level of service the company has provided since its beginnings at the turn of the century. During the transition from a regulated to a competitive industry, PSE&G has resolved to continue to provide energy and energy services its customers can count on, and to act as a deeply committed resource for the state, its people, and its businesses.

A PSE&G crew works to maintain power. © PSE&G

UTILITIES 103

NEW JERSEY–AMERICAN WATER COMPANY

NEW JERSEY–AMERICAN WATER COMPANY IS COMMITTED TO PROVIDING ITS CUSTOMERS WITH A SAFE WATER SUPPLY THEY CAN ENJOY AND USE WITH CONFIDENCE AND WITH SERVICE THAT IS PROMPT, EFFICIENT, AND CONVENIENT

"When communities and businesses rely solely on you to deliver safe, reliable drinking water, there is only one standard—excellence," says Daniel L. Kelleher, president of New Jersey–American Water Company.

Noted for its water-quality expertise and outstanding customer service, the company has provided clean, reliable drinking water to New Jersey residents for more than one hundred years. It has grown into a company that employs approximately 600 highly trained and dedicated associates, serving about one out of every eight New Jersey residents.

New Jersey–American is a statewide water utility providing water for more than one million residents in 120 communities in Atlantic, Burlington, Cape May, Camden, Essex, Gloucester, Hunterdon, Middlesex, Morris, Monmouth, Ocean, Passaic, Somerset, Union, and Warren Counties. It provides service from six operating centers across the state: Shrewsbury, Short Hills, Washington, Haddon Heights, Lakewood, and Egg Harbor Township. New Jersey–American's corporate office, which includes a centralized customer service center and a payment remittance center, is in Haddon Heights.

The company owns and operates sewage collection systems in Lakewood, Ocean City, and Howell. It also owns and maintains more than 20,000 fire hydrants to provide reliable fire protection service.

New Jersey–American Water Company is an investor-owned business and the largest New Jersey water utility. Its parent company, American Water Works Company, is the largest

New Jersey–American's Delaware River Regional Water Treatment Plant in southern New Jersey uses the latest technology to produce superior water for up to 500,000 people in Burlington, Camden, and Gloucester counties. The plant is helping to protect and preserve the area's natural resources by relieving stress on a major groundwater supply source.

"When you're providing the water your families and your neighbors drink," Dan Kelleher, New Jersey–American president, says, "There is only one standard—excellence."

investor-owned and most geographically diverse water utility business in the United States. Through its twenty-three regulated subsidiaries, the parent company serves more than 870 communities with a total population of more than seven million in twenty-two states.

Providing clean, reliable water supply and wastewater services for families and businesses in New Jersey is a point of pride for New Jersey–American. It produces more than 45,000 million gallons of water each year.

New Jersey–American conducts an internal proficiency program that is six times more extensive than required, to ensure its customers analytical data in which they can have the highest degree of confidence.

The company analyzes all its water samples in one of its own five state-certified laboratories or at its affiliated state-certified American Water System laboratory in Belleville, Illinois. The central quality control and research laboratory in Illinois has been dedicated to the analysis of drinking water since its inception in 1981. It has accumulated a database

CREATING THE FUTURE

of more than two million data points representing water quality in twenty-two states.

All states regulating the utilities of the American Water System have conducted extensive audits of the facility and have granted certification under the Safe Drinking Water Act. In addition to performing all required regulatory inorganic and organic drinking water tests for compliance purposes, the laboratory tests for contaminants that the Environmental Protection Agency (EPA) plans to regulate in the future. Because of the laboratory's unique capabilities, it routinely interacts with other nationally and internationally prominent researchers, universities, and institutions.

The Monmouth County Planning Board recognized New Jersey–American in 1998 for its role in efforts to protect source water quality. "This program is unique and was recognized by the EPA as one of the premier volunteer programs in the country," says Kevin Dixon, the company's director of water quality.

"We are proud to assure our customers a water supply they can enjoy and use with confidence," president Kelleher says. "All over New Jersey our customers have the comfort of knowing that they can fill a glass from their tap in the middle of the night without turning the light on."

Providing superior customer service is a priority for New Jersey–American Water Company. Customers have direct access to customer service and operations associates twenty-four hours a day. Translation assistance allows customers to communicate with the company in their primary language. The company is on-line

Whether the source is surface water, such as the water in the Jumping Brook Reservoir (shown above), or groundwater deep in the earth, New Jersey–American's highly trained, diligent staff works every day to provide drinking water that is second to none.

with the Board of Public Utilities for even more prompt and efficient response to customer concerns. New Jersey–American even makes paying bills convenient, offering a direct debit program and approximately one hundred payment locations, more than any other water company in the state.

The company prides itself on being a good corporate neighbor and becomes actively involved in the communities it serves. It has donated used laboratory equipment to schools, donated used computers to schools and other worthy groups, and sponsored trips to the New Jersey State Aquarium for children in special education programs. Company associates volunteer their own time for the community as well, assisting as fire protection personnel, emergency medical technicians, and community and government leaders.

The company also is involved in efforts around the world to ensure safe, reliable water for people in need. For example, New Jersey–American and its parent, American Water Works, hosted Ukrainian visitors from Lviv Vodokanal, the water and wastewater authority serving the city of Lviv. The meeting was part of a cooperative effort by the United States Agency for International Development and Water For People, the American Water Works Association's nonprofit humanitarian aid organization.

From assuring water quality to serving its customers' water needs, to providing support and expertise in the local and global communities, New Jersey–American Water Company is a leader in the water industry and in the communities it serves.

Mark Campbell (left), Leonard Eggers (seated in truck), and Mike Austin (kneeling in front) are among the 600 New Jersey–American Water Company associates dedicated to providing the best water and the best service to customers across the state. © H. Mark Weidman

UTILITIES 105

SOUTH JERSEY INDUSTRIES, INC.

GROWTH-ORIENTED SOUTH JERSEY INDUSTRIES, INC., SUPPLIES NATURAL GAS FOR SOUTHERN NEW JERSEY, TOTAL-ENERGY MANAGEMENT FOR THE EASTERN SEABOARD, AND WHOLESALE ENERGY NATIONWIDE

South Jersey Industries, Inc., is headquartered in Folsom, New Jersey, along with its three subsidiary companies, South Jersey Gas Company, South Jersey Energy Company, and SJ EnerTrade. © Bill Bodine/SJG

South Jersey Industries, Inc. (SJI), is an energy services company that is redefining itself to meet the demands of a changing industry and the needs of its customers. It is facilitating growth via corporate restructuring, three subsidiary companies, and strategic affiliations with other energy firms.

SOUTH JERSEY GAS COMPANY

SJI's principal subsidiary is South Jersey Gas Company, which provides regulated natural gas service to 264,000 residential, commercial, and industrial customers in southern New Jersey. The company traces its roots back to 1910 when the Atlantic City Gas and Water Company was merged with the Atlantic City Gas Company, owned by entrepreneur Clarence H. Geist.

South Jersey Gas Company's basic objectives are customer growth, revenue increase from new or enhanced services, and ongoing cost control. Future growth for South Jersey Gas will come as a result of economic development throughout the entire service area, with homes and small businesses sprouting up at a rapid pace. In particular, the second wave of casino expansion in Atlantic City, which is still in its infancy, will serve as a catalyst for this growth.

Homeowners in South Jersey Gas Company's service area overwhelmingly

The second wave of Atlantic City casino expansion, still in its beginning stages, projects future growth for South Jersey Industries. A laser-illuminated lighthouse marks the city's new grand entrance corridor, which links the convention center with the boardwalk. © Bill Bodine/SJG

prefer natural gas as their heating fuel, and most new houses built with access to its mains use natural gas for heat. As evidence of customer preference for natural gas, during 1997 the company recorded the highest number of conversions from other fuels in the last seven years. Conversions to natural gas from other fuels remain an important part of the company's growth, accounting for nearly one-third of its new customers each year.

Because delivering natural gas in southern New Jersey will continue to be SJI's primary business in the foreseeable future, the company is investing significantly in the business, to effectively serve customers. SJI's commitment to this business is evidenced by its plans to spend approximately $150 million from 1997 through 1999 to improve existing pipelines and install new mains and services.

In 1998 SJI introduced an expanded Service Sentry program to customers. Changes to this appliance service program were driven by customer demand and the company's desire to increase revenues by capturing a larger share of the heating, air conditioning, and appliance repair market. By participating in this program, customers will have more service contract choices and the benefit of South Jersey Gas Company's long-standing expertise in the appliance repair business.

The company's new automated dispatch system (ADS) allows South Jersey Gas Company to dispatch its crews via a computer network linking its phone representatives, divisions, service supervisors, and field service personnel. ADS also helps South Jersey Gas Company respond faster to emergencies because the system recognizes and dispatches the serviceperson closest to the site of the problem.

106 CREATING THE FUTURE

SOUTH JERSEY ENERGY COMPANY

Another key to SJI's growth lies in increasing its role in the deregulated energy marketplace. SJI subsidiary South Jersey Energy Company markets energy management services throughout the eastern United States, including natural gas, electricity, and consulting services.

As New Jersey's first and most established energy marketing company, Energy Company's goal is to maximize its customers' energy savings by using its experience, knowledge, and synergies with utility and other wholesale energy companies while providing a high level of customer service. Energy Company's services include natural gas supply purchasing, sales, and transportation administration for residential, commercial, and industrial customers; comprehensive historical energy analyses; and natural gas storage, capacity, and delivery management. As a federally licensed power marketer, Energy Company trades electricity on the Pennsylvania–New Jersey–Maryland grid and arranges for bulk power transactions among municipal and regional electric utilities and energy marketers. When the electric industry is further deregulated, the company will add electricity sales to its package of retail energy services.

Energy Company is the most successful residential energy marketing company in southern New Jersey. In 1998 it achieved the highest level of customer participation in South Jersey Gas Company's residential transportation program, adding about 50 percent of the eligible customers while competing with several other marketers.

SJ ENERTRADE, INC.

SJ EnerTrade, Inc., a subsidiary of South Jersey Energy Company, was formed in 1997 to separate the wholesale energy marketing and asset management operations from its predecessor company, South Jersey Fuel, Inc. EnerTrade sells natural gas to energy marketers, electric and natural gas utilities, and other wholesale users in the mid-Atlantic and southern regions of the country. Also, EnerTrade has a 50 percent share in South Jersey Resources Group, LLC, a company formed through an alliance with Union Pacific Fuels, Inc. Through South Jersey Resources, EnerTrade actively manages and profits from its own portfolio of natural gas assets, including storage and the assets of several large, natural gas utilities. The positioning of EnerTrade, along with the Resources Group alliance, are fundamental to SJI's ongoing success.

"We are enthusiastic about the opportunities brought about by natural gas and electric deregulation," says Richard L. Dunham, SJI's chairman of the board and chief executive officer. "We have prepared and repositioned ourselves based on the needs and demands of increasingly aware energy consumers and a rapidly evolving market. We are in the process of making changes in South Jersey Gas Company's corporate structure to facilitate our growth in the face of a changing industry environment. We emphasize the importance of our customers to our success, and we will continue to improve our ability to meet their needs."

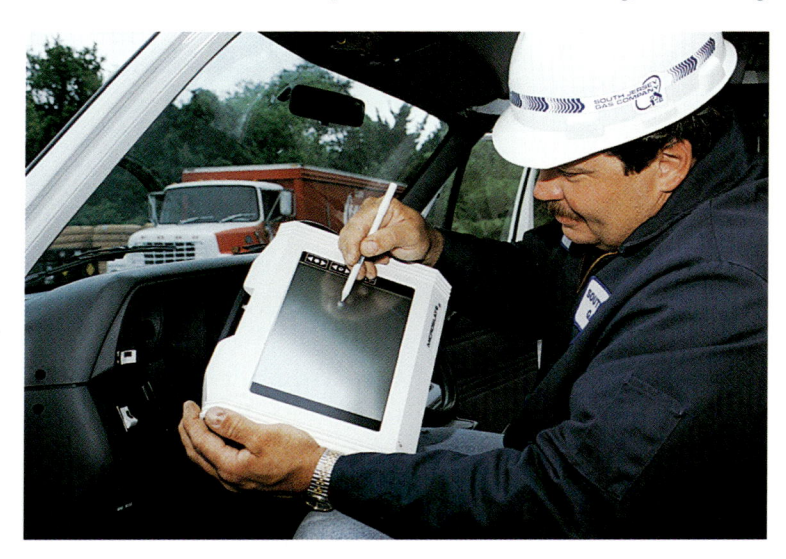

Throughout South Jersey Gas Company's service area, homes and small businesses are sprouting up at a rapid pace. The company is making a significant investment in its pipeline infrastructure to accommodate the area's growth. © Bill Bodine/SJG

South Jersey Gas Company's automated dispatch system uses wireless data transmission to process customers' service requests and coordinate service employees' activities in the field. In-house company employees designed and programmed the system and selected the equipment. © Bill Bodine/SJG

UTILITIES 107

ELIZABETHTOWN WATER COMPANY

CLEAR GOALS FOR A BETTER VALUE... ELIZABETHTOWN WATER COMPANY INVESTS IN PROVIDING THE HIGHEST-QUALITY WATER, BUILDING ITS COMPETITIVE RESOURCES FOR FUTURE GROWTH

Elizabethtown Water Company (Elizabethtown), is the sixth-largest investor-owned water utility in the United States based on gallons of water pumped annually. Elizabethtown provides water service to a population of half a million people in central New Jersey, with more than 2,900 miles of water main and more than 200,000 customers. Elizabethtown is the principal operating subsidiary of E'town Corporation (NYSE: ETW). Elizabethtown and its subsidiary, The Mount Holly Water Company, provide water service to fifty-four municipalities in eight New Jersey counties.

Company employees are working around-the-clock to ensure that Elizabethtown's water meets the highest standards of quality. The company is proud of the high-quality water that it has been supplying for more than 140 years. It is committed to providing the highest level of service into the future.

The Canal Road Water Treatment Plant (shown above), the Raritan-Millstone Plant, and improvements that have been made to the water transmission and distribution system during the past decade enable Elizabethtown Water Company to meet the needs of its customers.

Elizabethtown's facilities are continually being upgraded and expanded to handle customer growth. To better meet its customers' needs, in 1996 Elizabethtown completed the building of the largest single-construction project in its history—the Canal Road Water Treatment Plant. Together, the Canal Road Plant and the company's existing Raritan-Millstone Plant have a treatment capacity of 195 million gallons per day. The two plants are located at the confluence of the Raritan and Millstone Rivers, close to the Delaware & Raritan Canal. This increase in capacity has allowed Elizabethtown to better serve existing customers and add new ones.

Providing the highest-quality water is critical to meeting customers' needs, and Elizabethtown's state-of-the-art treatment, testing, and data management procedures ensure that the company meets or exceeds all state and federal

CREATING THE FUTURE

standards for water quality. Through its voluntary participation in the Partnership for Safe Water, in cooperation with the United States Environmental Protection Agency, the company strives for continuous improvement in its facilities and operations.

Elizabethtown makes customer service a top priority. Customers who call for service have shorter waiting times because of the company's improved information system, which handles billing, customer inquiries, and collection activities.

Consolidation and privatization are changing the water industry. In the face of these changes, E'town Corporation (E'town) is expanding through privatization of water systems and water and wastewater acquisitions.

Customer growth continues as a result of success in winning opportunities to operate municipal systems under contract and to build new water and wastewater systems. In 1998 E'town went back to its roots and began operating the city of Elizabeth's 17,300-customer water system under a forty-year contract. Elizabethtown was founded in the city of Elizabeth in 1854. The company also has taken over operation of Edison Township's 11,200-customer water system under a twenty-year contract. With success in these two privatization contracts, Elizabethtown hopes to continue to expand its customer base.

MAP LEGEND

RETAIL FRANCHISED AREAS

■ ELIZABETHTOWN WATER COMPANY

■ MOUNT HOLLY WATER COMPANY

■ WHOLESALE SERVICE AREAS

SYSTEMS OPERATED UNDER CONTRACT

◆ EDISON WATER COMPANY

❖ LIBERTY WATER COMPANY

▼ AWM FACILITIES*

● LAND OWNED

Service area is located in suburban New Jersey, with above-average customer growth and an ample water supply.

*AWM owns and operates more than 70 facilities in the tristate metropolitan area.

In 1998 E'town Corporation exercised an option to acquire its joint venture partner, Applied Wastewater Group (AWG). The new subsidiary, called Applied Water Management, Inc. (AWM), designs, builds, and operates water and wastewater facilities and ultimately operates them as regulated utilities. AWM is committed to creating balance by offering products and services that protect our natural resources while allowing communities and business to flourish. AWM currently owns and operates more than seventy water and wastewater facilities in the tristate metropolitan area.

"AWG brings us expertise in the design and construction of small water and wastewater facilities," says Andrew M. Chapman, president of E'town Corporation. "We expect the new subsidiary, AWM, to provide an excellent growth vehicle for Elizabethtown's utility business."

"In the future we will continue to focus on expansion efforts to increase sales and productivity improvements to further control costs," Chapman says. "E'town's goals include expanding into the municipal privatization market, continuing to deliver superior customer service, and maximizing productivity."

Elizabethtown's expertise in cost-effectively maintaining and improving aging water systems places it at a competitive advantage when bidding on water and wastewater systems. Because it is able to address long-standing water quality issues, Elizabethtown was selected by the township of Edison to operate its water system.

UTILITIES 109

NUI CORPORATION

FOR BUSINESS AND RESIDENTIAL ENERGY CUSTOMERS, NUI CORPORATION SERVES AS A SINGLE, CONVENIENT GATEWAY TO A MULTITUDE OF PRODUCTS AND SERVICES—FROM APPLIANCES AND SECURITY SYSTEMS TO A FULL ARRAY OF TELECOMMUNICATIONS SERVICES

Coming up with innovative solutions is nothing new for NUI Corporation. Nearly a century and a half ago the company was founded as Elizabethtown Gas Light Company for the purpose of providing a single service—a streetlighting solution for one of New Jersey's largest cities. Today, NUI and its affiliates across the country offer an array of products and services that are helping tens of thousands of businesses become more profitable, while helping hundreds of thousands of homeowners improve their comfort and lifestyle.

NUI's core business historically has been the distribution of natural gas. NUI's six natural gas distribution companies are Elizabethtown Gas in New Jersey, City Gas Company of Florida, North Carolina Gas, Elkton Gas in Maryland, Valley Cities Gas in Pennsylvania, and Waverly Gas in New York. These companies collectively serve nearly 370,000 residential, commercial, and industrial customers. Today, with the dramatic impact of deregulation on the natural gas industry, NUI has repositioned itself to begin offering a broad mix of products and services in addition to performing its traditional utility operation.

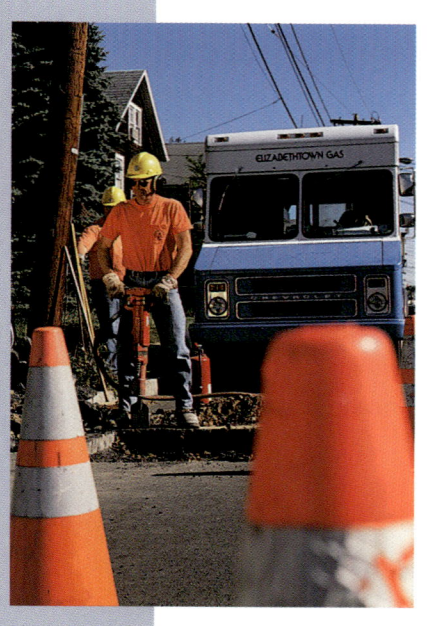

As a company focused on customer relationships, NUI is well positioned as a gateway through which customers can choose from an ever-growing menu of products and services. For residential customers, these options include the purchase or lease of household appliances; service contracts and maintenance programs for those appliances; and safety-related items ranging from carbon monoxide detectors to home security systems. For commercial and industrial

NUI's gas control center monitors the flow of natural gas for the firm's six utilities, as well as its wholesale and retail marketing affiliates.

An operations crew installs a natural gas service line for another new residential customer of Elizabethtown Gas, a distribution company of NUI Corporation.

customers, the choices include the purchase of energy supplies, supply portfolio and risk management services, energy consulting and project development services, and a full array of telecommunications services.

NUI Corporation also reaches business customers in thirty-eight states through TIC Enterprises, LLC, a national sales and marketing outsourcing firm. TIC provides Fortune 500 companies with a face-to-face sales solution to address the small- to medium-size business market. TIC's 520 sales representatives offer businesses telecommunications services and office equipment from leading providers including Lucent Technologies, LCI Communications, Nextel Communications, and Xerox.

"New Ideas. Traditional Values" is NUI's corporate theme, which defines its approach to business. "New Ideas" reflects the innovative and creative nature of the company and its employees, along with the exciting new business opportunities that are paving the way for NUI's future success. "Traditional Values" represents the timeless qualities of reliability, integrity, fair prices, and customer service that have been hallmarks of NUI for nearly 150 years. Taken together, "New Ideas. Traditional Values" represents the successful formula that is guiding NUI into the new millennium.

CREATING THE FUTURE

UTILITIES 111

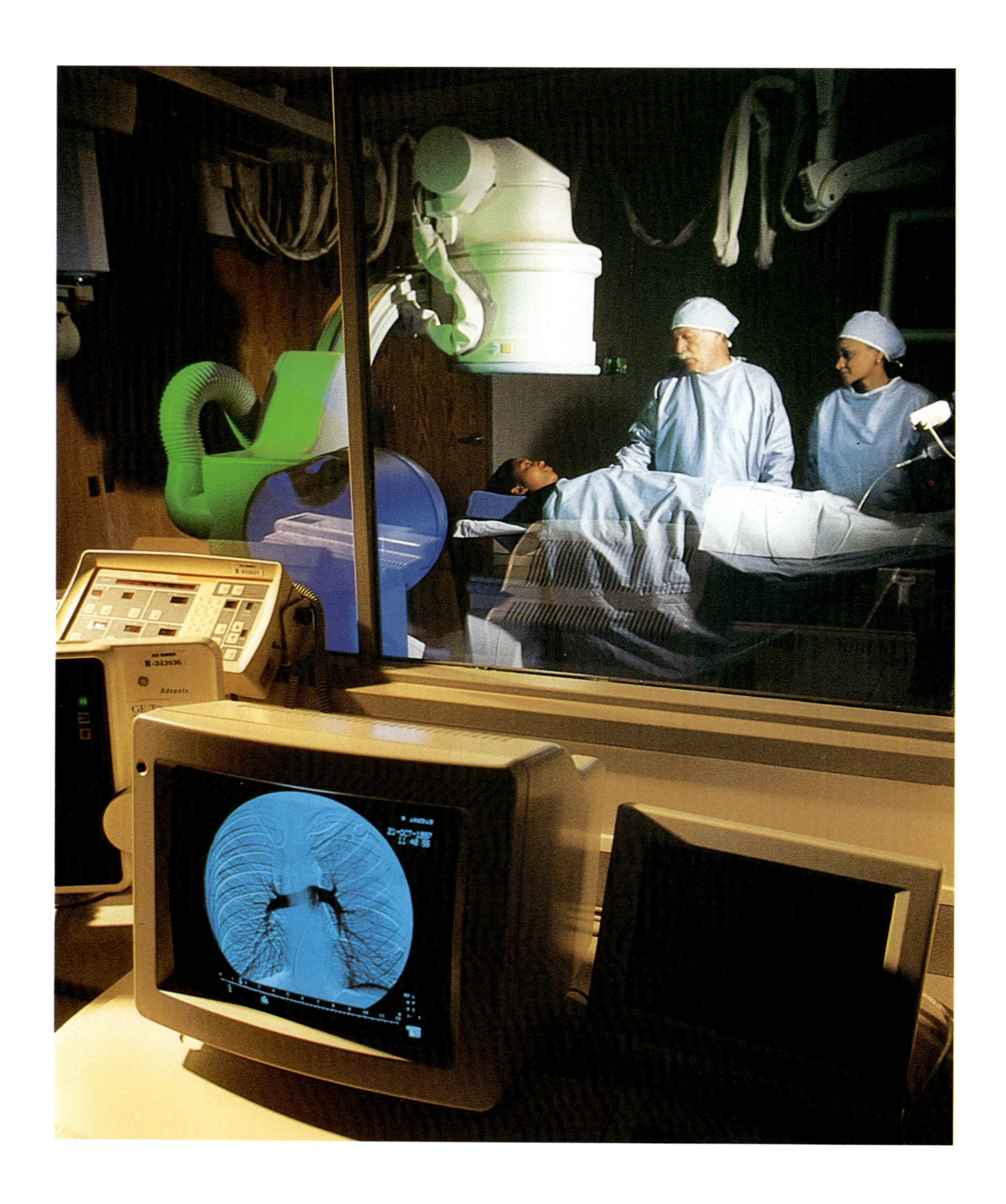

PEOPLE HELPING PEOPLE

112 CREATING THE FUTURE

CHAPTER FOURTEEN

NEW JERSEY HEALTH CARE CONSUMERS BENEFIT FROM A COMPETITIVE ENVIRONMENT FUELED BY MORE THAN ONE HUNDRED ACUTE-CARE HOSPITALS AND LONG-TERM OR SPECIALTY TREATMENT CENTERS THROUGHOUT THE STATE. MEANWHILE, DOZENS OF HEALTH MAINTENANCE ORGANIZATIONS AND PREFERRED PROVIDER ORGANIZATIONS IN THIS, ONE OF THE NATION'S MOST ACTIVE MANAGED-CARE STATES, VIE TO PROVIDE COVERAGE FOR CONSUMERS.

This active medical climate fosters the development of state-of-the-art medical facilities and top-quality medicine—both of which contribute to quality patient care.

Centers of Excellence

The University of Medicine and Dentistry of New Jersey (UMDNJ) is perhaps the largest player in the state's health care market. Besides the allopathic medical school in New Brunswick, its health care and education facilities include the UMDNJ–School of Osteopathic Medicine, the UMDNJ–University Hospital, the University Behavioral HealthCare facility, the UMDNJ–Graduate School of Biomedical Sciences, the UMDNJ–School of Health-Related Professions, and the UMDNJ–School of Nursing.

UMDNJ teaching hospitals include Cooper Hospital and University Medical Center in Camden, Kennedy Memorial Hospital and University Medical Center in Cherry Hill and Washington Township, and the Robert Wood Johnson University Hospital in New Brunswick.

Robert Wood Johnson University Hospital has sixty-seven doctors on staff who have been named among the "Best Doctors in America." The hospital is a partner with the Cancer Institute of New Jersey, the state's first cancer center designated by the National Cancer Institute. Robert Wood Johnson University Hospital also hosts a pediatric AIDS volunteer program, which received the Governor's Volunteer Award. The hospital is one of just thirteen nationwide to receive the Magnet Award for nursing excellence.

Help When and Where It is Needed

The trauma system in New Jersey is considered one of the finest in the United States. It is a network of ten trauma centers that are geographically situated so that one is within fifteen minutes by helicopter of any place in the

Quality health care is a successful marriage of technology and humanity. OPPOSITE: *Sophisticated tools, such as this angiography system used to generate X-ray photographs of blood vessels, aid in the process of diagnosis.* © Scott Barrow. ABOVE: *Ultimately, a tool is only as good as the hand that uses it. Here, a student at the University of Medicine and Dentistry of New Jersey stops to take a break during rounds at one of New Jersey's several major health care facilities.* © Peter Tenzer/International Stock

PEOPLE HELPING PEOPLE 113

> ESTABLISHED IN 1993, THE MAGNET HOSPITAL RECOGNITION STATUS FOR EXCELLENCE IN NURSING SERVICE IS THE HIGHEST AWARD GRANTED TO ORGANIZED NURSING SERVICES BY THE AMERICAN NURSES CREDENTIALING CENTER (ANCC). THE AWARD RECOGNIZES EXCELLENCE IN NURSING SERVICES, DEVELOPMENT OF A PROFESSIONAL MILIEU, AND GROWTH AND DEVELOPMENT OF THE NURSING STAFF. SIX OF THE THIRTEEN NATIONAL MAGNET FACILITIES ARE IN NEW JERSEY: HACKENSACK UNIVERSITY MEDICAL CENTER, HACKENSACK; ROBERT WOOD JOHNSON UNIVERSITY HOSPITAL, NEW BRUNSWICK; JERSEY SHORE MEDICAL CENTER, NEPTUNE; ST. PETER'S UNIVERSITY HOSPITAL, NEW BRUNSWICK; MEDICAL CENTER OF OCEAN COUNTY, POINT PLEASANT; AND RIVERVIEW MEDICAL CENTER, RED BANK.

state. Centers offering the highest level of care are in Newark, New Brunswick, and Camden. Other centers are located in Morristown, Hackensack, Jersey City, Paterson, Neptune, Atlantic City, and Trenton.

What makes these trauma centers different from the typical hospital emergency room is that they have teams of specially trained doctors and nurses, backed up by high-tech equipment, on duty at all times. These centers have care waiting for patients, versus patients waiting for the appropriate level of care. A trauma surgeon is in the building, rather than on call. There's no waiting for beepers to go off, which can mean the difference between life and death in the critical hour after a patient suffers serious trauma.

In addition, New Jersey's eighty-four acute-care hospitals are frequently lauded for being on the cutting edge of quality care in a variety of areas. Englewood Hospital and Medical Center, affiliated with Mount Sinai School of Medicine in New York City, was featured in *Time* magazine for its pioneering work in the area of bloodless medicine and surgery. The hospital performs procedures that traditionally involve blood loss and transfusion without either of these risks. The hospital's successful bloodless procedures have included liver resections, hip replacements, hysterectomies, and brain surgery. Englewood also features the latest technology in breast cancer detection

An important part of New Jersey's premier trauma system, paramedics get a head start on an accident victim's treatment before leaving for the hospital. © Bruce Ayres/Tony Stone Images

with Aurora, a new magnetic resonance imaging system dedicated solely to breast imaging and used for clinical diagnosis and management of breast disease.

Hackensack University Medical Center was the first New Jersey hospital to receive the Magnet Award for attracting the best nurses. It also has received more national rankings by medical specialty in *U.S. News & World Report*'s *America's Best Hospitals* than any other New Jersey Hospital, as well as a Quality Leader Award from the National Research Corporation.

And with the close of the twentieth century, New Jersey hospitals continue to make significant capital investments to meet community needs and assure state citizens of high-quality health care long into the twenty-

HEALTH CARE PIONEER

IN THE 1680S DR. WILLIAM ROBINSON WAS ONE OF NEW JERSEY'S FIRST PRACTICING PHYSICIANS. IN THE UNION COUNTY TOWN OF CLARK, ROBINSON WAS AMONG THE FIRST DOCTORS IN THE COLONIES TO DO DISSECTIONS FOR ANATOMICAL STUDY.

The patient below is about to undergo a CAT scan. The machine uses a series of cross-sectional images to compute the three-dimensional structure of the part of the body being studied. © Scott Barrow

first century. Here are a few of the projects that have been completed recently: a new, comprehensive, state-of-the-art, $2.3-million cardiac catheterization suite at Bayonne Hospital so residents do not have to travel for sophisticated cardiac testing; a $6.1-million same-day surgery center at Overlook Hospital in Summit, which uses up-to-date laser and fluoroscopic technologies; and a $49-million patient tower at JFK Medical Center in Edison, which includes a handsomely appointed maternity ward and a simulated downtown environment so visitors can bank and shop at the hospital.

In 1998, in what is considered the largest hospital donation in New Jersey history, millionaire toy maker and philanthropist Russell Berrie gave $5 million to Englewood Hospital and Medical Center for a new facility that maintains a "human touch" with its patients. The $25-million, three-story outpatient pavilion, which will have the word "humanistic" in its name, will offer expanded outpatient services, such as centers for breast care and imaging, outpatient surgery, comprehensive rehabilitation, and pain management.

Surgeons discuss a patient's condition before going into the operating room. Taking into account all the variables is part of well-considered medical care. © Scott Barrow

HEALTH CARE HERO

EARLY IN THE TWENTIETH CENTURY, MILLIONS OF AMERICANS PRAISED THE NAME CLARA LOUISE MAASS. THIS COURAGEOUS, SELFLESS NURSE FROM EAST ORANGE DIED OF YELLOW FEVER IN THE COURSE OF AN EXPERIMENT THAT LED TO THE DISCOVERY OF THE LETHAL INFECTION'S CAUSE.

SERVING COMMUNITIES

The state also houses a number of long-term therapy, counseling, and treatment facilities. These hospitals are created based on the needs of the community, and the variety of skill and expertise complement one another, providing New Jersey residents with a diverse network of quality health care. Specialty hospitals also are excellent training grounds for residents probing specialized areas.

The Kessler Institute for Rehabilitation tops the state's special treatment facilities list with its brain injury program. The largest physical medicine and rehabilitation hospital in New Jersey, with locations in four cities, Kessler offers comprehensive treatment for adults and adolescents suffering from both traumatic and mild brain injuries. The Johnson Rehabilitation Institute and New Jersey Neuroscience Institute at the JFK Medical Center in Edison also provide cutting-edge treatment for traumatic brain injury patients.

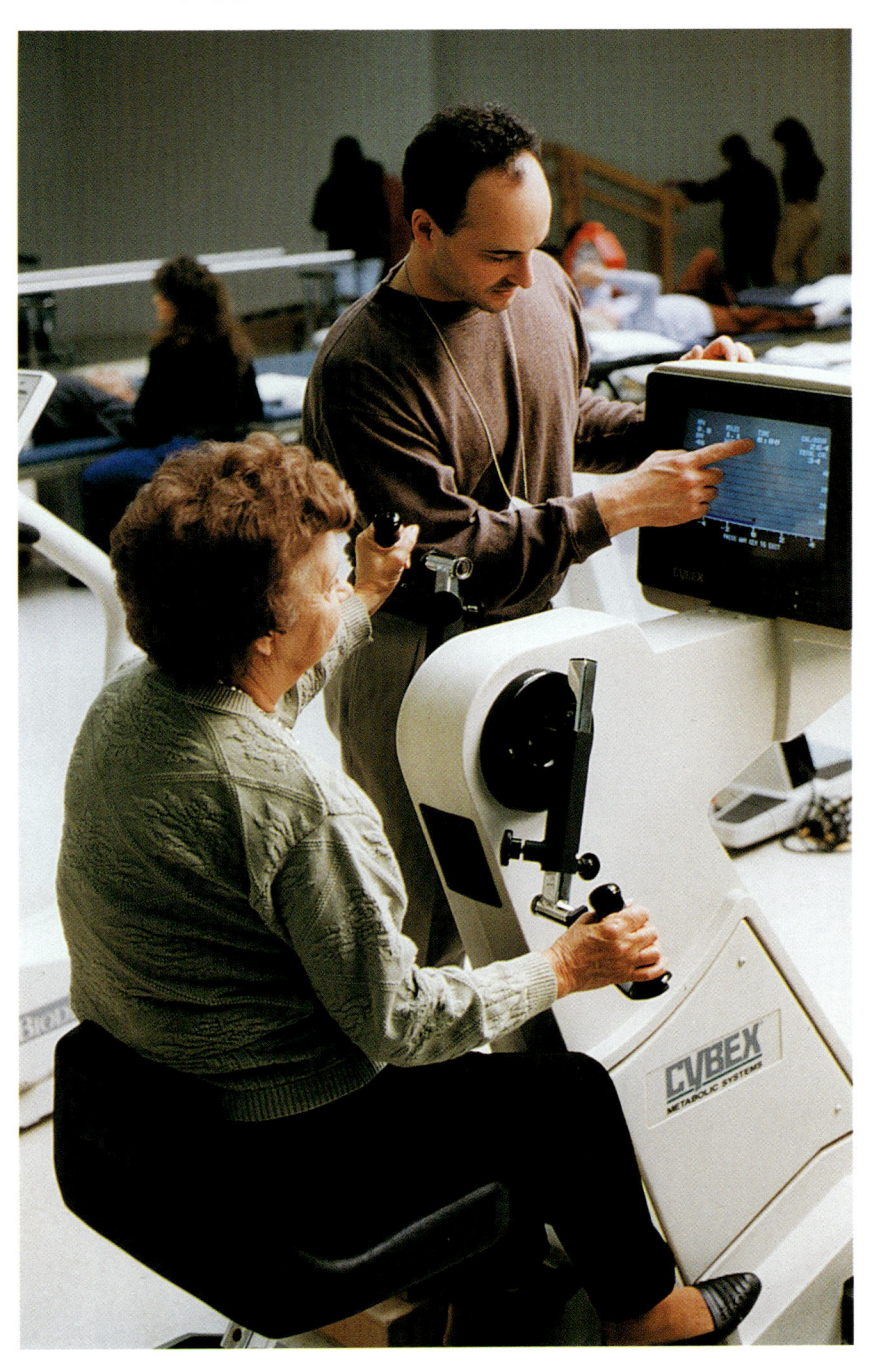

> ## THANKS, MOM
>
> FOURTEEN-MONTH-OLD DONTAY FRANCOIS OF LINDEN BECAME ONE OF THE WORLD'S YOUNGEST RECIPIENTS OF A KIDNEY TRANSPLANT IN 1998 WHEN HE RECEIVED ONE OF HIS MOTHER'S KIDNEYS TO FIX A CONGENITAL OBSTRUCTION. THE OPERATION WAS PERFORMED AT SAINT BARNABAS MEDICAL CENTER IN LIVINGSTON.

The Traumatic Brain Injury Treatment and Cognitive Rehabilitation facility at Children's Specialized Hospital, with locations in Mountainside and Toms River, is dedicated to rehabilitating children and adolescents with brain injury. CSH also is at the forefront of studying and caring for children with Respiratory Syncytial Virus, which causes ninety thousand hospitalizations and forty-five hundred infant deaths in the nation annually.

Pediatric medicine is important at other institutions as well. Morristown Memorial Hospital is a leader in treating pediatric kidney diseases, while Robert Wood Johnson University Hospital in New Brunswick has a state-designated specialty Acute Care Children's Hospital with a pediatric intensive care unit. The seventy-bed facility is a hospital within a hospital, and its expertise ranges across forty-five specialties and sub-specialties.

Similarly, St. Peter's University Hospital & Health System, a major affiliate of the University of Medicine and Dentistry of New Jersey, is considered a national leader in caring for women and children. The Hospital for Women and Children, a four-story unit within the medical center complex, is a regional

The Johnson Rehabilitation Institute at JFK Medical Center is a comprehensive facility dedicated to helping disabled adults and children reach the utmost of their potential. Courtesy, Solaris Health System

PEOPLE HELPING PEOPLE 117

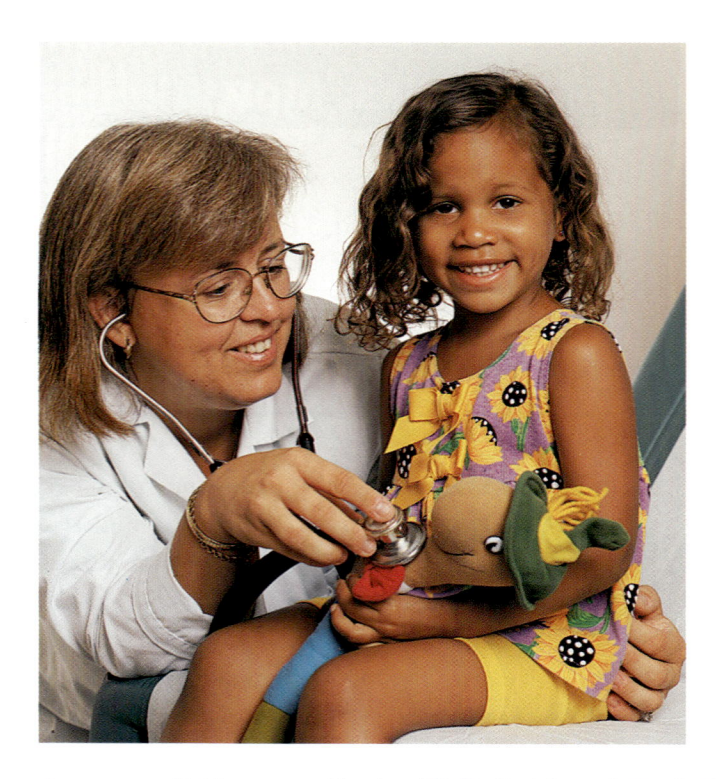

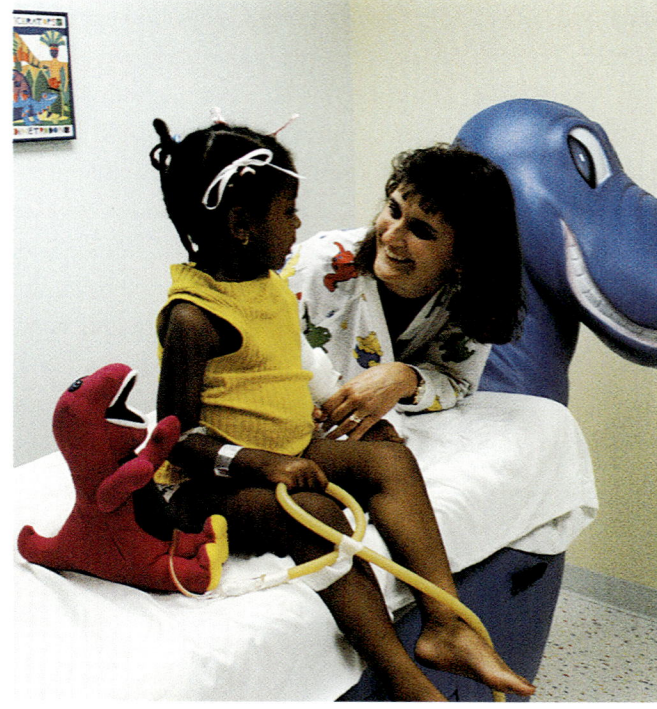

ABOVE LEFT: *Making a new friend at JFK Medical Center's Family Practice Center.* BELOW: *A doctor looks for clues at the New Jersey Neuroscience Institute at JFK Medical Center. Both photos © Sean O'Brien, Pompton Lakes, NJ/Courtesy, Solaris Health System.* ABOVE RIGHT: *The Pediatric Unit at St. Peter's Hospital for Women and Children. Courtesy, St. Peter's University Hospital & Health System*

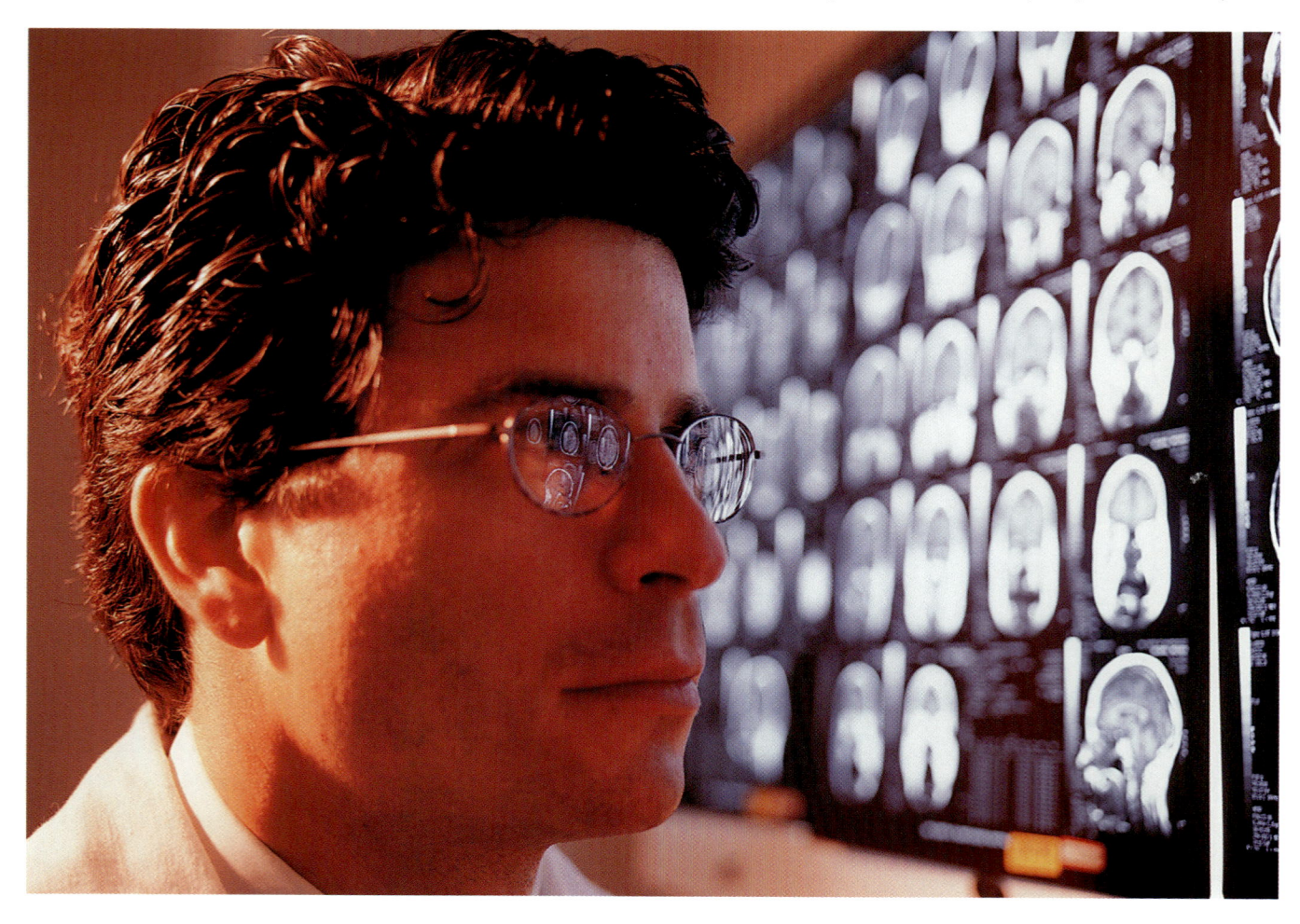

118   CREATING THE FUTURE

referral center for high-risk pregnancies and newborns, and offers the largest neonatal intensive care unit in the New Jersey/New York area. The state's only center of excellence in maternal-child health, St. Peter's was the first hospital in the country to offer a genetic sonogram service.

New Jersey's other specialty hospitals include the Joint Replacement Institute at Pascack Valley Hospital in Westwood. The institute is affiliated with New York Medical College and specializes in orthopedic procedures such as hip and knee replacements, and has been at the forefront of sports medicine for over twenty years. State residents can find quality psychiatric care at hospitals such as the Trenton Psychiatric Hospital, Ramapo Ridge Psychiatric Hospital, Ancora Psychiatric Hospital, and Greystone Park Psychiatric Hospital.

New Jersey is lucky enough to have experts in transplantation working here. Two affiliated hospitals, Saint Barnabas Medical Center in Livingston and Newark Beth Israel Medical Center, offer one of the top kidney transplantation programs in the United States and are at the forefront of research in kidney transplantation. The Liver Transplantation division at UMDNJ–University Hospital performed the first liver transplant in 1989 and continues to lead in that field of research. For a heart transplant or other heart surgery, New Jerseyans can turn

WATER LANDING

ON 3 MAY 1988, DR. GERALD CICCALESE SR. DELIVERED THE FIRST BABY UNDERWATER IN THE UNITED STATES AT CLARA MAASS MEDICAL CENTER IN BELLEVILLE. DONNA GARIBAM, WHO SHARES HER MOTHER'S NAME, WAS BORN IN A SPECIAL JACUZZI PROVIDED BY THE HOSPITAL. HER FATHER, WEARING BATHING TRUNKS, PARTICIPATED IN THE BIRTH.

Nurses with newborns in St. Peter's original facility, circa 1913. Today St. Peter's delivers nearly seven thousand babies a year. Courtesy, St. Peter's University Hospital & Health System

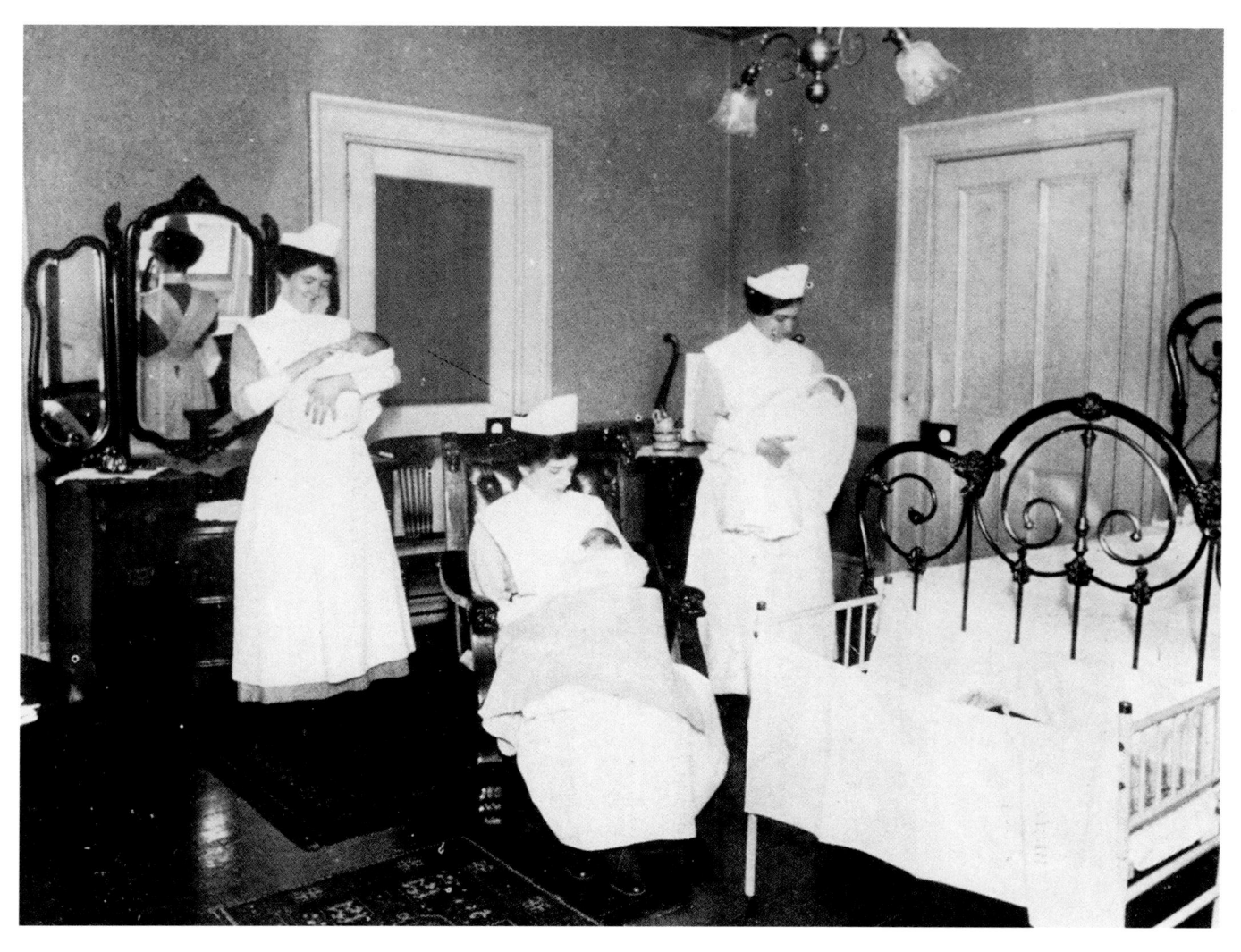

to the Newark Heart Institute at Saint Michael's Medical Center, where surgeons perform angioplasty, heart transplants, and the newest intervention techniques.

Saint Barnabas also operates New Jersey's only state-certified burn treatment facility. Recognized as one of the top medical facilities in the country treating burns, the Burn Center has taken care of more than seven thousand

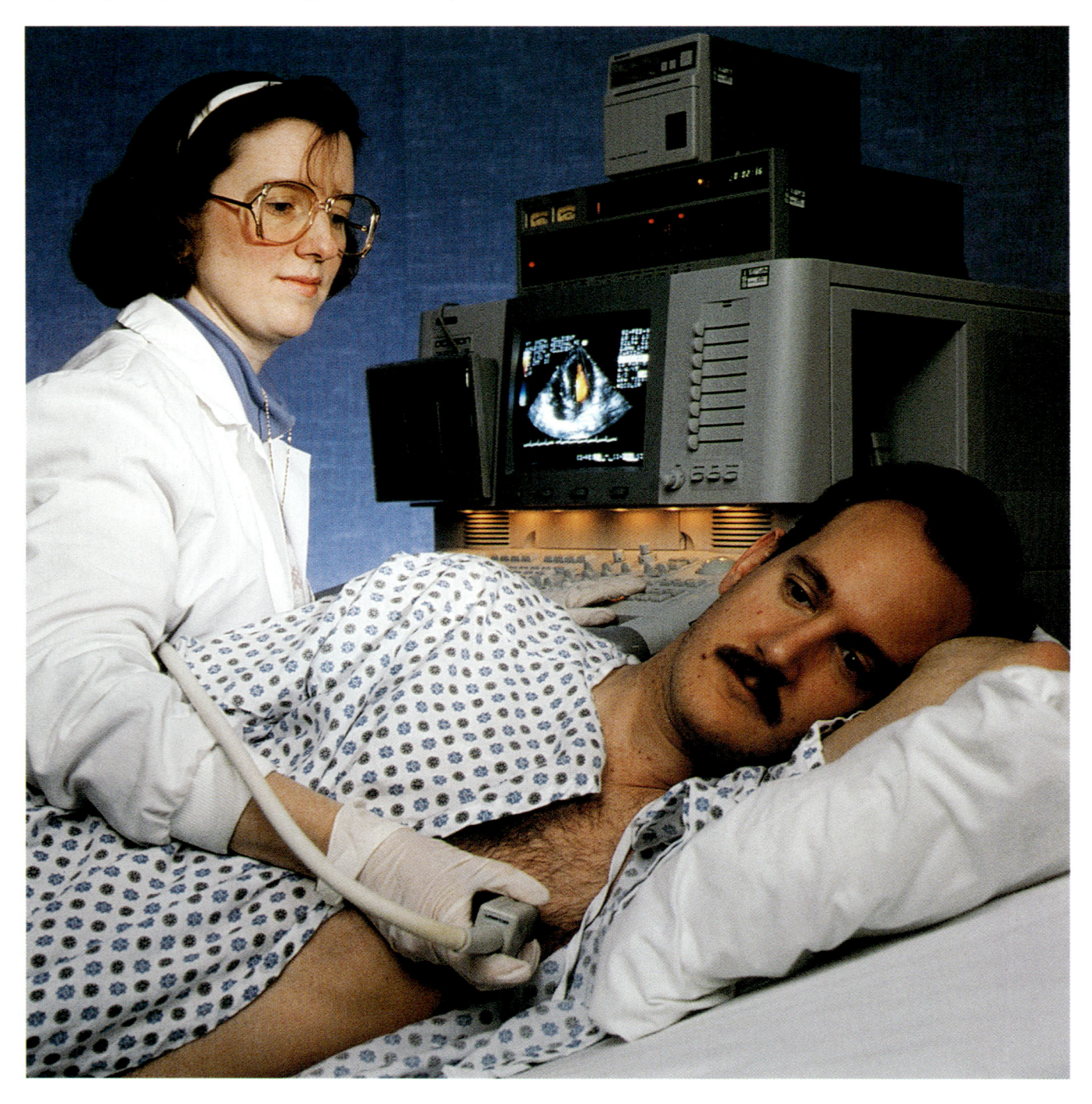

Technician Judith McCue performs an ultrasound at Muhlenbert Regional Medical Center, which offers high-technology tests for diagnosing heart problems. Courtesy, Solaris Health System

NEW JERSEYANS HAVE PLAYED HISTORIC ROLES IN THE STUDY AND TREATMENT OF HEART PROBLEMS. THE FIRST CARDIAC CLINIC IN AMERICA WAS ESTABLISHED BY DR. THOMAS J. WHITE IN 1926 IN JERSEY CITY. IN 1946 SAINT MICHAEL'S MEDICAL CENTER IN NEWARK BECAME THE FIRST COMMUNITY HOSPITAL TO PERFORM OPEN-HEART SURGERY.

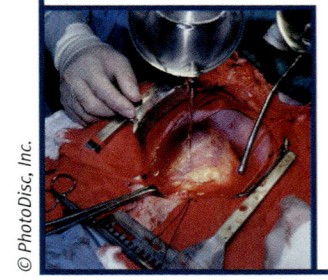

120 CREATING THE FUTURE

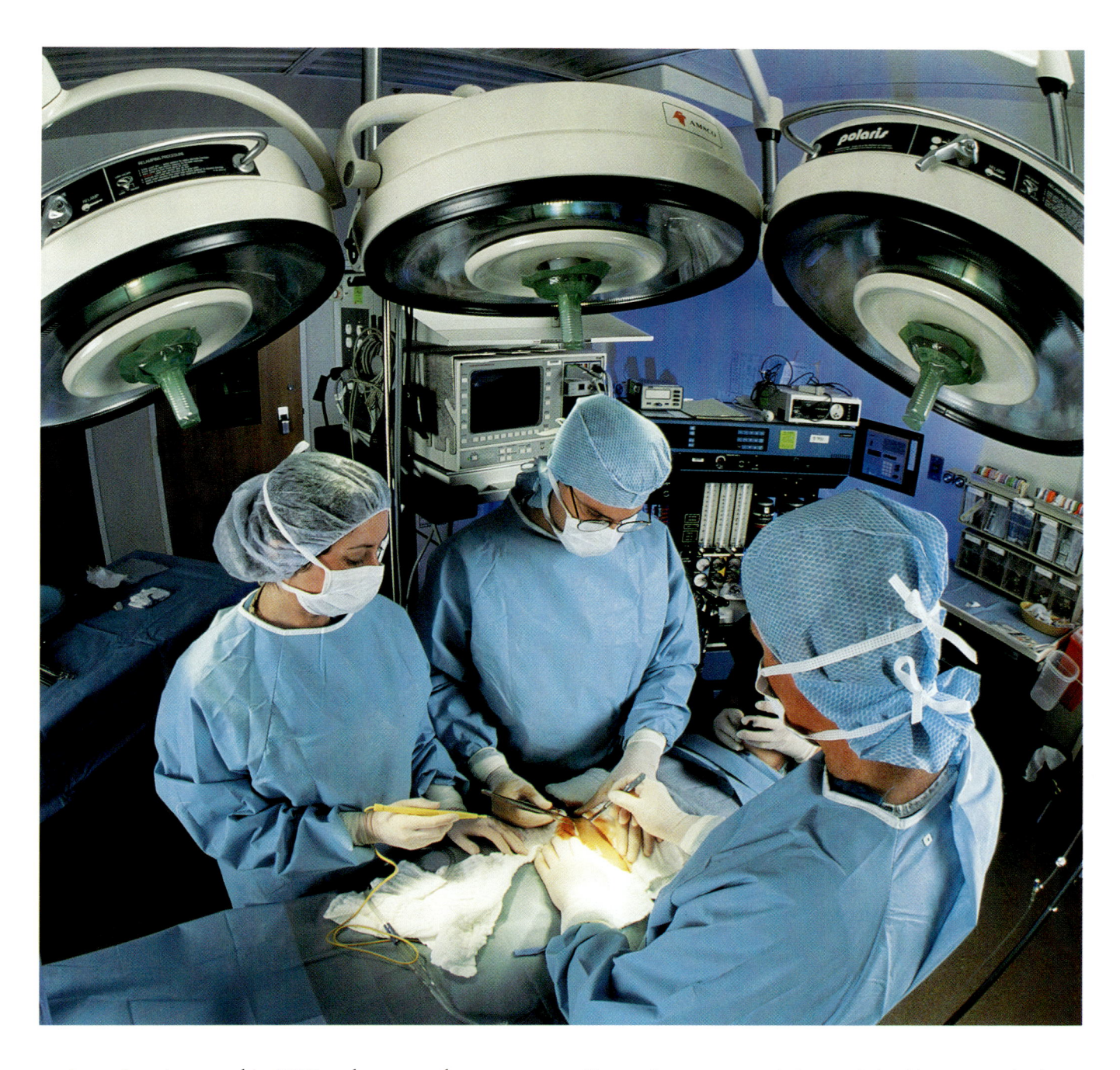

patients since it opened in 1977 and now employs a team of over ninety specialists.

Managing Health Care Costs

New Jersey is also home to a number of managed care organizations. The Northeast is one of the largest growth areas for managed care, and one-quarter of all New Jersey citizens, about two million people, are participating in one of nearly forty health maintenance organizations (HMOs) or preferred provider organizations (PPOs). In addition, fourteen HMOs and sixteen PPOs are based in the state, including such well-regarded names as HIP Health Plan of New Jersey, United Healthcare of New

Managed care programs help contain health care costs by determining when surgery is medically necessary. © Uniphoto, Inc.

LONG-LIFE BATTERIES

CONCEIVED BY DIRECTOR OF SURGERY VICTOR PARSONNET, M.D., AND GEORGE H. MYERS, PH.D., A BIOMEDICAL ENGINEERING CONSULTANT, THE COUNTRY'S FIRST NUCLEAR-POWERED PACEMAKER WAS IMPLANTED IN 1973. FIFTEEN HEART PATIENTS AT NEWARK BETH ISRAEL MEDICAL CENTER RECEIVED IMPLANTS THAT YEAR.

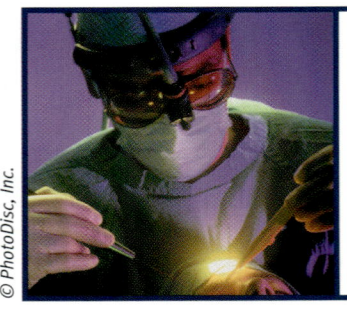

NEW JERSEY RANKS SIXTH AMONG THE FIFTY STATES IN THE NUMBER OF MEDICAL AND SURGICAL SPECIALISTS PER ONE HUNDRED THOUSAND PEOPLE.

Jersey, and the UMDNJ University Health Plans. PPOs include Consumer Health Network, AtlantiCare, and First Option Health Plan.

The impact of managed care has encouraged hospitals in New Jersey to consolidate, become more cost

LEFT: *Blue Cross and Blue Shield of New Jersey fosters a close cooperative relationship with health care providers. Pictured is BCBSNJ president and CEO William J. Marino. Courtesy, New Jersey Business & Industry Association.* BELOW: *New Jersey health care providers strive to safeguard the next generation from preventable illness and injury through patient education and appropriate care that begins at birth.* © Scott Barrow

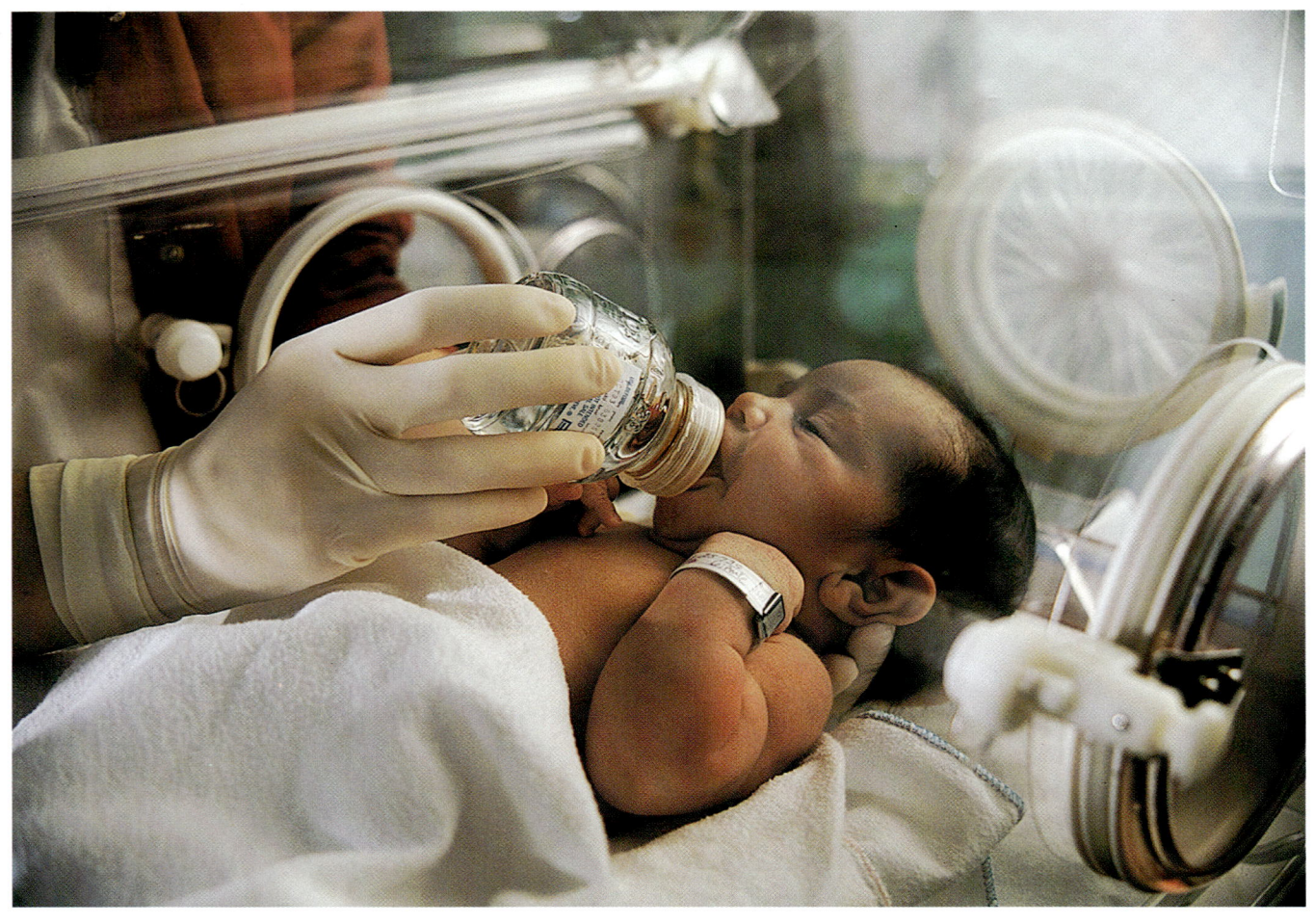

122 CREATING THE FUTURE

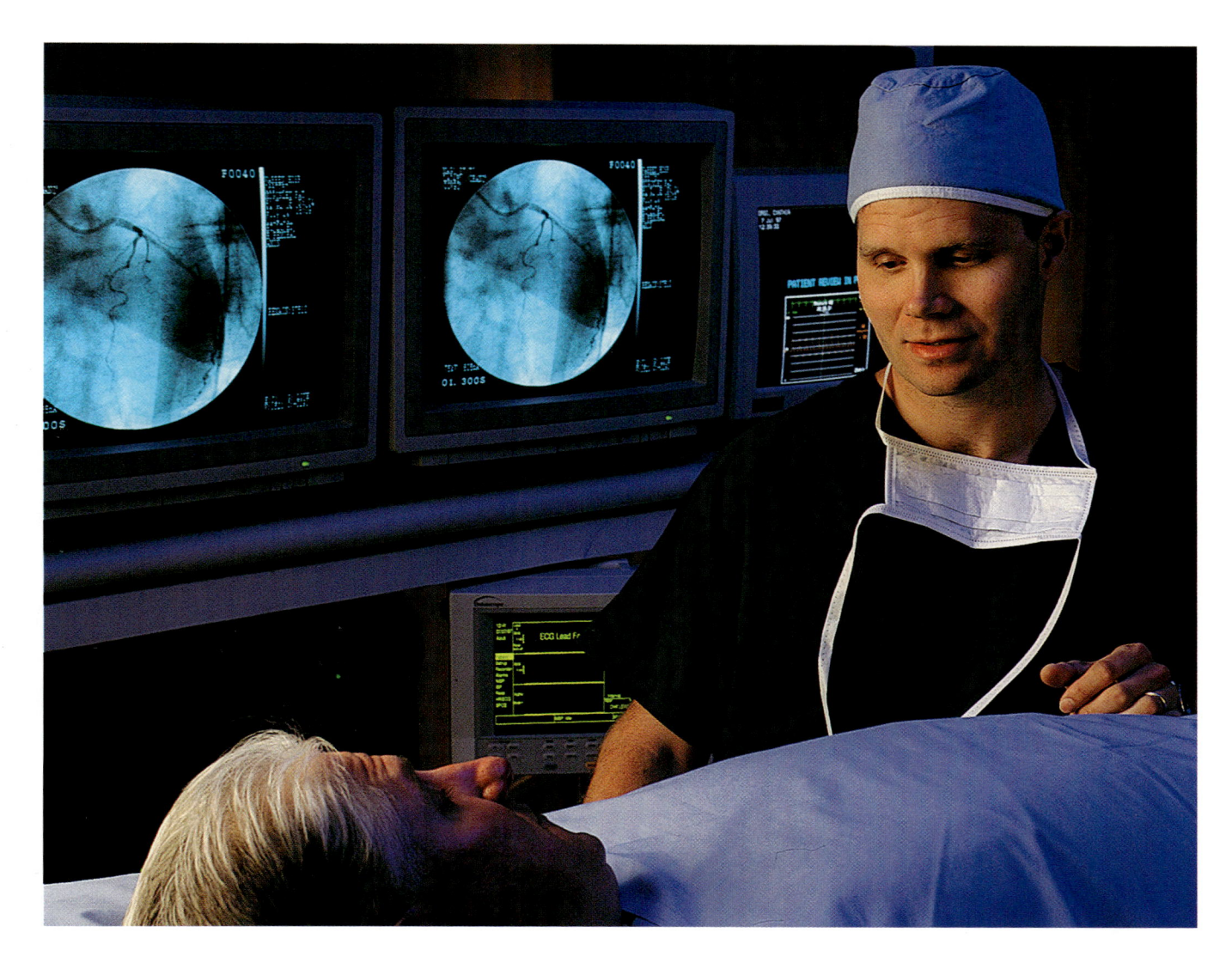

effective, and be better able to offer patients a continuum of services. Fourteen of the eighteen health care systems in the state were formed in the 1990s. These alliances and mergers tend to lead to improvements in existing facilities as well as a system that can easily refer patients in need of more specialized care. Moreover, the consolidation often means that hospitals in danger of going out of business are given a new life.

The largest group is the Saint Barnabas Health Care System, formed in 1996. Based in Livingston, the system has ten hospitals, 3,971 acute-care beds, and annual revenues exceeding $1.6 billion. The next-largest is the Robert Wood Johnson Health System with six hospitals, and the oldest is the Cathedral Healthcare System, which was formed in 1980.

All in all, these facilities and managed care organizations work together to provide state dwellers with unsurpassed choices in health care—a valuable asset in today's world.

No matter where you live in New Jersey, and no matter what type of insurance or managed care organization administers your medical program, New Jersey health care professionals stand ready, willing, and qualified to help. © Kelly/Mooney

THE 1997 BIRTH AT SAINT BARNABAS MEDICAL CENTER OF A HEALTHY BABY GIRL NAMED EMMA WAS THE FIRST IN THE WORLD TO RESULT FROM A NEW PROCESS CALLED CYTOPLASMIC TRANSFER. THE PROCESS REPAIRS MISSING OR ABNORMALLY FUNCTIONING PARTS OF A WOMAN'S EGGS. CYTOPLASMIC TRANSFER CAN HELP MANY COUPLES WHO OTHERWISE WOULD NEED DONOR EGGS TO HAVE CHILDREN. CHILDREN BORN THROUGH THIS NEW PROCESS ARE GENETIC OFFSPRING OF BOTH THE FATHER AND MOTHER.

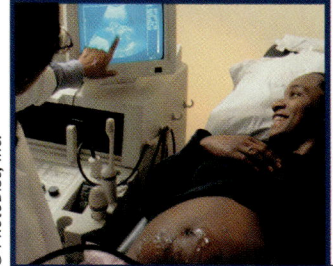

PEOPLE HELPING PEOPLE   123

124 CREATING THE FUTURE

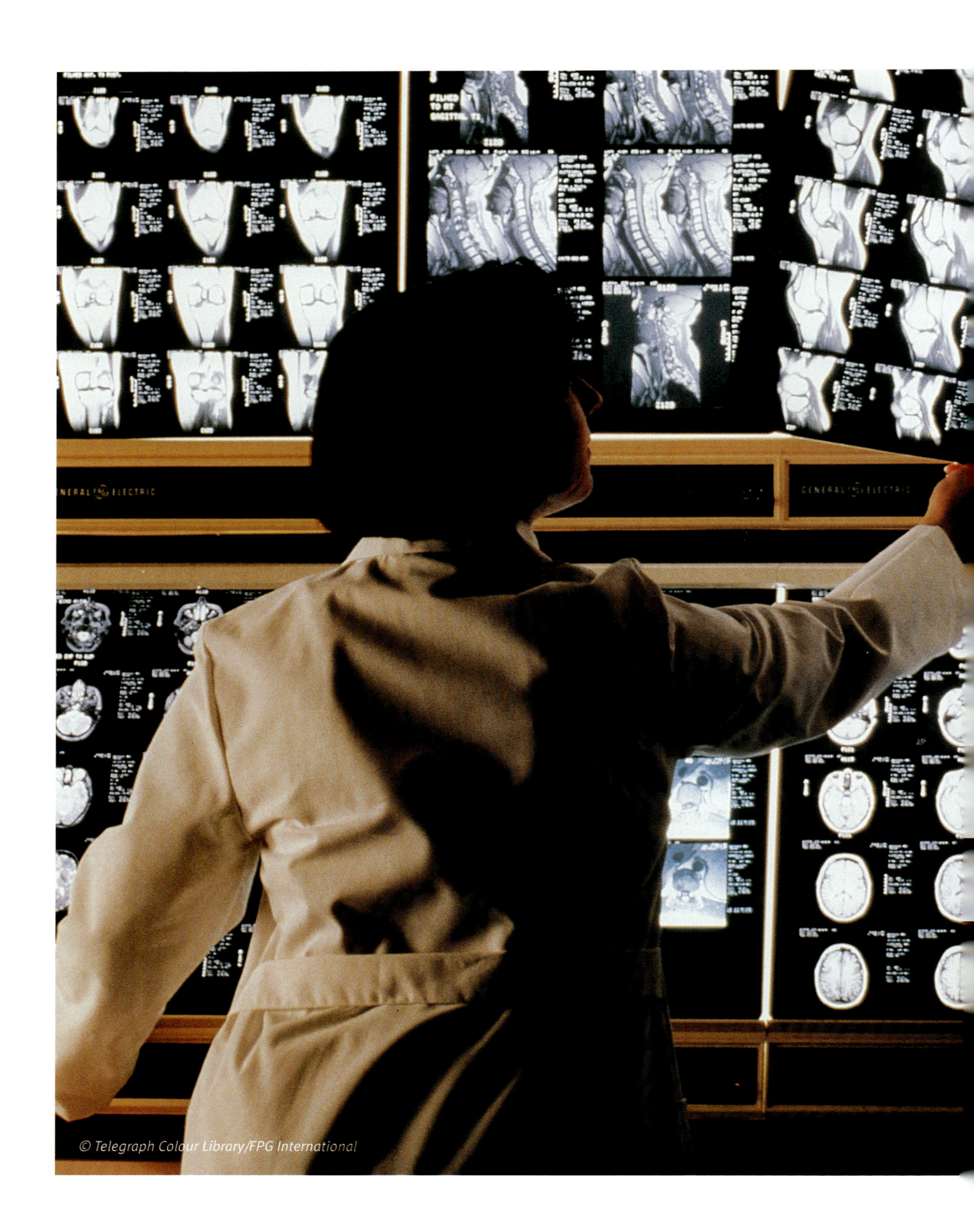

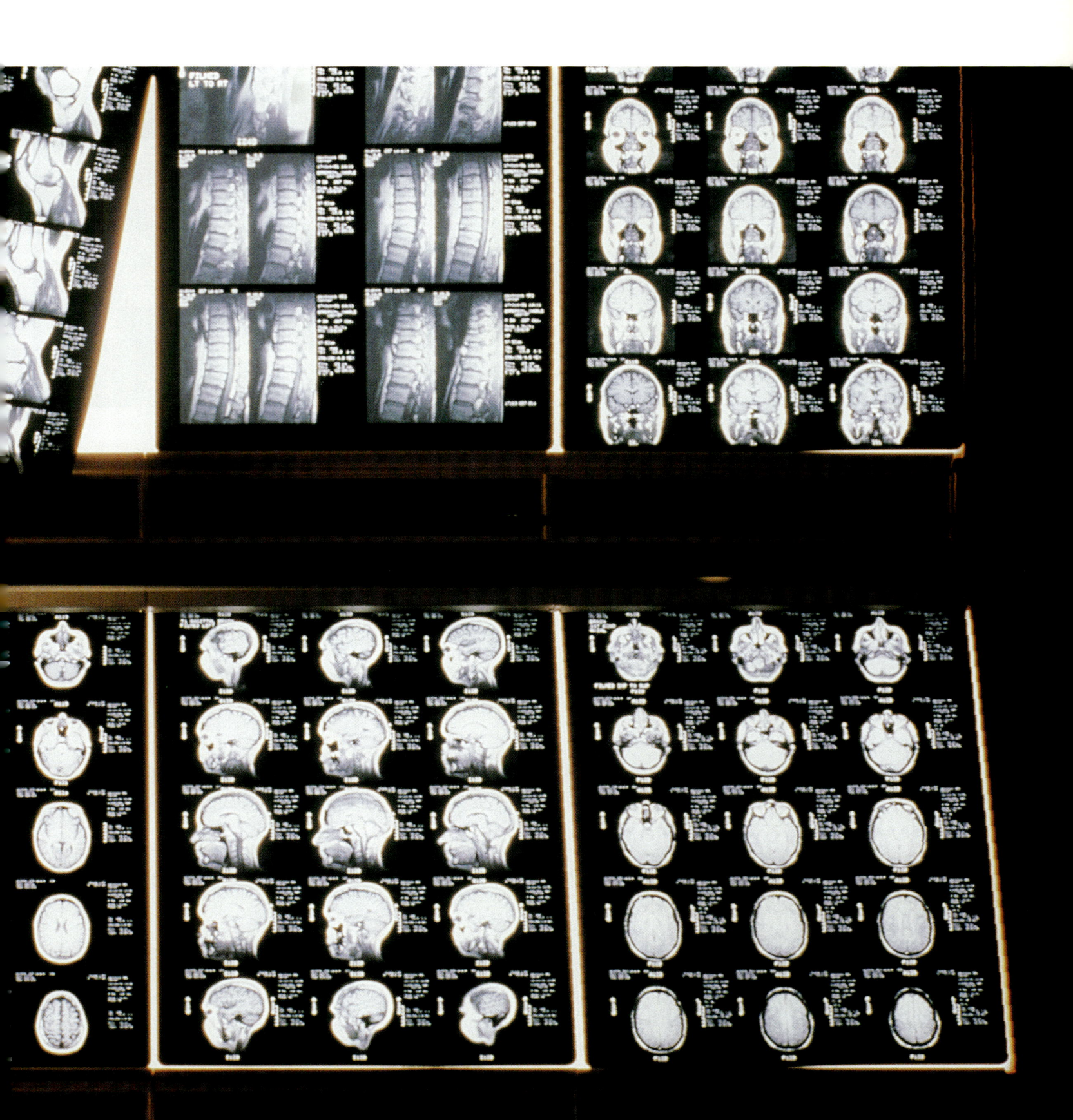

HEALTH CARE

ST. PETER'S UNIVERSITY HOSPITAL & HEALTH SYSTEM

ST. PETER'S UNIVERSITY HOSPITAL & HEALTH SYSTEM, A NATIONALLY RECOGNIZED LEADER IN THE DEVELOPMENT OF NEW PROCEDURES TO EVALUATE AND TREAT ILLNESSES, IS RENOWNED FOR ITS COMMITMENT TO EXCELLENCE IN PATIENT CARE

St. Peter's University Hospital and Health System is known nationally for its leadership in developing new procedures to evaluate and treat illness, and for its commitment to excellence in patient care. Founded in 1872 as a 16-bed hospital, St. Peter's has grown into a 416-bed core-teaching facility that is at the forefront of breakthroughs in medicine. Sponsored by the Diocese of Metuchen, St. Peter's has been rated one of the top hospitals in the country, receiving accreditation with commendation from the Joint Commission on Accreditation of Healthcare Organizations. St. Peter's became only the tenth hospital in the nation to receive the prestigious designation of Magnet status, conferred by the American Nurses Credentialing Center for excellence in nursing.

St. Peter's is a major teaching affiliate of the University of Medicine and Dentistry of New Jersey and employs 2,800 health care professionals and support personnel. In addition, more than 800 physicians and dentists have chosen to affiliate with the medical center.

NOBODY KNOWS MORE ABOUT HEALING

In its role as a University of Medicine and Dentistry of New Jersey/Robert Wood Johnson Medical School teaching affiliate, St. Peter's provides residency training for doctors specializing in pediatrics, orthopedic surgery, thoracic surgery, general surgery, primary care internal medicine, family practice, obstetrics and gynecology, radiology, and pathology. While medical advances help St. Peter's to provide better patient care than ever before, St. Peter's healing mission would be incomplete without a commitment that responds to the total, individual person, spiritually, emotionally, and physically.

An aerial view encompasses St. Peter's University Hospital, which is located on Easton Avenue in New Brunswick. © Nat Clymer

St. Peter's Neonatal Intensive Care Unit is the largest such unit in the tristate area, caring for more than 1,000 critically ill babies each year.

"We are proud that St. Peter's has become widely recognized for our lifetime continuum of services that combines compassionate care with the most modern health care technology," says John E. Matuska, president of St. Peter's University Hospital and Health System. "There is no doubt that medical advances help us to provide better patient care than ever before. However, at St. Peter's the process of healing would be incomplete without a commitment to the total, individual person."

The original St. Peter's Hospital was established in 1872 on the site where St. Peter's University Hospital stands today. Over the years it has continued to expand and add new state-of-the-art programs to meet community needs.

Recognizing that our world is changing rapidly, St. Peter's has devoted considerable time to developing an innovative response to the challenge of modern health care. Major factors contributing to St. Peter's success include its team of highly skilled physicians, nurses, and other health care professionals; the ongoing introduction of sophisticated technology; leadership in developing innovative medical procedures; and continued renovation and

CREATING THE FUTURE

expansion of programs. St. Peter's multifaceted medical programs include services for women and children, cancer care, and numerous specialized services.

A Leader in Women's and Children's Services

St. Peter's University Hospital and Health System is the state's only Center of Excellence in Maternal-Child Health, offering the most extensive maternity programs between Rhode Island and Baltimore. This center enables St. Peter's to handle all problems associated with pregnancy and childbirth. The four-story Hospital for Women and Children at St. Peter's is one of the top hospitals nationally in providing services for women and children throughout their lives. For many years, more babies have been born at St. Peter's than at any other hospital in New Jersey. It is a Level III Regional Referral Center for high-risk pregnancies and newborns, with perinatologists and neonatologists on staff and on-site around the clock. Continuing its commitment to statewide leadership, St. Peter's launched its Genetic Sonogram Service, the first of its kind in the United States; a Pregnancy Loss Evaluation Service, second of its kind in the country; and Fetal Echocardiograph Service, one of the few in the nation.

Women with urinary incontinence or pelvic organ prolapse can find help with a specialist in urogynecology at St. Peter's Health Center for Women, and programs for menopause and infertility are offered through the Mind/Body Medical Institute. The institute also has available relaxation classes for women undergoing breast, obstetrical, and gynecological procedures at the medical center.

A state-designated specialty acute care Children's Hospital, St. Peter's offers a vast array of pediatric specialties and sub-specialties through its Children's Health Network. These include the tristate area's largest Neonatal Intensive Care Unit, and programs for pediatric cardiology, allergies, anesthesiology, emergency care, cleft palate–craniofacial anomalies, urology, endocrinology, gastroenterology, psychology, surgery, ophthalmology, otolaryngology, dentistry, radiology, and development disability. St. Peter's also is home to the state's Sudden Infant Death Syndrome Center, a Regional Child Protection Center, the Pediatric Call Center, and Parents' Advice Line. St. Peter's Lou Damiano Pediatric Health Center is a model for pediatric primary and preventive care.

Comprehensive Cancer Care Program

The American College of Surgeons has approved St. Peter's for the Community Hospital Comprehensive Cancer Program, acknowledging the medical center's commitment to aggressive disease management through coordination and utilization of all available resources in order to deliver the highest quality care. The program's partnership with the Cancer Institute of New Jersey and an 11,000-square-foot Radiation Oncology Center allow St. Peter's to offer patients

---

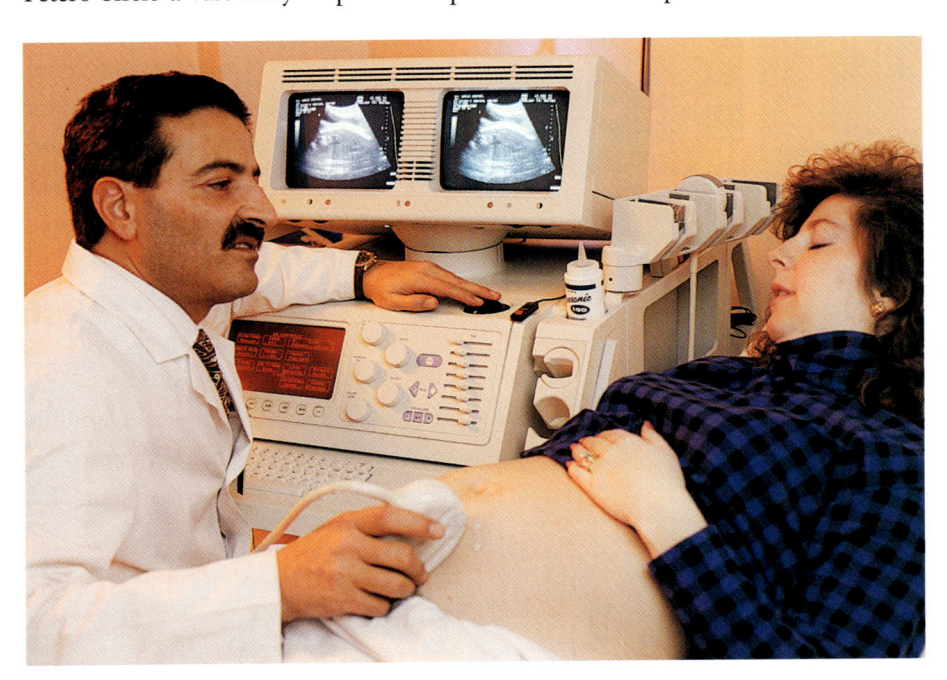

ST. PETER'S UNIVERSITY HOSPITAL & HEALTH SYSTEM'S MISSION STATEMENT

Keeping faith with the teachings of the Roman Catholic Church and guided by the Bishop of Metuchen, St. Peter's University Hospital & Health System is committed to humble service to humanity, especially the poor, through competence and good stewardship of resources.

We minister to the whole person, body and spirit, preserving the dignity and sacredness of each life. We are pledged to the creation of an environment of mutual support among our employees, physicians, and volunteers and to the education and training of health care personnel.

We are witnesses in our community to the highest ethical and moral principles in pursuit of excellence in all we do.

St. Peter's Antenatal Testing Unit offers patients obstetric ultrasound, antepartum fetal surveillance, and fetal echocardiography services. © Nat Clymer

ST. PETER'S UNIVERSITY HOSPITAL & HEALTH SYSTEM (CONTINUED)

technology not available anywhere else in New Jersey. The Cancer Institute of New Jersey is the state's only center designated as a Clinical Cancer Center by the National Cancer Institute.

The University Hospital's cancer programs continue to exemplify excellence in every aspect. The Oncology Nursing Unit, staffed by highly trained physicians, nurses, social workers, and clergy, is committed to the highest quality of care. Outpatient facilities, clinics, and the Radiation Oncology Department are equipped to respond to the ever-changing trends in cancer care and to participate in ongoing clinical research efforts. The staff takes a leadership role in its work with the Cancer Institute of New Jersey by assisting other facilities in developing quality oncology programs and standards of practice and by guiding them in taking an active approach in identifying cancer in its earlier and more treatable stages through screening programs.

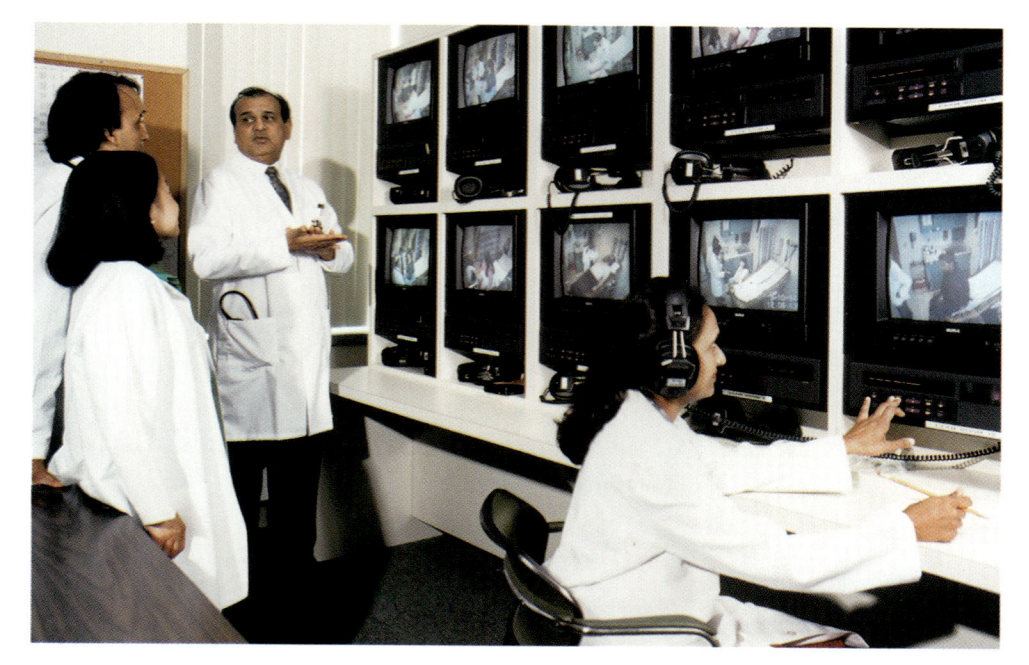

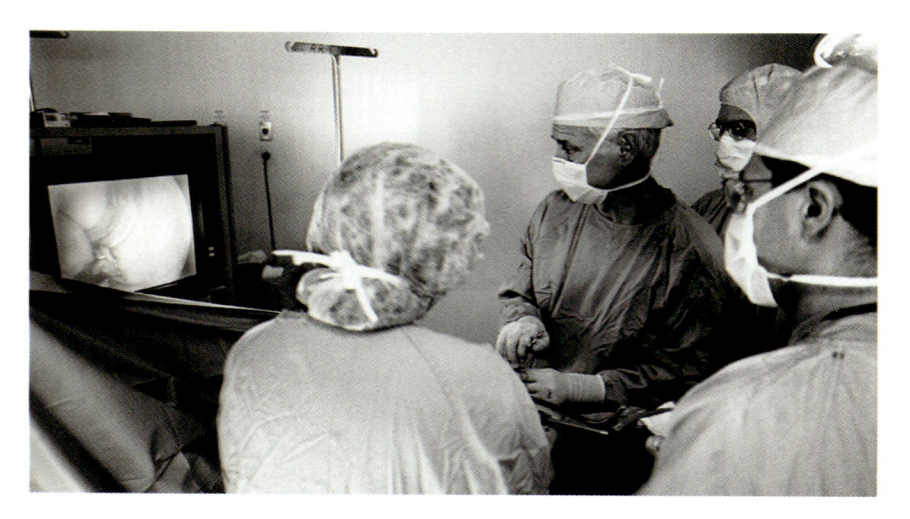

Video-assisted thoracic surgery, pioneered at St. Peter's in 1991, dramatically altered the way physicians perform chest surgery. © Nat Clymer

St. Peter's Numerous Specialized Services

The Center for Advanced Medicine and Surgery at St. Peter's encompasses a vast array of specialized services, including the Surgical Institute for Minimally Invasive Procedures; the Institute for Orthopedic Surgery; the Digestive Diseases Center; the Center for Diabetes Self-Management; the Wound Care Center; Asthma and Allergy Center; Center for Sleep and Breathing Disorders; Program for Addictions Consultation and Treatment; Nutritional Counseling and Weight Control; Institute for Molecular Diagnostics and Pathology; Speech and Hearing Services; Mind/Body Medical Institute; Physical Medicine and Rehabilitation; Community Care Homecare Services; Homecare America Health and Wellness Superstore; Electroencephalography; Vascular Lab; Adult Ambulatory Services; Ambulatory Surgery Center; Urology; Prostate Services; Family Practice Center; Endoscopy; Blood Donor Program; Pulmonary Function Lab; and Respiratory Therapy Services. ElderCare Services offer a specialized nursing care unit for the frail elderly, as well as the McCarrick Care Center, a 120-bed nursing home and Adult Medical Day Care Program in neighboring Franklin Township, and the Senior Health and Adult Medical Day Care Centers in Cranbury. The Cardiac Diagnostic and Treatment Center offers services from rehabilitation to catheterization.

St. Peter's prides itself on staying on the cutting edge of medical research and technology. For example, researchers at St. Peter's University Hospital have developed an advanced molecular test that significantly improves the diagnosis and management of Lyme disease. St. Peter's leadership in health care includes many unique programs and facilities, such as:

• The only Molecular Biology Laboratory in central New Jersey, which is equipped with the most sophisticated technology in the state
• The Breast Care Team, which provides a multi-disciplinary approach to breast cancer evaluation and treatment; services include mammography,

St. Peter's Clinical Competency Center was developed to promote, teach, and evaluate clinical competency at every level of training, from medical student to attending physician.

128 CREATING THE FUTURE

stereotactic breast biopsy, and instruction in breast self-examination
- Physical Medicine and Rehabilitation, whose services include physiatry, speech and hearing, and physical and occupational therapies
- The Institute for Reproductive and Perinatal Genetics, which offers pre- and postconceptional genetic counseling, prenatal diagnostic procedures and Level II ultrasonography, AFP/triplescreen testing, DNA diagnostic testing, paternity testing, teratogenic counseling, and pre- and postnatal genetic/pediatric evaluation
- Maternal Fetal Medicine, whose services include prepregnancy and perinatal consultation, pregnancy loss evaluation, and inpatient consultation
- The Antenatal Testing Unit, which offers obstetric ultrasounds, antepartum fetal surveillance, and fetal echocardiography
- The Fetal Alcohol Syndrome Prevention Program and the Center for Treatment of Pregnancy and Addiction
- The Cleft Palate Craniofacial Rehabilitation Center, which offers a team approach to the care necessary for the functional and cosmetic correction of children's facial malformations
- Natural Family Planning, which offers information and counseling on fertility

St. Peter's has a long tradition of community outreach and education. Programs on subjects such as Living with Diabetes, Lost A Spouse, and Caring for Your Elderly Loved Ones are held in the hospital and out in the community. The St. Peter's Mobile Health Unit, a specially equipped thirty-four-foot Winnebago, brings the resources of the medical center to underserved areas of the region. The Family Health Center was moved from the hospital campus to an area more accessible to the clients it serves.

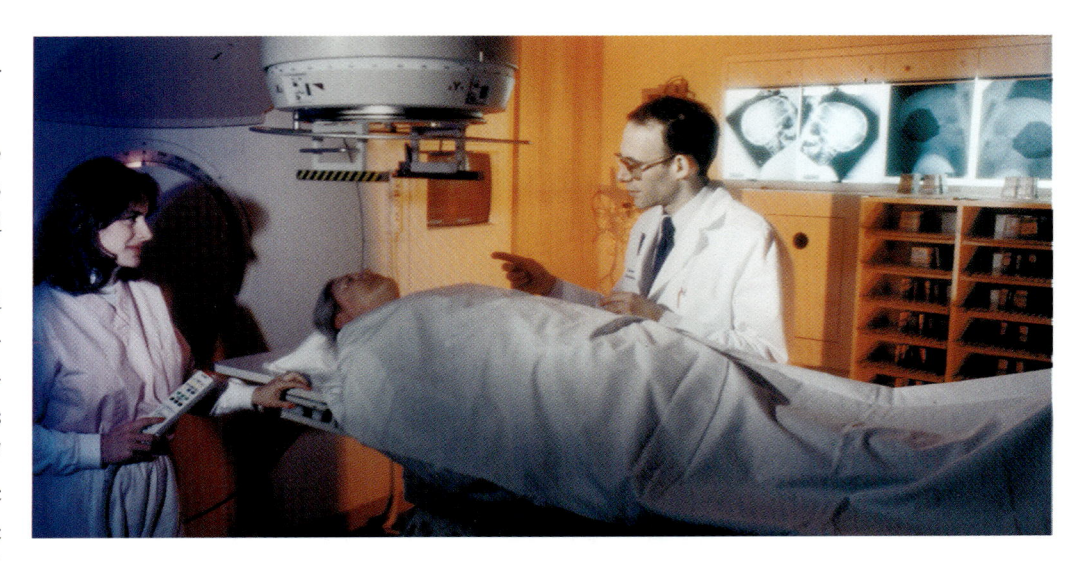

The Cancer Care Program at St. Peter's, accredited by the American College of Surgeons, offers a dedicated patient care oncology unit and a state-of-the-art radiation therapy center.

"At our heart and soul, St. Peter's is a community of people sharing a mission—essential values by which we choose to live and work. Our connectedness to God and the spirit of our different races, religions, ethnicities, and lifestyles energize our awareness that life is precious. Human dignity is a God-given right. We are servants pledged to give all we have to heal and to nurture our patients and each other. While patients are with us, their health and well-being are our most important concerns," says Monsignor William Capik, chairman of the board of trustees.

LEFT: *The Pediatric Emergency Room at St. Peter's provides physicians and nurses who are specially trained to care for children in crisis.*
INSET ABOVE: *St. Peter's offers residency training for doctors in a variety of specialties, from orthopedics to pediatrics.*

HEALTH CARE 129

HACKENSACK UNIVERSITY MEDICAL CENTER

OFFERING A COMPREHENSIVE, PERSONALIZED APPROACH TO HEALTH CARE, HACKENSACK UNIVERSITY MEDICAL CENTER ENCOMPASSES A BROAD DIVERSITY OF MEDICAL SPECIALTIES AND CONDUCTS ADVANCED RESEARCH

Hackensack University Medical Center is a regional-care teaching hospital that serves as a primary center of health care in northern New Jersey.

An outstanding medical facility offering a wide range of health care services, Hackensack University Medical Center received more national rankings by medical specialty than any other hospital in New Jersey, according to *America's Best Hospitals*, a consumer guide published by *U.S. News & World Report*. Hackensack University Medical Center received six national "Top 100" rankings, including cardiology, gastroenterology, geriatrics, orthopedics, otolaryngology, and rheumatology.

"This report firmly establishes Hackensack University Medical Center as a premier hospital in the state of New Jersey," says John P. Ferguson, medical center president and chief executive officer. "It also is a

Hackensack University Medical Center is one of New Jersey's preeminent teaching and tertiary hospitals, combining top medical expertise with high-level services and state-of-the-art technology.

tribute to the hard work and dedication of our fine medical and dental staff, nurses, employees, and volunteers, as well as the outstanding leadership of our board of governors."

The publication also cited Hackensack University Medical Center as one of the first Magnet hospitals in the nation recognized for nursing excellence by The American Nurses Credentialing Center.

"The notable rankings received by the medical center in *America's Best Hospitals* add credibility to our already excellent reputation," says George T. Croonquist, chairman of the medical center's board of governors. "It also confirms Hackensack University Medical Center's commitment to excellence in all areas of health care delivery."

"As America moves into a new era of health care delivery, Hackensack University Medical Center is in a unique position to lead the way in New Jersey, as is evident by this report," says John Ferguson.

The recognition by *U.S. News & World Report* is one of many accolades the medical center has

The DON IMUS—WFAN Pediatric Center for Tomorrows Children houses one of the largest and most comprehensive programs in New Jersey for children with cancer and blood disorders.

130 CREATING THE FUTURE

been awarded. It received the Magnet Award in 1995, the highest recognition in nursing excellence, which is given to hospitals where nurses are regarded as medical experts and where the patient-satisfaction rate is more than 90 percent. The medical center received the Quality Leader Award from the National Research Corporation in 1996, 1997, and 1998. Reflecting the outstanding work of its talented medical staff, the center was cited as having the "Highest Risk-Adjusted Survival Rate in Coronary Artery Bypass Surgery" by the New Jersey Department of Health, which also gave it a designation as a Kidney Transplant Center.

With an approved, licensed bed capacity of 629, the center provides the largest number of admissions of any hospital in the state. Hackensack University Medical Center has an annual operating revenue of nearly $400 million and is Bergen County's largest employer, with more than 4,500 on staff. The staff includes more than 800 physicians, representing many different medical specialties. Approximately 33,000 patients are served annually in the center's outpatient clinics, located both on and off the Hackensack University Medical Center campus. Every effort is made to provide comprehensive yet personalized health care services.

The hospital trains more then 250 students and 90 resident physicians each year. The medical center is a major affiliate of the University of Medicine and Dentistry of New Jersey–New Jersey Medical School and a member of the University Health System of New Jersey.

The Sarkis and Siran Gabrellian Child Care Learning Center, a 30,000-square-foot facility, provides day care for up to 370 children ages three months to six years.

The following provides an overview of many of Hackensack University Medical Center's programs. The diversity of the programs reflects the medical center's comprehensive approach to health care.

- Hackensack University Medical Center is a state-designated **Trauma Center**, staffed and equipped twenty-four hours a day, seven days a week to receive patients with major and life-threatening injuries.
- The medical center's **Heart Center**, which includes both noninvasive and invasive programs—offers a full range of state-of-the-art diagnostic and treatment services and is a New Jersey state–designated regional referral center for cardiac catheterization, cardiac surgery, and electrophysiology studies. In November 1997 the medical center received mortality data from the New Jersey Department of Health. This report showed that Hackensack University Medical Center's cardiac surgery team had the lowest risk-adjusted mortality rates for coronary bypass surgery of any hospital in New Jersey.
- One of the largest and most comprehensive programs in New Jersey for children with cancer and blood disorders, **The Tomorrows Children's Institute for Cancer and Blood Disorders**, is located in the DON IMUS–WFAN Pediatric Center for Tomorrows Children at Hackensack University Medical Center.
- The DON IMUS–WFAN Pediatric Center for Tomorrows Children at the medical center is also home to the Toys "R" Us/Kids "R" Us **Institute for Child Development** (ICD), an internationally recognized evaluation and treatment

COMMUNITY OUTREACH PROGRAMS

Hackensack University Medical Center provides many community outreach programs, including:
- Postpartum Depression Program
- Addiction Treatment Center
- The Body Shop
- Bone Marrow Transplant Support Group
- Cardiac Prevention and Rehabilitation Program
- Children's Arthritis Program
- Corporate Wellness
- Diabetes Education Program
- Genetics Counseling
- Head Trauma Program
- Health Awareness Regional Program
- Home Health Agency
- SIDS Center of New Jersey

HACKENSACK UNIVERSITY MEDICAL CENTER (CONTINUED)

center for children and adolescents with developmental and behavioral disorders.

- Hackensack University Medical Center's seventeen-bed **Neonatal Intensive Care Unit** (NICU), started in 1975, is now providing care for more than 4,400 patient days per year. It is a state-designated Level II program with eight intermediate bassinets and nine intensive care bassinets.
- The medical center's **Sarkis and Siran Gabrellian Child Care Learning Center** is a 30,000-square-foot facility that provides day care for up to 370 children ages three months to six years.
- The **Northern New Jersey Cancer Center** (NNJCC) at Hackensack University Medical Center is New Jersey's largest and most comprehensive adult outpatient center for cancer treatment. The NNJCC integrates and centralizes a full range of adult clinical and psychological support services in one location and aims to increase understanding of cancer and blood disorders and improve treatment through research. The NNJCC is affiliated with the Eastern Cooperative Oncology Group, National Cancer Institute, and the University of Rochester Cancer Center. Equipped with ultramodern facilities, a faculty of the highest caliber, and a well-trained staff, the NNJCC offers patients innovative, state-of-the-art medical treatment options, such as peripheral stem cell transplantation and bone marrow transplants.
- The **Bone Marrow Transplant Program**—a treatment for patients with certain leukemias and other cancers that are not curable by either chemotherapy or radiotherapy—is the only such program in Bergen and Hudson Counties. The center performs more bone marrow transplants than any other hospital in the state.
- The **Institute for Breast Care** at the medical center provides quick and efficient care in the patient's time of need. The center was created to provide all diagnostic and related services under one roof to promote the most effective treatment.
- Hackensack University Medical Center's **Institute for Radiosurgery** is a premier facility delivering one of today's most advanced treatments for a wide variety of intracranial lesions, including brain tumors and arteriovenous malformations. It is affiliated with the University of Medicine and Dentistry of New Jersey–New Jersey Medical School and the Cancer Institute of New Jersey.
- Excimer laser treatment for correction of nearsightedness, recently approved by the Food & Drug Administration, is now available at the the medical center's **Cornea and Laser Vision Institute**. The procedure, which reduces reliance on eyeglasses and contact lenses, is known as "photorefractive keratectomy" (PRK). It corrects nearsightedness by using excimer laser technology to reshape a patient's cornea.
- The **Center for Bloodless Medicine and Surgery** is committed to providing the highest standard of care to patients who object to the use of blood transfusions. The concept of bloodless medicine and surgery is not new. Today many people are concerned about health risks associated

The nine-story, 270,000-square-foot Hackensack University Medical Plaza is conveniently connected to the medical center's Patient Pavilion by an adjoining corridor. The medical plaza houses both private physician offices and an array of medical center programs, including The Center for Ambulatory Surgery, a 36,000-square-foot state-of-the-art-facility.

The Jeffrey M. Creamer Trauma Center at Hackensack University Medical Center is a state-designated trauma center capable of treating patients with major or life-threatening injuries at any time, day or night.

with blood transfusions, but for years there have been patients who refuse transfusions for religious reasons.

- The **Renal Dialysis Unit** was first instituted at Hackensack University Medical Center in 1966. It has twenty-one patient stations and the newest microprocessor-controlled dialysis machines. The machines have the ability to interface with various computer programs, allowing for monitoring and trend analysis to ensure accurate, optimum treatments.
- The medical center's **AIDS Outreach Program** provides AIDS patients with funds for primary medical care, including specialized medicines, outpatient programs, community and professional education, research studies, and other supportive services.
- Addiction and recovery facilities at Hackensack University Medical Center include the **Addiction Treatment Center (ATC)**. ATC offers a thirty-six-week intensive approach to outpatient detoxification that includes evaluation and assessment; orientation; individual, group, and family therapy; and supportive aftercare programs. For more information contact ATC at (201) 996-3560. The center's facilities also include the **Adolescent Drug and Alcohol Prevention & Treatment Program** (ADAPT), which offers a twenty-five-week outpatient intensive treatment approach for adolescents and teenagers with substance abuse problems. The program includes outpatient detoxification; medical supervision; individual, group, and family therapy;

The medical center's new state-of-the-art, 54,334-square-foot, five-story research facility will house laboratories for molecular biology, immunology, pharmacology, and virology studies. The center also will contain a 100-seat lecture hall, a computer center, and a center dedicated to clinical research.

and supportive aftercare programs. For more information, contact ADAPT at (201) 996-5999.

- The **Dave Winfield Nutrition Counseling Center** provides individual nutrition counseling and support services. Its expert staff helps patients develop a diet plan and make lifestyle changes. The center helps patients with weight management, high cholesterol, diabetes, and many other medical problems.
- With the recent establishment of the **Continence Center** at Hackensack University Medical Center, help is readily available for people who suffer from urinary incontinence. Staffed by highly skilled, board-certified urologists and incontinence specialists, the center is equipped with state-of-the-art technology for the evaluation, diagnosis, and outpatient treatment of urinary incontinence of all types and degrees.
- The medical center has the oldest **Hospice Program** in Bergen County, serving a wider area than any other Bergen County hospice by reaching all seventy communities in the county as well as residents of Hudson County.
- The foundation of any modern health care institution is its ability to deliver the latest, most advanced medical treatments. Intrinsic to accomplishing this goal is clinical and basic science research. At Hackensack University Medical Center, the **Institute for Biomedical Research** is a vital component in building and expanding clinical, educational, and research activities conducted at the medical center. The institute is charged with initiating and managing academic-level research at the medical center and serving medical center researchers, and pharmaceutical companies, governmental agencies, and private foundations.

SPECIALTY SERVICES ADDRESS MANY HEALTH CARE NEEDS

The medical center's specialty services include allergy, cardiac, dental, eye, family planning, gynecology, prenatal, pediatrics, neurology, and others, such as

- Physical Therapy
- Preparation for Breast-feeding
- Prostate Cancer Screening and Support Group
- Institute for Sleep-Wake Disorders
- Speakers' Bureau
- Steven Bader Immunological Institute
- Trauma Management Lecture

ROBERT WOOD JOHNSON UNIVERSITY HOSPITAL

ROBERT WOOD JOHNSON UNIVERSITY HOSPITAL OFFERS A FULL RANGE OF HEALTH CARE SERVICES, MEDICAL EDUCATION, ADVANCED RESEARCH, AND COMMUNITY OUTREACH PROGRAMS

Robert Wood Johnson University Hospital (RWJUH), one of the nation's leading academic health centers, captures the latest advances in medicine and brings these innovations immediately to New Jersey residents. In some cases, Robert Wood Johnson University Hospital physicians pioneer clinical trials that provide new medical science to the nation and the world.

"What really distinguishes us as an academic health center," says Harvey A. Holzberg, FACHE, president and CEO, "is our combination of the very best health care practitioners, state-of-the-art technology, and the experience and expertise to diagnose and treat the full spectrum of disease, from prevention and screenings to the most critical illness. We bring innovation to the practice of medicine that sets standards of care around the world.

"Another aspect that sets us apart," Holzberg says, "is that although we are a complex and sophisticated tertiary and quaternary academic health care center, we treat patients with highly personalized care, regarding our patients as partners in the healing process."

Robert Wood Johnson University Hospital is the core teaching hospital for the University of Medicine and Dentistry of New Jersey–Robert Wood Johnson Medical School. The hospital also is a member of University HealthSystem Consortium and the Robert Wood Johnson Health System and Network.

New Jersey's Commissioner of Health, Len Fishman, noted that patients of the hospital gain many benefits as a result of its status as a core teaching institution. He also commended Robert Wood Johnson University Hospital for demonstrating "its commitment to providing access to the medically and economically underserved populations of this state."

The Children's Hospital at Robert Wood Johnson University Hospital is one of an elite group of hospitals in the nation that offers minimally invasive surgery for pediatric patients.

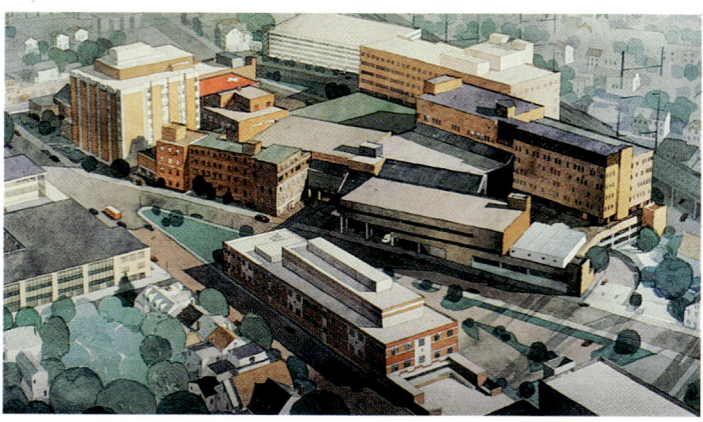

The Robert Wood Johnson University Hospital campus is located in New Brunswick.

ROBERT WOOD JOHNSON HEALTH SYSTEM AND NETWORK

The Robert Wood Johnson Health System is an alliance of leading health care providers throughout New Jersey. The Robert Wood Johnson Health Network includes hospitals, federally qualified health centers, long-term care facilities, and numerous satellite facilities. It is the only health care network in New Jersey that includes a medical school. Through research, educational forums, and identification of the most advanced procedures, the medical school enhances the ability of all member hospitals and health centers to provide the finest care available on a national standard. Members of the Health System and the Health Network share information and services and work together to assure that their patients have the most advanced health care close to home.

> **MISSION**
>
> Robert Wood Johnson University Hospital is committed to a fourfold mission—patient care, research, education of tomorrow's health professionals, and community outreach programs.

CENTERS OF EXCELLENCE

Treating more than 100,000 patients annually, RWJUH offers comprehensive services in every medical specialty including:
- The Heart Center of New Jersey
- The Vascular Center of New Jersey

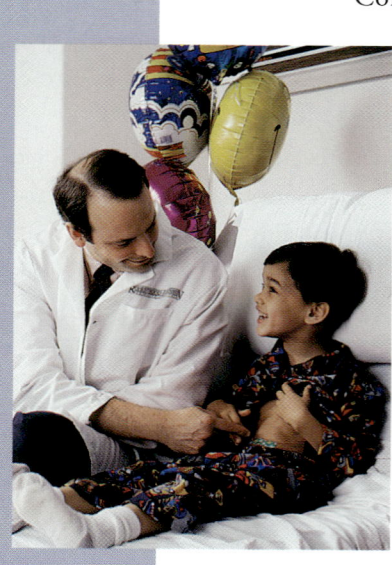

134 CREATING THE FUTURE

- The Cancer Institute of New Jersey
- The Children's Hospital—a state-designated specialty acute care hospital
- The Clinical Neurosciences Center
- Level I Trauma Center
- Center for Digestive Diseases
- The Women's Wellness and Healthcare Connection
- The Maternity Center and Special Care Nursery
- The Center for Heart and Kidney Transplantation
- The Center for Innovations in Bloodless Surgery and Medicine

The **Heart Center of New Jersey** is a 125-bed "hospital within a hospital" offering the latest diagnostic and treatment techniques for cardiovascular disease, including catheterization, angioplasty, open heart surgery, minimally invasive techniques, electrophysiology, and stents. Heart transplantation completes the full comprehensive range of options offered to treat cardiovascular disease. The Heart Center of New Jersey houses one of the busiest cardiac catheterization programs in the nation, with several high-risk catheterization laboratories in continuous operation. The Heart Center recently introduced the newest laser protocol to bring oxygen-rich blood to deprived heart muscle via tiny channels burned directly into the heart tissue.

The **Vascular Center of New Jersey**, the referral center of choice for vascular surgeries that are the most complex, uses a multidisciplinary approach. Physicians from the diagnostic, surgical, and medical specialties treat diseases of the veins using the latest spectrum of procedures, from minimally invasive ultrasound to highly complex surgery. Services include the Wound Care Center, the Vein Center, the Renovascular Center, Invasive Radiology, Vascular Surgery, and Thrombosis Prevention.

The **Cancer Institute of New Jersey**'s (CINJ) $26 million facility, located across the street from Robert Wood Johnson University Hospital, serves as the nucleus of the most innovative cancer treatment and research in the state. The Cancer Institute of New Jersey is the first and only site in New Jersey to receive the coveted designation of clinical cancer center from the National Cancer Institute, a branch of the National Institutes of Health. Robert Wood Johnson University Hospital was one of the founding partners of the Cancer Institute of New Jersey and has maintained a close working relationship to provide advanced clinical care and to conduct world-class cancer research.

Research, which is an important component of the hospital's mission, is conducted in collaboration with partners at UMDNJ–Robert Wood Johnson Medical School and the Cancer Institute of New Jersey.

In partnership with CINJ, Robert Wood Johnson University Hospital offers sophisticated cancer treatment for both children and adults. Hospital facilities include medical and surgical oncology units, same-day outpatient chemotherapy units, a bone marrow transplant center, and a pediatric hematology/oncology unit. In 1998 the hospital added an oncology Urgent Care Center for cancer patients needing prompt medical care.

The renowned seventy-bed **Children's Hospital** at Robert Wood Johnson University Hospital is home to the region's only Pediatric Intensive Care Unit and offers more than forty-five pediatric specialties under the clinical leadership of UMDNJ–Robert Wood Johnson Medical School. In keeping with its family-centered philosophy, the Children's Hospital features the largest and most comprehensive Child Life Program in the state, with professional caregivers available seven days a week to help meet the emotional needs of young patients. A special Family Teaching Program is provided for all children having surgery, including minimally invasive and same-day procedures.

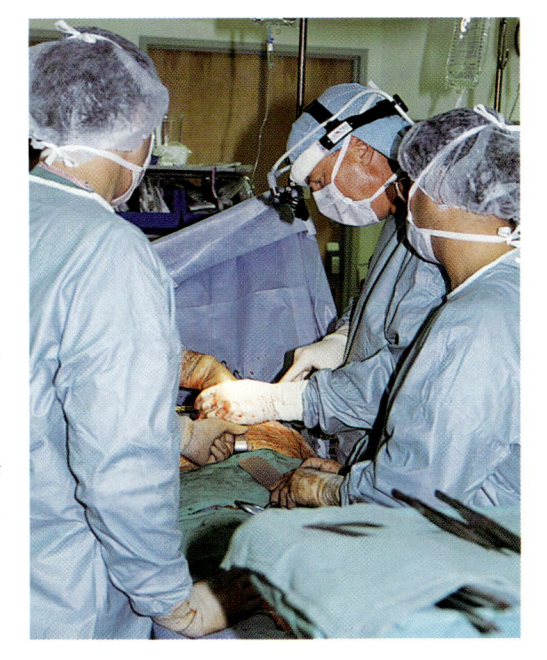

The Vascular Center of New Jersey at Robert Wood Johnson University Hospital is the referral center of choice for vascular surgeries that are the most technically difficult.
© Conrad Gloos

HEALTH CARE 135

ROBERT WOOD JOHNSON UNIVERSITY HOSPITAL (CONTINUED)

The hospital is building a new facility designed expressly for children and their families. It will consolidate the hospital's six existing pediatric and adolescent units and have its own dedicated entrance, a Pediatric Emergency Department, an expanded Child Life Center, and a new Family Center and School Room.

"I am very proud that Robert Wood Johnson University Hospital will be the home of a world-class facility for all children," said Holzberg at the groundbreaking ceremony. "It will be a special building designed to protect and nurture a child's view of the world and one that recognizes that the needs of the entire family must be taken into consideration when a child is hospitalized."

The **Clinical Neurosciences Center** at RWJUH is dedicated to research and medical and surgical treatment of a wide range of neurological disorders, including Parkinson's disease, stroke, and epilepsy. A nineteen-bed unit in the CORE Pavilion offers comprehensive services for neurology patients.

The hospital is home to central New Jersey's only **Level I Trauma Center**. A skilled shock/trauma team is available twenty-four hours a day for patients who are brought in by ambulance or helicopter. The trauma team includes general, orthopedic, cardiac, and vascular physicians; neurosurgeons; and attending pediatricians. The latest equipment, including MRI (magnetic resonance imaging) and CAT (computerized axial tomography) scan imagery is used for diagnosis and treatment. The Level I Trauma Center also sponsors numerous seminars and programs for the community on safety and injury prevention.

Specialists at RWJUH's **Center for Digestive Diseases** make use of sophisticated diagnostic tools and breakthrough methods of treatment to combat disorders such as indigestion; ulcers; and liver, gall bladder, and intestinal diseases. The Crohn's and Colitis Center of New Jersey, housed at the medical school, offers a multidisciplinary approach for diagnosing and treating Crohn's disease and colitis, both of which are chronic inflammatory bowel diseases with unknown causes. The center offers a full spectrum of diagnostic, medical, and surgical therapies.

The **Women's Wellness and Healthcare Connection** (WWHC) at the hospital is dedicated to the enhancement

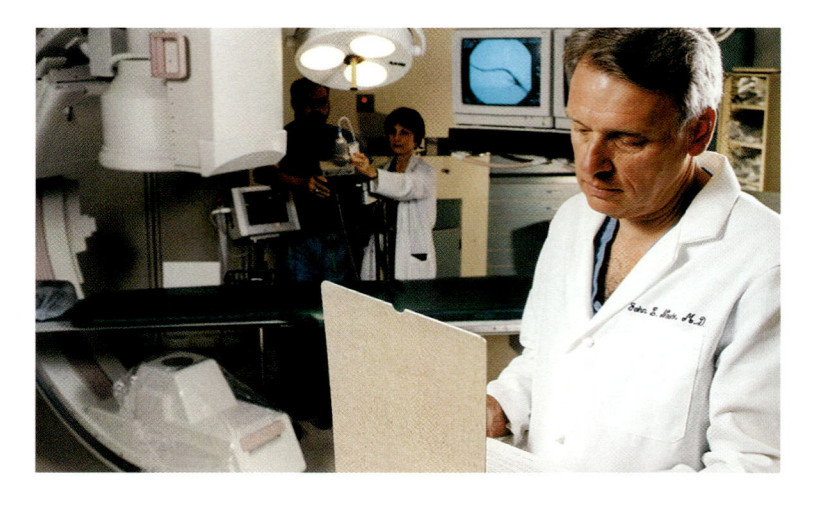

The hospital's Radiology Department offers the most sophisticated technologies available, including minimally invasive techniques that help some patients avoid surgery.

The Children's Hospital at Robert Wood Johnson University Hospital offers more than 45 specialties and the most comprehensive Child Life Program in the state.

of a woman's overall well-being. The primary mission is to provide women with health information and clinical services that promote healthy living practices. Teaching skills for disease prevention and health maintenance are an integral part of the Women's Wellness and Healthcare Connection's philosophy of care for women. As the only provider in the state of the Spirit of Women initiative, with cosponsors Johnson & Johnson, Ortho-McNeil, and *Prevention* magazine, the WWHC is one component of a range of services for women at the hospital, including the Maternity Center, the Center for Nurse Midwifery, and comprehensive obstetric and gynecologic services. A second-opinion service for women considering surgery is offered through the medical school. In another innovative program, a new treatment for uterine fibroids helps some women avoid hysterectomies.

The Robert Wood Johnson University Hospital Maternity Center and Special Care Nursery provide personalized, family-centered support in all aspects of prenatal, labor, delivery, and postpartum care. Modern labor/delivery/recovery rooms combine a homelike atmosphere with advanced facilities. Additionally, two postpartum Celebration Suites allow room for fathers to stay with mothers and babies in a hotel-like setting. A full range of parenting preparation courses is offered, including Lamaze, exercise, and breast-feeding programs.

The **Center for Heart and Kidney Transplantation** at Robert Wood Johnson University Hospital offers new programs in both heart and kidney solid organ transplantation.

"We are privileged to have earned the approval to begin two transplant programs simultaneously," states Holzberg. "As one of the nation's leading academic health centers, we are working in partnership with the UMDNJ–Robert Wood Johnson Medical School to bring a world-class transplantation center to the people of our state."

Robert Wood Johnson University Hospital is establishing satellite centers on the campuses of various affiliates of the Robert Wood Johnson Health Network to offer pre- and post-surgical care to transplant patients. These satellite centers further enhance the ability of transplant patients to receive care in their own communities, near their families and friends. Each multidisciplinary transplant team is led by physicians and surgeons with superb technical skills who are academic leaders in the field of transplantation and caring advocates for patients.

The **Center for Innovations in Bloodless Surgery and Medicine** offers a multidisciplinary team of physicians, nurses, and health care professionals who set a national standard in providing bloodless treatment approaches for a variety of elective as well as emergency procedures. This outstanding team is committed to ensuring community access to superior medical and surgical care that respects patients' religious beliefs and personal preferences regarding the avoidance of blood transfusions. Robert Wood Johnson University Hospital is one of the elite health centers in the United States that offers bloodless techniques in every surgical and medical specialty.

ADDITIONAL COMPREHENSIVE SERVICES

The hospital also is home to the Same Day Surgery Suite, the Skin Laser Center, the Center for Alternative and Complementary Medicine, the Chinese-American Medicine Initiative, the New Jersey Pain Institute, and the Comprehensive Sleep Disorders Center; in addition, special centers focus on the diagnosis and treatment of lupus and Lyme disease. Other programs provide Home Care and Hospice services. Through the Community Education Department, the hospital sponsors more than forty support groups as well as weekly health and wellness programs.

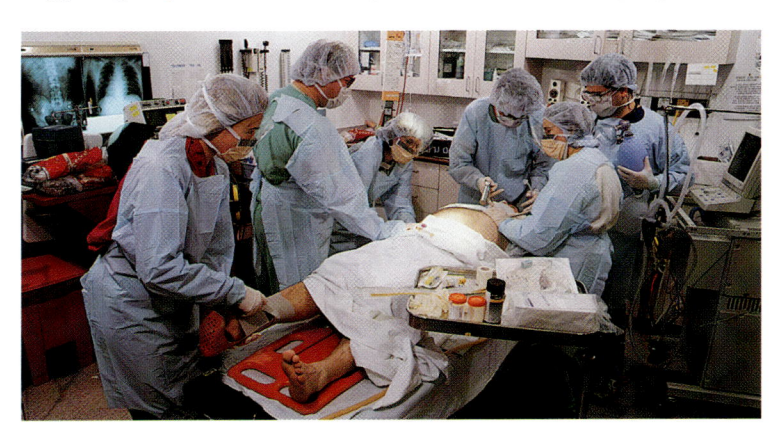

Nurses at Robert Wood Johnson University Hospital are encouraged to continue their education; approximately half of the registered nurses also are certified in their specialties, such as cardiology, oncology, or surgery.

The Community Health Promotion Program (CHPP) offers extensive outreach services to the local community with special attention to the health needs of immigrant and non-English-speaking residents. The hospital also supports initiatives to provide health information and services of special benefit to the African American community. The hallmark of the CHPP is a focus on creating programs off the hospital campus so that local residents can more conveniently access these services.

NATIONAL RECOGNITION

Excellence in health care at Robert Wood Johnson University Hospital has been repeatedly recognized with the awarding of Accreditation with Commendation from the Joint Commission on the Accreditation of Healthcare Organizations. An extraordinary summary score of 97 out of 100 points places Robert Wood Johnson University Hospital among the top 20 percent of hospitals surveyed. Even with such high scores, not all hospitals receive the extra letter of Commendation. The entire hospital staff takes great pride in this achievement.

Robert Wood Johnson University Hospital led the nation as one of the first hospitals to achieve Magnet designation from the American Nurses Credentialing Center in recognition of excellence in all aspects of nursing services.

LOOKING TO THE FUTURE

As Robert Wood Johnson University Hospital approaches the millennium, the hospital and the Robert Wood Johnson Health System and Network will continue as national leaders in the development of new and advanced protocols to save lives and to improve the quality of life. Working closely with UMDNJ–Robert Wood Johnson Medical School, the hospital will build on its international reputation for combining world-class research with innovative treatments to achieve the highest level of patient care.

The hospital's Level I Trauma Center was the first in New Jersey to pass three successive verification site visits by the American College of Surgeons. The center received a Pediatric Commitment verification in 1997.

HEALTH CARE 137

SAINT BARNABAS HEALTH CARE SYSTEM

NEW JERSEY'S LARGEST INTEGRATED HEALTH CARE DELIVERY SYSTEM, SAINT BARNABAS HEALTH CARE SYSTEM STRIVES TO PROVIDE THE HIGHEST LEVELS OF PATIENT CARE AND PATIENT SATISFACTION

The Saint Barnabas Health Care System is New Jersey's largest integrated health care delivery system. With many diverse health care facilities working as one system, all its affiliates share a common mission and vision to provide high-quality, cost-efficient health care to the residents of New Jersey.

"Throughout the Saint Barnabas Health Care System, our dedicated physicians, nurses, and health professionals are committed to providing the highest quality of patient care and health education to the community and the region," says Ronald J. Del Mauro, president and chief executive officer. "Our patients and their family members must know that they can expect the highest level of care, delivered cost-effectively, wherever they see our name."

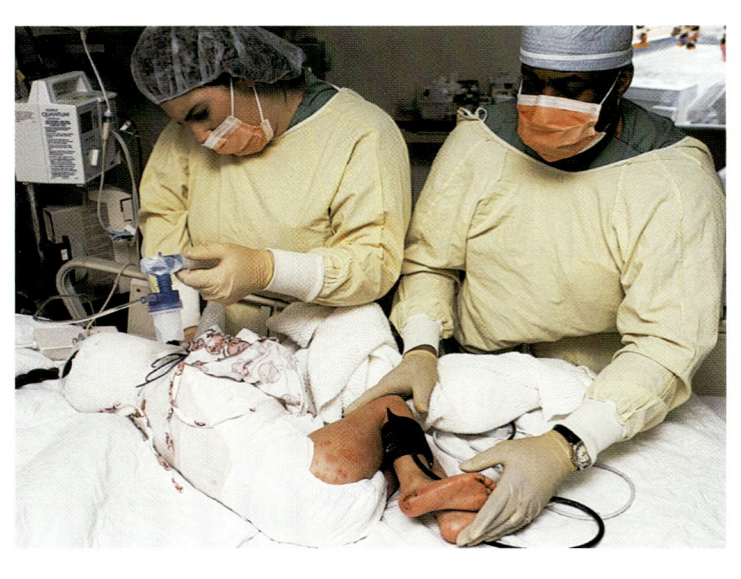

Within the Saint Barnabas system, each facility has unique strengths and attributes. This individuality is enhanced and, at the same time, a high level of consistency has been developed to ensure that quality pervades every facility. To this end, a Department of Patient Satisfaction has been established in each of the system's hospitals—a first in New Jersey, and possibly in the nation.

The Saint Barnabas Health Care System includes 22,300 employees—making it the state's second largest private employer; 4,620 physicians; and 443 residents. The system provides treatment and services for more than 185,000 in-patients and same-day-surgery patients, 342,000 emergency department patients, and more than 1.32 million outpatients each year and delivers more than 16,000 infants annually. Within the next two years projections are that it will serve the health needs of two million New Jerseyans, one-fourth of the state's population.

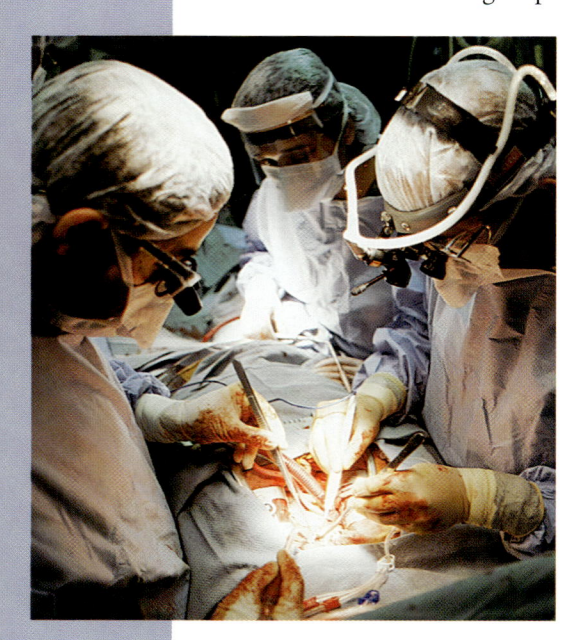

The Burn Center at Saint Barnabas Medical Center is New Jersey's only certified burn-treatment facility, caring for more than 400 patients per year. The center is equipped to treat pediatric through geriatric patients, with a full range of specialized services.

The Heart Hospital of New Jersey at Newark Beth Israel Medical Center offers patients access to a world-class team of experienced and dedicated professionals who provide cardiac services that are the state's most comprehensive—including pediatric and adult cardiac surgery and heart transplantation.

The Saint Barnabas system's hospitals include:
- Clara Maass Medical Center in Belleville
- Community Medical Center in Toms River
- Irvington General Hospital in Irvington
- Kimball Medical Center in Lakewood
- Monmouth Medical Center in Long Branch
- Newark Beth Israel Medical Center in Newark
- Saint Barnabas Medical Center in Livingston
- Union Hospital in Union
- Wayne General Hospital in Wayne
- West Hudson Hospital in Kearny

The system also has ten nursing homes with more than 1,400 beds, forty ambulatory care centers, three geriatric centers, one psychiatric facility, a statewide behavioral health network, and comprehensive home care and hospice programs.

Among the Saint Barnabas Health Care System's nationally recognized services and facilities are New Jersey's only certified burn-treatment facility; comprehensive cardiac surgery services for adults and, by volume, one of the top five pediatric cardiac surgery services in the nation in affiliation with the Cardiac Surgery Program at the Children's

Hospital of Philadelphia; the state's only heart and lung transplant center; two of New Jersey's three kidney transplant centers, which together are the sixth largest of 240 programs in the nation; the Joslin Diabetes Center, affiliate of the internationally recognized Joslin Diabetes Center in Boston; the world-class Institute for Reproductive Medicine and Science at Saint Barnabas; nationally recognized geriatric services; the acclaimed Institute of Neurology and Neurosurgery; state-of-the-art oncology services; and renowned women's and children's services, including Children's Hospital of New Jersey at Newark Beth Israel Medical Center.

The Mount Sinai Medical Center in New York City is collaborating with the Saint Barnabas Health Care System to enhance medical education, patient care, and managed care contracting. Saint Barnabas and Newark Beth Israel are major teaching affiliates of The Mount Sinai School of Medicine. Monmouth Medical Center is a major teaching affiliate of MCP-Hahnemann Medical School in Philadelphia. The Saint Barnabas system is a major clinical campus for the New York College of Osteopathic Medicine.

The commitment of Saint Barnabas to the communities it serves is integral to its mission. For example, Saint Barnabas is helping to create 400 jobs for Newark residents by building a laundry facility in Newark; and, as part of the South Ward Community Rehabilitation Project, the Saint Barnabas system,

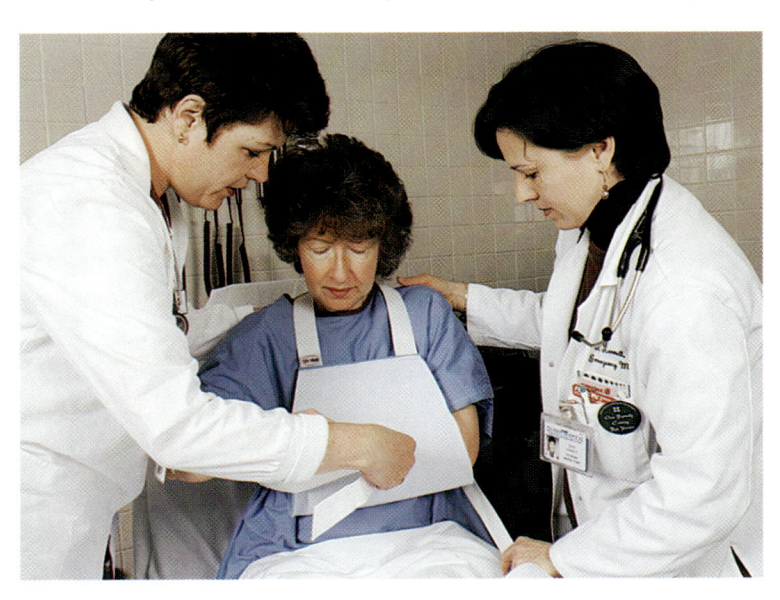

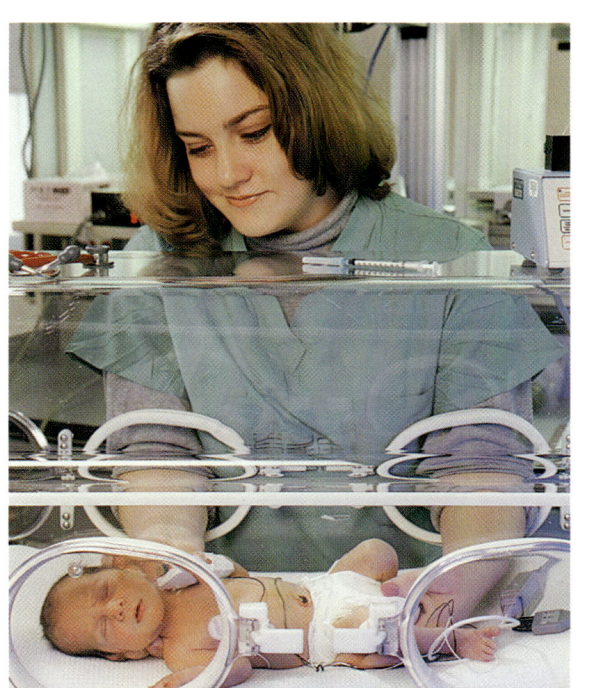

Monmouth Medical Center's Regional Newborn Center includes a Level III neonatal intensive care unit (NICU), one of three in the Saint Barnabas system designated by the state for high-risk births. Saint Barnabas Medical Center's NICU is one of only sixteen in the nation to treat more than 1,000 infants per year. Saint Barnabas is one of just twenty-two hospitals in the United States to deliver more than 6,000 babies each year.

Newark Beth Israel Medical Center, and the city of Newark are collaborating to rehabilitate the homes, commercial buildings, and stores surrounding Newark Beth Israel. In partnership with Newark's St. James A.M.E. Church, Saint Barnabas opened the Center for Family Life at St. James, the first collaboration of its kind in New Jersey between a church and a large health care system.

The system's new center for ambulatory care in Livingston is among the nation's most sophisticated outpatient facilities. "The Saint Barnabas Ambulatory Care Center is providing the highest quality medical care in an environment designed to set new standards for patient satisfaction," states Del Mauro. Designed to accommodate a patient's every need, the Ambulatory Care Center uses advanced information technology systems and a revolutionary concept in imaging services. Radiology images are transmitted throughout the facility, Saint Barnabas Medical Center, and will ultimately be transmitted to private physician offices, allowing for faster reporting of test results to physicians and patients.

"The Saint Barnabas Health Care System will continually strive to not only meet but also exceed the expectations of our patients," says Del Mauro. "Our outstanding physicians, employees, and facilities have made a measurable difference to the patients we serve. We will continue to work to bring even greater health care services to the residents of New Jersey and beyond."

SAINT BARNABAS
HEALTH CARE SYSTEM
NEW JERSEY

Saint Barnabas Health Care System's Union Hospital emergency department recently was ranked number one in patient satisfaction out of forty-one hospital emergency departments in New Jersey, according to the nationally recognized research firm Press, Ganey Associates, Inc.

HEALTH CARE 139

SOLARIS HEALTH SYSTEM

COMBINING JFK MEDICAL CENTER AND MUHLENBERG REGIONAL MEDICAL CENTER, SOLARIS HEALTH SYSTEM OFFERS A FULL SPECTRUM OF HIGH-QUALITY, COST-EFFICIENT HEALTH SERVICES

The word *solaris* means the sun—an essential source of energy and warmth. It also is a word describing a bright new light in New Jersey—the Solaris Health System, whose values and range of comprehensive health care services reflect the new age of health care.

In 1997 JFK Medical Center and its affiliates in Edison and Muhlenberg Regional Medical Center and its affiliates in Plainfield launched Solaris as a new community-based, nonprofit health care organization. Together the two hospitals have 5,600 employees, 850 affiliated doctors, and 1,575 beds. While each institution retains its original name and identity, as a consolidated organization they complement each other's strengths. Both JFK and Muhlenberg have strong ties to the community, established reputations in the region, quality medical staffs, and strong clinical programs. The new system enhances their ability to provide a full spectrum of high-quality, cost-efficient services to the residents of central New Jersey.

"The Solaris Health System is a hospital system created by the community to serve the people of the community," says John P. McGee, president and chief executive officer of Solaris Health System. "The people we serve and their personal accomplishments are our measure of success. As we move ahead, we will continually add advanced technology and new services to meet the changing needs of our community."

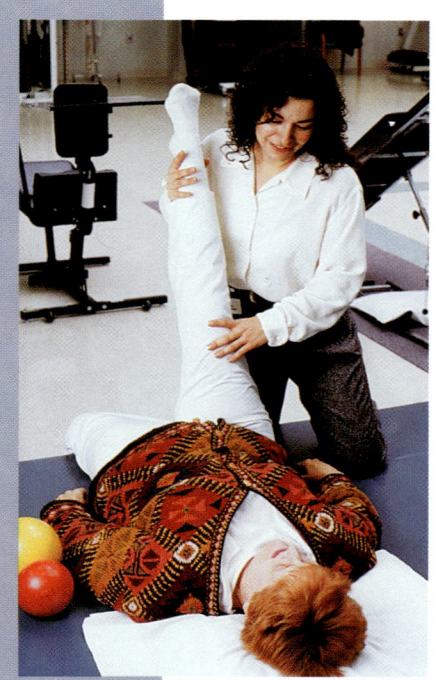

JFK MEDICAL CENTER

Founded in 1967, the 535-bed JFK Medical Center is noted for its innovative health care management and quality patient care. JFK records approximately 20,000 admissions annually, nearly 2,000 births, and more than 40,000 emergency room visits. JFK consists of the 441-bed Anthony M. Yelencsics Community Hospital and the adjacent 94-bed JFK Johnson Rehabilitation Institute. The medical center features a complete array of services, from emergency care and surgery to maternity and pediatrics, as well as specialty services.

Also at JFK is The New Jersey Neuroscience Institute, a nationally recognized comprehensive center for the diagnosis, treatment, and study of neurological disease. Staffed by a team of top neuroscience experts from across the United States, the institute also works to promote investigative efforts in basic and clinical research.

The JFK Johnson Rehabilitation Institute and its satellite facilities compose one of the first rehabilitation centers in the nation to recognize that individuals with acquired traumatic brain injury require a specialized treatment environment. With its unprecedented, comprehensive approach to care, the institute's Center for Head Injuries is regarded as pioneering in head trauma evaluation and treatment. In addition, the institute's Pediatric Rehabilitation Department provides children with the adaptive and coping skills they need to achieve success in everyday life through such special disciplines as physical therapy and occupational therapy. The institute also offers inpatient and day rehabilitation, outpatient therapies, and prosthetics and orthotics.

Muhlenberg Regional Medical Center's ChildBirth Center offers compassionate care in a homelike setting. Services include tours and educational classes prior to giving birth, comprehensive teaching during a new mother's hospital stay, and follow-up seminars throughout the year. © Nat Clymer

JFK Johnson Rehabilitation Institute offers comprehensive inpatient, subacute, and outpatient rehabilitation services to help children and adults regain the highest possible level of independence and quality of life.

CREATING THE FUTURE

JFK's Cancer Center features state-of-the-art cancer diagnosis and treatment capabilities, hospice care, and participation in nationwide cancer research networks. JFK's outpatient Mediplex Surgery Center provides same-day procedures, including laser, endoscopic, and arthroscopic surgery. The JFK Imaging Center and its Breast Center offer a full range of diagnostic examinations, including CAT (computerized axial tomography) scan and MRI (magnetic imaging resonance) services. Among other JFK Medical Center facilities are the Fitness and Conference Center and the Family Practice Center.

There are three JFK Hartwyck Nursing, Convalescent & Rehabilitation Centers, which provide a wide range of special services for long-term and residential care. All offer skilled nursing services and respite care in pleasant, comfortable surroundings. In addition, each facility is complemented by the medical and rehabilitation services offered by JFK Medical Center and JFK Johnson Rehabilitation Institute.

MUHLENBERG REGIONAL MEDICAL CENTER

Founded in 1877, the 396-bed, university-affiliated teaching medical center Muhlenberg Regional Medical Center offers services in all major medical specialties and most subspecialties. Its innovative Fitch Pavilion provides patients and visitors with a modern ChildBirth Center, Emergency Department, Intensive Care Unit, Operating Suites, and Post-Anesthesia Care Unit. The medical center offers sophisticated, state-of-the-art equipment and high-quality care. Its 1,700 employees and 350 physicians serve residents in Union, Somerset, and Middlesex counties.

In addition, Muhlenberg's special facilities include The Diabetes Center of New Jersey, the Anorectal Physiology Laboratory, the Thyroid Center, the Osteoporosis Center, and the Breast Health and Mammography Center. Other services include cardiac catheterization, chemical dependency treatment, hemodialysis, home care, hospice care, adult medical day care, subacute care, and community health education. Muhlenberg also operates SurgiCare of Central Jersey, a freestanding same-day surgery facility, and the Schools of Nursing and Allied Health, which offer diplomas in nursing, radiography, and nuclear medicine, plus associate in science degrees from Union County College.

"Beyond new facilities and programs, we are staying in touch with industry trends," says McGee. "We are looking ahead at the prospect of forming links with other hospitals and organizations to create a health system that will continue to meet the needs of the people in our community. Our goals are to improve our patients' access to care, expand the range of services we offer, and continue to offer high-quality care to the men, women, and children of central New Jersey. These steps toward progress are part of our commitment to continue as a health care leader."

JFK Hartwyck Nursing, Convalescent & Rehabilitation Centers offer skilled nursing services and respite care in pleasant and comfortable surroundings. Specialized programs include adult medical and Alzheimer's day care, subacute rehabilitation, and the state's first unit dedicated solely to the treatment of patients with Huntington's disease.

The New Jersey Neuroscience Institute at JFK Medical Center is designed exclusively for the diagnosis, treatment, and research of complex neurological disorders in adults and children. Services include programs for balance and dizziness disorders, epilepsy, spine and brain tumors, stroke, and movement disorders.

SOLARIS HEALTH SYSTEM AFFILIATES

- JFK Medical Center
- Muhlenberg Regional Medical Center
- Muhlenberg Foundation
- JFK Medical Center Foundation
- JFK Johnson Rehabilitation Institute
- JFK Hartwyck Nursing, Convalescent & Rehabilitation Centers
- Diabetes Center of New Jersey
- JFK Healthshare
- JFK LIFEStyle Institute
- Muhlenberg Schools of Nursing & Allied Health
- New Jersey Neuroscience Institute
- SurgiCare of Central Jersey

HEALTH CARE 141

THE COOPER HEALTH SYSTEM

Offering a technologically advanced, patient-centered delivery system, The Cooper Health System provides integrated health care services to southern New Jersey and the Delaware Valley

From its founding in 1887 as a small community hospital, The Cooper Health System has grown to become a dynamic, integrated health care delivery system serving an entire region.

In recent years, Cooper has adapted to meet the medical challenges of a geographically dispersed patient population and a rapidly changing health care environment. In the face of the economic challenge resulting from the advent of managed care, Cooper has redefined itself. In doing so, it has always kept patients as its first priority. By balancing economic reality with the ideal of quality patient care, today Cooper is a model academic health center for the twenty-first century.

"Changes in the economic climate, medical technology, and pharmacology will consistently drive the need for health care providers to keep pace and change the way we provide the care people need," says The Cooper Health System president and chief executive officer, Kevin G. Halpern. "The key is to operate leaner and more efficiently while always keeping quality of care as our first priority."

The Cooper Health System hospital administrators and physicians recognize that health care in the twenty-first century will be directed at managing the complete health care needs of a defined population, not simply providing care when patients are ill. Toward that goal, the entire Cooper Health System has shifted from a hospital-based system in Camden to a patient-centered delivery system throughout southern New Jersey.

Cooper Hospital/University Medical Center has been a cornerstone in the Camden community for more than 100 years. During the spring and summer, its active campus life spills onto its manicured grounds.

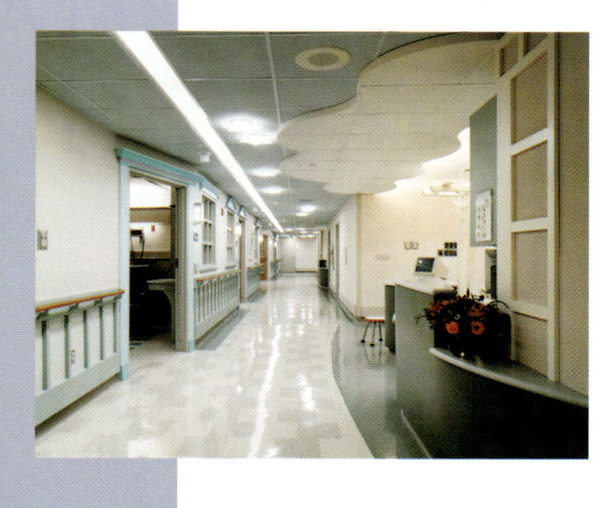

The Children's Regional Hospital at Cooper, a hospital-within-a-hospital, boasts a child-friendly decor in a medically progressive environment.

"A patient-centered delivery system is organized for the needs of the patient, rather than for the convenience of the staff. Cooper has changed staff members' jobs, the scope of their responsibilities, and the clinical process so that its services make sense from the patient's point of view—from expanding our hours to adding new services," says Halpern.

To The Cooper Health System, "patient-centered" means offering everything from the most sophisticated, technologically advanced medicine at Cooper Hospital/University Medical Center in Camden to a full array of primary care, preventive care, and wellness resources located at more than fifty sites throughout southern New Jersey.

The Cooper Health System's full range of services includes prevention, home health care, primary care, specialty ambulatory services, all levels of inpatient care, and subacute care. Today Cooper is recognized as a leader in the treatment of cancer, heart disease, geriatrics, trauma, and pediatrics.

CREATING THE FUTURE

As the clinical campus of the University of Medicine and Dentistry/Robert Wood Johnson Medical School, Cooper also is the major teaching hospital in southern New Jersey. Cooper Hospital/University Medical Center, located in Camden, is a 554–licensed bed, nonprofit academic medical center that specializes in the treatment of seriously ill and critically injured patients.

A "hospital-within-our-hospital," the Children's Regional Hospital at Cooper provides pediatric services that are among the finest available to the children of southern New Jersey. Designated by the State Department of Health as a specialty acute care children's hospital, it is uniquely equipped and carefully staffed to treat the region's most critically ill and seriously injured children, from newborns to adolescents. Its physicians and surgeons are recruited from the best children's hospitals in the nation. As experts in their field, they also are faculty members at the medical school.

The Cooper Health System at Voorhees is an impressive seventy-thousand-square-foot facility that houses offices for physicians representing a wide range of medical and surgical specialties, diagnostic imaging services, and a state-of-the-art outpatient surgery center—all in one convenient, suburban setting.

Cooper has grown by expanding the number of medical services it offers and by adding new facilities in the area surrounding Camden. By broadening its geographic focus, Cooper has become an important economic and social force throughout the region. Despite this change, Cooper has remained true to its mission to serve its local community. Even with economic pressure to move, Cooper has remained committed to the city of Camden—providing family health care as well as a major source of employment for city residents.

On 25 June 1996 The Cooper Health System Board of Trustees adopted the following mission statement:

"The mission of The Cooper Health System is to be a major provider of integrated health care services to southern New Jersey and the Delaware Valley in partnership with affiliated organizations. The Cooper Health System also acknowledges and respects our ongoing and continuing commitment to our immediate neighbors. Utilizing the highest ethical and professional standards, our goal is to continuously enhance the health of the people we serve and to improve the value of the care we provide. These goals will be accomplished without regard for any differentiating or discriminatory factors. The Cooper Health System is committed to providing the means for managing health care risk and ensuring the fiscal stability needed to maintain a vital and growing environment for our provider and payer partners and patients."

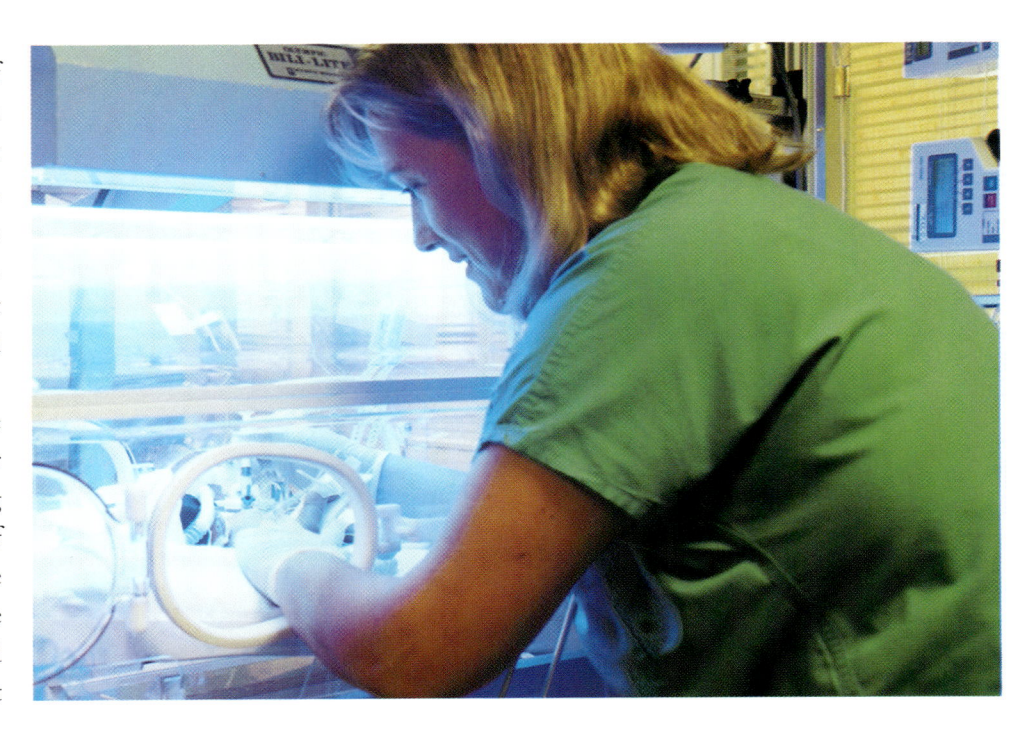

The neonatal intensive care unit of the Children's Regional Hospital has the highest designation for a neonatal center that is available in the state of New Jersey.

The Cooper Health System at Voorhees is an impressive seventy-thousand-square-foot facility with diagnostic imaging, a state-of-the-art outpatient surgery center, and offices for physicians representing a wide range of medical and surgical specialties.

FRANCISCAN HEALTH SYSTEM OF NEW JERSEY

Franciscan Health System of New Jersey, including St. Mary Hospital of Hoboken and St. Francis Hospital of Jersey City, offers comprehensive health care services for Hudson County

Founded in 1863, St. Mary Hospital of Hoboken is the longest-established hospital in New Jersey. A year later St. Francis Hospital of Jersey City was founded. Today the two hospitals are joined as the Franciscan Health System of New Jersey. Their mission remains the same as when they were founded—to provide the best medical care to Hudson County residents.

In the Franciscan Health System of New Jersey, there are approximately 1,700 employees, 700 members of the medical staff, and almost 200 volunteers. In addition to St. Mary and St. Francis Hospitals, the system operates FAITH services, which provides case-management services for people with AIDS; the St. Francis Hospital School of Nursing; the Community Mental Health Center; the Center for Family Health; and the Franciscan Home and Rehabilitation Center.

St. Mary Hospital and St. Francis Hospital have an affiliation agreement with Hackensack University Medical Center and Pascack Valley Hospital. This agreement brings their doctors and patients a wide range of medical expertise without their ever leaving Hudson County.

The Franciscan Health System offers Hudson County residents many services and centers of excellence.

Comprehensive **maternal health services** are offered at St. Mary Hospital, including many not found at other Hudson County hospitals. These services include a nationally recognized perinatologist, a

Shown at left, the Center for Family Health of St. Mary Hospital in Hoboken provides comprehensive family health care for patients of all ages.

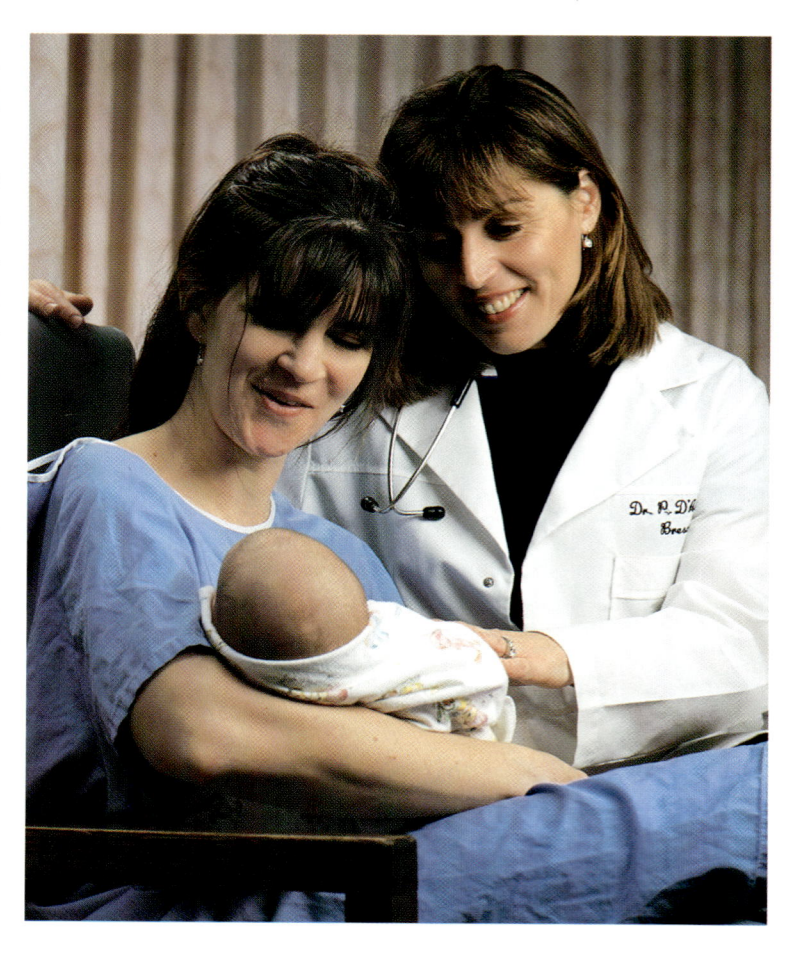

Franciscan Health System of New Jersey's St. Mary Hospital provides comprehensive maternal health services.

first-class perinatal unit on site, a neonatal intensive care unit, and round-the-clock coverage by an obstetrician, a neonatologist, a pediatrician, and an anesthesiologist. As part of its expanded maternal health services, St. Mary Hospital is collaborating with Hackensack University Medical Center on a high-tech program designed to help diagnose and treat pregnant women undergoing prenatal difficulties. Via telemedicine technology, ultrasound images can be transmitted by telephone lines. This technology allows St. Mary physicians to consult with specialists at Hackensack as a medical test is occurring. In effect, this allows doctors at the two locations to examine a patient simultaneously.

The **Center for Family Health of St. Mary Hospital** was opened in Hoboken in 1998. The center offers services for patients of all ages. It also is the site for St. Mary's family practice residency program, which has existed for more than twenty

144 CREATING THE FUTURE

years. The residency program is affiliated with the University of Medicine and Dentistry of New Jersey (UMDNJ)–New Jersey Medical School, giving doctors access to the latest in medical research and to leading faculty from UMDNJ's medical school. St. Mary is the only hospital in Hudson County fully accredited by the American College of Graduate Medical Education to teach medical doctors the specialty of family practice.

St. Mary Hospital has a newly remodeled thirty-eight bed inpatient unit to care for oncology, urology, and nephrology patients. The unit includes an on-site pharmacy to improve response time for physician requests and to allow caregivers to spend more time at patients' bedsides. "We're bringing state-of-the-art health care to our community," says Robert S. Chaloner, president and CEO of Franciscan Health System of New Jersey. "This new unit is a model for high-tech, high-touch inpatient care."

In 1997 St. Francis Hospital opened a **rehabilitation unit**—the first inpatient rehabilitation unit in Hudson County in more than a decade. The unit specializes in stroke recovery, orthopedic procedures, amputations, neurological disorders, and joint replacements. St. Francis also opened its newly remodeled pediatric unit in 1997.

In 1998 St. Francis Hospital opened a new **subacute unit** to provide transitional care for seniors who are recovering from hospitalization. The unit is designed to help ease the transition from hospital to home by providing skilled nursing and integrated medical care in a homelike environment.

St. Mary and St. Francis Hospitals are the only Hudson County hospitals that offer specialized inpatient behavioral health services for patients of all ages, from children through senior citizens. Services at St. Mary include the child crisis intervention unit, the only dedicated inpatient crisis intervention unit for children and adolescents in Hudson County; an inpatient adult psychiatric unit; and outpatient services coordinated by the Community Mental Health Center, which is affiliated with St. Mary. In addition, St. Francis Hospital has a center that specializes in psychiatric care for seniors, the only unit of its kind in Hudson County. Its nationally recognized experts treat seniors who have feelings of deep loss due to chronic illness, substance abuse, death of a spouse or friends, loss of a job, retirement, or change in appearance.

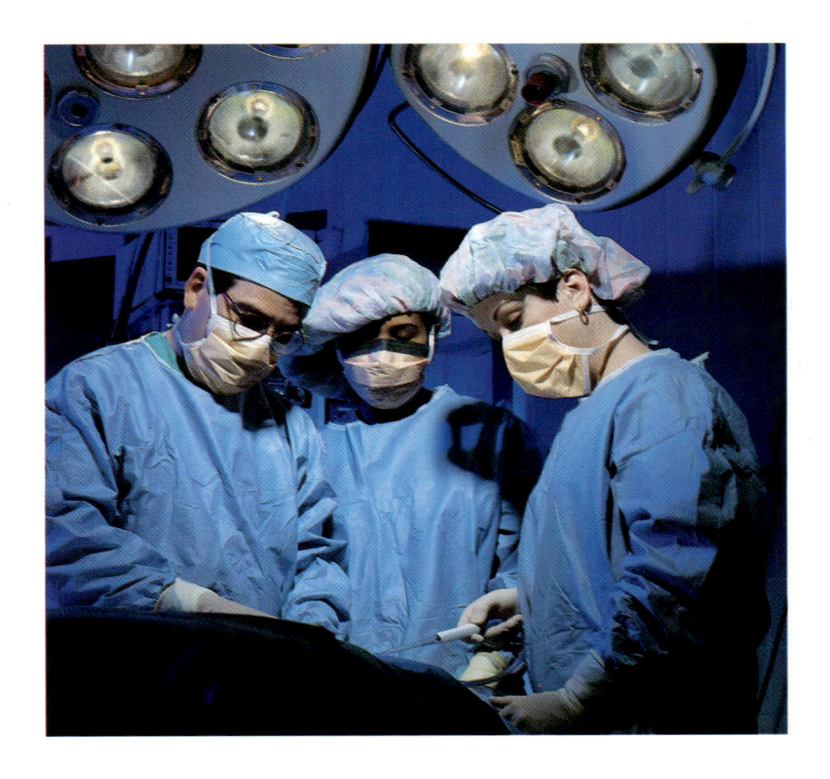

St. Mary and St. Francis Hospitals feature advanced technology that can help ensure a smooth and fast recovery, whether after same-day or inpatient surgery.

The newly acquired **Franciscan Home and Rehabilitation Center** is a 183-bed geriatric center that provides long-term care for seniors. It also includes a Meals-On-Wheels Program, an Alzheimer's Day Care Program, and a Geriatric Medical Clinic.

St. Mary Hospital and St. Francis Hospital have launched a new educational outreach program that gives Hudson County residents greater access to health care professionals. Called **Healthy Neighbors**, the program promotes healthy living through informative programs, including screenings, workshops, childbirth education classes, professional seminars, and community health fairs.

"As we face the future, we will continually work toward implementing new strategic initiatives that strengthen our ability to meet the community's need for cost-effective, high-quality health care services," Chaloner says.

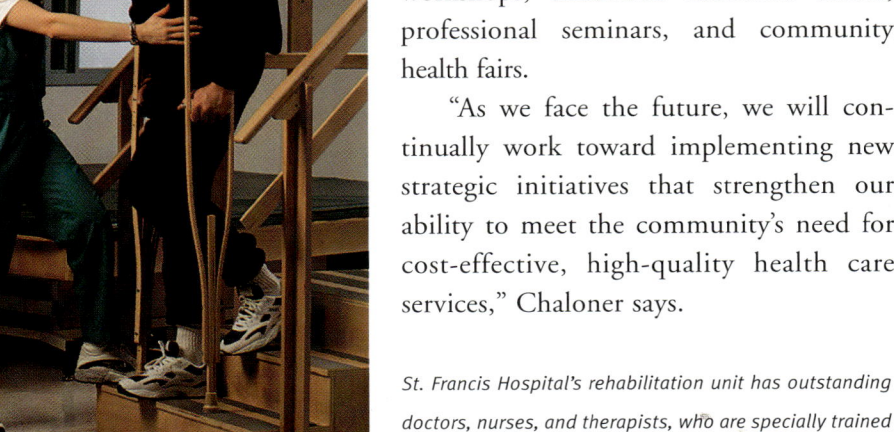

St. Francis Hospital's rehabilitation unit has outstanding doctors, nurses, and therapists, who are specially trained in rehabilitation.

A worker checks the contents of containers in a clean room at Merck & Co., Inc. These jars contain vaccines that have been produced in a sterile environment. © Bob Krist

AN EXPANDING FUTURE

The wealth of talent and resources in New Jersey has been a magnet for the nascent biotechnology industry. The state offers an abundance of scientists, engineers, and research institutions. The Garden State is fertile land for these cash-starved, entrepreneurial operations thanks in part to its proximity to the Wall Street investment community and to some of the world's leading biotech venture capitalists.

According to the Biotechnology Council of New Jersey, the state boasts over one hundred biotechnology firms, and some fifteen of these are public companies with a combined market capitalization of more than $2.5 billion. Together, they employ over five thousand people

IN 1987 MERCK & CO., INC., PLEDGED THAT MECTIZAN, ITS MEDICINE FOR PEOPLE SUFFERING FROM THE DEBILITATING DISEASE KNOWN AS "RIVER BLINDNESS," WOULD BE AVAILABLE FOR FREE TO ALL WHO NEEDED IT. BY 1997, APPROXIMATELY EIGHTEEN MILLION PEOPLE IN AFRICA, LATIN AMERICA, AND YEMEN WERE BEING TREATED WITH MECTIZAN THROUGH THE COMBINED EFFORTS OF THE WORLD HEALTH ORGANIZATION, THE WORLD BANK, OVER A DOZEN NONGOVERNMENTAL DEVELOPMENT ORGANIZATIONS, AND NUMEROUS MINISTRIES OF HEALTH. THAT SAME YEAR, MERCK REAFFIRMED ITS COMMITMENT TO DONATE MECTIZAN WHEREVER IT IS NEEDED, FOR AS LONG AS IT IS NEEDED, TO COMBAT THE DISEASE.

MODERN MEDICINE'S TOOLS 155

In 1997 the HealthCare Institute of New Jersey helped state legislators push for reform of the FDA's review process to help bring life-saving drugs and medical devices to patients more quickly. © Patrick Ramsey/International Stock

and have a payroll that exceeds $250 million. What makes these firms vital to the state's economy is their proven track record at raising equity via venture capital and stock offerings. They have formed dozens of strategic alliances worth several hundred million dollars, and have over twenty new products approved for use by the Food and Drug Administration or in the advanced trial stage.

OF 48 SIGNIFICANT NEW DRUGS APPROVED BY THE FDA IN 1997, 17 OF THEM WERE FROM NEW JERSEY–BASED COMPANIES.
THIS WAS THE HIGHEST NUMBER FOR ANY SINGLE STATE.

(Source: HealthCare Institute of New Jersey)

COMPANY	DRUG	TREATMENT
AHP/Wyeth-Ayerst	Normiflo	Vein thrombosis
AHP/Wyeth-Ayerst	Duract	Pain management
Bristol-Myers Squibb Company	Avapro	Hypertension
Bristol-Myers Squibb Company	Plavix	Heart attack/stroke
Hoechst Marion Roussel	Anzemet	Anti-nausea from chemotherapy
Hoffmann–La Roche	Posicor	Hypertension/angina
Hoffmann–La Roche	Zenapax	Transplant anti-rejection
Johnson & Johnson/Ortho-McNeil	Regranex	Diabetic ulcers
Knoll Pharmaceutical	Meridia	Obesity
Novartis Pharmaceuticals Corporation	Femara	Advanced breast cancer
Nycomed Amersham Imaging	Teslascan	Imaging of liver lesions
Schering-Plough	Fareston	Metastatic breast cancer
Warner-Lambert	Omnicef	Antibiotic
Cytogen	Quadremet	Pain relief in bone cancer
Novo Nordisk	Prandin	Type 2 diabetes
Roberts Pharmaceutical	Agrylin	Essential thromocythemia

Among the state's largest biotechnology firms are Alpharma, in Fort Lee, with nearly $500 million in annual sales of cold remedies and other antibiotics; and West Orange–based Organon, which develops pharmaceutical preparations and has sales of about $300 million. Sybron Chemicals, in Birmingham, is one of the fastest-

In addition to human pharmaceuticals, the international biotechnology firm Alpharma also produces animal health products such as feed additives. They are the largest producer of fish vaccines in the world. © Don Spiro/Courtesy, Alpharma

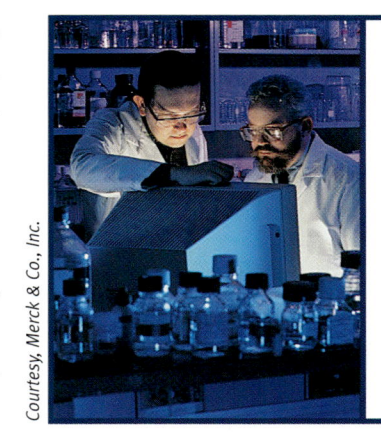

IN 1996 NEW JERSEY'S MAJOR PHARMACEUTICAL COMPANIES HAD INVESTIGATED OVER SEVEN HUNDRED COMPOUNDS FOR NEW DRUGS THAT WERE IN VARIOUS STAGES OF REVIEW BY THE FEDERAL FOOD AND DRUG ADMINISTRATION.

PHARMACEUTICALS DOMINATE NEW JERSEY MANUFACTURING

(SOURCES: NEW JERSEY DEPARTMENT OF COMMERCE; HEALTHCARE INSTITUTE OF NEW JERSEY)

INDUSTRY	NUMBER OF COMPANIES	NUMBER OF EMPLOYEES	TOTAL VALUE OF PRODUCTS (IN BILLIONS)	% OF STATE TOTAL
PHARMACEUTICALS	186	45,581	$10.7	11.6
OIL REFINING	18	5,057	$5.7	6.2
SOAPS, CLEANERS	194	18,672	$4.5	4.9
CHEMICALS	98	11,731	$4.0	4.4
PLASTICS	529	24,411	$3.9	4.3

MODERN MEDICINE'S TOOLS

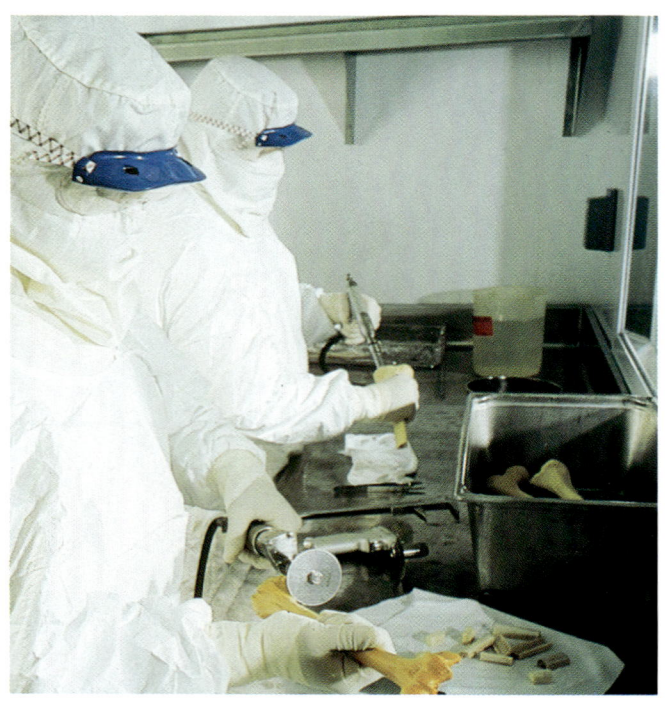

growing biotech firms, with a compound annual growth rate of 34 percent. Annadale-based Medarex has six products in clinical trials for cancer, AIDS, autoimmune disease, and prevention of cataracts; and Pharmacopeia, in Princeton, designs and synthesizes large collections of small-molecule compounds for pharmaceutical research.

New Jersey also is home to companies such as Osteotech. The Eatontown-based high-tech firm is the world's largest processor of human bones, ligaments, and tendons for transplantation. On an exclusive basis for the American Red Cross and Musculoskeletal Transplant Foundation, Osteotech produces materials that are used in grafting procedures to facilitate the healing and growth of bones.

Researchers at the biotechnology firm of Osteotech process bones for transplantation (LEFT) and examine processed tissue under a microscope (BELOW). Both photos courtesy, Osteotech

New Jersey's pharmaceutical companies have played a major role in fueling the growth of biotechnology in the state, both through alliances and an ever-growing pot of dollars. The state government also has taken aggressive steps to encourage investment in biotech research and development. New laws reduce the tax liability of emerging biotech companies, direct the state's Economic Development Authority to provide financial assistance, and prohibit local regulation of the industry.

In addition, the Economic Development Authority is currently constructing the Technology Centre of New Jersey in North Brunswick. This fifty-acre, high-tech research park will offer laboratory space at an affordable price to biotechnology firms. It also will complement the considerable resources and research brainpower already located at the Waksman Institute at Rutgers University; the Center for Biomedical Engineering at the New Jersey Institute of Technology; and the two centers at the University of Medicine and Dentistry of New Jersey, one for Advanced Biotechnology and one for Molecular Medicine.

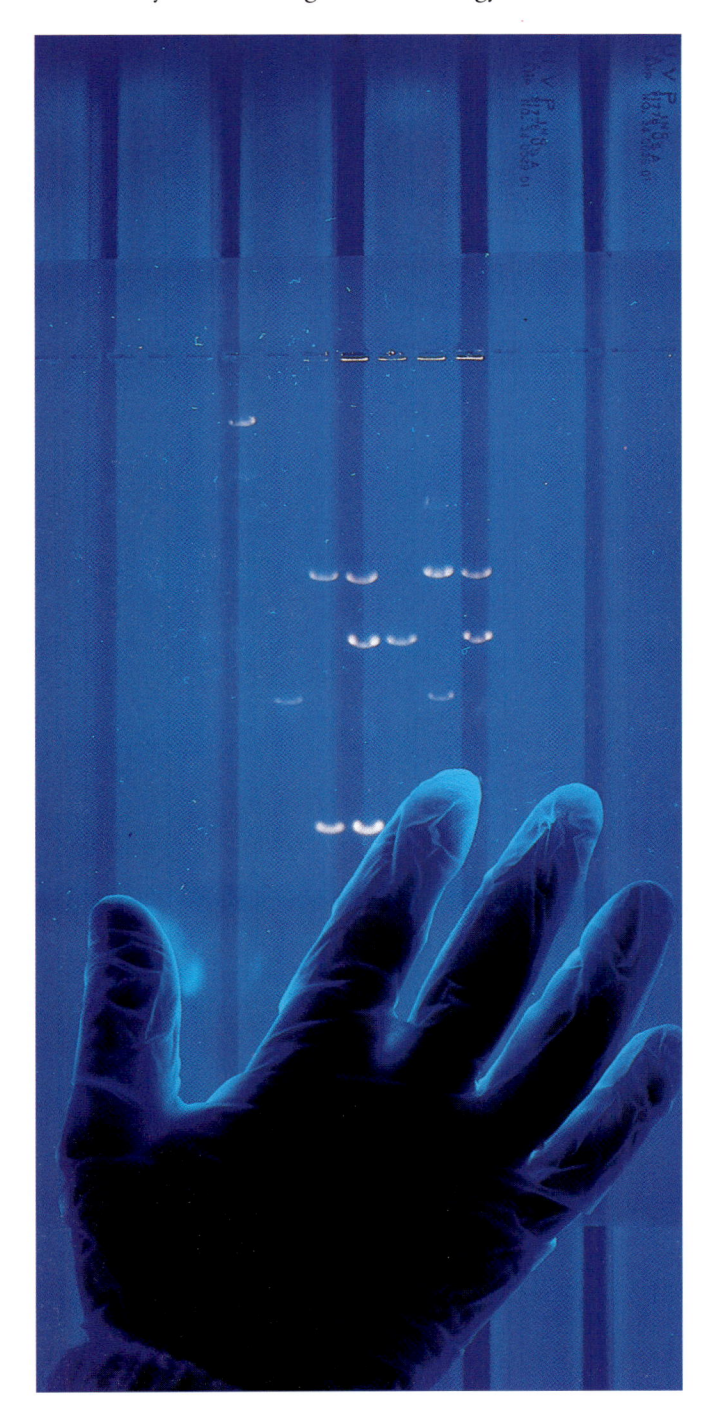

ABOVE: *A researcher at Wyeth-Ayerst Laboratories draws samples of an experimental compound for testing.* © Kelly/Mooney.
LEFT: *At Merck & Co., Inc., research into the nature and properties of DNA continues to lead to breakthroughs in our understanding of genetic and other life processes.* © Bob Krist

MODERN MEDICINE'S TOOLS 159

© Jorge Ramirez/International Stock

160 CREATING THE FUTURE

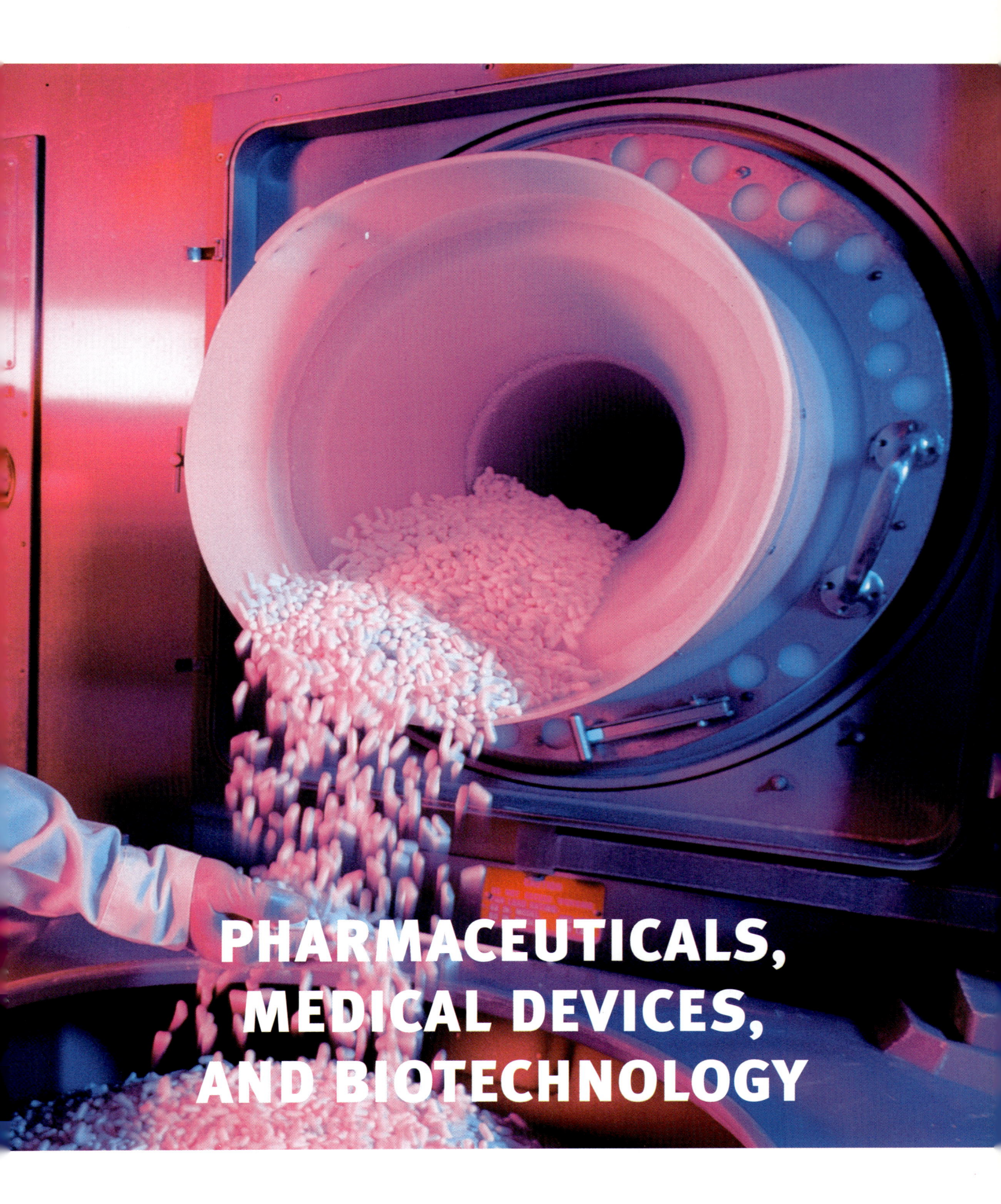

PHARMACEUTICALS, MEDICAL DEVICES, AND BIOTECHNOLOGY

NEUMAN DISTRIBUTORS, INC.

PRIVATELY HELD WHOLESALE PHARMACEUTICAL PRODUCTS AND SERVICES PROVIDER NEUMAN DISTRIBUTORS, INC., USES TECHNOLOGY, ACQUISITIONS, AND STRATEGIC ALLIANCES TO ACCOMMODATE CUSTOMERS AND PURSUE CONTINUED GROWTH

Neuman Distributors, Inc., is one of the nation's largest privately held wholesale pharmaceutical products and services providers. Founded in 1951 as the Silver Rod Supply Company in Clifton, New Jersey, Neuman has a history marked by expansion, innovation, and excellence.

Today Neuman has an extensive customer base serving nearly 3,000 independent and chain drugstores as well as more than 350 hospitals and managed care organizations. Neuman offers expedient service with more than 24,000 pharmaceutical, health, and beauty care items stocked, as well as more than 3,500 home health care and durable medical equipment products from more than 900 leading national manufacturers. Neuman has become a leader in many categories of the health care industry, ranking in the top 100 on *Forbes* magazine's 1997 list of the 500 largest privately held companies. With its decades of experience in a constantly changing marketplace, Neuman plans for more growth.

"Neuman Distributors is one of the fastest-growing companies in our industry," says Samuel Toscano Jr., chairman and chief executive officer. "We will continue to expand and evolve until we are the premier services provider to our customers."

The corporate offices for Neuman Distributors are housed in this 70,000-square-foot modern glass structure in Moonachie, New Jersey. Neuman's customer service, human resources, marketing, finance, purchasing, and management team offices are located here, along with the company's computer center.

Neuman's growth as a business began when the Silver Rod Supply Company's name was changed to Madison Drug in 1955. Madison Drug acquired Neuman Wholesale Drug Company and chose to keep the Neuman name. This was the first in a series of strategic acquisitions, which have served to position Neuman Distributors as the versatile industry leader it is today. Samuel Toscano Jr. assumed leadership of Neuman Distributors in the 1970s. The parent company of Neuman Distributors is Neuman Health Services, which is owned by Toscano, chairman and CEO.

The 1980s were a time of tremendous growth for Neuman Distributors, Inc. The company ventured into a broad range of health and beauty care products.

In the 1990s the company grew further through a series of acquisitions that diversified its business and increased its access to new markets. In the early and mid-1990s Neuman Distributors acquired H. K. Hineline, James Wholesale, and

Neuman Distributors, Inc.

162 CREATING THE FUTURE

Ketchum/OCP. In 1997 it acquired the assets of Drug Guild, becoming the sixth largest wholesale pharmaceuticals distributor in the United States, with combined sales approaching $2 billion.

Continuing its innovative business strategy, in 1998 Neuman Distributors established the NeuCare network to offer independent pharmacists rebates from manufacturers' market-share contracts. This network is designed to enable independent pharmacies to earn manufacturers' rebates equal to those enjoyed by large pharmacy chains and other customer classes. There are no costs to pharmacies to join NeuCare, no ongoing fees, and no transaction expenses. The program has no purchasing requirements and no requirement to accept all managed care plans. NeuCare provides independent pharmacists with a no-risk way to participate in a variety of performance-oriented contracts, and the network has rapidly grown to include nearly 1,000 participating stores.

To strengthen its position as a link between suppliers and pharmacists, Neuman also has acquired several pharmacy-related businesses, expanding its range of services to include pharmacy benefits and disease-state management. In addition Neuman has investments in many sectors of the health services industry. Neuman's partnerships include Strategic Health Outcomes, Inc., Mediview, Universal Benefit Systems, and KVM Technologies, Inc. Through these alliances, Neuman is able to offer a great many exclusive services, including:

- The Consumer and Health Care Information Center, which allows retail consumers at participating pharmacies access to information about selected products and services via on-site kiosks using Internet technology;
- NeuStar, a user-friendly order-entry system for pharmacies that allows pharmacists access to customized product-ordering data and reports;
- Envoy™, a highly efficient automated dispensing system that enables hospitals and institutions to create customized patient profiles on-line;
- The Universal Benefits Systems' pharmacy benefits management program, which analyzes and recommends ways for pharmacists to maximize profits and customer service;
- The Strategic Health Outcomes disease management network facilitates accredited training for pharmacists, enabling them to receive reimbursement from insurance companies for cognitive services rendered.

Neuman Distributors has distribution centers in Ridgefield, Secaucus, and Glen Rock, New Jersey; Brooklyn, New York; Newington, Connecticut; and Detroit, Michigan. The company recently opened a new 320,000-square-foot, state-of-the-art warehouse and distribution facility in Teterboro, New Jersey. Cutting-edge technology at this facility will ensure product availability and order accuracy, offering customers superior service and selection.

To further enhance its operations and effectiveness, in January 1998 Neuman Distributors moved its corporate offices to its present headquarters in Moonachie, New Jersey. Neuman's headquarters houses its customer service, human resources, marketing, finance, purchasing, and management team offices here, along with its computer center. At present, Neuman employs almost 1,000 people in various positions and locations. By restructuring and streamlining all departments and bringing them together under one roof, a cohesive organization with a broadened scope of programs and services is now available to customers, trading partners, and managed care groups alike.

This new, state-of-the-art warehouse and distribution center, located in Teterboro, New Jersey, was custom-built for Neuman Distributors. The 320,000-square-foot facility has 32-foot-high ceilings, and boasts the most globally innovative distribution technology, moving Neuman to the forefront as one of the industry's most progressive and cost-effective operators.

"With our continuing expansion plans, we needed the new headquarters to have additional space to accommodate the growing volume of our businesses and the changing requirements of our valued customers," says Toscano. "This move is part of our continuing strategy for growth and expansion as we move into the next century."

Neuman Distributors' corporate office is located at 250 Moonachie Road, Moonachie, New Jersey 07074; (201) 931-0022.

NEUMAN DISTRIBUTORS' SERVICES

Neuman Distributors offers the following exclusive services:
- The Consumer and Health Care Information Center
- NeuStar, a user-friendly pharmaceutical order-entry system
- Envoy™, a highly efficient automated dispensing system
- Universal Benefits Systems' pharmacy benefits management program
- The Strategic Health Outcomes disease management program

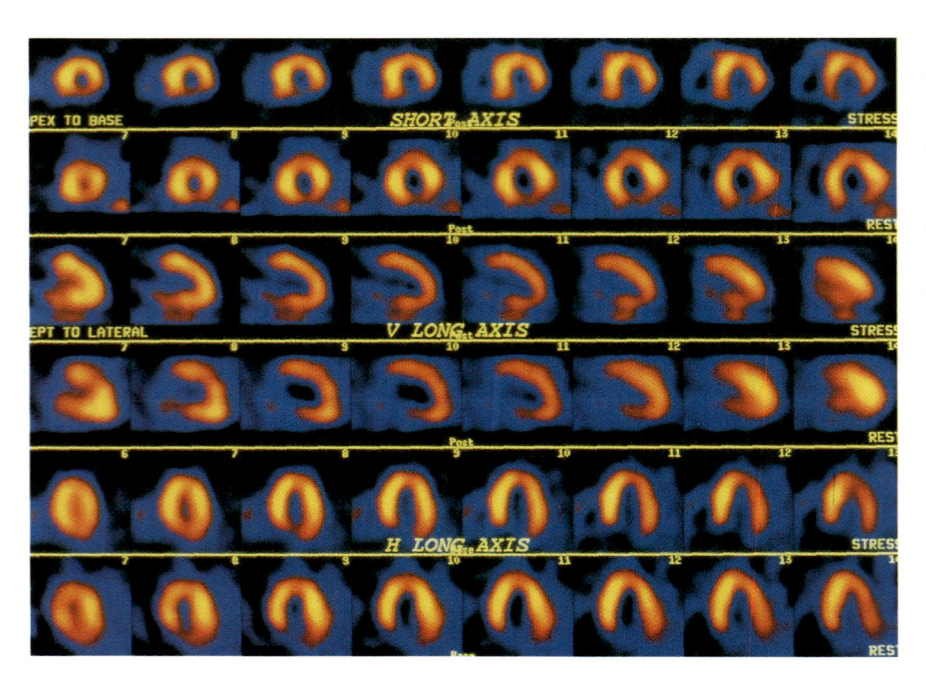

NYCOMED AMERSHAM IMAGING

A LEADER IN DIAGNOSTIC IMAGING AND ONCOLOGY, NYCOMED AMERSHAM IMAGING IS PART OF A GLOBAL COMMUNITY COMMITTED TO HELPING DOCTORS HELP PATIENTS LIVE LONGER, HEALTHIER LIVES

Scans of heart, enhanced with Myoview™, show blood flow within the heart.

Doctors at a community hospital review X-ray films hoping to better understand the cause of a patient's symptoms. A cardiologist completes an angiography confident that he knows the severity of disease involving his patient's heart. A man awaits his discharge from the hospital outpatient center having completed the procedure that may help him beat prostate cancer.

These patients represent only three of the millions who share a connection with a company that provides doctors with tools to assist in the more accurate diagnosis of illnesses of the bloodstream as well as the brain, heart, liver, and other organs. The patients have all benefited from the products developed, manufactured, and marketed by a New Jersey company that is part of a global commitment to improving health. These products are linked to Nycomed Amersham Imaging in the Americas, a leader in diagnostic imaging and oncology products.

Most people never give any thought to the contrast agents used to make X rays, MRIs (magnetic resonance imaging), CT (computerized tomography) scans, and nuclear imaging scans more vivid and revealing.

Yet for over half a century the scientists at Nycomed Amersham Imaging have repeatedly revolutionized the contrast agents used to enhance visualization, resulting in safer, more comfortable procedures for the patient and more information for the physician.

On the eve of the new millennium, Nycomed Amersham Imaging is poised to bring new imaging agents and oncology therapies to the arsenal of products available to help doctors help patients live longer, healthier lives. Nycomed Amersham Imaging continues to strengthen its leadership through product innovation, complemented by a commitment to customer service that matches the excellence of its science.

Headquartered in Princeton, New Jersey, Nycomed Amersham Imaging is a fully integrated research and development, manufacturing, and marketing organization that has operational responsibilities in the Americas (North, Central, and South) and the Caribbean.

REVOLUTIONIZING IMAGING

Nycomed Amersham revolutionized diagnostic imaging in 1974 with the introduction of the world's first nonionic X-ray contrast medium, which provided significant safety benefits for

Nycomed Amersham Imaging is uniquely positioned to offer a wide range of third-party development and manufacturing capabilities to the chemical and pharmaceutical industry.

164 CREATING THE FUTURE

patients. In 1982 the introduction of the Omnipaque® imaging agent set the gold standard for nonionic contrast agents. The X-ray imaging franchise was further expanded in 1996 with the introduction of Visipaque®, a third-generation product.

However, Nycomed Amersham Imaging is more than X-ray imaging. The company's research teams have developed agents that allow doctors to use MRI technology to see blood vessels more clearly, bringing a new dimension to MRI visualization of the blood system and liver lesions. The market for MRI contrast media is rapidly expanding; it is currently growing at double-digit rates worldwide. While MRI imaging was initially for the head, neck, and spine, the concept is now being expanded to the rest of the body.

Radioactive tracers also are part of the Nycomed Amersham portfolio of imaging products. Radiopharmaceuticals such as Myoview™, AcuTect™, and Ceretec® are used with nuclear imaging technology to study the heart, brain, and body.

In addition, contrast agents are being developed to enhance the ability of ultrasound scanning to visualize blood flow to the heart. This enhanced ability would allow doctors to determine more readily if a cardiac infarction exists, as well as to monitor thrombolytic treatment.

Nycomed Amersham's global leadership in diagnostic imaging is complemented by oncology products that are effective in the treatment of prostate cancer and in relieving bone pain associated with metastatic cancers. Use of Nycomed Amersham's proprietary I-125 RAPIDStrand™ and I-125 Seeds® implants

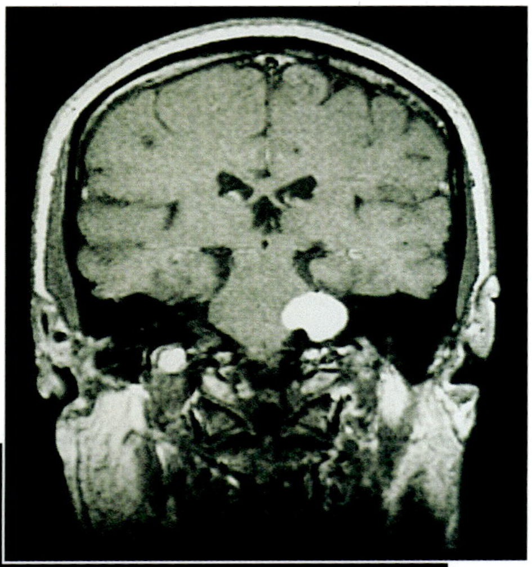

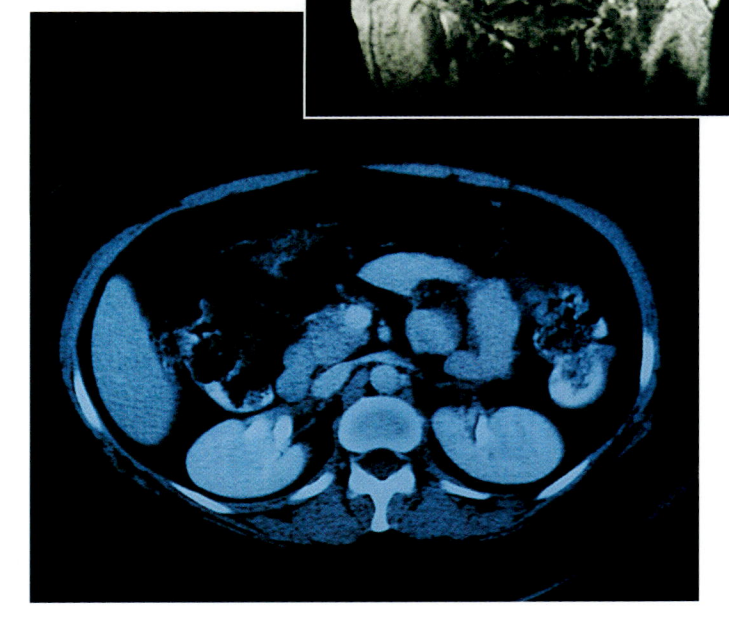

RIGHT: *This MRI (magnetic resonance imaging) scan of a brain was produced using Nycomed Amersham Imaging's Omniscan®.* BELOW: *This image of an abdomen is an Omnipaque-enhanced CT (computerized tomography) scan.*

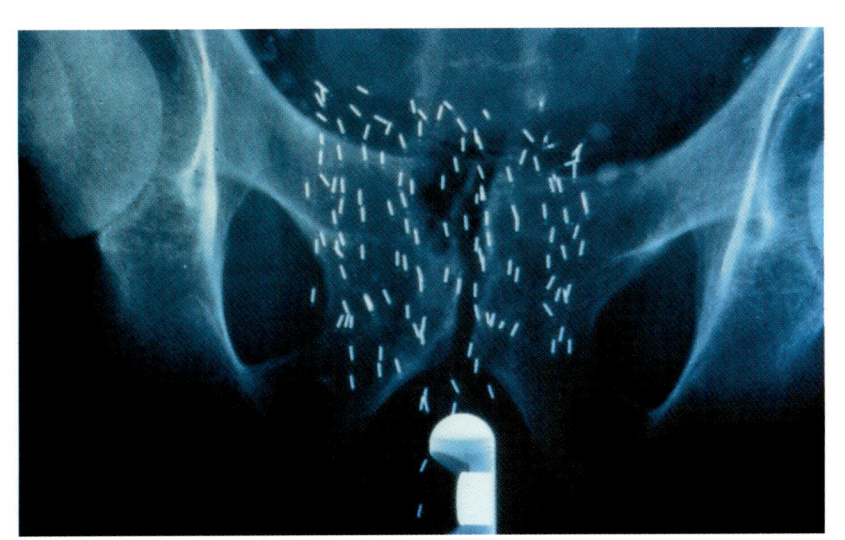

LEFT: *The actual size of I-125 Seeds® is shown in comparison to a dime.* BELOW: *A CT scan of I-125 Seeds, which are implanted and distributed throughout the prostate.*

for the treatment of prostate cancer has increased rapidly in recent years, as their efficacy and reduced side-effect profiles have become better known in the United States.

To support this growing acceptance, Nycomed Amersham Imaging makes ongoing major plant and personnel investments to ensure it continues to meet customer demand.

NEW PRODUCT PIPELINE

For more than half a century, Nycomed Amersham Imaging has been introducing products that have established its leadership in diagnostic imaging and radiopharmaceuticals. Today the company is aggressively developing new ways to provide physicians with a better view into the workings of the human body and the mechanisms of disease. The company has a number of contrast media under development that are intended to enhance visualization of blood vessels, lung disease, myocardial and brain perfusion, and tumors. The portfolio of compounds in development may ultimately improve the diagnosis of Parkinson's-like syndromes and tumor imaging.

NYCOMED AMERSHAM IMAGING (CONTINUED)

A GLOBAL FAMILY

Nycomed Amersham Imaging is a proud member of Nycomed Amersham plc, which has its global headquarters in Buckinghamshire, United Kingdom. Nycomed Amersham is a world leader in in vivo diagnostic imaging and one of the largest research-based biotechnology suppliers to global markets, with more than 11,000 employees on its worldwide team. Global revenues for the past year were in excess of $2 billion.

The company's mission is to generate technologies to link the frontiers of bioscience with society's needs for better and more cost-effective health care. Nycomed Amersham is innovation driven, with a strong product and technology portfolio in each of its principal businesses.

Nycomed Amersham is also committed to being a world leader in the provision of research-based biotechnology to support academia and the pharmaceutical industry in the development process, from genetic research to production of medicines based on that research. The company is a leading player in providing the systems to the pharmaceutical sector to help it take genes into medicines. These systems, including instruments, software, and reagents, enable research into genes and proteins, the subsequent discovery and development of drugs, and the manufacture of drugs based on biological molecules.

Additionally, Nycomed Amersham operates a European pharmaceutical business and intends to expand its portfolio of therapeutics, over-the-counter medicines, and diagnostics for its franchises in this market.

Nycomed Amersham Imaging headquarters is situated in a parklike setting in Princeton, New Jersey.

VISION FOR THE NEW MILLENNIUM

Nycomed Amersham Imaging in the Americas anticipates continued success in the world's largest and most important market—North America. To ensure that success, the company has a simple recipe for growth: the people of Nycomed Amersham Imaging are committed to providing leadership in medical imaging and oncology and intend to meet changing medical needs through product innovation and excellence in customer service.

As medical technology changes, requiring new imaging agents, and as new treatment opportunities emerge for oncology, Nycomed Amersham Imaging will be there with the products that redefine imaging, oncology, and disease prevention.

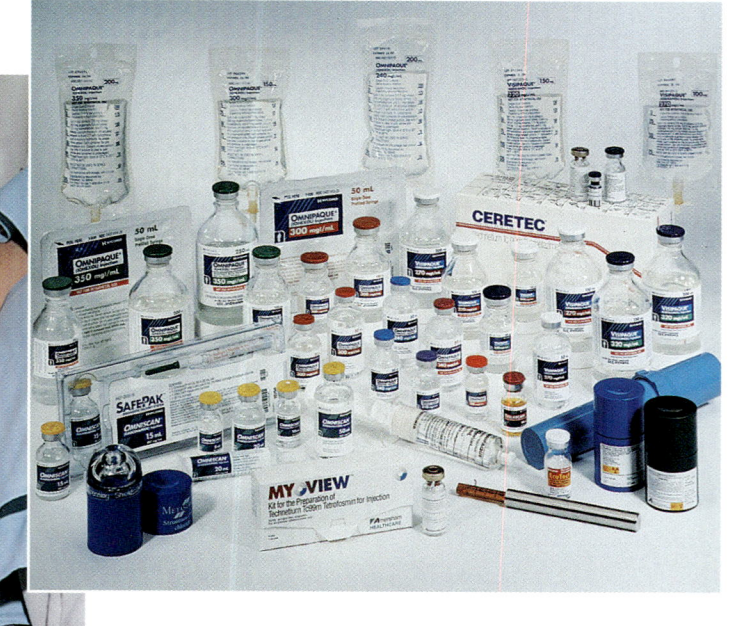

ABOVE: *The Nycomed Amersham Imaging family of X-ray, CT, MR imaging, nuclear imaging, and oncology products helps physicians to accurately detect, diagnose, and treat a wide range of diseases.* LEFT: *A scrubbed and gloved technician prepares a patient in the MRI suite by administering a contrast agent prior to the procedure.*

166 CREATING THE FUTURE

NYCOMED AMERSHAM IMAGING GLOSSARY

TERMS

- Contrast media: Fluids injected into the bloodstream to enhance images of body structures, organs, or functions during diagnostic imaging procedures
- X ray: Electromagnetic radiation sent through the body and absorbed by higher density structures, producing an image that is captured on film
- CT scan: Computerized tomography, a process by which a computer captures X-ray images to create cross-sectional views
- In vivo: Biological processes in living organisms
- MRI: Magnetic resonance imaging, a technique that uses a magnetic field and radio waves to produce detailed, high-resolution images of the body
- Nuclear imaging: The process of creating images of the heart, brain, or other body areas that take up injected radioactive tracers, or radiopharmaceuticals through scintigraphy (technique using a camera that emits gamma rays) to demonstrate areas of disease, abnormal function, and infection
- Ultrasound: A sonic wave sent through the body, partly reflected by tissues and used to build up an image of different organs

KEY PRODUCTS

Nycomed Amersham Imaging markets oncology products and a family of contrast agents that are used in X-ray imaging, CT scans, MRI, and nuclear imaging. Contrast agents allow physicians to more accurately detect, diagnose, and treat diseases and functional abnormalities.

X-ray and CT Scan Agents

- Omnipaque® (iohexol) Injection: Introduced in the United States in 1982, Omnipaque has been used with more than 100 million patients worldwide. A low osmolar, nonionic, iodinated contrast agent, Omnipaque is used in intravascular diagnostic procedures such as coronary angiography; aortography; visceral, cerebral, and peripheral arteriography; and excretory urography. It is also indicated for spinal cord imaging as well as shoulder, knee joint, and pelvic organ procedures.
- Visipaque® (iodixanol) Injection: Approved in 1996, Visipaque is the first of a new class of contrast agents that provides an extra level of safety. Visipaque is used for imaging the blood vessels of the heart, kidney, brain, and extremities.

MRI Agents

- Omniscan® (gadodiamide) Injection: Omniscan was launched in 1993 to provide contrast enhancement of the central nervous system (CNS) to detect lesions of the brain, spinal cord, and associated tissues. Since its introduction, Omniscan has received approval for both the adult (high dose) and pediatric CNS and was approved in 1997 for body imaging in children two years and older.
- Teslascan® (mangafodipir trisodium) Injection: Teslascan, which was approved in 1997 and launched in 1998, is the world's first hepatocyte-specific contrast medium used in the detection, characterization, localization, and evaluation of liver lesions.

Nuclear Imaging Agents

- Myoview™ (technetium Tc99m tetrofosmin): Myoview, a cardiac imaging agent that, when labeled with the technetium-99 radioisotope, is useful in the diagnosis and localization of reversible myocardial ischemia.
- Ceretec® (technetium Tc99m exametazime): Ceretec, an imaging agent that, when labeled with the technetium-99 radioisotope, can be used to visualize blood flow in the brain of stroke patients. It can also be used to identify infection and inflammation in the abdomen and other sites.
- AcuTect™ (technetium Tc99m apcitide): Approved in September 1998, AcuTect is the first and only modality to create images of acute venous thrombosis in the lower extremities. Nycomed Amersham Imaging copromotes this product with Diatide, Inc., the owner of AcuTect.

Oncology Products

In addition to a full line of imaging agents, Nycomed Amersham Imaging has a line of oncology products that is used for the treatment of cancer or for palliation of the side effects of cancer.

- Metastron® (strontium-89 chloride): Metastron is an intravenously administered radioisotope that provides pain relief for cancer patients suffering from bone pain due to metastasis associated with prostate cancer.
- I-125 Seeds® and RAPIDStrand™: RAPIDStrand is a nonsurgical delivery system for implanting individual seeds irradiated with iodine-125. Approved in 1994, this technique is used to treat prostate cancer. A six-year study concluded in 1995 documented a 95 percent success rate. The tiny I-125 seeds are distributed in a rigid, absorbable suture material that fits into an implant needle. The procedure is performed on an outpatient basis.

BRISTOL-MYERS SQUIBB COMPANY

RANKED AMONG THE TOP PERFORMERS IN ITS INDUSTRY, BRISTOL-MYERS SQUIBB COMPANY SUPPLIES THE WORLD WITH HEALTH AND PERSONAL CARE PRODUCTS, FROM THE FAMILIAR TO THE CUTTING EDGE

Bristol-Myers Squibb Company is a leading global health care and personal care company whose mission is to extend and enhance human life. The company employs 54,000 people worldwide and its products are available in virtually every country. Its principal products are pharmaceuticals, consumer medications, personal care products, nutritional products, and medical devices. Worldwide sales in 1997 were $16.7 billion, with more than sixty-three product lines producing annual sales greater than $50 million each. More than $1.3 billion was spent on research and development.

Bristol-Myers Squibb has been a major presence in New Jersey since 1905, when E. R. Squibb and Sons established a large ether plant on a ninety-six-acre site in New Brunswick, a facility that would later become one of the world's largest penicillin manufacturing plants. In 1938 the New Brunswick campus also became home to the Squibb Institute for Medical Research—one of the first industry-based research facilities of its kind and a forerunner of the current Bristol-Myers Squibb Pharmaceutical Research Institute.

The institute has been the scene of many major scientific advances, including the first crystallization of penicillin (1943), which greatly improved the drug's quality and safety; crystallization of streptomycin (1945), representing the next generation of antibiotics after penicillin; development of one of the earliest antihypertensive drug compounds, Raudixin (1954); and introduction of radiopharmaceutical and contrast-imaging agents to enhance noninvasive diagnostic procedures (1967). In 1975 scientists at the institute developed the first ACE inhibitor, Capoten (captopril), from an enzyme isolated from snake venom, which ushered in a new era in the treatment of hypertension and congestive heart failure.

The Bristol-Myers Squibb Worldwide Medicines Group and Pharmaceutical Research Institute are headquartered on a 276-acre site in Princeton. Inset: In the Bristol-Myers Squibb Department of Applied Genomics, researchers link genetic information to the development of disease to help discover innovative new medicines.

At left are products made by Bristol-Myers Squibb's Mead Johnson Nutritionals subsidiary, which studies show is the leading infant formula company in the world.

168 CREATING THE FUTURE

The Delaware River Port Authority building, designed by Michael Graves Architect, features a boardroom that affords a commanding view of city lights and the river below. © Matt Wargo

century comes to a close. Thanks largely to technology—fax machines and e-mail, desktop publishing software, and more—marketing professionals can opt for a New Jersey location and still communicate with clients around the world. Likewise, the rise of the information age and the widespread acceptance of the Internet have driven the need for more sophisticated marketing-communications support among the state's corporate leaders.

In the 1990s the MWW Group of East Rutherford grew to become one of the country's ten largest independent public relations firms. Named the nation's "hottest" agency by *Inside PR* magazine, MWW brings a fresh perspective to complex business problems for clients such as Continental Airlines and Bally Fitness. One of the state's largest advertising agencies, Dugan Valva Contess, is recognized nationally for the creative energy it brings to marketing for such clients as AT&T and IBM. It was recently named "Agency of the Year" by *Promo* magazine.

In the twenty-first century, New Jersey marketing experts expect to see a steady migration to direct mail, telemarketing, and the World Wide Web, and they are confident that the state's marketers will be at the forefront of this transformation.

OTHER PROFESSIONAL AND CONSUMER SERVICES

The expansion of outsourcing is expected to be a major twenty-first-century business trend; and New Jersey, already home to several major corporations that provide "outsourcing" services, is well positioned to be a national leader in this area.

A GOOD SPOT

NEWARK-BASED MCCARTER AND ENGLISH, NEW JERSEY'S OLDEST AND LARGEST LAW FIRM, FIRST OPENED FOR BUSINESS IN 1844 IN NEWTON. THAT RURAL TOWN WAS A HUB OF COMMERCE AT THE TIME BECAUSE OF THE NEWLY COMPLETED MORRIS CANAL, WHICH LINKED THE ATLANTIC COAST AND THE DELAWARE RIVER.

Poised and well-prepared, this New Jersey businesswoman gives a compelling presentation to her colleagues. © Dan Bosler/Tony Stone Images

The largest and most profitable among these companies is Automatic Data Processing of Roseland, the largest payroll services provider in the world. Begun in 1949 with just eight accounts, ADP now manages payroll and tax-processing for four hundred thousand small and large businesses. Effective management and a focused strategy have enabled the company to produce double-digit earnings growth for nearly four decades. International expansion and the development of new financial-management services should help keep that record intact.

Though much smaller than ADP, Digital Solutions of South Plainfield provides payroll services to over thirteen hundred clients in forty states, and also offers services in staff leasing, contract staffing, and human resources management consulting. The BISYS Group of Little Falls offers transaction processing, document imaging, and other support services for more than six thousand financial institutions. Similarly, Hackensack-based First Data Corporation is a leading provider of billing and transaction processing services for credit card issuers. New areas of growth include processing on-line sales, check verification services, and health care claims processing.

United Parcel Service (UPS) provides another function that businesses find indispensable. UPS got its start in 1907 before most people had telephones and before the United States Postal Service was equipped to deliver packages. Today UPS moves over 3.1 billion packages and documents a year worldwide. An employee-owned company with centers all over the world, UPS has over thirteen thousand employees in New Jersey.

Some major corporate players in retail, credit, and other service areas operate out of New Jersey, as well. Parsippany-based Cendant Corporation, formed by a 1997 merger between CUC International and HFS, is a leading business and consumer services company. Cendant owns Entertainment Publishing, a top discount coupon publisher, and more than fifty-four hundred hotel properties—as well as the country's top four real estate brokers. Among Cendant's offerings are real estate, relocation, and mortgage services; home improvement referrals; and many member-based services such as shopping, travel, dining, health products, and credit card and checking-account enhancement packages. Their brands include Century 21, Ramada, and Shoppers Advantage.

188 CREATING THE FUTURE

WALTER L. JACOBS INVENTED THE CAR RENTAL BUSINESS IN 1918 WHEN HE FOUNDED THE COMPANY THAT WOULD BECOME HERTZ. HEADQUARTERED IN PARK RIDGE, HERTZ IS THE WORLD'S LEADING CAR RENTAL COMPANY. WITH THIRTEEN HUNDRED U.S. LOCATIONS AND FOUR THOUSAND MORE ABROAD, HERTZ'S WORLDWIDE RESERVATIONS CENTER HANDLES SEVENTEEN MILLION RESERVATIONS A YEAR. AMONG HERTZ'S "FIRSTS" ARE THE "FLY-DRIVE" CAR RENTAL; COMPUTERIZED DRIVING DIRECTIONS; AND THE "INSTANT RETURN," WHERE THE AGENT MEETS THE RETURNING CUSTOMER IN THE LOT WITH A HAND-HELD COMPUTER. HERTZ ALSO RENTS EQUIPMENT, SELLS USED RENTAL CARS, MANAGES LIABILITY CLAIMS, AND PROVIDES CORPORATE CONSULTING SERVICES.

Liberty Travel, based in Ramsey, is the largest leisure travel company in the United States. Ninety percent of Liberty's sales are vacation trips. Liberty and its sister company, GOGO Worldwide Vacations, are planning ahead by offering agent training and growth programs; more new offices; and new trip packages, such as those specially designed for golfers, scuba divers, and skiers.

On the retail side of things, Bed Bath and Beyond is one of the biggest home furnishings store chains in the United States. Their Union-based company has more than 140 outlets in twenty-nine states.

If you ask any child to name his or her favorite store, he or she probably will say, "Toys "R" Us." No wonder, since it is the world's largest retailer of toys, with fourteen hundred stores, more than three hundred outside the United States. Toys "R" Us recently introduced a new store layout called Concept 2000, and is opening new ninety-thousand-square-foot superstores.

New Jersey also is home to three major supermarket chains. The Great Atlantic and Pacific Tea Company (A & P) has stores in nineteen states; Washington, D.C.; and Canada. Founded in 1859, A & P has gone through many changes over the years. Most recently the company has experimented with a new, energy-efficient supermarket called an "Earth Smart Store." Pathmark Stores has 144 stores, all within one hundred miles of its Woodbridge headquarters. This location gives Pathmark access to one out of ten food shoppers in the country. Pathmark, too, has plans for the new millennium in the form of Pathmark 2000 stores with wider aisles, larger selections, and more services. Elizabeth-based Wakefern Food Corporation is the United States' number-two supermarket co-op, as well as the largest retailer-owned food wholesaler. Wakefern offers its members standardized processing, a say in corporate policy, and "ShopRite University" training programs.

As the service sector continues to shape the national economy in new and surprising ways in the next millennium, New Jersey is sure to be at the forefront of innovation and change.

Atlantic City's Ocean One mall is a superlative example of New Jersey's retailing style and expertise. © Scott Barrow

SERVICES THAT SUCCEED 189

190 CREATING THE FUTURE

ACCOUNTING

KPMG PEAT MARWICK LLP

TAX MINIMIZATION, INFORMATION RISK MANAGEMENT, ELECTRONIC COMMERCE, INTERNAL AUDIT— TODAY'S PROFESSIONAL SERVICES FIRMS MUST GO BEYOND ASSURANCE, TAX, AND CONSULTING. KPMG PEAT MARWICK LLP PROVIDES SERVICES THAT CAN HELP NEW JERSEY BUSINESSES PREPARE FOR THE NEW MILLENNIUM

Since 1922 when KPMG opened its first New Jersey office in Newark, it has been committed to serving the state's business community. Today the firm's United States headquarters in Montvale is home to 1,200 KPMG professionals. The firm also has offices in Short Hills and Princeton, plus an additional 200 professionals and support staff based in its new office in Woodcliff Lake.

"The firm that would become KPMG Peat Marwick LLP was, in fact, the first accounting firm to recognize the myriad business and commercial opportunities available in the Garden State," says Edward Lazor, KPMG's Short Hills managing partner. "Seventy-six years later KPMG is an international professional services firm offering assurance, tax, and consulting services. We have a major presence in the state, with 2,100 employees who serve the needs of New Jersey's business and public sectors and their communities."

KPMG's New Jersey practice serves many of the state's largest and best-known companies. As a corporate citizen dedicated to the state's overall development, the firm actively contributes to the communities in which its employees live and work by supporting a broad range of civic, educational, and charitable organizations.

"There is a huge international presence here, with numerous subsidiaries of major foreign companies," says Lazor. "The state's biotechnology, pharmaceutical, technology, and financial services

Founding partners (clockwise, from left) James Marwick, S. Roger Mitchell, and Sir William Peat. Marwick's philosophy still guides the firm: Maintain the highest standards and take very good care of your customers.

KPMG's New Jersey office managing partners are, from left, Paul D. Merrill (Princeton office) and Edward J. Lazor (Short Hills office).

industries are booming, and we have an excellent system of colleges and universities. As they've grown, so has our list of services. And as the business climate in the state has changed, KPMG has adapted to better serve those companies."

New Jersey's **Financial Services** sector, comprising banking, finance, and insurance companies, was the first to be served by KPMG in New Jersey. KPMG has been a market leader in banking since 1922. There are more than 150 banking institutions in the state, including commercial banks, savings and loans, and mutual thrifts, as well as a number of out-of-state institutions doing business in New Jersey. KPMG serves about 30 percent of these banks, from smaller "hometown" banks to larger institutions, such as Summit Bank; overall, the banks served by KPMG represent about 70 percent of all deposits in the state. Other significant New Jersey financial services clients include The CIT Group, Inc.; Selective Insurance Group; and American Re corporation.

KPMG's experience extends well beyond the financial services industry. The firm's **Information, Communications, and Entertainment** (ICE) practice, for example, helps young technology companies navigate a constantly changing—and consolidating—marketplace.

To position the firm at the forefront of the new knowledge economy and to help achieve its own growth objective, in 1997 KPMG struck a series of major alliances with information-based

192 CREATING THE FUTURE

companies that lead in the markets they serve. These alliances also focus on business solutions for network integration and migration, electronic commerce, on-line call centers, and sales automation. In addition, KPMG provides two *Insider* editions for the PointCast Business Network, broadcasting financial news and analysis via the Internet.

The **Consumer Markets** and **Industrial Markets** practices serve clients in a multitude of industries, including some of the most familiar names in the automotive, chemical and energy, and retailing sectors. The firm's **Health Care & Public Sector** practice has been serving New Jersey's health, education, and government organizations for more than half a century.

The state's largest hospitals and pharmaceutical and biotechnology companies rely on KPMG to help them excel in today's increasingly complex and highly competitive health care environment. The firm performs assurance, tax, or consulting services for more than one-third of the hospitals in New Jersey, and it is the only professional services firm with a national biotechnology and life sciences practice headquartered in the state.

To help ensure that New Jersey's colleges and universities can continue to produce a highly skilled workforce, KPMG's Higher Education team assists more than fifteen public, private, and independent institutions throughout the state. "Colleges and universities throughout the nation are faced with shifting student demographics, new and uncertain investment opportunities, and rising costs," says Paul Merrill, managing partner of KPMG's Princeton office and an experienced professional in the area of higher education. "We've made a commitment to helping the higher education community figure out how to make it all work with fewer resources and less money.

"Government agencies are also searching for ways to cut costs and optimize their resources," Merrill adds. "We try to impress upon them that they have options they may not have considered."

KPMG's Business Measurement Process (BMP) is one of the tools the firm uses to help New Jersey's public and private sector organizations clarify those options. A proprietary audit methodology, BMP goes beyond the traditional audit to provide clients with an industry-specific analysis of their organization by redefining the audit process in terms of current economic realities. In other words, BMP looks at the operations behind the numbers that compose financial statements, to identify potential risks and opportunities to improve performance.

KPMG has long been a supporter of the New Jersey World Trade Council, which featured a daylong World Trade Conference, "Hong Kong: America's Business Partner in Asia." Among those attending the event were (from left) KPMG partner Robert P. Evans, chairman of the New Jersey World Trade Council; Qiu Shengyun, ambassador consul general, People's Republic of China; and Christine Todd Whitman, governor of New Jersey.

BMP enables KPMG professionals to "live" the philosophy of KPMG's founder, James Marwick: Maintain the highest standards and take very good care of your customers.

As Joseph T. Boyle, KPMG area managing partner for the Northeast, says, "Throughout this century and certainly during the more than seventy-five years we've been in New Jersey, we've never lost sight of our founder's goal."

ACCOUNTING 193

BEDERSON & COMPANY

BASED ON EACH CLIENT'S PARTICULAR REQUIREMENTS, BEDERSON & COMPANY FORMS A TEAM OF SPECIALISTS TO HELP PLAN AND MANAGE CLIENT FINANCIAL AND BUSINESS OPERATIONS

Although Bederson & Company is best known as a nationally recognized firm providing insolvency, reorganization, and investigative services, these services are fully integrated with its expertise in such areas as business appraisals, valuations, and other litigation services.

Bederson's broad scope of services also includes complex audits for large corporations, aggressive strategies for expansion-oriented firms, information services for midsize companies, progressive financial solutions, consultations, estate and income tax services, and financial planning for individuals and businesses. Bederson is able to use its range of capabilities to develop long-term client relationships and provide ongoing financial consulting.

Founded in 1937, Bederson has a reputation for integrity and outstanding client relations, and has become a leader in the state and a major force in the business community. Its clients range from large and growth-minded companies to midsize firms, small businesses, and individuals. The firm is noted for its fast response time in meeting clients' needs. To help clients stay prepared for economic, legislative, and technological changes, Bederson also conducts ongoing seminars for its clients.

Bederson & Company is a four-time winner of *CPA Digest*'s Digest 50 AWARD, and has received national recognition for its growth, profitability, innovative practice management, community service, and noteworthy contributions to the profession.

The staff at Bederson includes experts in a multitude of financial and commercial sectors. Bederson's professionals consist of certified public accountants (CPAs), management consultants, and certified financial planners (CFPs). These

Above, from left, are Al Rozell, Ed Bond, and Tim King, partners, of Bederson & Company's Insolvency and Litigation Services Department.

Edward P. Bond, at left, is managing partner of Bederson & Company, LLP, and past president of the New Jersey State Board of Accountancy.

specialists embody a high degree of technical competence, an extensive range of business experience, and an in-depth understanding of specific business segments, as represented by the credentials held by Bederson partners, such as: Certified Fraud Examiners, Certified Valuation Analysts, Certified Insolvency and Reorganization Accountants, Masters of Science in Taxation, and Masters of Science in Business.

The full complement of services that Bederson & Company makes available includes:
- Accounting and auditing
- Business and succession planning
- Business valuations
- Computer and technology consulting
- Consulting services
- Forensic services
- Insolvency, reorganization, turnaround, and litigation services
- Matrimonial litigation support and mediation services
- Mergers, acquisitions, and capital financing
- Nonprofit services
- Real estate services
- SEC and regulatory compliance
- Tax, estate, and financial planning

Based on a client's requirements, the firm brings together an exceptional team of such specialists, who are leaders in their fields. The team

CREATING THE FUTURE

works together to help clients resolve complex financial issues and develop strategies to increase profitability. Bederson helps clients structure their financial future; clients view the firm as their partner in financial growth.

Bederson & Company gears all its client operations to state-of-the-art accounting and tax practices. Its sophisticated internal networking systems allow the firm to research and access critical data to help clients make key business decisions. Its management information specialists help clients select accounting software systems that help cut costs, save time, improve efficiency, and access timely information. Bederson's experts also are helping clients prepare their computer systems for the year 2000 (Y2K) date change. Providing technology in conjunction with computer consultants is one of many ways the firm serves its clients' business management and financial needs. In addition, Bederson is licensed to provide electronic commerce (E-commerce) services leading to the issuance of a WebTrust Seal for commercial Web sites.

Bederson is a New Jersey–area member of TAG, an international association of leading accounting firms established to provide benefits to its member firms, their clients, and the communities they serve. This is accomplished through a continuous exchange of technical, product, and managerial information; export and import assistance; and seminars for specific industry groups.

Bederson also is a business-turnaround specialist, helping clients analyze and redefine their operations so they can function more effectively and profitably. Issues Bederson addresses include capital management, quality of supervision, and personnel effectiveness. Bederson & Company is listed among the top regional bankruptcy accounting firms by the industry publication *Turnarounds & Workouts*.

Above are, from left, Maribel Kane, Bederson & Company's director of Information Systems, and Sy Bressler, partner.

"Turnaround services require specialized expertise and a close working relationship with clients," says Bederson managing partner Edward P. Bond. "To make a turnaround happen, you have to analyze the situation, understand the marketplace, conduct marketing studies, and evaluate personnel. Ideally, clients call us in before they have major problems that threaten their solvency. Just as important as our services and expertise is the client's commitment to change. Even in a good economy, companies can have problems if they don't keep up with the times."

For more than thirty-five years Bond has maintained a leadership position in the financial and business community, including two consecutive appointments to the New Jersey State Board of Accountancy, where he formerly served as president. Renowned for significant contributions in the field of insolvency, reorganization, and turnarounds, he is a member of the American Bankruptcy Institute, the Association of Insolvency Accountants, and the National Association of Bankruptcy Trustees. Bond is dually licensed as a Certified Insolvency and Reorganization Accountant and as a Certified Fraud Examiner.

"Throughout Bederson's history we have experienced rapid growth thanks to our many loyal clients," Bond says. "As far as we're concerned, our clients are our partners. Our personalized service makes us unique—we work on a one-on-one basis with clients. We feel that the results we have achieved for our clients speak for themselves."

Shown at left is the reception and message center of Bederson & Company's offices in West Orange, New Jersey.

ACCOUNTING 195

DELOITTE & TOUCHE LLP

THE ONLY "BIG SIX" PROFESSIONAL SERVICES FIRM AMONG FORTUNE MAGAZINE'S "100 BEST COMPANIES TO WORK FOR IN AMERICA," GLOBAL LEADER DELOITTE & TOUCHE LLP PROVIDES ACCOUNTING AND MANAGEMENT CONSULTING TO PUBLIC AND PRIVATE ENTERPRISES

One of the nation's leading professional services firms, Deloitte & Touche LLP proactively identifies and delivers customized management solutions to help organizations stay competitive in a changing global environment. The firm provides a full range of accounting and auditing, management consulting, and tax services through 23,000 people in more than 100 cities in the United States, offering deep experience in mergers and acquisitions, employee benefits, real estate services, risk management, reengineering, electronic commerce, and computer security. Deloitte & Touche operates out of New Jersey, where it has five office locations, including Parsippany, Princeton, Trenton, East Brunswick, and Fairfield. The company is one of the largest accounting and auditing practices in the tristate region.

Deloitte & Touche LLP is part of Deloitte Touche Tohmatsu, a global leader in professional services with a staff of more than 72,000 people in 130 countries. Its combined practices around the world audit more than 700 companies with sales or assets in excess of U.S. $1 billion—approximately 20 percent of the world's most successful businesses. Deloitte Touche Tohmatsu serves thousands of enterprises in both the public and private sectors, including multinational and large national practices, public institutions, and tens of thousands of fast-growing smaller businesses.

Deloitte & Touche was recently ranked number fourteen on *Fortune* magazine's list of the "100 Best Companies to Work for in America," which is compiled to honor the organizations with the most advanced and innovative human resources initiatives. The selection of the firm is further distinguished by the fact that it was the only "Big Six" professional services firm included on the list.

Fortune recognized Deloitte & Touche for its commitment to designing and implementing progressive programs that address a number of critical human resources issues, including flexible work arrangements; alternative officing strategies; balancing work and family obligations; personal time off; and support and guidance outside of the office.

Programs like these exemplify Deloitte & Touche's commitment to helping all of its employees achieve a more satisfying work/life balance. Mike Cook, United States chairman and chief executive officer, puts it this way: "Our goal is to create a workplace where dedicated professionals provide superior client services while they

Deloitte & Touche operates out of five offices in New Jersey: Parsippany (above), Princeton, Trenton, East Brunswick, and Fairfield. © A. J. Sundstrom Photography

Office managing partner Guy Budinscak and senior partner Rich Kabobjian work out of the Parsippany office. © A. J. Sundstrom Photography

CREATING THE FUTURE

themselves are offered exciting challenges and the flexibility to balance these challenges with their personal lives."

Deloitte & Touche's greatest resource is its intellectual capital, derived from the recruitment and cultivation of the very best people. Intellectual capital—the product of deep experience and expertise in many fields, and an appreciation of the nature of change across markets, cultures, and industries—provides the seamless connection between the firm's commitment to its people and its dedication to maintaining excellent client-service standards. It is through the competence and integrity of its professionals that Deloitte & Touche is able to build client relationships based on superior service and absolute trust, and to help clients gain excellent value no matter what the challenge.

"Our mission," says Mr. Cook, "is 'to be the professional services firm that consistently exceeds the expectations of its clients and its staff.' Nothing is more important to us than our dedication to client service. We believe it takes more than mere competence—more, even, than excellence—to properly serve our clients. It takes, among other things, the willingness and ability to understand each client's current and future needs, to create and implement effective client-service plans, and to provide insights and maintain open communication with every client, every step of the way. In short, to earn their complete trust and confidence."

Beyond its extensive client-service commitments, Deloitte & Touche is constantly striving to help better the business community. The firm's current business initiatives include helping to promote safer business on the Internet; sponsoring a World Education program to provide companies with strategies and resources that help them compete more successfully in the international market; publishing various industry surveys and information booklets; conducting outreach efforts to small businesses; and advising governments on matters of national and international financial affairs.

Deloitte & Touche has one of the largest accounting and auditing practices in the tristate region. © A. J. Sundstrom Photography

On a global level, Deloitte Touche Tohmatsu is making impressive headway in important international markets, such as Hong Kong. According to Ed Kangas, the firm's worldwide chairman and chief executive officer, "Deloitte's merger with Kwan Wong Tan & Fong created Hong Kong's biggest accounting firm, which now audits 27 of the 100 largest companies on the Hong Kong stock exchange.

"The qualities that distinguish Deloitte & Touche are alive in every office of the firm, in every corner of the world," Kangas continues. "Ours is a truly global organization, shaped by a set of values and standards that remains constant year in and year out—values and standards upon which our clients and our people can depend, no matter where in the world they're conducting business."

Deloitte & Touche's greatest resource is its intellectual capital, derived from the recruitment and cultivation of the very best people. © A. J. Sundstrom Photography

ACCOUNTING 197

J. H. COHN LLP

KNOWN AS "THE BUSINESSPERSON'S CPA," J. H. COHN LLP, ONE OF THE NATION'S LEADING INDEPENDENT ACCOUNTING AND CONSULTING FIRMS, SERVES MORE THAN 1,500 BUSINESSES WITH PROGRESSIVE THINKING, EXPERTISE, AND CLOSE PERSONAL ATTENTION

One of the leading independent accounting and consulting firms in the nation, J. H. Cohn LLP, based in Roseland, New Jersey, is known as "the businessperson's CPA" due to the way its professionals think like entrepreneurs and understand business far beyond financial numbers, tax returns, and audits.

With the American Institute of Certified Public Accountants (AICPA) as a longtime client, J. H. Cohn might also be called the "accountant's accountant." It is not only New Jersey's largest accounting firm, but also one of the country's twenty-five largest.

Its 36 partners, 150 other professionals, and more than 40 other staff members provide accounting, auditing, tax compliance, tax advisory, and a wide range of management and information-system consulting services at J. H. Cohn's headquarters and its offices in Englewood Cliffs and Lawrenceville, New Jersey; Bronxville and New York, New York; and San Diego, California.

The firm's growth can be attributed to three factors that have been consistent since its founding in 1919: the highest professional standards; the knowledgeable and progressive thinking furnished to clients; and the focus on personal service. While J. H. Cohn's more than 1,500 clients include many large, publicly traded companies, the majority of its practice is devoted to serving midsize, closely held proprietorships, partnerships, and corporations that desire a close relationship with their accounting firm.

Administrative assistant Angela Marinuzzi (left) and receptionist Jill Meibach greet clients in the lobby of J. H. Cohn LLP. © Ricken Studio

RANGE OF SERVICES

In keeping with its fundamental mission of helping clients earn more and keep more of what they earn, J. H. Cohn is organized into six major business groups:

- Financial Management
- Lender Services
- Tax Advisory Services
- Consulting and Financial Planning Services
- Nonprofit and Governmental Services
- Appraisal and Litigation Support Services

Within each of these business groups, the firm specializes further in particular service areas and/or industries. Through its specialized lines of business, J. H. Cohn is able to offer clients highly technical expertise tailored to specific industries.

ANTICIPATING ISSUES

The firm's partners and staff who consult with business owners and investors on **financing issues**, for instance, realize that this is a field in which "it's not just what you know but who you know."

William Kowals, Kelly Frank, and Jeffrey Bernstein discuss tax strategies for their clients. © Ricken Studio

198 CREATING THE FUTURE

They not only have extensive backgrounds in financing, banking, and business planning, but also are strongly networked within the New Jersey/New York metropolitan area financial community.

In the firm's **tax practice**, on the other hand, "it's not just what or who you know, but when you know it." J. H. Cohn's tax professionals are dedicated to planning for the future, from both strategic and operational perspectives. They recognize that the best tax practice is tax planning—best performed in anticipation of transactions or potential issues. J. H. Cohn also offers sound advice, alternatives, and practical approaches to the tax consequences of completed transactions.

J. H. Cohn's tax department is large enough to have been able to develop many areas of specialization, including tax expertise for corporations; partnerships; individuals; state, local, and foreign tax filings; mergers and acquisitions; estates and trusts; and pension, profit-sharing, and deferred compensation tax plans, among others.

The **management consulting** department assists clients in many management functions, including computer system design and implementation, profitability improvement strategies, organizational and compensation reviews, software selection and implementation, treasury and cash management, and succession planning.

As **not-for-profit** groups play a larger role in local economies, J. H. Cohn has developed expertise to serve these organizations' special tax, budgeting, and accounting needs.

The firm is highly regarded throughout the legal, banking, and general business communities as well as in the CPA profession—one reason its appraisal and **litigation support service practice** is so strong.

J. H. Cohn's **Financial Planning Services** group offers strategic advice on short- and long-term asset allocation. The group helps clients map out and achieve financial goals, from buying property or saving for college bills or retirement needs to estate planning.

JHC Software Associates, incorporated in 1985 as a subsidiary of J. H. Cohn, helps clients find cost-effective solutions to their frequently changing hardware, software, networking, and consulting needs, for accounting, financial, and business-management functions. JHC Software Associates provides implementation, conversion, and on-site training and support. It has experience working with companies ranging from small- and medium-size family-owned businesses to large multinational corporations.

PEOPLE, PEOPLE, PEOPLE

Through the years, J. H. Cohn has earned and maintained its reputation by hiring outstanding people and offering them the opportunity to achieve their full professional potential.

The firm's corporate culture reflects the personality of its founder, emphasizing warm, personal attention to its employees, clients, and community. It has served some clients for three generations, and, with its progressive thinking and attitudes, especially vis-à-vis technology, J. H. Cohn hopes to serve them for generations to come. Its motto aptly expresses how it does business: "J. H. Cohn LLP—where the bottom line is you."

Steven P. Schenkel updates his staff on new technology methods and equipment.
© Ricken Studio

The management committee of J. H. Cohn LLP includes (standing, from left) co-managing partners Thomas J. Marino and Lawrence Zagarola; (seated, from left) Michael Cohen, James Heinze, Michael Goodman, Eugene Berl, and Kenneth Kanter; and (not pictured) Richard Puzo and Richard Schurig.
© Ricken Studio

PRICEWATERHOUSECOOPERS

BUILDING UPON THE BUSINESS KNOWLEDGE AND CLIENT SERVICE ORIENTATION OF THE COMPANY'S FOUNDING FIRMS, THE 140,000 WORLDWIDE PROFESSIONALS OF PRICEWATERHOUSECOOPERS ARE SHAPING THE FUTURE OF GLOBAL BUSINESS

PricewaterhouseCoopers (www.pwcglobal.com), the world's largest professional services organization, helps its clients build value, manage risk, and improve their performance. Drawing on the talents of more than 140,000 people in 152 countries, PricewaterhouseCoopers (PwC) provides a full range of business advisory services to leading global, national, and local companies and public institutions.

In New Jersey, PricewaterhouseCoopers has the largest professional services practice in the state. With 3,000 people working in seven offices across New Jersey, the firm has a powerful presence in the market, and with its proximity to large practice offices in both New York and Philadelphia, it can meet virtually any client need with experienced local resources.

"Our practice in New Jersey reflects the strategic importance of the state as a business center and regional operating hub to the firm," says Mary Beth Backof, managing partner of the PricewaterhouseCoopers New Jersey practice. "Many factors are driving our business growth. The generally strong economy has played an important part, as have

At left is Mary Beth Backof, PricewaterhouseCoopers New Jersey managing partner.

The new PricewaterhouseCoopers Florham Park office is a focal point for the firm's New Jersey operations and is home base for more than 900 partners and staff.

industry consolidation, corporate 'rightsizing,' outsourcing, and a rapidly changing information technology environment. All in all, New Jersey is an outstanding environment in which to continue to grow our business."

PwC's New Jersey resources include all those available through the global firm, including audit services, business advisory services, tax compliance and consulting, human resources advisory services, management and systems consulting, and financial advisory services. The firm also has a number of resident specialty practices, such as valuation, expatriate tax services, and personal financial services. PricewaterhouseCoopers has extensive expertise in a wide range of industries dominant in New Jersey, including pharmaceuticals, telecommunications, consumer products, manufacturing, high technology, and biotechnology, to name just a few.

Stephen Karnas, a senior audit partner with the firm, says, "Because of the many leading companies headquartered here, we have a rich client base in the state. We have built a dynamic, multidisciplinary practice to support our clients'

200   CREATING THE FUTURE

needs. We have the best resources available, from the standpoint of human capital. We feel it's not just about numbers in our business, it's really about people."

Reflecting its commitment to support and nurture its staff, PricewaterhouseCoopers provides an outstanding workplace for its employees. Culturally diverse, the firm has received several awards. Recently it was selected for the fourth consecutive year by *Working Mother* magazine as one of the 100 best companies for working mothers.

With each firm having more than 100 years of history, the 1998 merger harnessed the collective power of two venerable firms, Price Waterhouse and Coopers & Lybrand. Building on their legacies, the newly merged partnership, PricewaterhouseCoopers, was launched on 1 July 1998.

"The merger is linked to our firm's strategy of 'knowledge, worlds, and people' that emphasizes our people's knowledge, skills, and expertise in connecting with our clients," says Backof.

Both of these "legacy" firms have a rich history of active involvement in New Jersey, ranging from work on state initiatives such as the New Jersey Master Plan Commission and international trade missions to supporting numerous charitable and cultural organizations such as the New Jersey Performing Arts Center, in Newark.

"We take a broad view when we look at opportunities in New Jersey," says Bob Roche, regional leader of the firm's middle market practice. "Clearly large companies are an important part of our business here, but we are also committed to serving the middle market, which is one of the key sectors in our overall growth strategy."

The merger offers clients access to substantially greater resources locally and worldwide, with faster deployment of specialists, new products, and services. It also provides enormous scope and operational scale in critically important markets. In addition, the firm's ability to increase investment in technology and knowledge management ensures that clients have access to leading-edge solutions.

A strong team approach to business characterizes the firm's service philosophy. Pictured above, from left, are Bob Roche, Pete Solano, Raj Tatta, Steve Karnas, and Dick Stolz.

"We are exceedingly proud of the people employed by PricewaterhouseCoopers, who are at the cusp of an exciting era in professional services," says Nicholas G. Moore, chairman of PricewaterhouseCoopers. James J. Schiro, chief executive officer of the merged organization, continues that line of thought: "The front-edge thinking that is embodied in our people, our ability to leverage that reasoning for all of our employees around the world, and our success in using it to create value for clients will be what define this new organization in the days and years ahead."

Says Karnas, "We feel that as New Jersey goes, so goes the country. The state is a vibrant marketplace with enormous opportunities and challenges for our clients, which makes it a very important place for our firm to have a strong role. From both a global perspective and a local New Jersey perspective, our expanded multidisciplinary capabilities offer clients access to products and services supported by very talented people."

PRICEWATERHOUSECOOPERS

Shown here, some of the firm's key partners who are based in New Jersey include (seated, from left) Raj Tatta, Mary Beth Backof, Steve Karnas, and Vince Colman; and (standing, from left) Greg Prow, Dick Stolz, Tom Colligan, and Bob Roche.

ACCOUNTING 201

© Jeff Zaruba/Tony Stone Images

202 CREATING THE FUTURE

LAW

GIORDANO, HALLERAN & CIESLA, P.C.

SERVING CLIENTS LOCALLY AND THROUGHOUT THE METROPOLITAN AREA, GIORDANO, HALLERAN & CIESLA, P.C., COMBINES THE ADVANTAGES OF A SMALL LAW PRACTICE WITH THE EXPERTISE AND RESOURCES OF MAJOR CITY FIRMS

The success of the law firm of Giordano, Halleran & Ciesla, P.C. (GH&C), is attributable to its ability to combine the attentiveness to clients typically seen in a small law firm with the range of comprehensive services found in a large law firm. GH&C employs more than fifty-five attorneys who are supported by a staff of ninety.

GH&C's broad client base includes real estate companies, developers, banks and financial institutions, health care institutions, and service businesses. Its business clients range from new, small entrepreneurial ventures to established Fortune 500 corporations. The firm also maintains a large and well-respected criminal defense and personal injury practice.

While GH&C has a strong local commitment, its presence extends beyond the bounds of New Jersey. Its central New Jersey location, nearly equidistant

In the four decades since Giordano, Halleran & Ciesla (GH&C) was founded, the nearby town of Red Bank, New Jersey, shown above in the 1950s, has blossomed into a cosmopolitan center, recently named the "hippest town in New Jersey" by New Jersey Monthly *magazine.*

Offering the sophisticated breadth of expertise typical of law firms in major cities, GH&C's practice is conveniently located in central New Jersey. Shown at left is the firm's Middletown headquarters.

A FULL RANGE OF LEGAL SERVICES

- Business and Banking Law
- Commercial Litigation
- Corporate Finance and Securities
- Criminal Defense and Personal Injury
- Environmental Law
- Health and Hospital Law
- Intellectual Property Law
- Labor and Employment Law
- Land Use and Development Law
- Property Taxation
- Technology Law
- Workers' Compensation and Social Security Law

between Philadelphia and New York, makes it easily accessible to corporate clients. In addition to its Middletown office, near downtown Red Bank, the firm also has an office in Trenton, near the seat of state government as well as federal and state courts.

"We are unique in that we have a sophisticated practice based in Monmouth County and extending throughout the state and beyond," says the firm's managing partner Michael Gross. "We deal with the larger New York firms on an equal footing. However, our location allows our attorneys to be easily accessible when a client in New Jersey has a matter that requires a high level of experience."

Since its founding in 1959, GH&C has evolved into a full-service regional law firm, organized into several diverse practice areas to serve the community. As its clients' requirements have grown, the firm has developed new services, enabling clients to stay ahead of changing business trends, economic cycles, and political tides. For example, the firm developed its Employment Law and Technology Law practices to reflect the times.

Each of GH&C's major practice areas offers expertise comparable to highly specialized "boutique" law firms. At the same time, by operating under the umbrella of a larger firm, GH&C attorneys can immediately draw on the firm's broad range of internal resources to assist its clients as needed. This synergy allows the firm to handle complicated cases that require several types of expertise, such as combining the litigation skills needed to effectively handle a class-action lawsuit with a thorough knowledge of technical legal issues pertaining to environmental, health care, or labor law. The firm also has a network of professionals in allied technical fields providing expert support as needed.

"We offer each of our clients the resources of a large, full-service firm while also providing personal attention," says Gross. "Each of our practice areas is managed by talented attorneys with substantial experience in their specialty. We provide our clients with high-quality attorneys and high-quality services."

Some of GH&C's partners were cited for the firm's strengths in corporate, environmental, and real estate law in *New Jersey Monthly* magazine's "Best Lawyers in New Jersey" listing, which was derived from the Woodward/White Inc. "Best Lawyers in America" national listings.

While GH&C can point with pride to many of its former partners, Susan D. Davis is among those who exemplify the exceptional level of the firm's talent. When she became a partner, Davis was one of just four African American women partners in a major New Jersey law firm. In 1997 she was appointed United States magistrate judge, becoming the first African American to hold the position in New Jersey and the youngest judge on the federal bench in the state.

Giordano, Halleran & Ciesla's senior partners John R. Halleran (left), John C. Giordano Jr. (center) and Frank R. Ciesla (right) gather on a balcony at the firm's headquarters in Middletown, an area that has been heavily influenced by the law firm's clients for the past forty years.

In addition to the publication of its partners' works in such periodicals as the *New Jersey Law Journal* and *New Jersey Lawyer*, the firm takes an active role in industry associations, ranging from the local bar to national business organizations. GH&C also is a strong proponent of keeping its clients and the general public well-informed about legal issues that have a direct impact on their lives. The firm regularly sponsors seminars at Monmouth University on topics such as environmental law or land-use law, and two of its partners are instructors in the school's graduate-level Real Estate Certificate program. Four times each year the firm conducts a New Jersey Issues Forum at its offices, where people from across the state participate to update their knowledge of the law.

GH&C also produces a cable TV show called "Environmental Straight Talk" that is taped at Brookdale Community College. Firm members take an active role in the community by sponsoring community events and sitting on the boards of associations and charitable organizations.

As GH&C reaches its fortieth anniversary, in 1999, it continues building on its strong history and diverse talents to expand its services, and meet clients' needs in the future.

GH&C

Advantage client.

GIBBONS, DEL DEO, DOLAN, GRIFFINGER & VECCHIONE

THE MORE THAN 135 ATTORNEYS AT THE LAW FIRM OF GIBBONS, DEL DEO, DOLAN, GRIFFINGER & VECCHIONE PROVIDE A FULL RANGE OF DOMESTIC AND INTERNATIONAL LEGAL SERVICES

The firm's senior named partners and managing partner are, from left, Ralph N. Del Deo; John T. Dolan; John J. Gibbons; Michael R. Griffinger; David J. Sheehan, managing partner; and Frank J. Vecchione.

The law firm of Gibbons, Del Deo, Dolan, Griffinger & Vecchione has a long and rich history. The firm, which opened its doors in 1926 as Rossbach & Crummy, was founded by Andrew Crummy. He had been an Internal Revenue Service agent and then attended Harvard Law School. Upon graduation, he set up practice with another attorney, Adam Rossbach. When Rossbach passed away in the mid-1930s, Andrew Crummy continued on his own, specializing in taxation and bankruptcy reorganization law.

During World War II Crummy worked on legal matters for the Manhattan Project, where he met Colonel William Consodine, who was serving as the project's general counsel. When Consodine left the military in late 1945, the two became partners, and Crummy & Consodine was formed.

In the early 1950s John J. Gibbons and Thomas J. O'Neill joined the firm as partners. In the 1950s William Consodine (later a Superior Court judge) left the firm, and it became Crummy, Gibbons & O'Neill. It evolved in the 1970s and 1980s to Crummy, Del Deo, Dolan, Griffinger & Vecchione after John Gibbons became a judge on the United States Third Circuit Court of Appeals. In 1981 Andrew Crummy passed away, and in 1990, Judge Gibbons rejoined the firm, which then became Gibbons, Del Deo, Dolan, Griffinger & Vecchione, as it is known today.

The law firm is one of the oldest in New Jersey, and it also is one of the largest. More than 135 lawyers are engaged in a diversified full-service domestic and international practice. The law firm has nine major departments. These areas encompass litigation, corporate, intellectual property, real estate, banking, land use and municipal finance, and tax and insolvency law.

"We pride ourselves on being a full-service firm for both the private

The firm's Women Directors Business Networking Group includes, from left, partners Susanne Peticolas, Karen A. Giannelli, Alyce C. Halchak, Christine A. Amalfe, Geraldine E. Ponto, Elizabeth S. Kardos, and (not pictured) Angela D. Slater.

206 CREATING THE FUTURE

and public sectors, able to perform the complete range of litigation and transactional services. We handle sophisticated antitrust cases, product liability and employment matters, trademark and copyright cases, patent litigation, and intellectual property disputes for substantial corporate entities," says David J. Sheehan, managing partner. "And the reputation of our insolvency department has been and continues to be at the highest level," he observes.

The firm has provided representation on such diverse and complex matters as the reorganization of a private institution of higher education and the reorganization of a financially troubled Atlantic City casino. Along with advising debtor companies with regard to prebankruptcy planning and conducting the reorganization proceedings, the insolvency department also provides advice to secured and general creditors of debtor companies involved in insolvency situations.

The real estate department deals in matters ranging from simple to highly complex; and the banking department represents not only borrowers, but often one of the major banking institutions in the state, by way of its commercial and mortgage lending activities and its corporate trust work.

Along with its law practice the firm performs extensive pro bono work. "One of our proudest achievements has been the creation of the Gibbons Fellowship in Public Interest and Constitutional Law," Sheehan says. "It was begun in 1990 when Judge Gibbons retired from the federal bench and rejoined the firm. We sponsor two full-time associates for two-year stints to provide counsel on public issues, individual rights, and societal concerns."

This fellowship program was honored by the American Bar Association's first service award, in 1991, and is considered a national model for the participation of the private bar in pro bono cases. It provides the two sponsored associates, under the supervision of John J. Gibbons and attorney Lawrence S. Lustberg, a partner and director of the fellowship, an opportunity to write, teach, and litigate cases addressing significant issues such as homelessness; the death penalty and other criminal procedural issues; prison conditions; the rights of the AIDS-afflicted; welfare reform; domestic violence and other family-law issues; school finance; human rights; and consumer protection.

"We are proud to have the Gibbons Fellowship to speak for the poor and disenfranchised in the federal and state trial and appellate courts," says Sheehan.

The law firm has always been a part of the greater community of Newark. Its headquarters today is at Newark's state-of-the-art law building, called the Legal Center. The firm also maintains a regional office in midtown Manhattan.

The commitment of Gibbons, Del Deo, Dolan, Griffinger & Vecchione to the City of Newark is as strong now as it was when the firm first began—as the small, growing law practice that was founded by young Andrew Crummy more than seventy years ago.

Members of the firm's Employment and Labor Law department include, from left, Heather L. Akawie, John A. Ridley, Kerry M. Parker, Lana H. Coutros, Christine A. Amalfe, Katherin Nukk-Freeman, Thomas N. Lyons*, Richard S. Zackin, Joseph Maddaloni Jr., Kerrie R. Heslin, and Courtney E. Redfern.

*Former partner of the firm; appointed Judge, Superior Court of New Jersey, Union County.

For further information, contact Gibbons, Del Deo, Dolan, Griffinger & Vecchione at:

One Riverfront Plaza, Newark, New Jersey, 07102-5497;

telephone: (973) 596-4500; facsimile: (973) 596-0545; or,

1633 Broadway, New York, New York, 10019-6708;

telephone: (212) 649-4700; facsimile: (212) 333-5980;

E-mail: firm@gibbonslaw.com • Web site: www.gibbonslaw.com

GREENBAUM, ROWE, SMITH, RAVIN, DAVIS & HIMMEL LLP

THE HIGHLY REGARDED LAW FIRM OF GREENBAUM, ROWE, SMITH, RAVIN, DAVIS & HIMMEL LLP PROVIDES SOPHISTICATED LEGAL SERVICES IN ALL MAJOR AREAS OF LAW WITH A REPUTATION FOR RESPONSIVENESS AND COMMITMENT

The law firm of Greenbaum, Rowe, Smith, Ravin, Davis & Himmel LLP, established more than eighty years ago, has a tradition and reputation based upon an unfailing commitment to the highest professional standards and a keen personal interest in its clients. At the same time, the firm's approach to practicing law is cutting edge—giving it the knowledge and skills necessary to meet the sophisticated demands placed on its clients by the modern world. The firm today has the distinction of having several partners, representing virtually all areas of its disciplines, listed in the book *The Best Lawyers in America*.

Greenbaum, Rowe, Smith, Ravin, Davis & Himmel is recognized throughout the New Jersey business community as one of its major law firms. Its offices are located in Woodbridge and Roseland, providing easy access for clients. The firm is composed of five major departments: litigation; corporate; banking and creditors' rights; tax, trusts, and estates; and real estate. It also has many collaborative practice groups that transcend departmental lines. These include white collar criminal defense, intellectual property and patents, health care, environmental, employment, administrative, land use, and community association law.

The litigation department is one of the largest and most comprehensive of its kind serving business and industry in New Jersey today. The department provides a full complement of commercial and civil litigation services. It is particularly distinguished by its ability to handle complex matters and manage some of the largest and most sophisticated business litigation in the state. Companies represented range from major public corporations and Fortune 500 companies to established medium and small, publicly and privately held businesses, as well as general and limited partnerships of all scales. More than half of the firm's attorneys are litigators who maintain concentrated practices in all primary areas of the law, ensuring full coverage of all points of a dispute. These attorneys practice at the trial and appellate levels in state and federal courts and before administrative agencies and other regulatory bodies, arbitration tribunals, and mediators.

The corporate department provides a full range of general business representation, from basic counseling to the complex transactional services necessary to respond to the diverse needs of today's demanding business climate. Greenbaum, Rowe, Smith, Ravin, Davis & Himmel represents and advises corporate directors, executives, and business leaders of large family-owned businesses and Fortune 1000 companies.

The GRSRD&H Management Committee, above, includes (seated) Paul A. Rowe, managing partner and chair, Litigation Department; and (standing, from left) Arthur M. Greenbaum, partner; Michael B. Himmel, partner and chair of the White Collar Criminal Defense Group; and Alan E. Davis, partner and chair of the Corporate Department. © A. J. Sundstrom Photography

Members of the law firm include (seated) Wendell A. Smith, partner; and (standing, from left) Alan S. Naar, partner; and David L. Bruck, partner and chair, Banking and Creditors' Rights Department. © A. J. Sundstrom Photography

CREATING THE FUTURE

The banking and creditors' rights department provides comprehensive counseling to institutional lenders, creditors, and other participants in loan transactions, banking matters, and related litigation. A high degree of sophistication has been developed in representing clientele in workouts and other out-of-court procedures, with the goal being to maximize the return to the client in the most cost-conscious and expeditious manner.

The tax, trusts, and estates department renders complete tax services that encompass all phases of federal and state tax planning, and practices before all courts, including the New Jersey and United States Tax Courts. The department's services in this area consist of tax audits, appeals, and rulings; tax structuring for all business formats and transactions; and counsel in the areas of employee benefits and executive compensation.

The firm's real estate department has been prominently associated with New Jersey's real estate development and financing industries for several decades. It has provided legal guidance for leading developers, condominium and community associations, landlords, banks, and real estate brokers in all facets of their involvement throughout the state, and has successfully handled many landmark cases affecting the interests of realtors, developers,

Shown at left are (seated, from left) Margaret Goodzeit, partner; Mark H. Sobel, partner; and (standing) Michael A. Backer, partner and co-chair, Tax, Trusts & Estates Department. © A. J. Sundstrom Photography

or lenders in this arena. Additionally, the department represents life insurance companies, banks, and pension funds in connection with construction and permanent financing and in their work-out programs, and handles all facets of land use regulation, environmental and utility concerns, and condemnation.

The character of Greenbaum, Rowe, Smith, Ravin, Davis & Himmel is best reflected in the many enduring relationships that the firm's lawyers have enjoyed with its clients over the years, and is enhanced by the professional reputation, dedication, collective experience, and talent of its attorneys. Many of its current partners have been with the firm since graduating from law school, often working side by side with individual clients over several decades. The firm's associates, who are selected from the nation's best law schools, are encouraged to develop and to learn from its more seasoned practitioners.

The activities of many of the attorneys are multidimensional in scope. Some lawyers have served and continue to serve in leadership roles in bar associations and other professional groups; in state and local government; and with civic and charitable organizations, hospitals, and educational institutions. Others have taught at law schools and have authored treatises, books, and numerous articles in legal and business publications. All are encouraged to and most do participate in continuing legal education, seminars, and panels in a wide variety of professional and civic activities.

The partners of Greenbaum, Rowe, Smith, Ravin, Davis & Himmel believe that the most important asset a law firm has is its reputation. With that, they also believe it is only by providing the highest quality legal counseling that a firm can achieve a reputation for responsiveness and commitment. The firm is proud of its reputation among its colleagues, clients, and the business community, and continues to take pride in its ability to provide the highest caliber of legal services in all areas of practice.

Gathered at left are (seated, from left) Robert C. Schachter, partner and chair, Real Estate Department; Robert S. Greenbaum, partner; and (standing, from left) Martin L. Lepelstat, partner and co-chair, Tax, Trusts & Estates Department; and James E. Patterson, partner and chair, Labor & Employment Law Group. © A. J. Sundstrom Photography

Denver Library, designed by Michael Graves Architect. © Tim Hursley

ARCHITECTURE

DICARA MALASITS AND ROSENBERG ARCHITECTS

DiCara Malasits and Rosenberg Architects has truly helped to develop the landscape of New Jersey

If indeed history repeats itself, the twenty-first century looks bright for DiCara Malasits and Rosenberg Architects (DMR). Located in the suburban community of Maywood in northern New Jersey's Bergen County, the firm's offices have expanded significantly since DMR's 1991 inception. This full-service architectural firm has experienced growth in all aspects of its practice, including project diversity, staff size, and project recognition. DMR has become one of New Jersey's leading architectural firms, and the reason is simple—complete dedication and unwavering commitment to its clients.

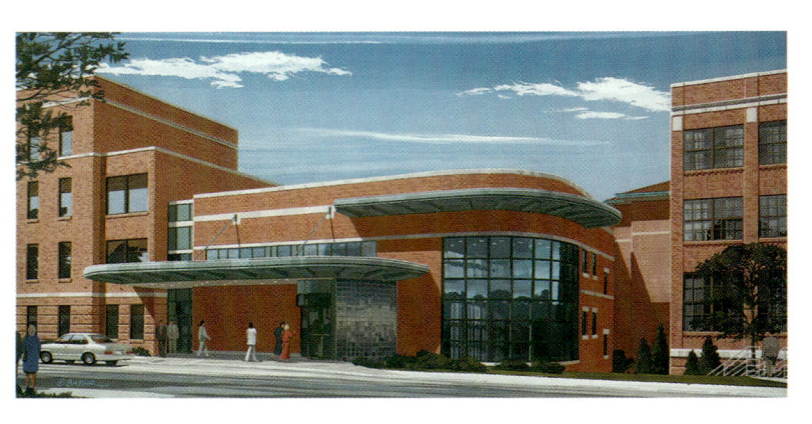

The three principals of the firm, Lloyd A. Rosenberg, AIA; Joseph DiCara, AIA; and Emery Malasits, AIA, share a common goal that is practiced by all staff members—to complete each and every project to the client's complete satisfaction.

In order to fulfill this goal without exception, a unique approach is used. Each project awarded to the firm is directly administered by a principal. This assures the client continuity, attention, and responsiveness by a decision maker at all times.

DMR Architects is a collaboration of talented, knowledgeable, and skilled professionals further complemented by efficient and responsive administrative personnel and an in-house marketing staff. Public relations services are offered to clients through the marketing department when the need arises to introduce information to the community. This is of particular interest to educational administrators and nonprofit organizations for whom the success of a project may rely on public opinion and funding.

DMR Architects' offices are fully networked with the latest technologies; the firm is poised to move ahead into the twenty-first century.

AN A+ IN SCHOOL DESIGN

DMR's clients include more than 100 of New Jersey's school districts. DMR

The new Regional Cancer Center shown above was designed by DiCara Malasits and Rosenberg Architects for its client Holy Name Hospital in Teaneck, New Jersey.

Principals of the firm are, from left, Emery Malasits, AIA; Lloyd Rosenberg, AIA; Joseph DiCara, AIA; and associates John Scheckel, AIA, and Gregg Stopa, AIA.

has served the Franklin Lakes, Butler, Millstone Township, Frelinghuysen, and Hasbrouck Heights school districts, to name a few. Recently completed is the 106,000-square-foot middle school in Lacey Township and additions and renovations to the Sparta Township district's high school. Also under way in Sparta is a new 133,000-square-foot middle school. In Jersey City, DMR is the owners' representative and design architect for the community's first charter school. Also in Jersey City, DMR served as architect for an early childhood development center for the public school system. All of DMR's designs satisfy the clients' program objectives, and often the firm receives recognition for its design excellence. For example, firm management provided the creative inspiration behind an award-winning design in a River Edge, New Jersey, school for a Discovery Classroom. This unique project transformed a storage closet into a hands-on science learning environment for elementary school students.

College-level students also benefit from DMR's expertise. The design and construction of a new academic building on Fairleigh Dickinson University's Florham-Madison campus has created a modern teaching facility on a campus rich with historic architecture and tradition.

DMR considers the educational market an exciting area for its work; the firm provides the most modern technology and building designs to allow teaching environments to reach into the twenty-first century.

CREATING THE FUTURE

DMR's design for an academic building on Fairleigh Dickinson University's Florham-Madison campus remained true to the existing Georgian-style architecture prevalent on the historic campus. © Victor J. Fiore Photography

HELPING OTHERS TO HEAL

Another market in New Jersey served by DMR is the health care sector. DMR works closely with Holy Name Hospital in Teaneck, New Jersey, and has completed renovations to the psychiatric unit, operating rooms, doctors' suites, and nursing stations. DMR's interior design staff was responsible for a complete renovation of the hospital's main boardroom and its lobby. The hospital's new 16,000-square-foot Regional Cancer Center, which includes the housing of linear accelerators, was designed by DMR. The new center's detailed design and its convenient location, connected to the existing hospital building, will allow the hospital to continue to care for area patients well into the millennium.

Also in the health care sector, DMR has provided schematic plans for a subacute wing at the former United Hospital in Newark, New Jersey, and has worked with the University of Medicine and Dentistry of New Jersey (UMDNJ) to renovate its C-level lobby. DMR is forging stronger relationships with the St. Barnabas Health Care System to expand upon its completed adult day care and medical offices project. The Hackensack University Medical Center also used DMR's services for its Wellness Center renovation project.

LOCAL GOVERNMENTS — DMR AND THE GARDEN STATE

DMR has worked with and is currently developing projects for various municipalities in the Garden State. These projects include a 75,000-square-foot municipal justice complex for Jersey City and a 256,000-square-foot administration building for Bergen County (in association with The Hillier Group). Completed projects include a 7,500-square-foot addition to the River Edge Free Public Library, a Senior Citizen Activity Center in Rutherford, New Jersey, and several other libraries, public safety buildings, and municipal complexes. DMR also is involved in the redevelopment of the City of Elizabeth waterfront. When completed, this project will create a new public space to be enjoyed by area residents for years to come.

CORPORATE ALLIANCES

DMR's architectural accomplishments also reach into the tristate area's corporate sector. DMR worked in collaboration with WJC Associates to provide renovations for Sony's Manhattan showroom and other retail stores. The recently completed 136,000-square-foot Liberty Plaza office building in New Brunswick, New Jersey, is the new home of UMDNJ's administrative and support services and several area merchants located on street level. The firm intends to strengthen its corporate presence by developing alliances with more of the state's Fortune 500 and Fortune 100 companies in preparation for growth in the next century.

HONORING THE PAST

DMR Architects had the privilege of providing pro bono construction administration services for the New Jersey Vietnam Veterans' Memorial, located in Holmdel, New Jersey. Situated on the memorial site is an Education Center, opened in September 1998, for which DMR was the architect of record. This Educational Center is the only one of its kind dedicated to the Vietnam War. The center contains a circular wall mural that depicts history, events, and culture throughout the Vietnam era.

WHAT THE FUTURE HOLDS

DiCara Malasits and Rosenberg Architects has truly helped to develop the landscape of New Jersey in the twentieth century. Scores of residents and business professionals have at some time visited, worked, learned, or healed in a facility created by DMR's professional staff.

The firm will continue its prolific, innovative, and creative designs and plans for myriad clients as DMR journeys into the new millennium.

DMR Architects is proud to serve as the architect of record for the New Jersey Vietnam Veterans' Memorial, located in Holmdel, New Jersey.

MICHAEL GRAVES, ARCHITECT

THE INFORMED AND DISTINCTIVE DESIGNS OF MICHAEL GRAVES, ARCHITECT—RANGING FROM OFFICES, HOTELS, AND PRIVATE RESIDENCES TO CENTERS FOR CULTURE AND RECREATION—ARE ADMIRED AROUND THE WORLD

Michael Graves, one of the world's leading architects, has been at the forefront of architecture and interior design since he began his practice in Princeton, New Jersey, in 1964. The distinctive work of his firm, Michael Graves, Architect, is fresh and contemporary, yet it also draws on a knowledge of history and local context. In projects in the United States and throughout the world, Graves has created highly original, award-winning designs that are functional, efficient, site-specific, and sensitive to the local cultural context.

The firm is known for the diversity of its practice. Projects have included large, multiuse urban developments; corporate headquarters and other office buildings; hotels and conference centers; sports and recreation centers; facilities for educational and cultural institutions; multiple-family housing; and private residences.

Numerous buildings produced by Graves and his staff have been highly acclaimed. The Humana Building, a corporate-headquarters office tower in Louisville, Kentucky, was cited by *Time* magazine as "one of the best buildings of the decade [1980s]." Other much-praised office buildings include the award-winning headquarters of the World Bank Group's

Michael Graves, Architect, was the design architect for the 1.1 million-square-foot headquarters building for the International Finance Corporation of the World Bank Group in Washington, D.C., including the interior design of the common spaces, such as the auditorium, cafeteria, and training center. © Andrew Lautman

International Finance Corporation, which is on Pennsylvania Avenue in Washington, D.C.; the headquarters and showrooms for Miele Appliances, located on Route One near Princeton; and the Delaware River Port Authority Headquarters, in Camden, New Jersey.

Among his international projects, Graves has designed the headquarters for the Ministry of Culture in The Hague. Graves also created the Hyatt Regency Hotel and Office Building in Fukuoka, Japan, which received one of Japan's highest awards for the design of commercial projects. The Disney corporate headquarters in Burbank, California, the Walt Disney World Swan and the Dolphin hotels, in Orlando, Florida, and the Hotel New York at Euro-Disneyland Park, Paris, demonstrate the architect's range of design skills while reflecting Disney's goals for significant architecture that also delights and entertains. Designs created by Michael Graves for residential apartment buildings in the Art Deco district of Miami Beach, as well as in New York City and in Japan, are each given their own architectural character appropriate to their surrounding contexts.

The Hyatt Regency Hotel and Office Building in Fukuoka, Japan, received one of Japan's highest design awards, the first ever received by an American company. The 260-room hospitality component functions in tandem with the attached 120,000-square-foot office building and convention center. © Toyota Photo Studio, courtesy of Maeda Corporation

214 CREATING THE FUTURE

Graves has received the New Jersey Governor's Walt Whitman Award for Creative Achievement, the Indiana Arts Award, and the National Sculpture Society's Henry Hering Medal for inclusion of sculpture in architecture, and is considered one of New Jersey's most distinguished arts advocates.

Architectural projects for cultural and educational institutions—museums, theaters, libraries, and universities—have constituted an important part of the firm's practice since its inception. Among other such projects, Michael Graves and his staff designed the Denver Central Library and Pittsburgh's O'Reilly Theater. In New Jersey, Graves has been the architect for The Newark Museum since the late 1960s, and was responsible for a major renovation, which was opened to the public in 1989. This renovation received numerous prestigious awards locally and nationally, including the Downtown New Jersey award and a citation from New Jersey's Business and Industry Association, establishing the reputation of Michael Graves in New Jersey as a designer of civic architecture that enriches the daily life of its citizens.

Michael Graves is the Schirmer Professor of Architecture at Princeton University, where he has taught since 1962. He has received nine honorary doctorates from universities including Rutgers and the New Jersey Institute of Technology. Thus Graves imparts to the educational projects undertaken by his firm the experience and knowledge of a member of an academic community. Representative university projects include an arts and sciences classroom building for Richard Stockton College of New Jersey; a residence hall for the New Jersey Institute of Technology; an engineering research laboratory for the University of Cincinnati; a classroom and office building for the University of Virginia; and two museums for Emory University in Atlanta. In addition, Graves is the design architect for the headquarters office building, conference center, and Hall of Champions for the National Collegiate Athletic Association (NCAA), in Indianapolis.

The firm's five senior architects—Patrick Burke, John Diebboll, Gary Lapera, Karen Nichols, and Tom Rowe—are responsible for the day-to-day management of the practice and, along with Donald Strum of the products department, are integral members of the design process. The participation of senior-level staff has allowed Michael Graves to devote his time to architectural design and to the diversification of the firm's services in interiors and product design.

The design services of Michael Graves, Architect, often extend to the design of consumer products, graphics, artwork, and exhibitions. For example, in his designs for New Jersey–based Lenox, Graves created a full corporate-identity program, including a new logo; packaging for Lenox china, glassware, and giftware; and numerous Lenox retail stores and boutiques throughout the United States. For the Italian manufacturer Alessi, Graves has designed more than 100 tabletop products since the 1980s. One of these is his famous teakettle that features a whistling bird.

Under the trade name Graves Design, the firm has developed its own collection of furniture; lighting fixtures; hardware; tabletop and decorative objects; and personal accessories. These products are made available through the firm's relationships with major national retailers. Graves also has his own Studio Store, in Princeton, which features Graves Design products.

As part of its commission by the Lenox company to design a new corporate identity program, logo, and packaging for its china, glassware, and giftware, Michael Graves, Architect, also designed several retail stores and boutiques. © Kim Sargeant

The twenty-six-story, 525,000-square-foot Humana Building in downtown Louisville, Kentucky, was designed as the health care company's corporate headquarters. Special attention was paid to orienting the building toward the Ohio River and relating it to historic town houses on one side and a modern office tower on the other. © Paschall/Taylor

ARCHITECTURE 215

CUH2A, INC.

PRINCETON-BASED ARCHITECTURE AND ENGINEERING FIRM CUH2A, INC., HANDLES DIVERSE, TECHNICALLY SOPHISTICATED PROJECTS, EXPANDING ITS OPERATIONS WITH OFFICES IN CHICAGO, ILLINOIS; WASHINGTON, D.C.; AND RICHMOND, VIRGINIA

From its distinguished beginnings, when it won the competition to design the New Jersey Pavilion at the 1964 New York World's Fair, CUH2A, Inc., has evolved as a world-class architecture and engineering firm. Today the multidisciplinary practice is one of the largest design firms in the nation and ranks as the largest architecture/engineering firm in New Jersey.

By offering architecture, engineering, planning, and interior design services, CUH2A integrates imaginative design with innovative technology to meet the unique needs of its clients.

The firm serves corporations, educational institutions, and government agencies nationwide in a broad range of markets, including science and technology, education, research, hospitality, and entertainment. It has designed facilities for many Fortune 500 firms, including Pfizer, Merck, Procter & Gamble, Rhône–Poulenc Rorer, AT&T, Mobil, and Eli Lilly. The group has established a reputation for excellence in design for diverse client needs and building types and is particularly recognized for its execution of technically sophisticated projects.

Since its founding in 1962, CUH2A has grown in size from three partners to several hundred design professionals. In addition to its headquarters in Princeton, the firm has offices in Washington, D.C.; Richmond, Virginia; and Chicago, Illinois.

The name "CUH2A" is an acronym derived from the first initials of the last names of the original five partners: Philip S. Collins, Harrison J. Uhl Jr., Richard W. Hoisington, Kurt M. Anderson,

The Pioneer Hi-Bred International corporate headquarters in Johnston, Iowa, was designed to accommodate the seed corn manufacturer's strong, consistent growth. The 132,000-square-foot building features three above-ground levels for offices and a lower level for building operations and a print shop. This project was awarded a bronze medal for design by the American Institute of Architects, New Jersey Chapter.

In the atrium of this Pfizer office building in Groton, Connecticut, the linear aspect of the floor plan is minimized by a curved handrail. The form creates an edge between private offices to the north and functional public spaces, such as training and conference rooms and a library, to the south. Above the atrium, a continuous skylight brings natural light into the center of the building.

and Ahmed A. Azmy. Collins founded the firm in 1962 when he won the design competition for the 1964 New York World's Fair New Jersey Pavilion.

Uhl and Hoisington joined him to assist with the pavilion's contract documents and field inspection. Anderson joined the firm in 1965. The firm adopted its present name in 1976 when Azmy joined, completing the "2A."

For years CUH2A was known as one of the nation's premier designers of academic and corporate science facilities. In the 1980s the firm focused on developing a niche market in the area of pharmaceutical facilities. In the 1990s the firm expanded into new markets, such as corporate strategic planning, themed entertainment, corporate offices, and interiors.

CUH2A's full range of design services includes architecture, landscape architecture, space planning, interior design, graphic design, and lighting design. The firm's in-house engineering disciplines provide structural, HVAC, electrical, plumbing, fire protection, security, energy management, and central utility engineering. CUH2A offers comprehensive planning services, including site selection and evaluation, site master planning, strategic facilities planning, facility programming, and

CREATING THE FUTURE

laboratory planning. The firm also provides cost estimating, information technology design, computer-aided facility management, move management, and construction administration services.

"Our mission is to serve our clients' business goals," says John R. Rivers, AIA, chairman of the board of directors. "With dynamic economic conditions, we must remain agile to help our clients respond to shifts within their own markets. To accomplish this, we mobilize the firm to provide solutions that meet our clients' evolving needs."

The firm has many high-profile projects in progress, including AT&T's 2.8 million-square-foot corporate research and development campus in Middletown, New Jersey. CUH2A is providing site planning, facility planning, and a full range of architectural and engineering services in support of AT&T's decision to colocate employees at its central New Jersey facility. When completed in 1999, the five-building complex will accommodate an employee population of 6,200.

In 1995 the New Jersey Economic Development Authority (NJEDA) hired CUH2A to design its new Technology Centre of New Jersey. The center provides laboratory and production facilities for emerging technology companies. CUH2A developed a multiphased master plan that allows for a total build-out of 836,000 square feet on the NJEDA's fifty-two-acre site in North Brunswick. Several buildings have been designed and the second new building, Tech II, a 60,000-square-foot research facility, is currently under construction.

In 1998 CUH2A acquired the Washington, D.C.–based architecture, interiors, and planning firm Cooper • Lecky Architects, PC, to serve the Washington area.

"This new entity increases our geographic base of operations, augmenting our Princeton office," says CUH2A president

The tower of the Health Sciences Facility at the University of Maryland at Baltimore is the institution's glowing symbol on the Baltimore cityscape. A functional integration of architectural image and mechanical systems, the tower houses fume-hood exhaust stacks to ensure that the fumes are discharged downwind of their intake. CUH2A designed this project in a joint venture with Ayers Saint Gross.

Richard L. Henry, AIA. "Having an affiliate office in Washington significantly enhances our ability to serve the federal market."

In 1998 CUH2A also established a branch office in Chicago, Illinois, to more effectively serve clients in the Midwest. The Chicago office provides the same comprehensive level of services offered by the firm's Princeton headquarters. Current projects under development by CUH2A's Chicago office include the design of additions and renovations to Nycomed Amersham's biotechnology facility in Arlington Heights, Illinois; the master plan for the existing thirty-acre research and development campus of USG Corporation, and new facilities in the Midwest for Duron Paint and Wallcoverings. Other projects include the design of renovations to the Marriott International hotels in downtown Chicago and Oak Brook, Illinois; and in St. Louis, Missouri.

Most recently CUH2A established CUH2A Entertainment, a new division devoted exclusively to the design of facilities for entertainment and entertainment-related uses. This division is an extension of CUH2A's continued diversification of its practice to include theme parks, hotels and resorts, themed retail stores, and restaurants.

As CUH2A continues to expand, to respond to the marketplace, and to build its history, it still is guided by its original mission statement: The people of CUH2A provide creative solutions in support of the goals of the firm's clients. "CUH2A has learned to grow and adjust to the ups and downs of the market," states Rivers. "Throughout the decades, our quality of service has never been compromised, as demonstrated in our ability to maintain long-standing relationships with clients well after their projects are completed."

The child care center for Merck & Co., Inc., in Whitehouse Station, New Jersey, provides a homelike setting for the children of the pharmaceutical company's employees. The 17,000-square-foot facility is articulated as a series of connected "houses" grouped along a skylighted corridor. This project received an Award of Merit from the National Commercial Builder's Council.

ARCHITECTURE 217

EDWARDS AND KELCEY, INC.

THE PLANNING AND DESIGN PROWESS OF EDWARDS AND KELCEY, INC., IS SEEN ACROSS THE STATE IN BRIDGES, TUNNELS, HIGHWAYS, HOSPITALS, OFFICES, AIRPORTS, RAILROADS, UTILITIES, AND COMMUNICATIONS FACILITIES

Edwards and Kelcey, Inc., was established in 1946 by Dean Edwards and Guy Kelcey, both pioneers in the field of transportation planning and engineering. Since its founding, Edwards and Kelcey has grown to be a highly respected, multidisciplinary planning, engineering, and consulting firm.

The company is privately held with headquarters in Morristown, New Jersey, and offices nationwide. Edwards and Kelcey is among the top 100 consulting and design firms in the nation, ranked by *Engineering News Record*'s Annual Survey.

With more than five decades of experience, the firm has proven accomplishments in the planning, design, and construction of the state's transportation and communication infrastructure. Edwards and Kelcey's professional consulting and engineering services have been applied to New Jersey's most challenging undertakings.

Edwards and Kelcey's staff of more than 650 engineers, architects, planners, environmental specialists, and construction inspectors provide the expertise and experience that has created a reputation of dependability within the industry. Edwards and Kelcey, Inc., also is the holding company for Edwards and Kelcey Wireless, LLC; Edwards and Kelcey Constructors, Inc.; Iffland Kavanaugh Waterbury; and Value Engineering Incorporated (VEI).

Edwards and Kelcey Wireless has been a leader in wireless communications for twenty-five years, providing construction services integrated with design, engineering, and architectural expertise to create complete systems.

Edwards and Kelcey's planning and design experience is evident throughout New Jersey. Shown here, the Secaucus Transfer Station.

Shown at left is the interchange of Route One and College Road in Princeton, designed by Edwards and Kelcey. © Leigh Photographic Group/Janice Ford

Edwards and Kelcey Constructors specializes in providing turnkey telecommunications construction of wireless facilities, including towers, antennas, and rooftop installations. Custom-designed site concealment towers reflect the company's commitment to creative structural solutions that address environmental, community, and zoning concerns.

Iffland Kavanaugh Waterbury is a structural engineering and architecture firm specializing in seismic analysis and retrofit design, structural rehabilitation and restoration design, and marine engineering design. VEI provides project/construction management, value engineering, claims analysis, and scheduling and cost-estimating services.

The firm's professionals are experienced at taking even the most complicated projects from concept through to completion. Edwards and Kelcey has performed construction management and inspection services for transportation and major building projects for the past four decades. These projects have included the construction and improvement of highways; bridges; tunnels; corporate headquarters, hospitals, offices, and other buildings; airports; railroads; utilities; and telecommunications facilities.

Says Edwards and Kelcey chairman and CEO Ronald A. Wiss, "Our firm provides complete professional services from initial planning through construction, and the ability to effectively respond to any issue that arises."

ARCHITECTURE

220 CREATING THE FUTURE

BUSINESS SERVICES AND RETAIL

UNITED PARCEL SERVICE

UNITED PARCEL SERVICE IMPROVES SHIPPING ACCURACY AND CREATES NEW CUSTOMER OPTIONS BY USING ADVANCED INFORMATION TECHNOLOGY, SUCH AS ITS NEW ELECTRONIC DOCUMENT PROCESSING SYSTEM

Founded in 1907, United Parcel Service (UPS) is one of the largest express carrier and package delivery companies in the world, serving more than 200 countries and territories with an unmatched array of product options and a firm commitment to service. Headquartered in Atlanta, Georgia, UPS has been named by *Fortune* magazine as the most admired company in the transportation industry for the past fifteen consecutive years. *Fortune* magazine also has rated UPS as the world's most admired mail, package, and freight delivery company.

UPS transports more than 3.1 billion parcels and documents annually—this translates to about 12 million packages per day. The value of the packages UPS handles each year in the United States is equal to about 5.5 percent of the nation's gross domestic product. To serve its customers,

UPS is committed to global commerce, as represented above by the Eiffel Tower, in Paris, France—one of 200 countries and territories served. The broad UPS portfolio offers time-definite, door-to-door shipping with single-carrier responsibility to and from locations worldwide.

UPS has more than 500 aircraft, 157,000 vehicles, and 1,713 facilities worldwide.

UPS has more than 329,000 employees around the world today, including about 14,900 people in its New Jersey workforce.

"I am proud to say that UPS has deep roots in New Jersey," says Jim Kelly, UPS chairman and CEO, a New Jersey native and alumnus of Rutgers University. "In our main data center in Mahwah, information regarding millions of packages is processed every day. It is the technological nerve center of our company, and it will play an enormous role in the future of UPS and the future of our industry."

In New Jersey and in many other states, UPS participates in Welfare to Work initiatives, which offer an opportunity for strong partnerships between the public and private sectors with the purpose of ensuring an educated workforce. UPS also has forged relationships with the states of Pennsylvania and New Jersey to help solve issues of

Today's UPS fleet began with the purchase of a single aircraft in 1981. It now is one of the ten largest airlines in the United States.

222 CREATING THE FUTURE

transportation for its Welfare to Work employees who work at the UPS hub in Philadelphia or the UPS regional air operation in Camden, across the river from Philadelphia. UPS worked with New Jersey Transit to implement a bus system between the cities to provide the needed transportation for employees.

UPS employees support and actively participate in many programs to benefit the community. As part of its employee-driven region/district grants program, UPS provides local nonprofit agencies with the support and funding necessary to meet existing and urgent needs of communities. Grants are awarded to community charitable organizations throughout the United States, including several in New Jersey. UPS also serves the greater community and, among other activities, was a partner in the 1998 Olympic Games, as it will be again in 2000.

In its core business of package delivery, UPS uses information technology to help improve shipping accuracy and to supply its customers with more ways to manage and track their shipments. UPS has been cited for its leadership in the use of technology, which was the basis for two Computerworld Smithsonian Awards the company received for creating an International Shipment Processing System and its global telecommunications network. UPS has invested more than $9 billion in its information technology infrastructure and systems. Worldwide, UPS has 165,000 PCs, 80,000 handheld computers, and one of the largest DB-2 databases in the world. UPS also is the world's largest user of cellular technology, with one million calls daily.

The UPS interactive Web site (www.ups.com), launched in December 1994, allows customers to download software, calculate and compare rates, prepare international documentation, locate drop-off centers, request a pickup, and track packages.

Expanding the UPS service portfolio to include electronic document delivery is the company's latest electronic commerce initiative. This new service, UPS Document Exchange, is now available worldwide. UPS Document Exchange is a suite of delivery and information management services for transmitting anything that can be converted to an electronic file. The service currently offers a choice of two Internet delivery options: UPS OnLine Courier and UPS OnLine Dossier.

UPS OnLine Courier allows customers to send documents to anyone, regardless of the E-mail software, operating system, and hardware used by either sender or receiver. Customers have several security options, including password protection and encryption.

UPS OnLine Dossier, an insured service, features a unique double-encryption process to provide the highest level of encryption and verification technology available globally for maximum security on a public network.

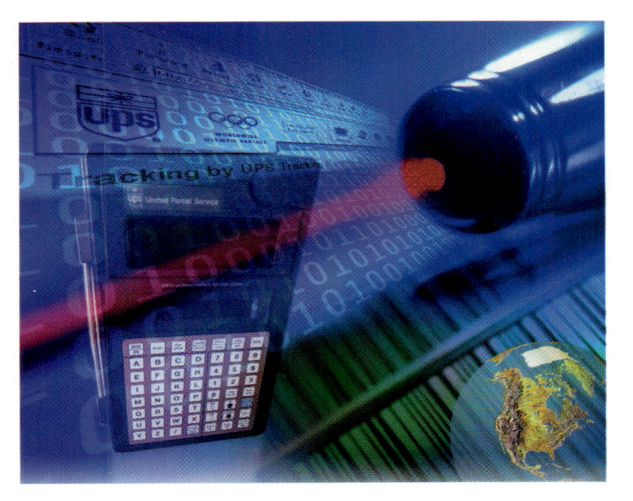

UPS is becoming as visible in the virtual world—evoked in the montage at left—as it is in the physical world, with a wide range of information technology systems that expand customers' shipping options.

In another of its recent innovations, UPS will offer the industry's first comprehensive guarantee of commercial ground service. Without any change in rates, customers shipping packages to a commercial address will be given a guaranteed delivery date—even when the package is being shipped by ground; if the package doesn't arrive by its guaranteed date, shipping is free. This initiative is a response to customers' needs for planned, scheduled deliveries with options for urgent express shipments. Based on current volume, the new guarantee will apply to more than 7 million commercial ground packages delivered daily by UPS, in addition to the 1.8 million air-express and international deliveries that already have guaranteed delivery.

"At UPS we insist that our people attain success not by cutting corners, but by doing things the right way," says CEO Kelly. "It is this philosophy that has helped UPS grow into a $22 billion company. UPS is employee-owned, which means that each of us has a big stake in seeing the company succeed."

The reputation of the UPS driver is synonymous with courteous, dependable service.

BUSINESS SERVICES AND RETAIL 223

TOYS "R" US

Toys "R" Us prides itself on providing what customers want most—huge merchandise selections, value pricing, brightly designed stores, and excellent customer service

The Toys "R" Us store above exemplifies the colorfully bright store design that customers recognize.

Against the backdrop of a country restoring its spirit after World War II, twenty-five-year-old Toys "R" Us founder Charles Lazarus set up his first baby store business. As he learned the ins and outs of running his first store, he realized that one of his most valuable skills was the ability to listen. He listened to his customers and provided what they needed. "I need a toy for my baby and some for my older children," was something he heard over and over. So he began to stock and sell toys.

In 1957 Lazarus put his first Toys "R" Us concept into action by selling toys in a large retail environment, offering a wide variety at discount prices. Moving into the 1980s fueled by energy, enthusiasm, and optimism, Toys "R" Us opened even more stores in the United States and began expanding internationally. Today Toys "R" Us is a name every parent and child knows, and its backward "R" logo is recognized everywhere.

With more than 1,450 stores in 27 countries, Toys "R" Us continues to mark milestone after milestone. In 1997 it acquired Baby Superstore and merged it with its own store Babies "R" Us, thereby expanding its business to encompass all the kinds of products purchased for babies. With this unique move, the company came full circle to Charles Lazarus's original concept—providing what customers need. Toys "R" Us continues to focus on what today's experienced, value-conscious consumer wants, with bright stores, baby and gift registries, and improved customer service. The company also is exploring new ways to reach consumers through a number of avenues, including the Internet, at www.toysrus.com. Its traditional offering of a great selection of merchandise priced for good value is as strong today as it was fifty years ago.

Toys "R" Us is dedicated to giving back to its employees, customers, and communities. The company is a leader in offering equal opportunity employment and workforce diversity. In addition, it established the Toys "R" Us Children's Benefit Fund to provide support for programs and health initiatives that benefit children. Toys "R" Us also is a leader in recognizing the needs of differently abled children; in conjunction with the National Lekotek Center, it produced a *Toy Guide for Differently-Abled Kids* to assist customers in making informed decisions about toy selection for children with special needs.

"I think we are in the best business in the whole world," Lazarus says.

As shown at left, the founder's original concept for the success of Toys "R" Us prevails: a large retail environment offering a variety of toys at discount prices.

224 CREATING THE FUTURE

BUSINESS SERVICES AND RETAIL 225

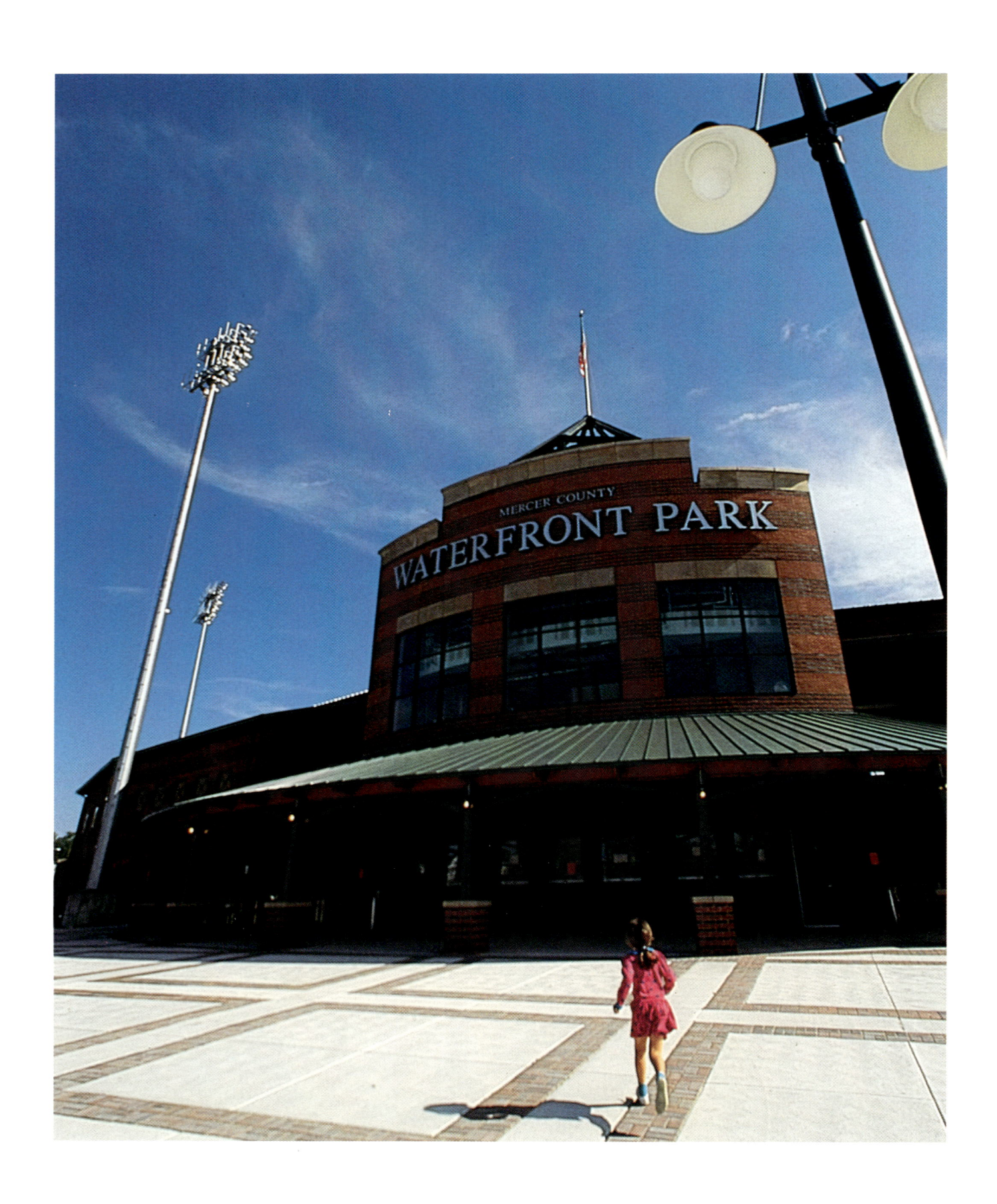

LOCATION, LOCATION, LOCATION

226 CREATING THE FUTURE

CHAPTER SEVENTEEN

NO VACANCY. THESE WORDS BRING SMILES TO THE FACES OF COMMERCIAL DEVELOPERS. AND THEY APTLY CAPTURE THE NEW JERSEY REAL ESTATE MARKET AT THE BEGINNING OF THE NEW MILLENNIUM. AFTER A SLOW START, REAL ESTATE SPECULATION SOARED IN THE LATTER PART OF THE 1990S. IN 1997 ALONE, INDUSTRY EXPERTS ESTIMATE THAT THERE WAS SOME $630 MILLION IN NEW COMMERCIAL AND INDUSTRIAL CONSTRUCTION STATEWIDE.

Growth in the current office market is even greater than it was during the bull market of the mid-1980s.

You might not even describe what is going on in New Jersey as speculative development anymore. The northern part of the state comprises the sixth-largest office market in the country, and over 70 percent of the space in buildings that have recently sprouted there has been pre-leased in build-to-suit situations. At the same time, an industry once ruled by small, family-owned businesses is increasingly dominated by Real Estate Investment Trusts, or REITs.

Prime Real Estate

The fast-paced tempo of the real estate market reflects the obvious advantages that New Jersey has offered companies for over two centuries. The state is perfectly situated, near the metropolitan hubs of New York and Philadelphia, and today it boasts an infrastructure of top-quality interstate highways, rail lines, airports, and shipping ports. The recent boom also reflects an aggressive effort by Governor Christie Whitman to encourage corporate relocations to the Garden State. "Open for Business" is one of the slogans the state has been using in its marketing efforts.

Morris County, where office vacancy rates were more than 30 percent at the height of the recession, is now one of the strongest markets in the state. The sub-region around Morristown, an area populated by law firms, accounting firms, and corporate offices of the Fortune 100, has seen its vacancy rates tumble to below 5 percent. According to the New Jersey Chapter of the National Association of Industrial and Office Properties, Middlesex and Morris Counties lead the state in new office and industrial construction, followed by

OPPOSITE: *The Mercer County Waterfront Park stadium is the scene of many a good time for Trenton Thunder minor-league baseball fans. Completed in 1994 at a cost of $17.2 million, the 6,341-seat stadium features two picnic areas for group outings, standing-room-only viewing from the concourse, sixteen luxury suites, and a Stadium Club Restaurant. The concourse level bustles with activity during the games as fans visit the concessions, gift shop, newsstand, inflatable speed-pitch area for children, and information booth.* © Scott Barrow. ABOVE: *New construction projects flourish in New Jersey at the end of the twentieth century.* © Kelly/Mooney

LOCATION, LOCATION, LOCATION 227

PROPERTY VALUES

THE PASTORAL VALLEYS OF MORRIS AND SOMERSET COUNTIES CONTAIN SOME OF THE WORLD'S MOST OPULENT ESTATES. THEIR PAST AND PRESENT OWNERS HAVE SUCH NOTABLE NAMES AS VANDERBILT, ROCKEFELLER, ONASSIS, AND KING HASSAN II OF MOROCCO.

Mercer and Bergen Counties. Overall office vacancy rates have been hovering around 12 percent.

In the late 1990s the state saw a flood of mega-deals and capital-raising as institutional investors and banks formed REITs, mutual funds that raise money to invest in real estate. Saddle Brook–based Vornado Realty Trust is one of the nation's most aggressive REITs. Its holdings include Chicago's world-famous Merchandise Mart, a property long owned by the Kennedy family. Mack-Cali Realty in Cranford is a $3.5-billion REIT formed in 1997 through a merger of two veteran developer families, the Macks and the Calis. The firm already controls some 8 percent of New Jersey's office space, including about 20 percent of all Class A facilities, and has plans for six new office projects totaling over five million square feet in Jersey City.

BRINGING THE PAST INTO THE FUTURE

New construction isn't the only reason the state is experiencing a strong commercial real estate market. Gale and Wentworth, LLC, of Florham Park, has led the way on major revitalization projects, in which old corporate structures are re-engineered for new corporate tenants. The 575,000-square-foot former IBM campus in Franklin Lakes has been altered to suit the needs of Merck-Medco, while the 410,000-square-foot former Prentice-Hall office complex in Englewood Cliffs now serves Citibank.

Moreover, keen developers are redeveloping and renovating dilapidated buildings and formerly unusable sites throughout the state, providing both an economic benefit

A raceway was built on the Passaic River to harness the power of the Great Falls for the city of Paterson. Today visitors to Paterson can see the partially restored structure. Shown here, an 1888 construction site. Courtesy, Great Falls Visitor Center

228 CREATING THE FUTURE

ABOVE: *The old makes way as this Newark complex is demolished. © Fred Charles/Tony Stone Images.* BELOW: *Parsippany-based Sordoni Skanska engineers at the site of a $300-million AT&T complex. Courtesy, New Jersey Business & Industry Association*

and an aesthetic one to the surrounding areas. Many of New Jersey's commercial buildings date as far back as the 1800s when the state was an industrial powerhouse, and a great many of these sites sat vacant until recently. The ability of developers to adapt existing properties has prolonged the lives of historic buildings. One classic example is the former Maxwell House Coffee plant in Hoboken, with its magnificent views of the Hudson River and the New York City skyline. It now houses both residential and retail tenants.

But that's only the beginning. In Summit the old county courthouse has been transformed into a stylish office headquarters. In Paterson the city spearheaded the conversion of its old redbrick factories and warehouses surrounding the historic Great Falls into a major downtown art center. Private developers recently rescued one of New Jersey's oldest buildings, the Essex County Courthouse in Newark, designed by Cass Gilbert, the renowned architect of the United States Custom House and the Woolworth Building in New York City.

Major redevelopment projects are also happening on inner-city land that was once thought unsalvageable due to industrial contamination. Through the state's new "brownfields" program, generous tax breaks, liberal liability regulations, and minimal cleanup costs have encouraged companies to revitalize industrially tainted

GOOD FORTUNE

WITH TWENTY-THREE FORTUNE 500 COMPANIES HEADQUARTERED IN NEW JERSEY, THE STATE ARGUABLY HAS THE NATION'S LARGEST CONCENTRATION OF MAJOR CORPORATIONS.

land. The program was created by the 1993 Industrial Sites Recovery Act and has been utilized by several cities. Perth Amboy, which intends to revitalize no fewer than six sites, is one such city. By 1998 the state had already received about three hundred applications for brownfields projects.

The most famous brownfields turnaround happened in 1994, in Trenton, when the Trenton Thunder minor-league baseball team began playing on the green grass of the city's immaculate new Mercer County Waterfront Park. Previously, the site was contaminated with industrial waste. Trenton continues to lead the way in brownfields redevelopment, as two brand-new factories have sprouted on what was once the old Crane Pottery site and the old Champale Brewery. In 1998 Vice

A LONG HISTORY

FOUNDED IN 1664, ELIZABETH IS NEW JERSEY'S OLDEST ENGLISH TOWN. NAMED FOR ELIZABETH CARTERET, THE WIFE OF A BIG NEW JERSEY LANDOWNER, IT IS THE STATE'S FOURTH-LARGEST CITY TODAY.

Constructed and operated by the New Jersey Sports and Exposition Authority, the Meadowlands Sports Complex in East Rutherford is home to professional football, ice hockey, basketball, and soccer games, as well as horse racing, concerts, family shows, and world-class entertainment events. © SuperStock

230 CREATING THE FUTURE

a credit card. United National shares the income from the program with its partner, allowing funds to be earmarked for special needs, including youth recreational programs. It is through programs such as these that United National not only serves the needs of a community today, but just as importantly invests in its future.

Helping small and midsize businesses realize their dreams is the goal of the bank's business relationship managers. They understand that each business is different and has its own unique set of challenges, so they take the time to get to know each one and to understand its needs. At United National, businesses have quick and convenient access to a full menu of business banking services. The Capital Group, United National's newest subsidiary, stands ready to deliver the customized lending that some businesses need when traditional financing options are insufficient, highly restrictive, or unavailable altogether.

The bank's Trust and Investment Services Division has built its reputation by combining innovative services with a disciplined approach and a proven track record of outstanding performance. Employees maintain an active and responsive relationship with each of the bank's clients, putting client needs first while continuing to discover and capitalize upon new opportunities for them. In today's ever-changing financial marketplace, where more and more trust accounts are being serviced outside the state, United National is somewhat unique—all of its investment management and administrative decisions are still made in New Jersey.

Bank employees are involved and visible in the community. It is the bank's belief that an institution such as United National—true to its community roots—must have highly motivated employees who are readily accessible, responsive, and focused on creating value for customers.

"The communities we serve are our lifeblood," says Gregor. "In what is a true community partnership, they provide opportunities for our future growth and we, in turn, provide the resources for their mutual growth and prosperity." United National's continuing success is testimony to the drive, commitment, and hard work of its people and their willingness to challenge traditional ways of thinking. The bank brings together the breadth of products that today's consumers and businesses want, with a reputation for outstanding service. That, together with its tradition of promoting the growth and vitality of the communities it serves, forms the framework for the bank's business strategy of preserving its community bank culture.

"We look forward to the challenges and opportunities brought about through today's rapidly changing business environment," says Gregor. "United National has a strong history of responding to the needs of our customers and communities. We will continue to build on our success."

Being responsive to customer needs has long been a trademark of United National's philosophy. The bank's officers function as more than just bankers—they strive to serve as valued advisors who can not only implement solutions but also help to craft them. © Joe Diamond Photography

At left is a photograph, taken in 1926, of The Plainfield Trust Company, the predecessor to United National Bank. Largely unchanged and recently restored, the building today serves as United National's Park Avenue Office in Plainfield. © Howard Rowe Photographer

FINANCIAL SERVICES AND INSURANCE 251

COLUMBIA SAVINGS BANK

AN INDEPENDENT INSTITUTION WITH $1.7 BILLION IN ASSETS, COLUMBIA SAVINGS BANK IS COMMITTED TO THE LOCAL COMMUNITY AND TO PROVIDING PERSONAL SERVICE FOR BOTH BUSINESS AND INDIVIDUAL BANKING NEEDS

Columbia Savings Bank is the perfect choice for banking customers who want a full range of banking services provided with a personalized touch. As one of New Jersey's largest and strongest independent community banks, the institution continues to be a leader in financial services for individuals and businesses around the state.

"At Columbia Savings Bank we know our customers by name," says Abraham Mamary, Columbia Savings Bank's president and CEO. "We not only are part of the community, but we also are very much involved in community affairs. This close community involvement is what differentiates Columbia Savings Bank from large banks."

In every town where the bank has a branch, Columbia Savings forms a partnership with the community, joining organizations such as the Rotary Club and the Lion's Club, supporting charitable events, sponsoring sports teams, and providing scholarship opportunities. From its annual charity golf outing to its involvement with Habitat for Humanity, Columbia Savings demonstrates a strong commitment to the community.

"The rapport we have with our customers facilitates our role as a true community bank," Mamary says.

Abraham Mamary is president and chief executive officer of Columbia Savings Bank.

Columbia Savings Bank's new corporate headquarters in Fair Lawn, New Jersey, includes a full-service banking facility.

Columbia Savings Bank is really two banks in one—a bank providing both business and personal services. It offers a full range of consumer services for individuals and families and also specializes in commercial lending. As an SBA (Small Business Administration) Preferred Lender, the bank is strongly committed to meeting the financing needs of small-, medium-, and large-size businesses. It has the ability to approve SBA loans in-house.

Columbia Savings Bank, with $1.7 billion in assets, operates in Bergen, Burlington, Camden, Morris, Gloucester, Passaic, Union, Middlesex, and Monmouth Counties. The bank's future plans include further growth throughout New Jersey.

In 1996 the charter of Columbia Savings Bank as a mutual savings bank was changed to that of a mutual holding company. The move, which is similar to steps being taken by more and more community banks, allows the bank to raise capital in the capital markets when necessary, and gives it other operating advantages. This structure also provides strong protection against unwanted takeovers by other financial institutions.

"This restructuring makes a statement that Columbia Savings Bank is here to stay," says Mamary. "It solidifies our determination to remain a highly respected independent community savings institution."

Columbia Savings Bank's new, three-story, 68,000-square-foot corporate headquarters in Fair Lawn is a spacious complex that consolidates the bank's various divisions and serves as a full-service banking facility, including three drive-up windows and a twenty-four-hour drive-up ATM. By building its new headquarters in its hometown of Fair Lawn, Columbia Savings has reaffirmed its commitment to the community and its commitment to developing a statewide network of banking offices from its Garden State roots. According to expert real estate professionals, the headquarters is one of the first significant new office buildings in Bergen County since the end of the last construction boom in the early 1990s.

The new headquarters building is quite different from the bank's original home—an old schoolhouse where several Fair Lawn business leaders formed the Fair Lawn Building and Loan Association in 1927. The institution subsequently moved, first to a local lumber yard, then to quarters in Fair Lawn's Borough Hall and, in 1941, to its own building at Fair Lawn Avenue and River Road. The Fair Building and Loan Association was renamed the First Savings and Loan Association of Fair Lawn, in 1940, and later Columbia Savings Bank, in 1970.

"We were founded in Fair Lawn seventy years ago with a community-minded spirit that has followed our growth throughout the state," Mamary says. "Our new headquarters, fittingly still in Fair Lawn, reaffirms our strong, ongoing commitment to the banking needs of New Jersey residents, backed by quality service and financial products that people can always count on."

Columbia Savings Bank proudly celebrated its seventieth anniversary during 1997 and recorded another year of progress marked by healthy growth and further expansion. As a local bank, Columbia Savings is dedicated to serving the borrowing needs of individuals and commercial customers alike and looks forward to serving its home state well into the next millennium.

As part of an annual event, "Christmas in April," volunteers in partnership with Columbia Savings Bank refurbish and paint the homes of needy senior citizens. The bank's year-round community efforts help to improve the quality of life in the towns where it conducts business.

Columbia Savings Bank

President and CEO of Columbia Savings Bank, Abraham Mamary (front row, right), receives a plaque from SBA New Jersey deputy district director, James Kocsi (front row, left), designating the bank as a Small Business Administration (SBA) Preferred Lender, one of twenty-two in New Jersey. The bank now can approve SBA loans within twenty-four hours. In attendance are (from left) SBA New Jersey assistant district director, William Boone; Columbia Savings senior vice president and chief lending officer, Alex Grinewicz; and vice president of commercial lending, Mark Krukar.

FINANCIAL SERVICES AND INSURANCE 253

THE DUN & BRADSTREET CORPORATION

THE DUN & BRADSTREET CORPORATION ASSISTS CUSTOMERS IN MAKING MORE PROFITABLE DECISIONS BY PROVIDING INFORMATION THAT CAN HELP REDUCE RISK

Creating The Dun & Bradstreet Corporation of the twenty-first century is the focus today at the world's largest business information company. The corporation consists of the Dun & Bradstreet operating company (D&B), the leading provider of business-to-business credit, marketing and purchasing information, and receivables management services, and Moody's Investors Service (Moody's), the leading debt-rating agency and a major publisher of financial information for the capital markets.

Chairman and chief executive officer Volney Taylor and his senior management team are the architects of the current Dun & Bradstreet Corporation (NYSE: DNB), which employs approximately 13,000 people in 39 countries. The corporation's recent transformation began in 1996, when it spun off two corporations, Cognizant Corporation and ACNielsen Corporation. The Dun & Bradstreet Corporation then consisted of the D&B operating company, Moody's and Reuben H. Donnelley. In 1998 Donnelley, the largest independent marketer of Yellow Pages in the United States, and Dun & Bradstreet separated into two corporations.

"With a 157-year history, The Dun & Bradstreet Corporation is one of the oldest and most respected brand names in the business world," says Taylor. "As a result of the spin-offs, we are a leaner and better focused corporation that is poised for growth."

While The Dun & Bradstreet Corporation is new in many ways, its ability to serve its customers remains a constant. Customers rely on Dun & Bradstreet to provide the insights they need to build profitable, high-quality business relationships with their customers, investors, and business partners. The corporation is focused on transforming information from a variety of sources into a powerful decision-making resource that is a critical component in all decision-making and business processes.

MOODY'S INVESTORS SERVICE

Moody's, which was founded by John Moody in 1900 and acquired by The Dun & Bradstreet

Volney Taylor is chairman and chief executive officer of The Dun & Bradstreet Corporation.

Dun & Bradstreet executives (left to right) Ronald J. Burton, vice president–Business Development; Volney Taylor, chairman and chief executive officer; William F. Doescher, senior vice president and chief communications officer; and New Jersey governor Christine Todd Whitman gather for a ribbon-cutting ceremony at the 1997 opening of The Dun & Bradstreet Corporation headquarters in Murray Hill, New Jersey.

Corporation in 1962, is the leading global credit rating agency. It publishes credit opinions, research, and ratings on fixed-income securities and on issuers of securities and other credit obligations. It also provides a broad range of business and financial information.

Moody's employs approximately 600 analysts and has a total of 1,200 associates located around the world. The company maintains offices in 12 countries and provides ratings and information on governmental and commercial entities in more than 100 countries. The credit ratings help investors analyze the credit risks associated with fixed-income securities, as well as create efficiencies in fixed-income markets by providing reliable, credible, and independent assessments of credit risk. For issuers, Moody's services increase market liquidity and may reduce transaction costs.

In recent years Moody's has improved the depth of its analysis function and enhanced its research offerings. The move has helped bolster service to customers, which include investors, depositors, creditors, investment banks, commercial banks and other financial intermediaries, as well as a wide range of corporate and governmental issuers of securities.

Moody's publishes rating opinions on a broad range of credit obligations. These include various

254 CREATING THE FUTURE

United States corporate and governmental obligations, international cross-border notes and bonds, domestic obligations in foreign local markets, structured finance securities and commercial paper issues. In recent years, Moody's has moved beyond its traditional bond ratings activity, assigning ratings to insurance companies' obligations, bank loans, derivative product companies, bank deposits and other bank debt, managed funds, and derivatives. At the end of 1997, Moody's had outstanding ratings on approximately 85,000 corporate and 62,000 public finance obligations. Ratings are disseminated to the public through a variety of print and electronic media including real-time systems, widely used by securities traders and investors.

DUN & BRADSTREET

The D&B operating company is the world's leading provider of business-to-business information. Companies of all sizes in all industries around the world use D&B information in both the front and back office to better manage customers and suppliers. By embedding D&B information into business systems and processes, companies can achieve a direct and seamless link between back- and front-office operations.

D&B information includes global business identification and corporate linkage information on more than 50 million companies and risk-assessment information on more than 11 million companies in the United States. As the largest source of business information in the world, D&B can help companies:

- Analyze markets and identify profitable prospects,
- Maximize revenue from current customers,
- Evaluate, consolidate and leverage vendor relationships,
- Streamline and automate risk management,
- Improve cash flow through better collection efforts.

The integration of D&B information within the supply and demand chain begins by applying D&B's unique Data Universal Numbering System (D-U-N-S® Number) to a company's vendors and customers. The D&B D-U-N-S Number, the most widely used standard numbering system in the world, can identify companies by location, industry, country and corporate affiliations, linking a parent company to its branches, subsidiaries and divisions. D&B uses the numbering system to update files, eliminate duplicate records and analyze customers and vendors for increased sales

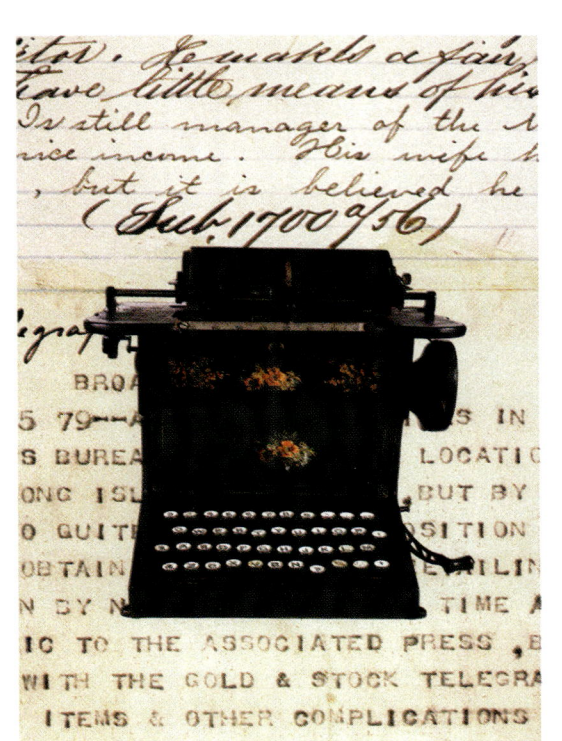

Dun & Bradstreet has always been a pioneer in adopting new technologies and innovations. In 1874 its predecessor, R. G. Dun & Company, was the first business to order a commercial typewriter, purchasing 100 "machines for writing," at a total cost of $5,500. The model, known as the "Remington No. 1," is shown at left. In the background is a handwritten report (at top) and an early typewriter report (below) for comparison.

and reduced spending. It has been adopted by governments, corporations, industries and trade associations as the way to improve the accuracy and usefulness of business information in databases.

"Companies can enhance their internal processes by integrating D&B information in their decision-support and analytical tools, enabling consistent and automated decision making," says Taylor. "As companies around the world turn to Enterprise Resource Planning and Enterprise Relationship Management, D&B is positioned to embed its information in these technologies and other decision-making systems."

D&B also uses the D-U-N-S Number to maintain and continually update its database. Every day the company makes 950,000 updates to its information. The company integrates hundreds of millions of pieces of information, ranging from trade styles to trade experiences to financial statements on both public and private companies into one easily accessible database.

D&B distributes its information through a variety of channels, including the Internet, partnerships, direct on-line access, paper, fax, telephone, and service consultants.

In 1841 Lewis Tappan (left) founded The Mercantile Agency with the purpose of helping merchants reduce credit risks. Its successful credit reporting was augmented by methods developed by John M. Bradstreet (center) and R. G. Dun (right), and the firm next became R. G. Dun & Company and ultimately today's Dun & Bradstreet Corporation.

The Dun & Bradstreet Corporation

FINANCIAL SERVICES AND INSURANCE 255

MERRILL LYNCH & CO., INC.

A LEADER IN GLOBAL FINANCIAL SERVICES, WITH CLIENT ASSETS OF MORE THAN $1.4 TRILLION, AND WITH 10,300 EMPLOYEES THROUGHOUT THE STATE, MERRILL LYNCH & CO., INC., IS EXPANDING ITS OPERATIONS IN NEW JERSEY

The Merrill Lynch corporate campus in Princeton encompasses training facilities and an administration building.

With locations throughout New Jersey, Merrill Lynch & Co., Inc., is not only one of the state's largest employers, but it also is a leading global financial management and advisory company with a presence in forty-five countries, across six continents. Merrill Lynch serves the needs of both individual and institutional clients with a diverse range of financial services, including:
- Financial planning
- Business financial services
- Securities underwriting
- Trading and brokering
- Investment banking and advisory services
- Foreign exchange trading
- Commodities and derivatives
- Banking and lending
- Mortgages and credit
  - Insurance
  - Retirement services
  - Research

With client assets totaling more than $1.4 trillion, Merrill Lynch is a leader in planning-based financial advice and management for individuals and small businesses. As an investment bank, according to Securities Data Company, Merrill Lynch has been the top global underwriter of debt and equity securities for eight years running and a leading strategic advisor to corporations, governments, institutions, and individuals worldwide. Through Merrill Lynch Asset Management and Merrill Lynch–Mercury Asset Management, the company operates one of the world's largest mutual fund groups.

In addition to numerous branch offices throughout New Jersey to serve its business and consumer customers, Merrill Lynch has a 250,000-square-foot office and a state-of-the-art conference and training center complex in Plainsboro. It also leases a 100,000-square-foot space in the Forrestal Center in Princeton.

Merrill Lynch has approximately 10,300 employees throughout New Jersey. This includes more than 4,000 employees in the Somerset area, where the firm's state-of-the-art technology platforms are developed and maintained and its award-winning network of client service representatives is located. In addition there are more than 2,300 employees at the Merrill Lynch facility in Jersey City who are responsible for the company's global operations and processing. In 1997 the company approved a plan to build a new facility in Hopewell Township to consolidate existing operations and allow for future

Members of the Merrill Lynch staff exchange ideas.

256 CREATING THE FUTURE

expansion. Initial occupancy will include 3,500 employees currently located at other sites in New Jersey, with space available for future expansion.

"Merrill Lynch is committed to New Jersey," says David H. Komansky, company chairman and chief executive officer. "As a leader in global financial services with more than 880 offices worldwide, we feel our office expansion in Hopewell makes sound business sense and gives us an opportunity to further attract a highly skilled and diversified workforce." The plan calls for the purchase of 450 acres to develop in the first phase up to six separate buildings, each to be approximately 160,000 square feet. Future phases will be constructed as business needs dictate. Construction of the first building is scheduled to start in spring 1999, with initial occupancy projected for late 2000.

"This is a very important and welcomed development for New Jersey," says Governor Christine Todd Whitman. "Merrill Lynch's decision to develop a new site in Hopewell Township retains 3,500 jobs and will potentially include an additional 1,500. We will continue to work with firms such as Merrill Lynch to help us shape our growth in a way that maintains New Jersey's beauty and quality of life," Whitman says.

On a global basis, Merrill Lynch is organized into four primary business groups. The **Corporate and Institutional Client Group** provides financing, trading, and strategic advisory services to corporations, large institutions, and governments worldwide.

The **Asset Management Group** is central to Merrill Lynch's overall business strategy. The group provides one of the widest arrays of investment services available from any company. It has grown to become one of the largest investment managers in the world, with almost $500 billion in assets under management.

Staff members gather to attend lectures and presentations at the Merrill Lynch training facility.

The **Private Client Group** represents the historical roots of Merrill Lynch. Its more than 13,000 financial consultants in 700 offices throughout the United States have relationships with more than 4.5 million households, including small businesses. They provide a complete range of financial services—planning, cash management, investments, home mortgages and other kinds of loans, trust accounts, and estate planning. Merrill Lynch financial consultants assist clients in addressing complex financial issues and help them for the future.

The **International Private Client Group** has evolved from initially providing United States securities brokerage services to offering a range of private banking services designed to address the asset, liability, and transition needs of high-net-worth clients abroad through its 1,100 Private Bankers in about forty offices in more than thirty countries. Merrill Lynch recently opened retail offices in Japan and Canada.

"Our clients have multiple needs, and those needs must be addressed in the context of a highly complex and fast-changing marketplace," says CEO Komansky. "They are eager for trusted relationships that deliver integrated solutions and continuity. We will continue to develop what we feel will be the best and most enduring competitive advantage of all—excellence. Being the best at what we do, wherever we do it, and whenever we do it."

Through its foundation grants, matching gifts program, scholarships, and volunteer service initiatives, Merrill Lynch strives to deliver on its corporate "Principle of Responsible Citizenship." Merrill Lynch has organized corporate donations and sponsorships, as well as employee volunteer efforts throughout the United States and in New Jersey. Through the Merrill Lynch & Co. Foundation, Inc., the company provides substantial grants to education, the arts, the environment, human services, health care organizations, hospitals, and civic groups.

The company's founder, Charles E. Merrill, believed that the opportunities of the markets should be accessible to everyone, so he set about his life's work of "bringing Wall Street to Main Street." That spirit lives on today in Merrill Lynch offices throughout New Jersey, the nation, and the world.

Shown at left is one of the many Merrill Lynch branch offices located across the state of New Jersey. © Tom Crane

FINANCIAL SERVICES AND INSURANCE 257

FIRST UNION NATIONAL BANK

SUCCESSFUL, CUSTOMER-FOCUSED FIRST UNION BANK FORMS KEY ALLIANCES TO OFFER A FULL RANGE OF FINANCIAL SERVICES, HEEDING THE PREFERENCES OF ITS CUSTOMERS AND REACHING OUT TO HELP ITS LOCAL COMMUNITIES

The sixth-largest banking company in the nation and the largest in New Jersey, First Union Bank is a leading provider of financial services to more than 16 million customers. With full-service offices located in Connecticut, Delaware, Florida, Georgia, Maryland, New York, North Carolina, Pennsylvania, South Carolina, Tennessee, Virginia, and Washington, D.C., First Union provides customers with easy access to its services along the entire East Coast.

More than simply a bank, First Union is a full-service financial services company. With approximately 1,900 branches and the nation's sixth-largest network of automated teller machines (ATMs), First Union offers a full range of financial services to corporations and individuals.

These financial services range from deposit accounts to investment management services, and from Wall Street–type corporate financing to credit and debit cards and the Internet (Web site: www.firstunion.com).

First Union's more than 200 additional diversified offices also provide such financial services as mortgage banking, home equity lending, leasing, insurance, securities brokerage, and capital markets services. With its policy of local decision-making for loan applications, First Union combines the advantages of the close working relationship typical of a hometown bank with the backing of the resources of one of the nation's largest financial services organizations.

First Union has succeeded by being responsive to its customers. Its Quality Customer Service and Total Quality Management programs have become models industrywide. Under these quality programs, First Union continuously trains employees

Although First Union customers benefit from the resources, technology, and expertise of the nation's sixth-largest financial services organization, they enjoy the benefits and convenience of a neighborhood bank. © A. J. Sundstrom Photography

Donald Parcells, president of First Union Atlantic, is responsible for First Union's banking operations in New Jersey, New York, and Connecticut. A. J. Sundstrom Photography

in improved techniques for customer service and sales. Employees earn cash incentives for achieving high standards of service. The corporation's incentive program is just one example of its commitment to provide quality service to its millions of customers and to continually attract new customers.

First Union Corporation was profiled as one of the "101 Companies That Profit from Customer Care" in *The Service Edge*, a 1989 book citing "role models for the new American manager." The book praises First Union for its quality programs and for its aggressive customer service research, including use of an independent firm's "mystery shopper" program and in-depth market research in customer definitions of what good service consists of.

Exemplifying this customer-centered approach, First Union has developed a new concept in banking called Future Bank, which responds to customers' diverse lifestyles by making financial services available to customers when, where, and the way they want them—twenty-four hours a day.

First Union also is dedicated to providing an excellent working environment in which employees are encouraged to develop as professionals. In 1995, 1996, and 1998 *Working Mother* magazine selected First Union as one of the 100 best employers for working mothers in the nation.

CREATING THE FUTURE

First Union also received the Corporate Award for the Advancement of Women in 1996 from the National Council of Women. In addition, *Hispanic* magazine recognized the company as one of the top 100 companies in the nation for providing the most opportunities for Hispanic employees.

In the past decade First Union has used the power of its firm foundation to grow via mergers with banks and other companies. By seeking merger partnerships with more than seventy other organizations that have compatible managements and philosophies, First Union has maintained its reputation for strong financial performance and high-quality products and service. As the operations of acquired companies have been consolidated, First Union has achieved efficiencies by standardizing products, procedures, and automation systems.

Although First Union is headquartered in Charlotte, North Carolina, it has strong New Jersey roots. First Union Bank was started after the turn of the twentieth century when an entrepreneur named H. M. Victor raised funds to open Union National Bank. Union National grew and eventually became First Union.

First Union Bank grew into a unique East Coast presence with the acquisition in 1996 of First Fidelity Bancorporation of Newark, New Jersey, and its 1998 acquisition of CoreStates Financial Corp., purchases that added the states of Pennsylvania, New York, Connecticut, and Delaware to the First Union family.

First Union also recently merged with The Money Store, which is based in Union, New Jersey, creating the nation's number one coast-to-coast provider of home equity and small-business association (SBA) loans and the number three provider of student loans. The Money Store operates 172 branches in fifty states, with call centers that primarily handle customer inquiries through its well-known 1-800-LOAN-YES line.

Tom Bracken (standing, left), head of Commercial and Government Banking for First Union–New Jersey, and Jay Bloom, executive director of Brand New Day, Inc., in Elizabeth, New Jersey, visit a day care center supported by First Union Bank.

Each year First Union channels financial contributions and employee volunteer resources into hundreds of programs and initiatives, from neighborhood revitalization to innovative programs for improving education. In addition, it develops financial products and services designed to meet the needs of low- to moderate-income families and individuals. First Union strives to make a positive impact on every First Union Bank community.

"At First Union our commitment to the communities in which we live and work is one of our highest priorities," says Don Parcells, president of First Union Atlantic. "We are fortunate to employ people who genuinely care about others and who dedicate themselves to making a difference in our neighborhoods."

Bank employees tutor, mentor, and provide educational programs for students at many schools throughout New Jersey. Here, First Union employee volunteers host a graduation party for students they have "adopted" from the Parker School in Trenton.

FINANCIAL SERVICES AND INSURANCE 259

MADE IN NEW JERSEY

CHAPTER NINETEEN

ONCE KNOWN AS THE "WORKSHOP OF THE NATION," NEW JERSEY HAS A RICH MANUFACTURING LEGACY THAT STRETCHES BACK TO THE AMERICAN REVOLUTION. THE STATE'S FIRST INDUSTRIAL BOOM BEGAN IN 1791 WHEN ALEXANDER HAMILTON SELECTED THE GREAT FALLS OF THE PASSAIC RIVER, LOCATED IN PATERSON, AS THE SITE FOR A MODEL FACTORY TOWN. THROUGHOUT THE NINETEENTH CENTURY PATERSON WAS THE SILK-MAKING

capital of the world, as well as home to innovators in gunsmithing and boat-building. Rail and steamboat service transformed Jersey City, Newark, Camden, and Trenton into leading industrial areas. As highway and other transportation systems improved in the early part of the twentieth century, the Garden State became a manufacturing giant, known for such products as soups, air conditioners, building materials, and electronics.

Today, at the dawn of the twenty-first century, the state's diverse manufacturing base accounts for one out of eight nonagricultural jobs, about 477,000 workers in all. And even with the shift to a more service-oriented economy, New Jersey remains a national leader in the making of chemicals, medicines, and soaps and cleaners; and the state is the headquarters for dozens of major manufacturing firms that have production facilities here and around the globe. Some of these companies have a familiar ring because they make products consumers know and love (Does "M'm! M'm! Good!" strike a chord?), while others are corporate powerhouses that manufacture everything from toilets to automobile air bags.

THE TASTE OF NEW JERSEY

Based in Camden since 1869, the Campbell Soup Company is the nation's leading producer of soup, vegetable juice, and picante sauce, and has in the

OPPOSITE: *An American icon, Campbell's soup accounts for 80 percent of the canned soup market in the United States. The company holds about 10 percent of the international market and is hoping for more, especially in Europe and Asia. The descendants of John Dorrance, who invented condensed soup, still own about 44 percent of the company. © Rick LaSalle/Tony Stone Images.* ABOVE: *The Great Falls of the Passaic River first thrilled Alexander Hamilton when he was an officer in Washington's army. Later, as Secretary of the Treasury, Hamilton enthusiastically supported the choice of a site near the falls for an industrial community. © Ellen Denuto*

MADE IN NEW JERSEY 261

> ### THE WHITE HOUSE'S CHINA
>
> TRENTON WAS ONE OF AMERICA'S MOST IMPORTANT POTTERY CENTERS IN THE 1800S. IT WAS ALSO THE BIRTHPLACE OF WALTER SCOTT LENOX, WHOSE EFFORTS TO PERFECT FINE AMERICAN CHINA LED TO THE CREAMY, LUSTROUS WARE KNOWN THROUGHOUT THE WORLD TODAY AS LENOX CHINA.

neighborhood of $8 billion in annual sales. Founded as a canning and preserving business by fruit merchant Joseph Campbell, the conservatively managed concern is ubiquitous in America's kitchens, and its soup cans have become a pop culture icon. Growth and expansion in the latter half of the twentieth century has come in part from key acquisitions, including V8 juice, Swanson frozen dinners, Godiva Chocolate, and Vlasic Pickles.

New Jersey has a healthy diet of food producers like Campbell. The best known among these companies is Nabisco Holdings Corporation, based in Parsippany, the largest cookie and cracker maker in the United States, with such popular brands as Oreo, Chips Ahoy!, Fig Newtons, SnackWells, and Ritz. Bestfoods of Englewood Cliffs is the world's leading producer of mayonnaise, sold under the Hellman's and Best Foods brands, but the $10-billion firm also makes market-leading Mazola corn oil, Thomas' English muffins, Skippy peanut butter, and Knorr soups and sauces.

Smaller companies with well-known products include Alpine Lace Brands of Maplewood, which makes a full line of low-fat cheeses for health-conscious consumers; Goya Foods of Secaucus, which makes more than 850 Hispanic and Caribbean grocery products; and J and J Snack Foods of Pennsauken, which makes and distributes soft pretzels, frozen beverages, baked goods, and other snacks.

MANUFACTURING POWERHOUSES

Major manufacturers that call New Jersey home include AlliedSignal of Morristown, a conglomerate that thrived in the 1990s thanks to a stronger focus on three main markets: aerospace, chemical and other engineered products, and automotive products. The company has an expansive product line and is the world's leading producer of hydrofluoric acid and a leading maker of nylon fibers.

Clinton-based Foster Wheeler Corporation also is organized into three business groups: one that builds chemical plants and oil refineries; another that manufactures steam-generating equipment; and a third that builds and operates power plants. Rock drills and air compressors supplied by Ingersoll-Rand Company helped create the Mount Rushmore monument, and the Woodcliff Lake company remains a leading manufacturer of construction machinery and industrial equipment. For over one hundred years, Engelhard Corporation of Edison has been one of the world's top producers of base materials used in the petroleum, chemical, and food industries.

The world's first air conditioner was manufactured in New Jersey, and two Garden State corporations are top producers of those cooling machines. For Piscataway-based American Standard Companies, air-conditioning systems account for more than half of its sales, with plumbing fixtures and automotive braking systems making up the rest. All of the company's industrial businesses are first or second in their markets. Meanwhile, Fedders Corporation of Liberty Corner owns a 30-percent share

Foster Wheeler's world headquarters in Clinton. Courtesy, Foster Wheeler Corporation

ABOVE: *Ingersoll-Rand air compressors provided power for tools and hoists used to build the English Channel tunnel.* BELOW LEFT: *Portable air compressors undergo final assembly and inspection. © Don O'Barski. Both photos courtesy, Ingersoll-Rand.* BELOW RIGHT: *Family-owned Goya Foods is one of the largest Hispanic-owned companies in the country. Goya controls over half the Hispanic foods market in the Northeast and Florida, and is working to become a household name among non-Hispanics as well. Courtesy, Goya Foods*

MADE IN NEW JERSEY 263

IN 1895 ITALO MARCHIONY OF HOBOKEN STARTED SELLING HIS ICE CREAM AND LEMON ICE IN LIQUOR GLASSES. MANY BROKE OR WERE STOLEN, AND THE REST HAD TO BE WASHED AFTER EACH USE. TO SERVE HIS CUSTOMERS SOMETHING THEY COULD TAKE WITH THEM, HE BAKED WAFFLES AND MOLDED THEM INTO THE SHAPE OF A CUP WHILE STILL HOT. THANKS TO HIS NEW INVENTION, MARCHIONY SOON BECAME THE MOST POPULAR PUSHCART VENDOR IN THE AREA.

Jersey is Union Camp Corporation of Wayne, a leading maker of fine papers, packaging, and chemical and wood products. The Sealed Air Corporation of Saddle Brook, which merged with W.R. Grace and Company in 1998 to form a $2.5 billion company, is the world's largest manufacturer of plastic bubble wrap, along with other kinds of protective and specialty packaging.

TRADITION AND CHANGE

Despite a decrease in the number of New Jersey–based manufacturing facilities, many companies continue to do of the residential market for room air conditioners and dehumidifiers, selling its products under the Fedders, Emerson, Quiet Kool, and Airtemp brands.

American Home Products Corporation is one New Jersey manufacturer that has been climbing the Fortune 500 list in recent years. Thanks to a string of acquisitions, the Madison-based company is not only one of the top five U.S. makers of prescription drugs, but is a leading maker of chemicals, herbicides, and animal health products. Another Fortune 500 manufacturer based in New

RIGHT: *Governor Whitman poses with Anheuser-Busch representatives on Made in New Jersey Day. Courtesy, New Jersey Business & Industry Association.* BELOW: *A fleet of early Benjamin Moore trucks stands ready. Courtesy, Benjamin Moore & Co.*

CREATING THE FUTURE

NEW JERSEY WAS AMERICA'S FIRST PETROCHEMICAL CENTER, AND IT REMAINS THE PETROLEUM AND CHEMICAL PROCESSING LEADER OF THE EAST COAST, SECOND ONLY TO OPERATIONS ON THE GULF COAST. AMONG THOSE ENTITIES MAINTAINING OPERATIONS IN THE STATE ARE OIL COMPANIES SUCH AS EXXON, CHEVRON, AND HESS; ALONG WITH CHEMICAL CONGLOMERATES SUCH AS AMERICAN CYANIMID, DU PONT, AND HOECHST CELANESE.

manufacturers annually ship some $20 billion in products to more than fifty countries, making the state the ninth-largest exporter of goods in the nation.

The New Jersey manufacturers who have stayed have devised creative solutions to make doing so easier and more profitable. The Langston Corporation, a Cherry Hill manufacturer of machinery used to make corrugated boxes, concluded that moving would be more expensive than staying put. Langston constantly looks at its machine designs and processes for greater cost effectiveness and functionality. The company also has been able to reduce its power costs by operating only at night and taking advantage of lower service rates. Besides, Langston is proud of its century-old history in the state.

Deep roots and tradition are just as important to Red Devil of Union, which makes hand tools and chemicals for the booming home-improvement industry. Family-owned since its inception in 1872, the company prides itself on worker training, and wouldn't want to move only because it could find cheaper labor somewhere else.

Other companies that have proudly celebrated the century mark in New Jersey are Tingley Rubber Corporation of South Plainfield, a maker of footwear for industrial applications; and McWilliams Forge Company in Rockaway, a top forging supplier to shipyards and to every major aerospace engine manufacturer.

In 1907 Ingersoll-Rand's Gordon stope drill beat its competitors in the South African Stope Drill Contest, helping to promote Ingersoll-Rand's worldwide reputation. Here, the drill is tested in Phillipsburg. Courtesy, Ingersoll-Rand

business in the Garden State, and their efforts are good for the economy. Moreover, some economists argue that the departure of many so-called "Three-D" jobs (dirty, deadly, and dangerous) has made New Jersey a better place and contributed to the economy's upward trend. In addition to enjoying safer work environments and cleaner communities, workers now command a higher minimum wage than the national one. And more and more manufacturing jobs require technical know-how and offer higher compensation in return. Manufacturing jobs pay an average annual salary of nearly $45,000, about 22 percent more than the national average. And

CONVERTING A CORNER GROCERY STORE INTO A SPACIOUS SUPERMARKET IN THE LATE 1800S, THE GREAT ATLANTIC AND PACIFIC TEA COMPANY OF MONTVALE LATER BECAME THE WORLD'S BIGGEST RETAIL FOOD CHAIN. THE COMPANY SELLS MORE THAN FIFTEEN HUNDRED OF ITS OWN PRODUCTS, INCLUDING THREE BRANDS OF COFFEE.

MADE IN NEW JERSEY 265

USING THE DESIGNS OF INVENTOR JOHN GEORGE LEYNER, INGERSOLL-RAND BEGAN MANUFACTURING THE JACKHAMER® DRILL IN 1921. INGERSOLL-RAND JACKHAMER DRILLS WERE SENT TO SOUTH DAKOTA IN 1927 TO HELP SHEER AWAY THE SURFACE OF MOUNT RUSHMORE SO THAT THE FACES OF THE PRESIDENTS COULD BE SCULPTED.

© Image Club Graphics

BETWEEN PRODUCER AND CONSUMER

Not just a manufacturer of goods and products, New Jersey has long been a leading warehouse and distribution center, in large part due to the state's strategic location on the eastern seaboard. With highways crisscrossing the state and huge port facilities, New Jersey is seen by manufacturers as an ideal place for storing and moving products.

As the twentieth century draws to a close, developers around the state have built larger warehouses for their clients—and sometimes built them without having committed tenants. Twenty-first-century warehouses are getting taller as new technologies allow companies to operate in storage facilities with higher ceilings. As a result, warehouses will be bigger, but not eat up as much precious land as they did in the past.

The bulk of the new warehouse building has been in Central New Jersey, mostly near exits of the New Jersey Turnpike. In 1998 Security Capital Industrial Trust broke ground on the first of six buildings that will comprise a total area of 1.26 million square feet. Demand from national clients for a base of operations in New Jersey compelled the Denver, Colorado–based real estate investment trust to build warehouse facilities in the Garden State near Exit 8. Heller Construction of Edison built a one-million-square-foot facility near

New Jersey warehouses can now hold more goods on less acreage, thanks to their ability to make use of more vertical space. Here, a worker takes inventory using a bar code scanner. © George Kavanagh/ Tony Stone Images

266 CREATING THE FUTURE

Exit 9 on speculation, and eventually signed up enough tenants to fill the warehouse to capacity. The unusually high thirty-eight-foot internal clearance was undoubtedly a major draw.

Looking to the Future

Once the engine of New Jersey's economy, manufacturing is now part of a more diverse business sector. But it remains vital to the state in terms of jobs and economic activity, and it generates products that are used the world over. The industrial complexion of New Jersey has evolved since Alexander Hamilton turned Paterson into a model factory town, but the commitment to nurturing manufacturers has remained constant. Indeed, in 1996, the New Jersey Business & Industry Association started an annual Made in New Jersey Day. And the exhibits by over forty companies—from glass producers in Cumberland County, to luxury yacht makers along the Jersey Shore—proved that "Made in New Jersey" is now, more than ever, a stamp of quality and pride.

A DOWN-ON-HIS-LUCK SALESMAN, CHARLES DARROW INVENTED THE GAME OF MONOPOLY IN 1930 AND NAMED THE STREETS AFTER THOSE IN ATLANTIC CITY, HIS FAVORITE VACATION SPOT. A PLAQUE AT THE CORNER OF PARK PLACE AND THE BOARDWALK HONORS DARROW.

© UPI/Corbis-Bettmann

At its Flanders facility, Benjamin Moore's technical staff develops new latex- and solvent-based coatings. The company has been based in New Jersey since shortly after its founding in 1883. Courtesy, Benjamin Moore & Co.

MADE IN NEW JERSEY 267

ABOVE: *Updated versions of Thomas Edison's 1879 invention still find their way into homes and offices all over the world. Here, lightbulbs undergo testing before being packaged and shipped.* © Lonny Kalfus/Tony Stone Images

A GOOD INVESTMENT

IN THE 1990S CHEMICAL MANUFACTURERS IN NEW JERSEY CUT THEIR EMISSIONS OF HAZARDOUS SUBSTANCES BY OVER 38 PERCENT. THIS ACHIEVEMENT CAN BE CREDITED TO OVER $700 MILLION IN PRODUCTION MODIFICATIONS AND NEW EQUIPMENT.

BELOW: *The George Washington Bridge is one of New Jersey's many links to the global market.* © Roberto Arakaki/International Stock. OPPOSITE: *Plastic packaging is among the products manufactured by Wayne-based Union Camp Corporation.* © Bob Krist

MOTHER'S HELPER

DURING WORLD WAR II WILLIAM MAXSON, A WEST ORANGE INVENTOR, CAME UP WITH THE IDEA OF FEEDING SOLDIERS ALREADY COOKED, FROZEN MEALS THAT COULD BE EASILY REHEATED. THE SOLDIERS LIKED THE IDEA; AND, AFTER THE WAR, THE GENERAL PUBLIC CAME TO LIKE WHAT BECAME KNOWN AS TV DINNERS.

MADE IN NEW JERSEY 269

© Frank Herholdt/Tony Stone Images

270 CREATING THE FUTURE

MANUFACTURING, DISTRIBUTION, AND WAREHOUSING

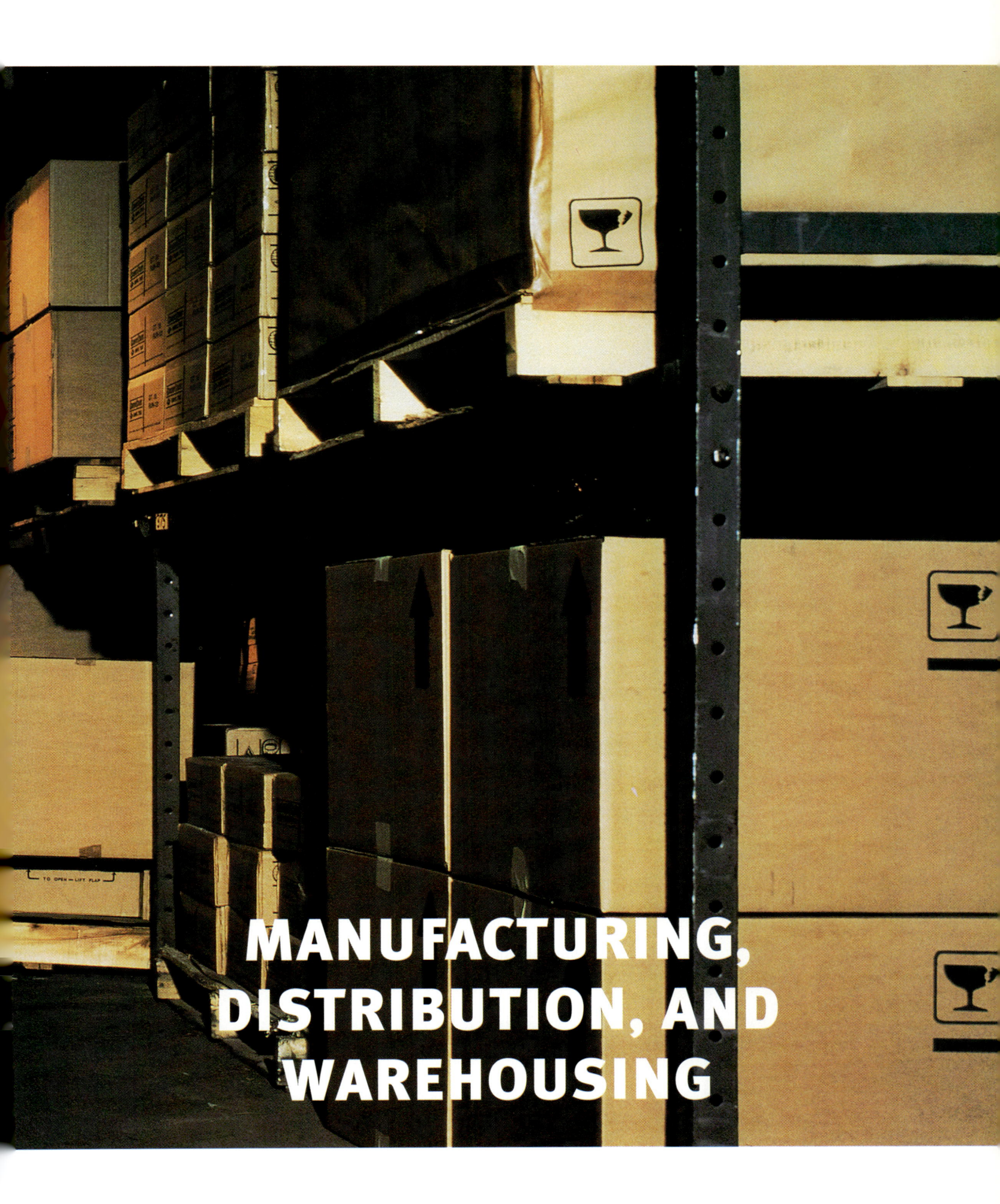

RICOH CORPORATION

RICOH CORPORATION IS A WORLD PIONEER IN DEVELOPING COMPUTER-CONNECTED, MULTIFUNCTIONAL OFFICE WORK FLOW SYSTEMS FOR EASY LOCAL OR REMOTE ACCESS AND TRANSFER OF IMAGES, WORDS, NUMBERS, AND SOUND

Ricoh Corporation, headquartered in West Caldwell, New Jersey, is a subsidiary of Ricoh Company Ltd., a sixty-two-year-old leading supplier of office automation equipment with 1997 sales in excess of $10.6 billion.

Ricoh Corporation also is a diversified office equipment and electronics manufacturer and, for the last two years, the number one manufacturer of black-and-white digital copiers in the United States. The company is a pioneer in the development of computer-connected and digital multifunctional document systems, a leader in the fast-growing color copier market, and a premier supplier of black-and-white copiers, facsimile machines, printers, and scanners. The company also manufactures and sells optical and magnetic storage devices, photographic equipment, and digital cameras.

Ricoh Corporation's mission is to create a digital office environment where images—information in its most basic form—are communicated with ease from any location. To achieve this, Ricoh Corporation recently launched its Image Communication initiative, a strategic vision that is the driving force behind all that Ricoh does. Image Communication takes place whenever an idea in its most basic form—the image—is communicated to another person. To that end, Ricoh is developing systems that enable people to create, modify, and process all types of images—text, numbers, illustrations, photographs, moving images, even voice—without limits.

Image Communication represents Ricoh's new view of the work environment. It is an innovative office model that has unprecedented flexibility and, therefore, requires solutions that mirror this flexibility. Ricoh's future product introductions and office solutions will be created through its new Image Communication strategy and will enable individuals to work from a home, mobile, or traditional corporate office while sharing, transferring, and storing central database information.

"Ricoh Corporation is committed to achieving a productive synergy between people and technology through our Image Communication strategy," says Katsumi "Kirk" Yoshida, chairman and chief executive officer of Ricoh Corporation. "We envision that a digitally connected work environment will increase speed and efficiency while creating a managed-paper workplace.

"With the combined efforts of all Ricoh companies throughout the world, including the United States, Japan, Canada, Latin America, and Europe, Ricoh's Image Communication strategy will create new and practical applications for existing systems and change the traditional interaction of people and information forever."

A Commitment to New Jersey

Ricoh Corporation established its national headquarters in New Jersey in 1969. Since then the company has continued to expand and prosper. Today Ricoh employs 1,300 people in New Jersey, occupying more than 180,000 square feet of office space in West Caldwell and Fairfield.

The top U.S. manufacturer of black-and-white digital office copiers, Ricoh Corporation, Inc., is headquartered in West Caldwell, New Jersey. The corporation is a subsidiary of Ricoh Company Ltd., a sixty-two-year-old leading supplier of office automation equipment, whose 1997 sales exceeded $10.6 billion.

Katsumi "Kirk" Yoshida is chairman and chief executive officer of Ricoh Corporation.

272 CREATING THE FUTURE

Through Ricoh's support of industry initiatives and many charities, the company has assumed an active role as a corporate citizen. Ricoh underwrites many fund-raising events, including sponsorship of events benefiting the Tomorrows Children's Institute and the New Jersey Cancer Research Fund.

KEY PRODUCT AREAS

Ricoh Corporation boasts one of the industry's broadest imaging product lines, which caters to all sizes of businesses, government agencies, and consumers, and is committed to developing and manufacturing the most advanced and technologically sound digital office products on the market. Through ongoing and comprehensive research and development (R&D), Ricoh continues to incorporate state-of-the-art features into its products, improving the output quality, efficiency, and cost-effectiveness of document imaging.

In addition to its award-winning line of analog and digital black-and-white copiers, Ricoh also manufactures digital color copiers designed to fulfill the color imaging needs of the corporate environment. Many of these digital products also have the ability to be connected to a network, print controller, or personal computer, giving users the option of configuring them as work group printers.

Ricoh's scanners and facsimile machines offer even more document imaging solutions for the corporate environment. With superior output quality and fast transmission times, Ricoh's scanners and facsimile machines allow people to digitally copy a document into a computer network or send a document around the globe. For specialty markets, Ricoh also manufacturers high-speed digital duplicators for environments that routinely make large quantities of copies of a single document, and wide-format copiers for environments, such as architecture or advertising firms, that require documents larger than eleven inches by seventeen inches.

Ricoh also realizes that having electronic access to documents while on the

The Ricoh Magio mininotebook computer is designed as a powerful, lightweight, full-featured solution for the computing and communication needs of the mobile executive.

The Ricoh Aficio FX10 is a deluxe personal imaging workstation that provides superior digital copy capabilities; fast plain-paper fax capabilities, including personal computer faxing; high-powered printing; and amazingly high-resolution scanning.

road is critical to success in today's business world. That is why the company introduced its first mininotebook computer, the Magio, in 1998. The Magio is a powerful, high-performance, full-featured mininotebook computer that weighs less than three pounds and can easily be taken anywhere.

For the consumer, Ricoh also manufactures 35 mm, point-and-shoot, and portable digital cameras that store and edit both still and moving images and sound, which can be viewed on a television or computer monitor.

INDUSTRY AWARDS

Ricoh is the leading manufacturer of digital office copiers, according to findings by industry analysts Dataquest and CAP Ventures. Independent research conducted by these firms shows that the Ricoh Group shipped more Ricoh-manufactured digital copiers for the 1997 calendar year than any competitor, with 23 percent market share for that product category. Ricoh also became the leader in black-and-white digital copiers among more than ten office product vendors for the first time in 1997, and the Ricoh Group attained the leading market share for the second consecutive year. Industry trade publication *Better Buys for Business* recently presented more Editor's Choice awards to Ricoh than to any other office product manufacturer.

The United States Environmental Protection Agency (EPA) recently awarded Ricoh the 1998 ENERGY STAR Imaging Equipment Partner of the Year Award, the EPA's highest industry award. Ricoh received the EPA's 1997 ENERGY STAR Office Equipment Copier of the Year Award and the 1996 Award for

RICOH CORPORATION (CONTINUED)

The Ricoh Aficio Color 5000 is designed for corporate graphics departments and color copy shops where quality, connectivity, and reliability are crucial.

For marketing and sales of its full line of Ricoh-brand office products, the company uses a nationwide network of independent dealers as well as its regional direct retail sales force. Additionally, Ricoh's three wholly owned subsidiaries sell Ricoh-brand office products.

Ricoh Corporation's territory is organized geographically, with a Ricoh Group sales organization for the United States, one for Canada, and one for Latin America. The Ricoh Group in the United States is further organized into two segments—the Ricoh Business Unit (RBU) based in West Caldwell, New Jersey, and the wholly owned Savin Corporation, headquartered in Stamford, Connecticut.

Excellence, Overall Office Equipment Partner of the Year. Ricoh also has been recognized for its leadership role in promoting the production and use of energy-efficient ENERGY STAR–rated copiers, facsimile equipment, and printers. Ricoh's Companywide Quality Control program was introduced in 1971 to establish the company as a high-technology leader. This program led to the company winning two Deming Prizes, awarded to companies that demonstrate an outstanding commitment to quality control by creating products or inventions that make exceptional advances in the pursuit of quality. Among the fewer than 100 companies that have won the Deming Prize, Ricoh was the first office equipment manufacturer to become a winner, and it is the only company to have won twice.

Additionally, Ricoh Corporation received the 1998 Digital Manufacturer of the Year award from *The Cannata Report*, a leading industry publication. The award was a result of *The Cannata Report*'s Thirteenth Annual Dealer Survey, which cites Ricoh's high-quality products and services as the compelling reasons the company is appreciated by its network of dealers.

Ricoh also has contributed to the growth of its sales business through strategic acquisitions. In 1993 Ricoh acquired American Office Equipment Company, Inc. (AOE). AOE/Ricoh, Inc., as it is now called, is a $60 million company based in New Jersey, with more than 300 employees. The areas it serves include northern and central New Jersey, and New York City and Rockland County, New York.

In 1995 Savin Corporation was acquired by Ricoh Corporation, becoming a wholly owned subsidiary. Savin markets Ricoh products and provides product support under the Savin brand name through its nationwide dealer network and direct retail sales branches.

In 1997 Ricoh acquired Imagetech and Selective Business Systems. Imagetech, headquartered in Seattle, Washington, is a $15 million company with 120 employees at four locations. The purchase of Imagetech marked Ricoh's first direct retail presence on the West Coast. The purchase of Selective Business Systems, in Detroit, Michigan, gave Ricoh a direct retail presence in the Midwest.

NORTH AMERICAN OPERATIONS

In the United States, Ricoh Corporation has more than sixty locations. It opened its first United States manufacturing plant in 1973 and currently operates eleven manufacturing facilities in Southern California and Georgia.

Ricoh Electronics, Inc., is headquartered in Tustin, California.

The Ricoh Aficio 650 is the flagship product of the Aficio black-and-white line and is optimally designed for the most demanding mid- to high-volume environments. The machine represents the ninth-generation digital engine that Ricoh has manufactured since entering the digital market in 1989.

"Ricoh, the Image Communication company for businesses and professionals who require first-class image capturing, processing, duplication, and transmission, will continue to be one of the world's leading manufacturers of office equipment," says Yoshida.

THE NEXT MILLENNIUM

Ricoh began its digitalization effort in the early 1980s and now is marketing its ninth-generation technology, while many competitors continue to introduce their first. Realizing the potential for a digital solution that could be integrated with other office equipment, Ricoh implemented intensive R&D programs to create a new digital products line called Aficio.

Introduced in 1996, Aficio products are specially designed to meet the changing needs of businesses by streamlining work flow. Aficio is Ricoh's response to the increasing demand for digital, multifunction products and the growing need for seamless network connectivity. Each Aficio product can perform in virtually any office environment, from a small office to a work group to a large corporation.

Ricoh realizes that the workplace of the future will continually evolve as a digital-imaging environment where customers will increasingly turn to technology that connects offices and people, to transmit information across the hall and around the world. To ensure delivery of these solutions into the corporate environment, Ricoh Corporation has reorganized its business units to better support its dealers and direct retail customers.

Under this new structure, each Ricoh business unit is separated into three distinct organizations: a dealer team, a retail team, and a business support team. This structure enables each business unit to focus on growth opportunities in a timely manner and concentrate on process improvements and total customer satisfaction. Ricoh also will continue to heavily support its R&D efforts for products that allow people to communicate better and faster than ever before.

Ricoh, with its prominence firmly established in the image-processing arena, its cutting-edge technology, and its commitment to customer service, stands ready to meet the exacting requirements of a changing marketplace in New Jersey and around the world.

Also in 1997, Ricoh acquired Custom Copy Services, Inc., located in Southern California. Together with Imagetech and Selective Business Systems, these dealerships constitute the Ricoh Business Systems, Inc., network.

Just over two decades ago, corporations took the first tentative steps in the workplace toward the reinvention of office processes, with the goal of creating more efficient management of information by the beginning of the twenty-first century. It was a time for new ideas and new technology, for innovation and experimentation.

Ricoh recognized this opportunity and established Ricoh Electronics, Inc. (REI), at the very dawn of this technological revolution. In the more than twenty years since, REI has developed the tools and resources necessary to make this goal a reality. With facilities in Orange County, California, and Lawrenceville, Georgia, REI manufactures copiers, toner, thermal media products, and an impressive array of parts specifically created to fill particular business requirements.

Ricoh conducts R&D at its California facility, Ricoh Silicon Valley, Inc. (RSV). Currently, these efforts are centered on making products that adhere to the guidelines of Ricoh's Image Communication vision. Ricoh plans to continue to develop and launch products that exemplify this corporate vision.

INTERNATIONAL OPERATIONS

Ricoh Company Ltd., in Tokyo, is one of the world's three largest manufacturers of copiers and facsimile equipment and maintains more than twenty manufacturing plants in Europe, Asia, and the United States. The company has 128 consolidated subsidiaries and affiliates in Japan and 205 abroad, which together employ more than 68,000 people.

MANUFACTURING, DISTRIBUTION, AND WAREHOUSING 275

SILVER LINE BUILDING PRODUCTS

DEDICATED TO INNOVATIVE PRODUCT DEVELOPMENT, HIGH-QUALITY MANUFACTURING, AND GOOD VALUE, SILVER LINE BUILDING PRODUCTS MAKES PREMIER VINYL WINDOWS AND PATIO DOORS FOR BUILDINGS ACROSS THE NATION

Founded in 1947, Silver Line Building Products has become one of the nation's largest manufacturers of vinyl windows and patio doors. Silver Line provides its products to building-supply companies, lumber yards, window dealers, and home centers.

Silver Line, a family-owned business founded by Arthur Silverman, originally produced tools, dies, and stampings for the production of jalousie windows. Shortly thereafter, responding to demand, Silver Line began to make jalousies and sliding glass doors in their Kenilworth, New Jersey, plant.

Early success led to a complete product line of aluminum windows for new construction and replacement. In 1984, after it already had outgrown three plants in Kenilworth, Silver Line expanded its manufacturing operations with the purchase of a 250,000-square-foot facility in Middlesex, New Jersey.

In 1986 Silver Line ventured into the vinyl window market. Its first line of vinyl replacement windows was an instant success. Once again, new products fueled company growth, and Silver Line again expanded, opening its South Plainfield, New Jersey, plant solely for the extruding of vinyl lineals and the fabrication of vinyl windows. A new construction vinyl product line was added in 1988.

The aesthetically pleasing Silver Line vinyl windows are also technologically advanced: each model is thermally efficient and virtually maintenance-free.

From left, Kenneth Silverman, Silver Line president and CEO, and Arthur Silverman, founder and chairman, work together to build innovative product lines.

"Vertical integration is the key to our success," says Silver Line president/CEO Kenneth Silverman. "Internally extruding our own window profiles and injection-molding window hardware enables Silver Line to better control quality, supply, and price, ensuring customers the best window value."

The Silver Line Vinyl Extrusion Division, in North Brunswick, New Jersey, is among the largest plastic pipe, profile, and tubing extrusion companies in North America, according to a dollar-based ranking published in the industry newspaper *Plastics News*. Pipe, profile, and tubing extrusion make up one of the primary segments of a plastics-product manufacturing industry that generates total shipments valued at more than $110 billion per year.

The process involves forcing (extruding) melted plastic under pressure through precision dies to make vinyl window lineals. These lineals are then fabricated into window components using state-of-the-art equipment in one of Silver Line's technologically advanced manufacturing plants.

Silver Line steadily gained market share in its vinyl window and patio door business, and opened another new facility, in Lithia Springs, Georgia. Several of the window styles produced in this plant are designed specifically for the southern United States market and for blocktype construction. Vinyl extrusion operations began in the Lithia Springs plant in 1998. Expansion already has started at this facility, with an additional 200,000 square feet of manufacturing area under construction.

Silver Line's flagship plant, an 880,000-square-foot facility in North Brunswick, New Jersey, was opened in the fall of 1995. This state-of-the-art manufacturing plant uses the latest technologies for extruding and fabrication of windows in order to continually supply its customers with high-quality, cost-effective products with consistent standards.

Silver Line's historic commitment to New Jersey is the reason Ken Silverman, the founder's son, purchased the former Johnson & Johnson plant for its North Brunswick site in 1994. The plant is a technologically advanced facility featuring vertically integrated production methods, which translate to greater quality control and better service. Its fifty extrusion lines and production of tens of thousands of windows per day demanded more workers, and the workforce of 1,500 was expanded to 2,400, thus bringing hundreds of new jobs to central New Jersey.

The addition of a new 300,000-square-foot plant in Lansing, Illinois, helps to further the company's expansion and is designed to increase its distribution to cover most of the continental United States. Extrusion presses in the Lansing

The Silver Line Vinyl Extrusion plant is located in North Brunswick at an advanced facility—the former Johnson & Johnson site—and features vertically integrated production methods for added quality control.

plant will be in full production in 1999. Another manufacturing plant, which is planned as the company's fifth facility, will be instrumental in attaining the company goal of comprehensive national distribution.

According to its mission statement, "Silver Line is committed to developing and manufacturing the highest quality, most innovative vinyl windows available today. We will effectively use all technologies and resources available in order to create the most proficient, quality-consistent production methods. By employing a highly competent and motivated workforce, dedicated to anticipating and satisfying our customers' requirements, we will meet or exceed these goals and continue to excel in our industry."

Says Kenneth Silverman, "By continually developing innovative products, refining manufacturing technologies, and providing unparalleled window values, Silver Line will continue broadening the gap between itself and the competition, while maintaining our status as one of the nation's premier vinyl window manufacturers."

improve productivity for builders and furniture makers. For example, AdvanTech® Flooring was designed to meet the construction industry's need for a premium-quality structural floor panel that is faster to install and provides greater dimensional stability than plywood.

NATURAL RESOURCES

One of the largest private landowners in the United States, Huber manages approximately one million acres of timberland. Through forest stewardship, **Huber Wood Products** practices sustainable forestry and manages 25 percent of its land for non-timber values such as wildlife and aesthetics.

Huber Energy, one of the larger privately owned energy production companies in North America, has been active in oil and gas exploration, development, and processing since 1919. Thanks to its strategy of using the best available technology and highly effective operating controls, it is one of the most cost-efficient producers of oil and gas in North America. The company also manages more than 100 million tons of economically recoverable coal reserves.

TECHNOLOGY-BASED SERVICES

Huber's **AVEX Electronics Inc.** provides contract manufacturing services for original equipment manufacturers of computers, communications equipment, and other high-tech electronics. AVEX produces specialized electronic circuit boards through

Huber Woods Environmental Center stands on 120 acres of property donated in 1974 by J. M. Huber Corporation to Monmouth County to be managed as a nature sanctuary. The Huber home, which was donated with the Huber Woods property, is now a wildlife center. © Robert Henschel

Huber's four primary businesses are (clockwise, from top left): Energy, Wood Products, AVEX Electronics Inc., and Engineered Materials.

completed product assemblies while contributing design, engineering, and manufacturing expertise throughout a customer's production processes. These contracted electronic services center on computer, telecommunications, and consumer products for companies such as IBM, Compaq, and General Instrument.

Throughout its history, Huber has been committed to long-term profitable growth. Joseph Maria Huber believed that to succeed, you must constantly search for new ideas and then make sure you have the resources to follow through. The J. M. Huber Corporation has held fast to this basic belief and developed its "family of solutions" to meet the needs of all its customers.

"Huber is able and willing to make investments that support our customers' needs at times when others are not," says Francis. "Because we are family owned, we are not driven by stock market fluctuations. We can steadily pursue both strong profitability and aggressive growth. We actively innovate to make our products and services the best they can be—to work better in our customers' applications, cost less, and add more value."

HUBER
A FAMILY OF SOLUTIONS

THE NEWARK GROUP

AS AN EXPERIENCED AND EXPERT RECYCLER, THE NEWARK GROUP IS A LEADING MAKER OF 100 PERCENT–RECYCLED PAPERBOARD OF NEARLY EVERY GRADE AND VARIETY, AND A POSITIVE FORCE ON BEHALF OF THE ENVIRONMENT

For more than 100 years, The Newark Group has been part of the development and growth of paper recycling in the United States. Pioneers in the company were experimenting with the recycling of old newspaper into paperboard in the 1890s and were issued a United States patent in 1893. The first paper mill owned by the company was founded in 1912 by these pioneers and still operates as Newark Boxboard in the Ironbound section of Newark.

Today Newark Group has more than sixty operations in the United States, providing a national network of paper recovery facilities, paperboard mills, and paperboard converting plants. The company is recognized by paper industry analysts as the largest manufacturer of 100 percent–recycled paperboard in the country. Paperboard is heavyweight paper that is sometimes referred to as cardboard. It makes up the largest class of paper products consumed in the United States.

Paperboard made from 100 percent–recycled paperboard is everywhere—it is found in books, toys, game boards, loose-leaf binders, cereal cartons, rigid boxes, notebook backs, picture backs, mailing tubes, furniture, wallboard facing paper, and more. Newark Group produces 3,500 tons of 100 percent–recycled paperboard every day, and each ton must be competitive against other materials to provide economic benefits, or it won't be sold. Recycling at Newark Group is not a passing environmental fancy, but an industrial enterprise that must make economic sense.

Recycling has become an environmental buzz word, but as Newark enters its second hundred years, paper recycling is finally getting recognition as a critical part of our nation's manufacturing base that also makes environmental sense.

Paper recycling has great public support. People feel good about recycling because they feel a shared responsibility not to squander natural resources—and they can participate in the process. The Newark Group is proud to provide a market for paper material collected in commercial and municipal programs throughout the United States. The company states, "We applaud the continued strength of the American public's recycling activities, which is the lifeblood of our business."

Corporate headquarters for The Newark Group is in Cranford, New Jersey.

The company's route system for pickups from supermarkets and retail stores generates large volumes of used corrugated containers.

288 CREATING THE FUTURE

Members of The Newark Group's management team have been active with local, state, and federal groups involved with the recycling industry and the environment. Edward K. Mullen, chairman of the Newark Group, has been a major force in both areas for many years. Ed Mullen joined the company in 1959, and over the years he has led its growth and acquisition strategy.

As major members of the paper industry became less attracted to the recycled paperboard market in the 1970s, Newark Group started moving to acquire mills. Three mills were acquired in 1971 and The Newark Group is still growing. In 1997 it acquired two mills. During this same time period the company grew in paperboard converting through its BCI Book Covers, Inc., and Newark Paperboard Products divisions. Collecting, sorting, and packing recovered paper was always an important function, and another division, Recycled Fibers, has become a player in both the domestic and international markets.

The growth strategy also has meant major investments in new facilities, technology, and products to satisfy the old and new markets. The fundamentals of paper recycling are old, but the speed and accuracy of today's converting equipment has created an entirely new set of standards for the simplest of paperboard products. Every process in the company has been improved or changed in the past twenty-five years. The entire process must now be measured and controlled to assure the level of quality that has been mandated by the customers of today.

The Newark Group's corporate office in Cranford, New Jersey, keeps close financial and planning control of the four distinct business units, but forces decisions down to the operating level whenever possible. The divisions' operating units have as much decision-making leeway as is practical. This structure gives The Newark Group the power of a large company with the entrepreneurial qualities of a smaller one.

The Mill Division has fifteen sites that operate twenty-two paper machines around the clock, seven days a week, and produce more than 1.3 million tons of superior-quality 100 percent–recycled paperboard annually. Approximately 35 percent of this tonnage is consumed within The Newark Group's own converting plants and 65 percent is sold to independent paperboard converters worldwide.

The primary product of BCI Book Covers is laminated paperboard in a wide range of calipers, sheet sizes, and custom-cut-to-size panels. BCI is North America's largest supplier of heavyweight paperboard for the stationery, loose-leaf, game board, and book publishing industries. Altogether, BCI serves twelve active and rapidly expanding markets.

This paperboard machine is at the Newark Paperboard Mill Division's Pacific mill.

Newark Paperboard Products is a nationwide supplier of tubes and cores for paper, film, fabric, and tape manufacturers. The division manufactures a full line of mill finishing supplies and offers a full spectrum of converting and finishing services.

The Recycled Fibers division has grown into one of the largest collectors and suppliers of high-quality recovered paper. It not only supplies its own paperboard mills with raw material, but it also sells half of what is processed to independent mills. Processing facilities in every region of the nation collect, sort, grade, and pack more than 2.5 million tons of recovered paper annually. This accounts for more than 5 percent of all recovered paper collected for recycling each year in the United States.

MAKERS OF
100% Recycled Paperboard™

A municipal collection of old newspapers is unloaded at the company's boxboard mill in Newark.

MANUFACTURING, DISTRIBUTION, AND WAREHOUSING 289

BENJAMIN MOORE & CO.

RECOGNIZED INDUSTRYWIDE FOR ITS RIGOROUS LABORATORY TESTING, BENJAMIN MOORE & CO. APPLIES ITS HIGH STANDARDS TO THE ART AND SCIENCE OF PRODUCING FINE PAINTS, STAINS, AND COATINGS FOR USE BY PROFESSIONALS AND DO-IT-YOURSELFERS

Benjamin Moore & Co. began as a small start-up manufacturer in 1883 and today is one of the country's largest producers of paints and stains. Its products are sold primarily throughout the United States and Canada through a network of authorized, independent retailers to paint users ranging from the professional painting contractor to the industrial maintenance specifier, from the interior designer to the do-it-yourself homeowner.

Benjamin Moore & Co. was founded by Benjamin Moore, a young, enterprising Irishman who began his paint business venture with his brother, Robert, in a small building in Brooklyn, New York. The brothers started by manufacturing a product called Calsom Finish, a calsomine coating for walls and ceilings. From its New York roots the company began its expansion in North America in the early part of this century. In 1972 it moved its headquarters to New Jersey.

In the twentieth century new technology accelerated the development of new paint products, including washable flat finishes, latex-based paints, and waterborne products that blended the best features of latex and oil coatings. The company grew steadily during the first half of the century and expanded dramatically after World War II. Today Benjamin Moore & Co., now headquartered in Montvale, New Jersey, has grown to produce paint in fifteen manufacturing facilities in North America.

Shown above, color transitions from Benjamin Moore & Co. that energize, inspire, and transform space include Benjamin Moore #076, Benjamin Moore #1372, and Benjamin Moore #1330.

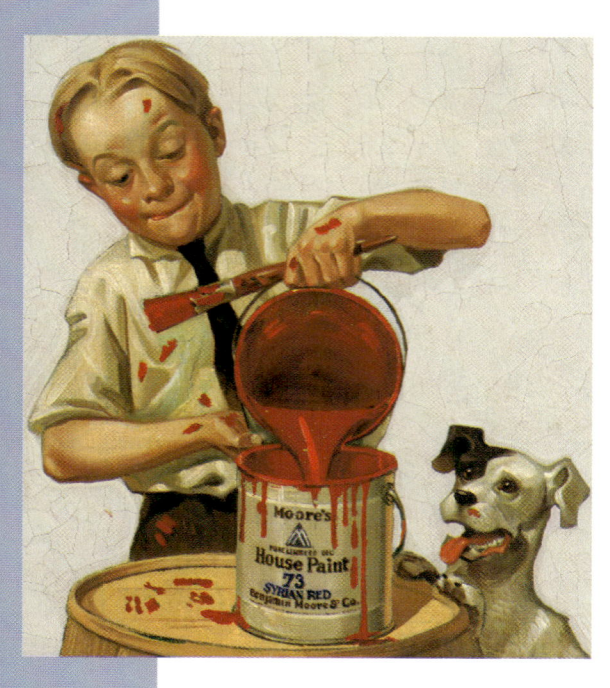

Benjamin Moore & Co.'s display advertisement from 1919 shows Benjamin Moore's quality product being enjoyed by a boy with support from his faithful companion.

The entire line of Benjamin Moore & Co. products is sold in North America at more than 4,000 independent paint retailers. These retailers, in turn, serve the needs of homeowners and professional and industrial painters with their expertise, extensive product knowledge, and personalized service.

"We still live by the philosophy and the standard of integrity set by Benjamin Moore," says Richard Roob, chairman and CEO of Benjamin Moore & Co., and it is upon those guidelines that the company's vision is based.

One reason Benjamin Moore & Co. consistently delivers the level of quality that its customers have grown to rely on is the ongoing, rigorous scientific testing to which all its products are subjected. More than 100 chemists, chemical engineers, technicians, and support staff maintain Benjamin Moore & Co.'s stringent product standards and develop new products. In addition, Benjamin Moore & Co. is committed to sound environmental management. Environmental considerations are included in the company's

CREATING THE FUTURE

facility design, product development, production, packaging, marketing, distribution, and end use.

At Benjamin Moore & Co., developing new paints is both a science and an art. The company's technical staff operates at numerous team-based laboratories located at the Benjamin Moore Technical & Administrative Center in Flanders, New Jersey. At each lab, equipped with state-of-the-art instruments, the staff focuses on a specific area of coating expertise. Together they develop all Benjamin Moore paint formulas. All the laboratories work with Benjamin Moore & Co.'s manufacturing plants and its marketing department to address the varied needs and demands of the professional, commercial, industrial, and do-it-yourself markets.

If formulation is the scientific side of the business, color development can be viewed as the artistic. However, that, too, is gained through exacting color standards and prescriptions created and monitored in the Color Development and the Color Assurance laboratories. The result is an unparalleled range of colors available at every Benjamin Moore & Co. dealer.

The Technical & Administrative Center operates the Benjamin Moore & Co.'s Exterior Testing Station, known as "the test farm." It is here that more than 20,000 painted and stained panels are exposed to the elements for periods of time ranging from six months to fifteen years. New exterior coatings are tested, as are existing product formulations and competitive coatings. Every known exterior surface condition that can plague paint or stain shows up either at the New Jersey testing station or in the harsh UV-saturated Florida sun, where a second testing station is located.

"Our technical facility is recognized in our industry as a model coatings research and development center," says company president Yvan Dupuy. "Our large professional staff is experienced and knowledgeable in all aspects of coatings technology, and they are supported by the most modern equipment and instrumentation

Benjamin Moore & Co. is known for its commitment to producing the highest-quality products and offering paints of unsurpassed colors, such as the hues shown above.

Benjamin Moore & Co. has been manufacturing premium quality paints and stains since 1883. The company recently introduced Benjamin Moore brushes and rollers.

BENJAMIN MOORE'S VALUES AND MISSION STATEMENTS

Benjamin Moore's original philosophy has endured while product offerings have expanded and changed. This philosophy is reflected in the company's values and mission statements.

BENJAMIN MOORE'S VALUES STATEMENT

- We are committed to maintaining the highest standards of fairness, honesty, and decency.
- We recognize an obligation to shareholders and employees to properly reward their respective contributions to company profitability and growth.
- We encourage learning so that each of us may seize the opportunities for self-fulfillment through personal growth.
- We strive to achieve mutually beneficial relationships with suppliers.
- We are committed to being good corporate citizens and to the protection of the environment.

BENJAMIN MOORE'S MISSION STATEMENT

Benjamin Moore & Co. is a high-performing, innovative provider of quality coatings and related goods and services for decoration and preservation.

available. The quality of the products they develop has earned us an outstanding reputation within both the industry and the marketplace."

MANUFACTURING, DISTRIBUTION, AND WAREHOUSING   291

RECKITT & COLMAN INC.

RECKITT & COLMAN INC. IS THE NAME BEHIND MANY OF THE BRANDS CONSUMERS KNOW AND TRUST— BRANDS LIKE LYSOL® CLEANERS AND DISINFECTANTS, RESOLVE® CARPET CLEANERS, SPRAY'N WASH® LAUNDRY STAIN REMOVERS, AND FRENCH'S® MUSTARDS

Reckitt & Colman Inc. makes, markets, and sells leading household and specialty food products in North America. The company's product portfolio includes Lysol® cleaners and disinfectants, Resolve® carpet cleaners, Spray'n Wash® laundry stain removers, French's® mustards, and Frank's® RedHot® sauces. These products are widely used in consumer households as well as in professional markets, such as hospitals and nursing homes, hotels and resorts, and schools and other institutions. Specialty food products also are sold to food manufacturers and the food service industry.

The company is a subsidiary of London-based Reckitt & Colman plc, which has grown from its United Kingdom roots to become a global company, making products in more than 30 countries and selling them in more than 170 countries across the world. Approximately one-third of Reckitt & Colman's overall business is in North America.

The production line for Lysol disinfectant spray at Reckitt & Colman's manufacturing facility in Belle Mead, New Jersey, is tended by Clara Valez and Sam Gangwer. © Reckitt & Colman Inc.

New Jersey–based Reckitt & Colman Inc. makes, markets, and sells household and specialty food products, including the leading Lysol®, Resolve®, Woolite®, French's®, and Frank's® RedHot® brands. © Reckitt & Colman Inc.

RECKITT & COLMAN

Reckitt & Colman's North American Regional and Resource Centers are located in Wayne, New Jersey, and its world-class Technical Center is in Montvale, New Jersey. In addition to a major manufacturing site in Belle Mead, New Jersey, the company also has offices, manufacturing facilities, and logistics centers throughout the United States, Canada, and Jamaica.

Reckitt & Colman was first established in North America in the 1920s with the purchase of the R. T. French Company. It has emerged as a dynamic consumer products company through a series of key acquisitions, including Airwick Industries, Durkee Famous Food, and the Boyle-Midway Division of American Home Products.

The 1994 acquisition of L&F Products, consisting of Lysol brand cleaners and disinfectants and other major brands, enabled Reckitt & Colman to strengthen its United States presence.

In 1998 Reckitt & Colman acquired several DowBrands products, including Spray'n Wash laundry stain removers and Glass Plus® glass and surface cleaner.

Reckitt & Colman's manufacturing facility in Belle Mead, New Jersey, which was first opened by the former L&F business in 1971, has expanded through the years to its current size of 415,000 square feet and has become one of the largest aerosol manufacturing facilities in the United States. The Lysol, Easy-On®, Easy-Off®, Wizard®, and Mop & Glo® brands are made here and then shipped to logistics centers in the United States and Canada. The Belle Mead team consists of more than 280 women and men who work in capacities ranging from equipment operators to engineering specialists.

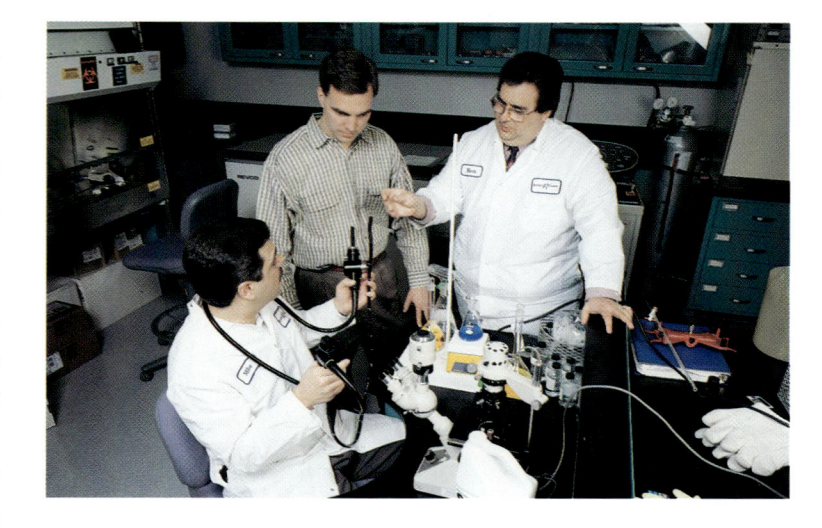

The Reckitt & Colman Technical Center in Montvale is a 78,000-square-foot, energy-efficient, state-of-the-art facility. It features highlights such as development and testing laboratories, microbiology and virology laboratories, food test kitchens, pilot plants where sample batches are made and tested, a sensory evaluation laboratory, and a research library. The facility houses more than 150 scientists, technicians, and support personnel and acts as the company's global technical center for its Surface Care and Fabrics Care products.

Reflecting its team-based work philosophy, the company renovated its Regional Center in Wayne, New Jersey, to eliminate traditional offices and other area floor plans that unintentionally formed barriers to the achievement of company goals. Reckitt & Colman's new open-plan work environment encourages more personal interaction among coworkers and greater information sharing and innovation in all areas of the company.

With regard to community involvement, the company takes pride in conducting an annual regionwide United Way campaign

From left, Mike Monticello, Phil Mazzini, and Ben Costa discuss product development at Reckitt & Colman Inc.'s world-class Technical Center in Montvale, New Jersey. © Reckitt & Colman Inc.

and offering employees matching gifts to charity and education programs. It also partners with the nonprofit disaster-relief agency AmeriCares to donate Lysol brand cleaners and disinfectants and educational materials to assist flood victims with cleanup efforts, and provides employees with a number of opportunities, such as Habitat for Humanity projects, to volunteer their time to help those in need. Initiatives such as these earned Reckitt & Colman the distinction of being named Corporate Citizen of the Year in 1997 by the Wayne Industrial and Economic Development Commission.

In addition to its focus on the business, Reckitt & Colman takes seriously its commitment to the environment. The company designs its products, processes, and packaging to minimize waste and ensure materials are safe for disposal. It also takes appropriate action to support and facilitate efforts to reduce waste, where possible, through reuse and recycling.

"Looking at the twenty-first century, we consider it a major advantage to be headquartered in New Jersey," says Joseph M. Healy, president and CEO. "New Jersey offers a talent pool that is rich in diversity and has a heritage focused on the health care industry, which is important to us with regard to the market-leading cleaning and disinfectant products we sell to consumers and to the professional marketplace. It's a great place to do business."

Regional operations for Reckitt & Colman Inc. are based on Valley Road in Wayne, New Jersey. © Reckitt & Colman Inc.

MANUFACTURING, DISTRIBUTION, AND WAREHOUSING 293

NEW JERSEY BUSINESS & INDUSTRY ASSOCIATION

Representing more than 16,000 member companies, the New Jersey Business & Industry Association offers representation before government agencies, strategic lobbying, insurance, seminars, and opportunities to network with peers

The New Jersey Business & Industry Association (NJBIA) is the leading voice for New Jersey enterprise. The nation's largest statewide employer association, NJBIA represents more than 16,000 member companies that together employ more than one million employees in New Jersey. Since 1910, when the organization was founded as the New Jersey Manufacturers Association, it has been a strong and effective advocate for business.

NJBIA is the chief representative of the state's business community before the legislature and state agencies. NJBIA appears frequently before the executive and legislative branches of state government on behalf of its member companies, addressing hundreds of legislative and regulatory initiatives in order to enhance the state economy. Consistently rated one of the top lobbying groups for its credibility and clout, NJBIA is regarded by public officials, pollsters, and peers as one of the most effective lobbying organizations in the state.

Located at 102 West State Street, across from the State Capitol, NJBIA is strategically located to give members an insider's view of politics in Trenton.

NJBIA members benefit from a variety of direct services. While NJBIA's government affairs work is important, it is just one of the many services the association offers. NJBIA provides many seminars and publications for members to help each business improve its bottom line. Participation in seminars, NJBIA policy committees, annual Golf & Tennis Day, county-based Employer Legislative Committees, and other programs provides many opportunities for members to meet, network, and learn.

As a member of NJBIA a company, along with its employees, is eligible to apply for insurance coverage with New Jersey Manufacturers Insurance Company (NJM), one of the state's largest property/casualty insurers. NJM provides coverage for workers' compensation and personal automobile and homeowners' insurance. The insurer has a top rating in its industry and pays annual dividends to policyholders.

"When it comes down to it, 'clout' comes from the numbers, and the larger and more powerful we are, the more people will listen," says NJBIA president Joe Gonzalez. "Each and every member counts. Our members guide our agenda for legislative action and tell us which programs are useful. Our members make us a dynamic and growing organization. We are committed to helping them succeed."

Association president Joe Gonzalez welcomes a crowd of 250 business leaders to NJBIA's 1997 Public Policy Forum in Woodbridge, New Jersey. © A. J. Sundstrom Photography

Joe Gonzalez chats with New Jersey governor Christine Todd Whitman at a bill signing ceremony in Edgewater, New Jersey, in January 1998.

CREATING THE FUTURE

MANUFACTURING, DISTRIBUTION, AND WAREHOUSING 295

LEADING IN EDUCATION

296   CREATING THE FUTURE

CHAPTER TWENTY

New Jerseyans care deeply about the quality of their education, and it shows. The state's eight million citizens are among the most educated in the nation, and one of the Garden State's greatest assets is its higher education system. Over 325,000 students, including over 50,000 graduate students, attend fifty-four public and private colleges and universities. Over 90 percent of these students hail from New Jersey secondary schools. The annual state budget for higher education is in excess of $3.2 billion.

Besides providing an outstanding education, New Jersey's institutions of higher education support economic growth in the state through research and development. Colleges and universities here have been prodigious when it comes to securing private and government funding. In 1994 alone, New Jersey schools accounted for over $400 million in research and development expenditures.

As the twenty-first century dawns, the state's public colleges—the backbone of New Jersey's system of higher education—have been moving aggressively to become "prestige" schools. In recent years an increasing number have switched their designation from "college" to "university." In the same vein, the school formerly known as Trenton State College has adopted the more refined name of the College of New Jersey to reflect its consistent ranking as the best public college in the mid-Atlantic region and as a "best buy" in national college surveys.

Choice Abounds

The diversity of choices is what makes New Jersey's system of higher education truly outstanding. The state's flagship public university, Rutgers, with nearly fifty thousand students on three campuses, is one of the oldest, most respected state schools in the United States. Of the twenty-eight top state universities, Rutgers ranks sixth in six-year graduation rates, thirteenth in freshman SAT scores, and first in minority enrollment.

OPPOSITE: *Students who hope to work in engineering, architecture, and similar fields must first master the tools of their trade. Today these tools include computer-aided design (CAD) systems. Here, an instructor and student at the New Jersey Institute of Technology confer over a computer-generated rendering. © Mike Peters/Courtesy, New Jersey Institute of Technology.* ABOVE: *The quest for knowledge has always turned our eyes and thoughts to the heavens. Here, a lone astronomer burns the night oil in the observatory of the Serin Physics building on Rutgers's Busch campus in Piscataway. © Rutgers/Nick Romanenko*

RUTGERS VS PRINCETON

More a violent free-for-all than an organized sport, college football was born on a cold Saturday afternoon in November 1869 when students from Princeton and Rutgers clashed on a large field in New Brunswick. About a hundred spectators saw Rutgers win 6 to 4.

But Rutgers is only the tip of the iceberg. New Jersey has two other public research universities, both with their main campuses in Newark. Two national magazines rank New Jersey Institute of Technology among the top universities. *Money* magazine, in its annual "Money Guide: Best College Buys," rates NJIT third among the nation's scientific and technological institutions. *U.S. News and World Report* places NJIT among the top one hundred "national universities" in its annual guide to "America's Best Colleges." NJIT's School of Architecture is the fifth-largest architecture school in the nation. Similarly, the University of Medicine and Dentistry of New Jersey is the largest freestanding health sciences university in the country.

New Jersey also has nineteen two-year community colleges across the state and eight four-year public colleges and universities, which combine affordability and quality. Finally, there are fourteen private institutions, which draw about 80 percent of their students from within the state. Among them are smaller, prestigious colleges such as Drew University in Madison, known for its strong liberal arts programs; Stevens Institute of Technology in Hoboken, which focuses on the sciences and technology; and Seton Hall University in South Orange, which is one of the country's top Catholic colleges and will celebrate its 150th anniversary in 2006. Then, of course, there's Princeton University, an Ivy League school whose tradition, history, and general excellence place it among an elite few in the nation.

Carrying On the Tradition

Princeton and Rutgers are two of the nation's oldest institutions of higher learning. Ironically, Princeton was

The graduating class of 1900 at the New Jersey Normal School, now known as the College of New Jersey, the "best public college in the mid-Atlantic region." Courtesy, the College of New Jersey

Montclair State University in Upper Montclair, William Paterson University in Wayne, Kean University in Union, and Monmouth University in Long Branch. Jersey City State College is expected to petition for university status, too. Several four-year institutions, including the College of New Jersey, Caldwell College, and Bloomfield College, feel strongly about remaining colleges. Since 1994 Richard Stockton College in Stockton, known for its small-sized classes and individualized attention, has been classified as one of only seven selective public liberal arts colleges in the country.

COMMUNITY COLLEGES

More than a third of New Jersey's students attend the state's nineteen community colleges, two-year schools designed to provide affordable access to career programs and training. About one-quarter of these students eventually transfer into New Jersey's public four-year colleges and universities.

Each county's college tailors its offerings to the unique needs of its residents. For instance, Atlantic Community College, in the shadow of Atlantic City's casino resorts, runs the nationally recognized Academy of Culinary Arts and the Casino Career Institute. Camden County College is a national leader in technology instruction. Passaic County Community College is known for its cultural programs, including its Poetry Center and Young People's Theater. Salem Community College, located in the heart of the state's glass-blowing industry, is the only school in the nation where you will find an associate's degree program in scientific glass technology.

In addition, New Jerseyans show a desire for lifelong learning. Over two hundred thousand citizens participate

Valerie Fitzhugh (center), a member of the Rutgers fencing team, shows off her swashbuckling equipment to friends on the Busch campus. Women's fencing is one of Rutgers–New Brunswick's thirty NCAA varsity sports teams. © Rutgers/Alan Goldsmith

THE PRINCETON UNIVERSITY CAMPUS OFFERS A 250-YEAR HISTORY OF ARCHITECTURE. BUILDING STYLES RANGE FROM THE COLLEGIATE GOTHIC TO THE ITALIANATE REVIVAL TO THE POST-MODERN. PROMINENT ARCHITECTS WHO HAVE DESIGNED CAMPUS BUILDINGS INCLUDE BENJAMIN LATROBE, RICHARD MORRIS HUNT, AND ROBERT VENTURI.

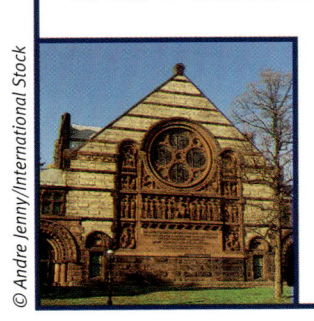

LEADING IN EDUCATION 303

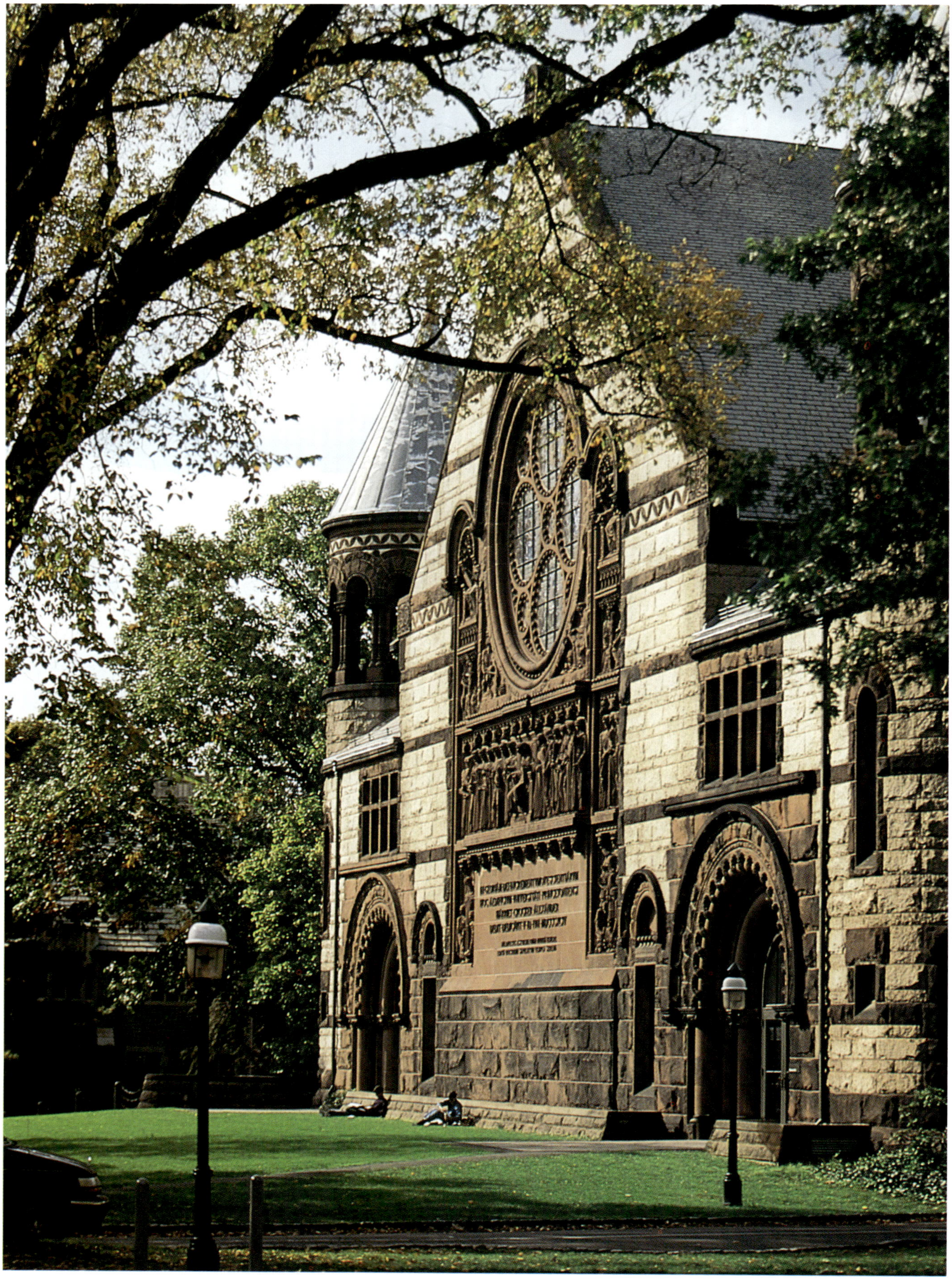

Seton Hall is one of the nation's largest and most respected Catholic institutions. Courtesy, Seton Hall University

The *New York Times* deemed Thomas Edison "one of the brighter stars in higher learning."

SPECIAL PROGRAMS AND PROJECTS

New Jersey works hard to keep its most promising high school students in-state. Eight public and private institutions participate in the Outstanding Scholars Recruitment Program, which offers roughly $2 million in grant scholarships to deserving students who choose to go to Rutgers University, The College of New Jersey, Drew, Fairleigh Dickinson, Montclair State University, NJIT, or Richard Stockton College.

In a further effort to attract students in and outside of New Jersey, universities and colleges throughout the state are spending millions of dollars to build new facilities, incorporate new programs into their curriculum, form alliances with other schools and with corporations, and update and expand their use of technology.

New construction and renovation projects include a new academic building on the Florham-Madison campus of Fairleigh Dickinson University; a new $12-million sports complex and $17 million in additions of labs and classrooms at Montclair State; and a $6-million renovation of Drew's Bowne Theater, which has been the site of the New Jersey Shakespeare Festival since 1962. The biggest capital project, which is expected to be completed as the new century begins, is the

annually in continuing education courses at New Jersey community colleges, and nearly half of those attending New Jersey colleges and universities are twenty-five years of age or older.

In response to so many adult students, the state founded the innovative Thomas Edison State College in 1972, which provides unique self-directed programs of study. The college offers no "classroom" courses. Instead, the college brings education directly to adults, wherever they live or work.

OPPOSITE: *Princeton University's venerable Alexander Hall stands in testament to the university's rich history and tradition of excellence.* © Scott Barrow. RIGHT: *Bergen Community College offers degree programs in eighty fields of study. Here, graduating seniors gather for commencement exercises.* Courtesy, Bergen Community College

LEADING IN EDUCATION 305

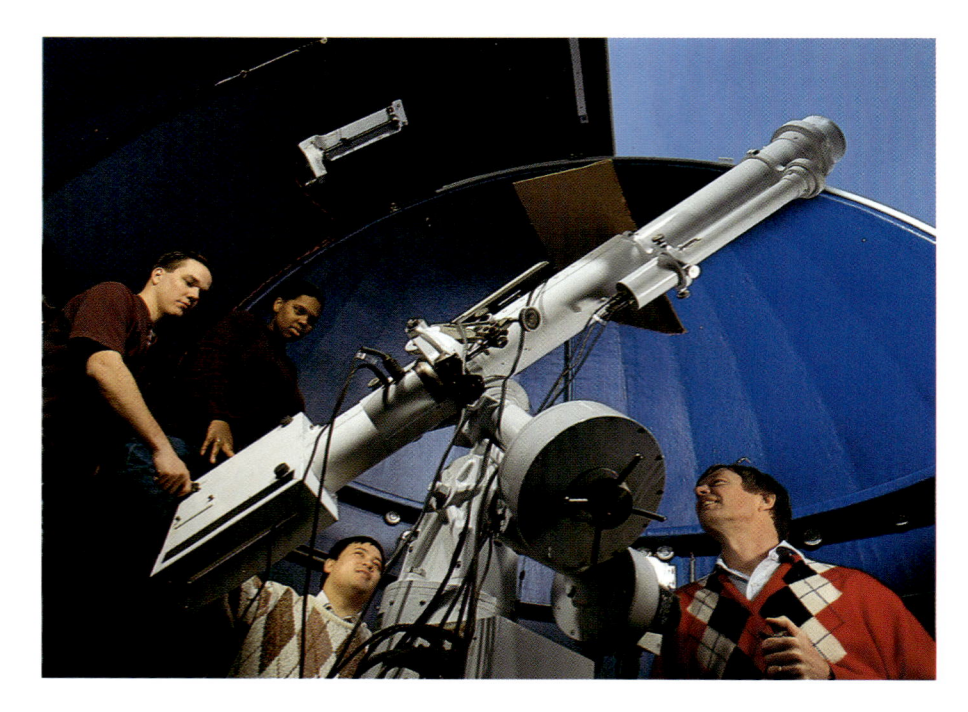

Science rules at New Jersey Institute of Technology. © Mike Peters/Courtesy, New Jersey Institute of Technology

$49-million Center for Law and Justice in Newark. This site will house the Rutgers School of Law and School of Criminal Justice.

The University of Medicine and Dentistry of New Jersey has recently introduced new doctoral programs in health sciences and biomedical informatics—fields of study that focus on the technology and delivery systems needed to respond to rapid changes in health care. Other new academic programs include a new course of study for entrepreneurs at Fairleigh Dickinson University's business school, a graduate degree in women's studies at Drew, two advanced programs in health law and policy at Seton Hall, and a master of arts in jazz history at Rutgers's Newark campus.

Technology continues to play a critical role in how students learn. Most institutions of higher learning in New Jersey have updated and expanded their computer labs and constructed campuswide networks. They also have rewired their lecture halls and residence buildings: Students can plug in their computers in class and get Internet access from their dorm rooms. At Seton Hall, the school's innovative alliance with IBM has fostered a number of initiatives, from providing incoming freshmen with notebook computers to be used in the classroom, to digitizing the library so that all materials are available on-line.

With so many great choices, it is easy to see why New Jersey's best and brightest high school seniors stay home for a first-rate college education.

BELOW: *Researchers use state-of-the-art greenhouse facilities on Rutgers's Cook campus in New Brunswick. © Rutgers/Nick Romanenko.* OPPOSITE: *The past and future intersect on Princeton's historied campus. © Scott Barrow*

306 CREATING THE FUTURE

LEADING IN EDUCATION 307

Asbury Hall at Drew University. © G. Steve Jordan/Drew University

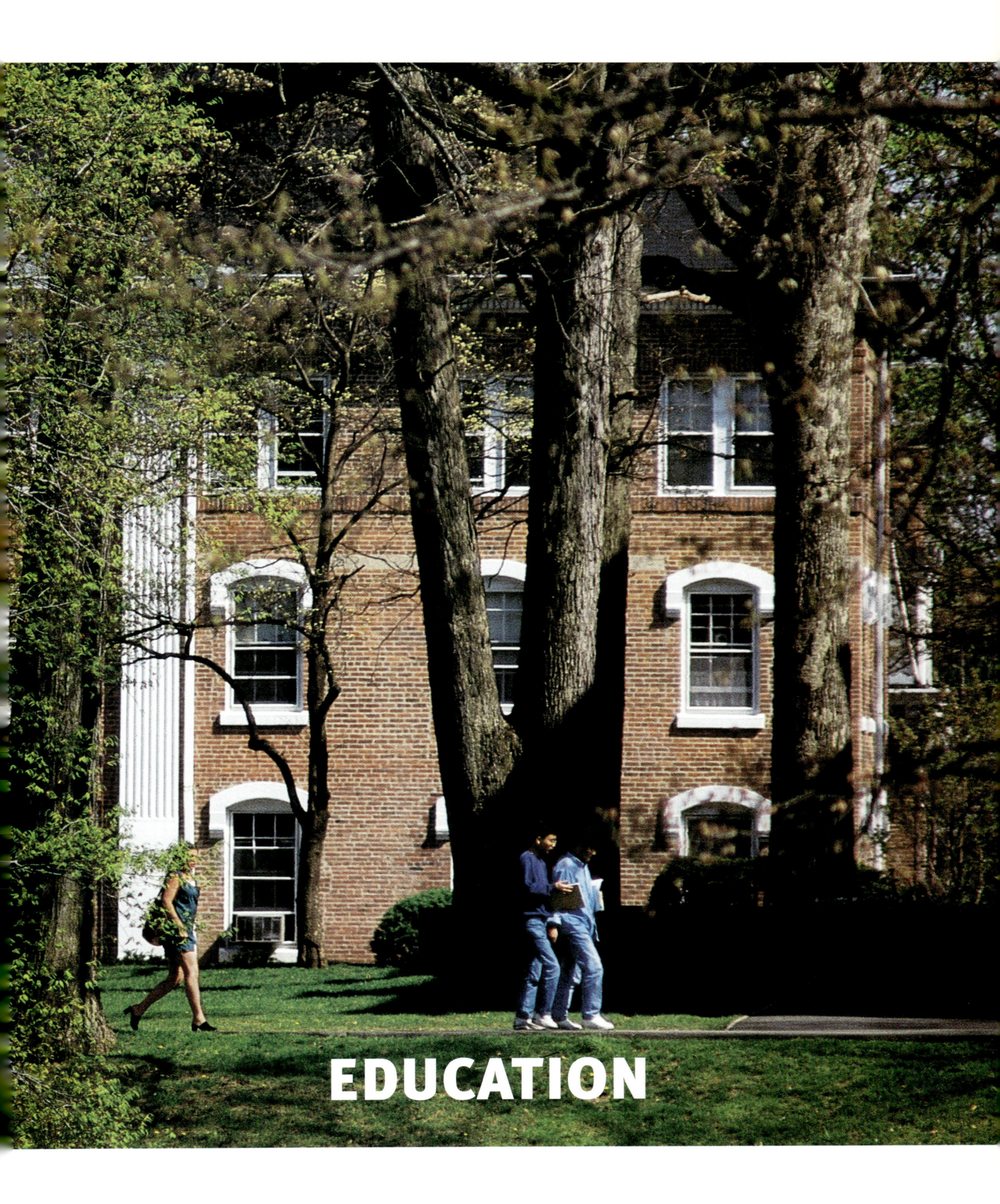

EDUCATION

BROOKDALE COMMUNITY COLLEGE

FULLY ACCREDITED BROOKDALE COMMUNITY COLLEGE COMBINES THE BEST TRADITIONS OF HIGHER EDUCATION WITH GOAL-ORIENTED CLASSES, PROVIDING UNIQUE OPPORTUNITIES FOR LIFELONG LEARNING AT ITS MAIN CAMPUS AND FIVE CENTERS IN MONMOUTH COUNTY

With its outstanding reputation for academic excellence and community service, Brookdale Community College, the County College of Monmouth, is positioned to play an increasingly important role in the development of the region's people and businesses. The school's ability to work closely with students to help them as they make transitions, learn new skills, and think critically has never been more important than it is in today's fast-paced and competitive world.

"Brookdale is a unique institution because it is very student focused," says Dr. Peter F. Burnham, president of Brookdale Community College. "The learning and teaching that occur here are based on providing as much individual support and attention as possible. At the heart of our learning process is attention to student achievement. I believe this personalized attention enables the Brookdale student to have a comprehensive and personal learning experience that helps prepare each one for work and life."

Brookdale's comprehensive approach to teaching benefits not only students but also the business community. The business courses that Brookdale offers are determined by demand in the job market and input from local employers. In addition to its new culinary degree—available through the Culinary Education Center, developed in cooperation with the Monmouth County Vocational School District—Brookdale is exploring other new degree fields and continuously assessing and improving its more than fifty degree and certificate programs.

Further meeting local needs, Brookdale's partnership with Rutgers University enables residents to acquire a four-year degree from a public institution without traveling outside of Monmouth County

The increasingly diverse student body at Brookdale Community College can take advantage of many clubs and activities offered through the Office of Student Life & Activities. Among the options are athletics; trips to metropolitan attractions, such as theaters and museums; performances by guest artists and musicians; Friday dinner cinemas; health programs; study abroad opportunities; and the International Center.

Robin Shannon broadcasts live from WBJB 90.5 FM, Brookdale's public radio station serving central New Jersey. Shannon, a Brookdale graduate, is the local host for Brookdale's broadcast of the popular National Public Radio show "Morning Edition."

to attend school. Other postassociate agreements are in development.

To prepare students for an increasingly technological business environment, Brookdale has recently completed a collegewide electronic network with connections to all departmental units and campuses and new PCs for all faculty members. Brookdale is also using the most current technology to teach classes at several sites simultaneously through its Interactive Television Viewing (ITV) classrooms.

Brookdale's curriculum emphasizes "experiential learning," in the form of internships, cooperative work experience, or service learning opportunities. These experiences give students a chance, in a supervised environment, to apply what they learn in school in the "real" world.

310 CREATING THE FUTURE

"One of the school's fundamental roles is to keep one of the most precious resources—young people—here in Monmouth County," says Burnham. "Brookdale is now enrolling more than one of every four Monmouth County high school graduates who are bound for college. This means that 25 percent of the youngsters of our community who are pursuing higher education are making Brookdale their college of first choice. Brookdale's reputation is made strong by several advantages it provides, including an education students can afford, the quality of the education, the ability to easily transfer credits to a four-year school, and the chance to enter the workforce fully prepared."

Brookdale affords an opportunity for thousands of currently employed citizens to renew and upgrade their skills to strengthen the workforce and economy of Monmouth County. The college works with unemployed and underemployed people of all ages and backgrounds. Brookdale is the perfect example of the way a community college helps to strengthen the economy of its community by reinvesting tax dollars that help citizens become more productive, thus generating more tax dollars and improving the quality of life for the entire community.

Brookdale offers the community a full array of noncredit workshops, seminars, trips, and intensive job training programs. The programs range from vocational courses to professional development. Courses are designed for different age groups, including children and adults of all ages. Brookdale also hosts several major events annually at the college as part of its community outreach program, including a Women's Conference and the African American Family Festival, and local high school graduation ceremonies.

Brookdale's Center for Business Services also provides custom-tailored training for local employers. Working directly with an employer's human resources department or with company executives, the Brookdale staff conducts an assessment of needs, identifies areas in which training would strengthen the company's operations, and tailors a training program for the company's employees. These programs can be presented on Brookdale's Lincroft campus, at one of its Learning Centers, or at the company's own site. Although the bulk of the on-site training is noncredit, the college can also, at the company's request, present courses for credit. Because Brookdale has tremendous professional resources within the college, the community at large, and among other community colleges, it can offer any kind of course or program a company needs, from English as a Second Language to highly technical skills training.

Brookdale continues to work in partnerships with business and industry, expanding its successful workforce training programs, continuing to build comprehensive services for retraining and worker assistance, and developing seamless education programs for all.

Brookdale Community College was founded in 1967 by the citizens of Monmouth County through the Board of Chosen Freeholders. The college is governed by a twelve-member board of trustees, all active professionals in the community. In addition to the college's main campus in Lincroft, there are five extension centers around Monmouth County: in Asbury Park, the Bayshore, Western Monmouth, Long Branch, and at Fort Monmouth. The college also maintains a Learning Center in Guayaquil, Ecuador.

This picturesque corn crib is a reminder of the original Brookdale Farm, owned by the Thompson family, where racehorses were bred and trained from the late 1800s to the 1940s. The college was established in 1967 after philanthropist and society leader Geraldine Thompson's sale of the farm on very generous terms to the Monmouth County Board of Chosen Freeholders.

Brookdale's Performing Arts Center, a 350-seat public theater, offers a seasonal calendar of drama, music, dance, and guest appearances by popular artists. The center is the site for Brookdale's unique Technical Theater I and II courses, where students learn computerized lighting, set design and construction, staging, and costume and makeup skills in a professionally equipped house; graduates are fully prepared to work behind the scenes in New York theaters.

EDUCATION 311

BERGEN COMMUNITY COLLEGE

COMPREHENSIVE RESOURCES COMPLEMENT THE HANDS-ON APPROACH TO EDUCATION AT 167-ACRE BERGEN COMMUNITY COLLEGE, A FULLY ACCREDITED INSTITUTION DEDICATED TO FOSTERING STUDENTS' POTENTIAL

The Bergen Community College megastructure, which includes many hands-on facilities, allows students to gain practical skills in their particular area of study.

As a community college, Bergen Community College (BCC) offers students many advantages that they may not find anywhere else: small classes, affordable tuition, faculty dedicated to classroom teaching, outstanding academic support services, flexible scheduling, a diverse student population, and a student-centered campus.

BCC is a comprehensive, publicly supported two-year college that is fully accredited by the Commission on Higher Education of the Middle States Association of Colleges and Schools. Through its open admissions policy, the college is committed to providing equal educational opportunities for all.

BCC offers three types of degree programs in more than eighty fields of study. Students can earn an associate in arts (A.A.), associate in science (A.S.), and an associate in applied science (A.A.S.) degree. In addition, the college offers one-year certificate programs and certificates of achievement that provide training for specific occupational skills.

Workforce training is a key element in the education mix at BCC. Credit and noncredit programs are designed to equip students with the technical skills and training needed to remain competitive in the workforce of tomorrow. The college has recently introduced several new programs specifically geared to the current workforce trends, including environmental technology, specialty imaging for radiographers, and a veterinary technology program.

Through its Division of Continuing Education and Institute for Corporate Training, Bergen Community College is able to meet the rapidly changing needs for computer training, English as a Second Language (ESL), and high-technology training, as well as provide professional development programs in health, management, real estate, construction, and more. In addition, the college offers customized training to business and industry, given on the Bergen and Paramus campuses. The Adult Learning Center in Hackensack, undergoing a comprehensive expansion, also offers a wide variety of programs, including adult-based literacy, high school equivalency, ESL, and employability skills workshops.

Students receive more than a degree at BCC; they gain practical skills and knowledge that they will continue to apply beyond the walls of the college. The school's hands-on approach to education reflects the faculty's focus on applying the concepts they teach to real-life situations. A student may be chef for the day in the Bergen Room restaurant as part of the school's Hotel-Restaurant Management program, work in the Child Development Center as part of the Early Childhood Education major, or use the commercial art computer labs while learning the tools of the trade as a graphic artist.

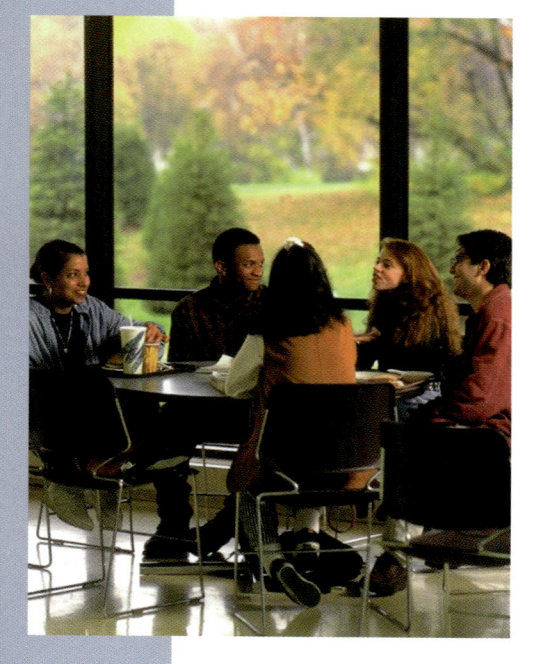

The cafeteria is just one of the campus locations where students gather to share ideas and get to know each other.

CREATING THE FUTURE

BCC offers comprehensive facilities and resources that support its academic programs. The allied health, drafting, robotics, and hotel-restaurant management departments all boast well-equipped labs. Some of the facilities, such as the Dental Hygiene Clinic and the Bergen Room restaurant, are open to the public. Whatever a student's major is, BCC has the resources for a hands-on education that will enhance the academic experience and prepare the student for the career of his or her choice.

Situated on a beautiful 167-acre campus, Bergen Community College is bordered by two golf courses and a county park. The campus grounds include a pool, tennis court, baseball fields, a par course, and a nine-lane track for jogging.

As a resource for study and intellectual enrichment, the Sidney Silverman Library is an integral part of the college's educational

Providing students with easy access to technology is a high priority at Bergen Community College. Computers are an integral part of the curriculum in every discipline.

programs. To support curricula, the library acquires, organizes, and maintains a wide variety of print and nonprint materials for individual and classroom use. CD-ROM computer workstations are networked to allow faculty and students to do research using a variety of sources, including magazines, newspapers, and government documents. Internet access is available in the library and in computing labs, and soon will be offered throughout the campus.

Transfer programs offer a course of study that corresponds to the freshman and sophomore offerings at most colleges and universities. After completing an associate's degree at Bergen, many students transfer to a bachelor's degree program at colleges in New Jersey and throughout the nation. The college also is involved in dual-admission programs with four-year colleges, including the New Jersey Institute of Technology, Ramapo College, and Montclair State University.

BCC's campus life is rich with student activities, clubs, and organizations. Students at Bergen are encouraged to participate in student government, clubs, student publications, and athletics. These activities provide a way to develop communication and leadership skills or simply to have fun and meet people. A number of athletic teams for men and women, as well as intramural opportunities, motivate students to get involved in sports.

"At BCC, we believe in being a 'learning' institution—one that learns at the same time it teaches. We continue to foster our own potential as we nurture students. Students' success in college is of the utmost importance to us. We are ready to help students in a variety of ways to ensure that each student's experience will be both productive and satisfying. Our faculty is dedicated to teaching and to sharing knowledge. Bergen Community College offers students the opportunity and assistance they need to be what they want to be. No matter where their personal journey may lead them—an exciting career, furthering their education, or the chance for new opportunities—BCC is ready to be our students' guide," says BCC president Dr. Judith K. Winn.

Intercollegiate athletics are an important part of student life at Bergen Community College. The women's volleyball team has won numerous regional tournaments over the years and also has competed on a national level.

EDUCATION 313

SETON HALL UNIVERSITY

FOUNDED IN 1856, SETON HALL UNIVERSITY MATCHES ITS CATHOLIC CONCERN FOR THE ETHICAL, SPIRITUAL, AND INTELLECTUAL DEVELOPMENT OF STUDENTS WITH THE HIGHEST QUALITY EDUCATION, CREATING A STIMULATING COMMUNITY OF GOODWILL

The largest and oldest diocesan university in the United States, Seton Hall University was founded in 1856 by Bishop James Roosevelt Bayley, the first bishop of Newark. He named it after his aunt, Elizabeth Ann Seton, a pioneer in Catholic education and the first American-born saint.

Nestled on fifty-eight acres in the suburban village of South Orange, New Jersey, Seton Hall's campus is home to eight schools: the College of Arts and Sciences, the W. Paul Stillman School of Business, the College of Education and Human Services, the College of Nursing, the School of Theology, the School of Diplomacy and International Relations, University College, and the School of Graduate Medical Education. Seton Hall's School of Law is located in Newark.

With a tradition of quality education based on Christian values, Seton Hall takes pride in its concern for the intellectual, ethical, and spiritual development of its undergraduate and graduate students. Catholic not only by its charter and mission, but also by its ongoing spirit and activity, the university holds as a basic tenet that religious faith is vital to life and its meaning.

At the same time, Seton Hall is committed to bringing together people of different races, cultures, religious traditions, and ethnic backgrounds into a respectful, supportive environment, helping to establish a truly multicultural community in which all people of goodwill are welcome.

The Mobile Computing Program is one of the cornerstones of Seton Hall University's initiative to make information access universal. All first-year students entering the university take part in a unique program that offers specifically designed sections of core courses that make use of notebook computers inside and outside the classroom.

Seton Hall University defines itself and its academic, student life, and community programs on a Catholic understanding of the nature of the world and the human person. The university takes pride in its concern for the intellectual, ethical, and spiritual development of its students.

"Our mission is to provide an educational experience that not only imparts concrete kinds of knowledge and skills but, equally as important, helps transform students into certain kinds of people, prepared to live lives anchored in a firm spiritual and moral center," says Seton Hall president Monsignor Robert Sheeran. "My vision is that all our academic endeavors and efforts be related to our values and faith convictions, and that our graduates and faculty be active participants and leaders in their professional, community, and family lives."

At Seton Hall, students find people who are willing to listen, offer support, and help them

CREATING THE FUTURE

achieve their goals. More than fifty priests of the Archdiocese of Newark serve the university community as administrators and staff members, and as professors on the university or seminary faculties. With nearly 350 full-time faculty and many adjunct faculty, the student-faculty ratio is 17 to 1. In addition to a highly dedicated and accessible faculty, the university offers comprehensive academic advising and career development programs as well as a diversity of special services designed to assist students in their academic, personal, professional, and spiritual development.

At the undergraduate level, Seton Hall offers more than forty majors as well as many minors, certificates, and interdisciplinary and other special programs. These curricula are continually evaluated and enhanced to meet the changing educational, professional, and technological demands of our increasingly complex society.

The university also encourages students to participate in extracurricular activities such as student government; student professional organizations; internships and cooperative education experiences; varsity, intramural, and club sports; recreation and fitness activities; fraternities and sororities; community service; cultural programs; and ethnic and other special interest organizations.

Seton Hall is in the midst of one of the world's most cosmopolitan centers of education, business, publishing, art, and entertainment. With New York City only fourteen miles from South Orange, students can explore the best that the Big Apple has to offer, such as museums, plays, concerts, and sporting events. In the city as well as throughout northern New Jersey, students take part in internships, cooperative education assignments, and community service activities. And with the increasing importance of international business, communication, and governmental cooperation, many students pursue international study programs as part of their undergraduate education.

Seton Hall is involved in the ongoing process of revitalizing its campus. In the fall of 1994 the university dedicated its $20 million, four-story Walsh Library, a facility that offers state-of-the-art study and research capabilities to undergraduate and graduate students, faculty, and scholars from around the world.

In 1997 the Kozlowski Hall academic building, with more than 126,000 square feet of academic space, opened on the South Orange campus. This multimedia facility houses the W. Paul Stillman School of Business, the College of Education and Human Services, the Center for Public Service, and the Department of Psychology. It also contains 156 faculty and administrative offices and teaching spaces that include seminar rooms and a 350-seat auditorium.

To make effective use of information technology in teaching and learning, Seton Hall has adopted an information-technology long-range plan. This $14 million, five-year plan is designed to improve the university's computing infrastructure and information services, providing students with the technological skills they need to succeed in the future. Highlights of this ambitious plan include the Mobile Computing Program, which provides undergraduate students with laptop computers and core curricula that incorporate the use of technology; and Seton-Worldwide, the cyber university, offering degree programs on-line.

The Kozlowski Hall academic building opened its doors in the fall of 1997. A major feature of the building is the technological capability it brings to the teaching and learning processes, including the most contemporary information and distance-learning technologies.

Located at the heart of the campus, Seton Hall's Walsh Library opened in the spring of 1994. Its facilities include a bibliographic instruction center, reading and group-study rooms, an exhibit and art gallery, a special collections center, and a media center.

EDUCATION 315

FAIRLEIGH DICKINSON UNIVERSITY

AT FAIRLEIGH DICKINSON UNIVERSITY THE CURRICULA EMPHASIZE ACADEMIC TRAINING COMBINED WITH APPLICATIONS DESIGNED TO HELP STUDENTS SUCCEED IN THE BUSINESS WORLD

For generations of Americans, higher education has been the path to opportunity. The child who is first in the family to attend college, the successful executive who desires an MBA degree, the owner of a small business who is studying entrepreneurship—each is in search of the optimum education; each has differing needs.

For more than half a century, such people have found the right education at Fairleigh Dickinson University (FDU). Today, more than 90,000 FDU alumni live and work in greater New Jersey and beyond. They are living testimony that the university's fulfilling its institutional mission—to provide education that addresses diverse needs—spells success.

Today, higher education faces new challenges. It must respond not only to the changing needs of individuals, but to the need to remain competitive in an increasingly technological, knowledge-based, global economy. With its focused mission and flexible programs, FDU is poised to meet those challenges. For more than half a century, FDU has had a proven record of providing education that serves the people and businesses of its region.

When FDU was founded, in 1942, the available choices for acquiring a higher education in New Jersey were few. The creation of a system of community colleges did

FDU's Dickinson Hall, located on the banks of the Hackensack River, is a 170,000-square-foot complex with state-of-the-art academic facilities.

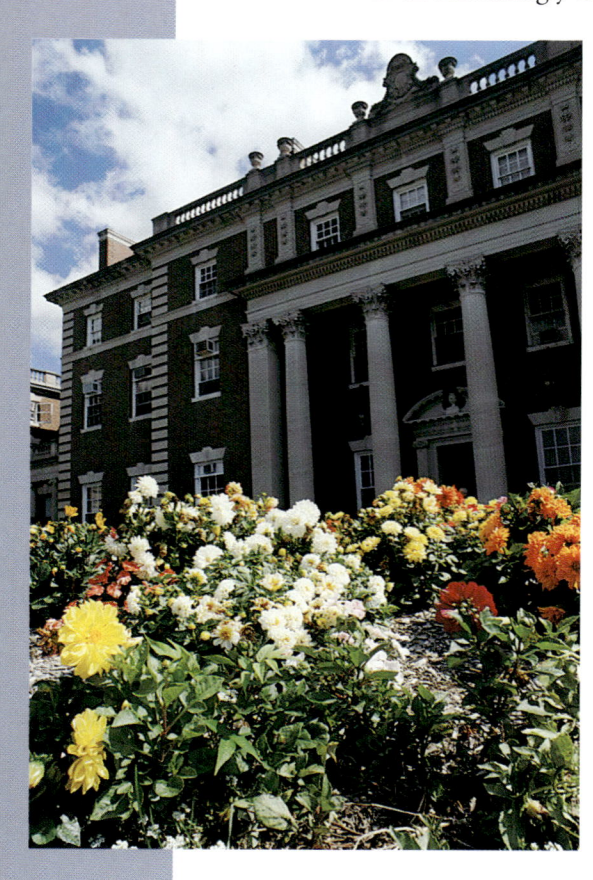

The picturesque Mansion on the Florham-Madison campus, once the centerpiece of the famous Vanderbilt-Twombly Estate, currently offers students a unique educational setting. © Shelley Kusnetz

not begin until the late 1960s, followed by the transformation of state teachers' colleges into comprehensive colleges and universities. Beginning as a two-year school, FDU made higher education in New Jersey possible for thousands of the state's residents. As the demand increased with a growing population and with the support of the GI Bill, FDU grew to new heights.

The school went from a two-year to a four-year institution, in Rutherford, and then to today's major university, with campuses at Teaneck-Hackensack and Florham-Madison, offering two-year and four-year undergraduate degrees, graduate education (including two doctoral programs), and professional training. As the New Jersey economy grew, creating demand for advanced training in business, the MBA program offered by FDU's Samuel J. Silberman College of Business Administration became one of the largest in the country, preparing executives for corporations throughout New Jersey, New York, and the region.

In addition, FDU always has considered a global perspective integral to a fulfilling educational experience. In England, the university owns and operates Wroxton College, near Oxford, while in Israel, FDU operates a branch campus in

316 CREATING THE FUTURE

FDU's Division I basketball team won the Northeast Conference championship in 1998 and advanced to the NCAA tournament, where the FDU Knights gave the University of Connecticut Huskies all they could handle. Shown at right, NEC First Team All-Star Rahshon Turner drives for two against the Huskies.

Tel Aviv. Also, the university has developed programs and cooperative agreements with institutions in Spain, Russia, Korea, and Thailand, among others.

FDU places an emphasis on curricula that combine academic training and real-world applications. "Higher education cannot exist in a vacuum," says FDU president Francis J. Mertz. "It must be relevant to the needs of society. At FDU, we seek to provide a dimension that goes beyond the classroom and creates opportunities for our students to bridge the gap between the classroom and the workplace."

To meet these needs, FDU has developed programs that expose students to the realities of the marketplace. FDU also has developed an ongoing effort to maintain a close relationship with industry, in order to keep abreast of the latest developments.

"We're proud of our many excellent relationships with leaders in the private sector," says President Mertz. "Our partners in industry have played invaluable roles in various university endeavors, from cooperative programs to curriculum development to student mentoring. In turn, we have worked to enhance their success by providing programs that respond to their needs and educating students who are poised to assume leadership roles in business."

Especially significant is the impact the university has had and continues to have on the New Jersey economy. FDU has enjoyed a rich history of providing the state with knowledgeable, creative business leadership. More than 1,000 FDU graduates hold the titles chief executive officer, chief financial officer, chief operating officer, president, or vice president, or are the proprietors of their own New Jersey businesses. In addition, large numbers of FDU alumni are employed in many of New Jersey's top firms. Overall, more than 38,000 alumni are working at companies in the state.

"While our focus and our main identification will remain as an undergraduate institution for full-time students, we also are committed to being the region's leading institution of lifelong learning. Part of our job increasingly will be to respond to a society where many people change not only their jobs but their careers as well. As we prepare students for a changing world, we must continue to assess ourselves," President Mertz says. "FDU's innovative academic offerings, our outreach efforts to serve nontraditional students, our devotion to improving our fiscal condition, and our significant upgrades point FDU in the right direction."

FDU students have the opportunity to learn while enjoying a collegiate experience in a tranquil, scenic environment.

MONTCLAIR STATE UNIVERSITY

RECOGNIZED AS VITAL AND FORWARD-LOOKING, WITH A NOTABLE FACULTY AND STRONG CURRICULA, MONTCLAIR STATE UNIVERSITY OFFERS DEGREES IN FORTY-FOUR UNDERGRADUATE MAJORS AND THIRTY-FOUR GRADUATE MAJORS

From its founding in 1908 in response to a growing demand for professionally trained teachers, Montclair State University (MSU) has evolved into a four-year comprehensive public university that offers a broad range of educational and cultural opportunities. Montclair State was awarded university status by the state of New Jersey in 1994, reflecting the school's commitment to teaching excellence, program diversity, and student access.

For ninety years Montclair State has evolved and grown with the times, fulfilling its mission to meet the changing needs of the people of New Jersey. Along the way, it has always been the place where those seeking an outstanding education at an affordable price could find it.

The second largest university in New Jersey, Montclair State is composed of the School of Business, the School of the Arts, the College of Humanities and Social Sciences, the College of Science and Mathematics, the College of Education and Human Services, and the Graduate School. With hundreds of majors, minors, and concentrations, it offers its 13,000 students the breadth and variety of a large university combined with the individual attention more typical of a small college.

Montclair State recognizes that a student's college experience is defined not only by academic programs but also by the delivery of student services. The best classroom education cannot be fully appreciated if registration, advising, and residence life are not centered on student needs. At MSU such services as the Academic Success Center, phone-in registration, and the Health and Wellness Center reflect the university's care for its students.

Montclair State has been designated by the state of New Jersey as a Center of Excellence in the fine and performing arts. Its proximity to the cultural centers of New York City has allowed the university to offer an extraordinary range of opportunities for performing arts students, at both graduate and undergraduate levels, to work with world-class musicians, artists, dancers, and actors in a program that combines professional training with the professional contacts that assist entry into careers in the arts.

MSU is a major player in the effort to reform and renew teacher education and the public schools. With the sole Center of Pedagogy in the nation, as well as the world headquarters of the Philosophy for Children movement and the home of the New Jersey Network for Educational Renewal, Montclair State has achieved international recognition for its work in improving our children's education. The Institute for the Advancement of Philosophy for Children attracts scholars from around the world, who learn about the application of logical thinking to the elementary school classroom. Montclair takes an active role in the Newark school system with programs for grade school children, college-bound students, and teachers. Its Institute for Critical Thinking has been recognized as a national model for faculty and curriculum development.

With a strong commitment to public service, Montclair State offers a variety of services to the community, ranging from business consulting to programs for gifted and talented children, from cultural events to environmental assessments,

One of the oldest buildings on campus, Morehead Hall houses one of the newest concepts in student services: the Academic Success Center. Here students can find advisors, tutorial services, career development assistance, and special programs, enabling them to have various needs met all in one place. © S. Hockstein/Harvard Studios, Inc.

Dickson Hall is the newest classroom and faculty office building on the Montclair State campus. © S. Hockstein/Harvard Studios, Inc.

CREATING THE FUTURE

and from tutoring elementary school children to providing psychological services in Spanish.

Each year more than 1,200 academically gifted students in kindergarten through eleventh grade take part in advanced instructional programs offered on weekends at the campus, while close to 500 artistically talented youngsters receive instruction through the Preparatory Center for the Arts. Summer camps are offered for academically, musically, and athletically talented children.

MSU's community service commitment is also supported by the School of Conservation, a 240-acre facility in Stokes State Forest—one of the largest college-operated environmental education centers in the world. The Psychoeducational Center provides special services to children with learning, reading, speech, and other disabilities. The Center for Continuing Education offers a variety of programs for adult learners. The School of Business provides consulting services on a wide range of topics and holds conferences, seminars, and workshops for small businesses interested in forming international partnerships.

Another aspect of Montclair State's service to the community became a reality with the recent opening of two new athletic and recreational facilities, Yogi Berra Stadium and the Floyd Hall Arena, which provide some of the best baseball and ice-skating facilities in the country. The stadium is the home of the New Jersey Jackals during the summer and the MSU Red Hawks during the college baseball season. The arena is available for use by hockey teams from area schools, competitive skaters seeking practice ice, and recreational skaters on all levels.

Its leadership role in higher education has allowed MSU to redefine the meaning of scholarship so that it more clearly fits the work done at a university where the focus is on teaching rather than research. A guiding factor in this evolution is the notion of the scholarship of application, turning knowledge into practice. This is what Montclair State perceives its vital role to be, a role it has played since its very beginning. As a university, Montclair State becomes more and more a practical resource for the community at the same time it enhances the education it offers. Opportunities such as the Urban Initiatives Program and the Paralegal Clinic afford students the experience of working where people need them and provide communities with the resource of intelligent, willing assistance supervised by knowledgeable faculty.

The history of Montclair State University has been one of change, growth, and distinction. Founded in 1908 as a normal school, the institution became Montclair State Teachers College in 1927, dedicated to the education of secondary school teachers through a four-year bachelor of arts degree program.

Part-time, extension, and summer courses were added to meet the professional needs of teachers, and in 1932 Montclair was authorized to offer the master's degree. With its strong emphasis on the liberal arts and sciences, in 1937 Montclair became one of the first teachers' colleges accredited by the Middle States Association of Colleges and Schools. Responding to rapid enrollment growth in the late 1940s and the 1950s with an expanded faculty and curriculum, the campus became Montclair State College in 1958 and a comprehensive, multipurpose institution in 1966. Recognizing the strengths of its academic programs and faculty and its commitment to excellence in instruction and research, the New Jersey Board of Higher Education designated Montclair State a teaching university on 27 April 1994 and approved the university's first doctoral program, leading to the Ed.D. in pedagogy, on 23 October 1998.

The university is entering a new era under the guiding hand of its new president Dr. Susan Cole. "I think Montclair State University is a grand institution and its potential is very exciting," she says. "I'm really looking forward to working with the faculty so that we can expand and enhance the university program and serve the state."

Montclair State University is a vital and forward-looking university, proud of its heritage and prepared to respond to the challenges and opportunities that lie ahead. As a result of the strength of its faculty and the comprehensiveness of its programs, the university expects to continue as a major contributor to the cultural and educational life of the region it serves.

LEFT: *Montclair State University Sprague Library's new addition doubled the capacity for books and nonprint items.* © S. Hockstein/Harvard Studios, Inc. ABOVE: *Students gather under the arch, the entrance to the College of Humanities and Social Sciences at Montclair State University.* © S. Hockstein/Harvard Studios, Inc.

THE COLLEGE OF NEW JERSEY

WELL-RANKED, THE COLLEGE OF NEW JERSEY OFFERS A PICTURESQUE CAMPUS, A HIGHLY QUALIFIED FACULTY, AND ALL THE TOP FACILITIES FOR AN EXCEPTIONAL UNDERGRADUATE PROGRAM

The history of The College of New Jersey (TCNJ) reaches back to 1855 when it was established by the state legislature as the New Jersey State Normal School. It was New Jersey's first, and the nation's ninth, teacher training school. The school flourished in the latter 1800s, and the first baccalaureate program was established in 1925. This change marked the beginning of TCNJ's transition to a four-year college.

Today, TCNJ has achieved national distinction for its commitment to excellence. For nine years the college has been ranked among the best schools of its type in *U.S. News & World Report*'s annual survey, and honored as the "Number One Public College in the North."

For the past eight years, *Money* magazine has ranked TCNJ as one of the top-ten schools nationally in its guide *Your Best College Buys*.

In *The Fiske Guide to Colleges,* Edward B. Fiske, former education editor of the *New York Times,* cites TCNJ as "fast becoming one

The College of New Jersey's tree-lined campus, which provides spectacular spring foliage, offers a beautiful residential setting for students all year long.

The clock tower above Green Hall, the main administration building, is a well-known symbol of The College of New Jersey. Since 1985 all new buildings have been designed to reflect the Georgian Colonial architecture of this building, one of the oldest on campus.

of the nation's premier public schools." TCNJ also is featured in *The Best 100 Colleges for African-American Students* and *Peterson's Competitive Colleges,* and is rated as "highly competitive" in *Barron's Profiles of American Colleges.*

"We are a mission-driven institution," says TCNJ president Harold W. Eickhoff. "Our students' education has always been the center of our mission. Our purpose has been steadfast since the Normal School was chartered in 1855: The preparation of educated minds to meet the needs of New Jersey."

The College of New Jersey emphasizes academic programs designed to provide students with an undergraduate education of exceptional quality. Students may choose from more than forty liberal arts and professional programs offered through the college's five schools: Arts and Sciences, Business, Education, Engineering, and Nursing.

Recognizing that the first year of college can set the tone for an entire college career, TCNJ has developed an award-winning program called First-Year Experience (FYE). Because college encompasses more than just classroom learning, FYE incorporates three interrelated components: the Interdisciplinary Core Curriculum, Service

CREATING THE FUTURE

Learning, and Residence Life. By addressing these three areas of a student's life, the college provides a strong foundation for undergraduate education.

Classes at The College of New Jersey are small (the student/faculty ratio is fourteen to one) and all are taught by faculty, not TCNJ graduate assistants. The 324 members of the full-time faculty are teachers and scholars. Teaching is their primary responsibility, but they also are active researchers, authors, artists, performers, and regular contributors in their academic disciplines.

In addition to winning the Bancroft Prize in History, professors have received grants and fellowships from the Guggenheim Foundation, the Fulbright Foundation, the National Institutes of Mental Health, the National Science Foundation, the National Endowment for the Humanities, and others.

The college's Roscoe L. West Library houses one of the largest, most comprehensive collections among institutions of its type in the region. Other campus facilities include television and radio studios, Kendall Hall Theater and studio theater, the College Art Gallery, a concert hall, and a full range of science, technology, and computer laboratories.

Students can pursue special interests and contribute to the campus community through more than 120 clubs and organizations, such as the student newspaper, ROTC, and the TCNJ Chorale. TCNJ also has maintained one of the best intercollegiate athletic programs among the nation's NCAA Division III colleges and universities. The program offers twenty-one varsity sports for men and women, distinguished by thirty-three national championships since 1979; and numerous intramural and recreational activities. Facilities include a lighted AstroTurf stadium, an NCAA-approved track, an aquatic center, and eight lighted tennis courts.

Many students spend time studying or relaxing by Lake Ceva, one of the two lakes that form part of the northern border of the college's suburban, 265-acre campus.

"The college has arrived as one of the best. And we are where we are because more than fifteen years ago we set out to be where we are today," President Eickhoff says. "But our having arrived is more than surveys and favorable national comparison.

"It is documented when you listen to the recordings of our music groups; when you review our faculty's impressive record of scholarship; when you attend a trustees' meeting to honor the faculty's research work; when you listen to the comments of teaching professionals from across this country who come here each year as graders of ETS advanced placement tests and hear them express admiration for this campus; when you see the display of student research; when you listen to the dean and leadership of the School of Education describe enthusiastically the revision of their curriculum to more clearly implement the college's mission of service; when you stop at a lunch table in Brower Student Center and sense the pride of our craftsmen and technical staff; when you see the wall of NCAA national championship trophies.

"All these examples, and dozens of others, reflect a remarkable record of accomplishment. And they are real because we at the college have made them real."

During freshman orientation students enjoy a game of sand volleyball outside of New Residence Hall.

EDUCATION 321

ROWAN UNIVERSITY

A ROWAN UNIVERSITY EDUCATION PREPARES STUDENTS FOR THEIR CAREERS AND THEIR LIVES BY FOSTERING KNOWLEDGE THROUGH STUDY, RESPONSIBILITY THROUGH SERVICE, AND CHARACTER THROUGH CHALLENGE

"Expect More. Achieve More." Rowan University's new slogan captures the essence of a Rowan education. The school's outstanding programs challenge students and help them form new expectations for their academic development, while faculty members work closely with each student to achieve his or her best. The end result is that, after completing study in one of the university's thirty-one majors within its six academic colleges, graduates leave Rowan with the full range of skills they need to succeed in their personal and professional lives.

As a regional public university committed to teaching, Rowan offers classes taught only by professors, not teaching assistants. Rowan combines liberal education with professional preparation and offers undergraduate through doctoral programs. The university's liberal arts–based curriculum extends students' academic reach by providing a wide range of learning experiences that complement the specific courses in their majors.

Since its founding in 1923 as Glassboro Normal School, Rowan University has gone from being a normal school (one that educates future teachers) to a comprehensive institution. Events in the school's more recent history, however, have virtually transformed it.

In 1992 industrialist Henry Rowan and his wife, Betty, donated $100 million to the college—at the time the largest contribution ever to a public institution. The gift served as a catalyst for dramatic change,

Rowan students are part of a close-knit community of learners. They live on a dynamic campus and attend small classes taught by professors, not teaching assistants.

Rowan's state-of-the-art facilities, nationally ranked academics and sports, exceptional professors, and superior resources provide its students with a valuable education.

including the institution's being renamed in Rowan's honor and attaining designation as a university. Rowan's funding also led to the establishment of the School of Engineering in 1995. In 1997 the university's doctorate program in educational leadership was approved—the first doctorate offered at any of the New Jersey state colleges.

The combined efforts of the Rowan Foundation and private donors have resulted in new facilities, including a $26 million engineering building, a $16.8 million library, and an $8.6 million recreation center—the newest and largest of all the New Jersey state college recreation facilities—as well as new scholarship programs. To support the teaching and learning processes, all Rowan students, faculty, and staff have access to the technologies they need and the training necessary to use the technologies intelligently in the classroom, the library, throughout the campus, and at their residences, on or off campus.

While these facilities offer the school's nearly 10,000 students access to the resources that typify a large university, among Rowan's strengths are the small class size and personal attention traditionally associated with a small college. The school has a student-to-faculty ratio of 17 to 1 and an average class size of 23 students.

CREATING THE FUTURE

The phrase "achieve more" in Rowan's slogan reflects the accomplishments of its students. All Rowan University biological science majors who were recommended for medical school in 1997 were accepted. Rowan accounting majors rank in the top 25 percent of those taking the New Jersey CPA exam. The school's exceptional program in communications has led to its students' having won more awards than any other chapter of the Public Relations Student Society of America in the nation. The master of business administration (MBA) program was ranked in the top 20 percent in a recent student satisfaction survey of seventy-nine part-time MBA programs nationwide. In sports, which also play an important role in student life at the university, the Rowan men's baseball, soccer, basketball, and track and field teams have won ten NCAA Division III national championships. More than 100 of the school's athletes have received All-American honors.

Rowan has implemented an exciting and bold five-year strategic plan setting it on course to become a nationally recognized regional university. The plan's initiatives include strengthening current academic programs, adding new ones, and integrating technology into the curriculum.

Although Rowan University holds international repute, enrolling students from as many as twenty-five foreign countries, it also makes a tremendous impact locally. Students from every county in New Jersey can be found in attendance. Thus, the university is helping to keep the state's best and brightest students at home. Rowan is one of three comprehensive public universities in the state, but it is the only one in South Jersey.

Rowan has one of the top Division III programs in the country. The university's eighteen varsity teams have won ten NCAA Division III national championships.

The university also has an important impact on the local and state economies. An economic impact study conducted in 1997 shows that the approximately $33 million annual state allocation to Rowan generates more than a sixfold return, or $212 million, for the New Jersey economy. Put another way, for every $1 received from the state, the university returns $6.50 to the economy. The study also found that the university's economic impact on Gloucester County, where it is situated, was $93 million, and on the town of Glassboro, $47 million. The report confirmed that the money flowing into the university from all sources then surges outward, affecting people and business throughout the state.

Rowan graduates are in demand. A total of 84 percent of the class of 1996 was employed full time within one year of graduation, and 28 percent had full-time jobs at graduation.

"In addition to Rowan's extending its range as a nationally recognized university attracting students throughout the country, it is also being recognized by local youth as a viable option to moving north or out of state to get a 'university' education. As we move forward into the twenty-first century and evolve as an institution, we are steadfast in our commitment to provide an exceptional environment for achievement," says Rowan University president Dr. Donald James Farish.

Rowan's thirty-one academic programs are complemented by outstanding facilities. Over the last few years the university has spent more than $50 million to build and renovate academic buildings, recreation facilities, and residence halls.

EDUCATION 323

UNIVERSITY OF MEDICINE AND DENTISTRY OF NEW JERSEY

THE UNIVERSITY OF MEDICINE AND DENTISTRY OF NEW JERSEY IS DEDICATED TO THE PURSUIT OF EXCELLENCE IN EDUCATION, RESEARCH, HEALTH CARE DELIVERY, AND COMMUNITY SERVICE

When the University of Medicine and Dentistry of New Jersey (UMDNJ) opened its doors in 1970 as a fledgling school on a makeshift campus in Newark, its mission was to develop high-quality medical and dental education for New Jersey residents.

In twenty-eight years, UMDNJ has evolved into the largest freestanding publicly funded health sciences university in the country and the only academic health center in New Jersey.

UMDNJ has eight schools on five campuses, a hospital, a behavioral health care system, and affiliations with more than 200 health care and higher education institutions. The university consists of the state's only three medical schools, its only dental school, a graduate school of biomedical sciences, a school of nursing, a school of health-related professions, and its most recent addition, a school of public health.

The growth and development of the university have been in large part a result of the vision and leadership of Dr. Stanley S. Bergen Jr., who was appointed as UMDNJ's first president in 1971 and served as its only president for twenty-seven years, and in June 1998 was appointed founding president emeritus.

Since its inception, UMDNJ has been committed to improving the health and well-being of all New Jerseyans. UMDNJ has identified major public health issues and designed solutions. Recent initiatives include:

- The Cancer Institute of New Jersey (CINJ), which offers world-class cancer care to patients through a statewide partnership of health care institutions so that patients can be treated without leaving the state. UMDNJ–Robert Wood Johnson Medical School faculty provide the core of physicians and researchers. CINJ is one of only fifteen centers nationwide designated as a National Cancer Institute clinical cancer center;
- The Violence Institute of New Jersey at UMDNJ, a statewide resource with programs focused on the treatment, research, and prevention of violence;
- University Heights Science Park, a collaborative project of the Council on Higher Education in Newark to develop a fifty-acre science and technology park. The anchor tenant of the park's biotechnology cluster will be a new International Center for Public Health, which will house the prestigious Public Health Research Institute, the New Jersey Medical School National Tuberculosis Center at UMDNJ, and the school's Department of Microbiology and Molecular Genetics.

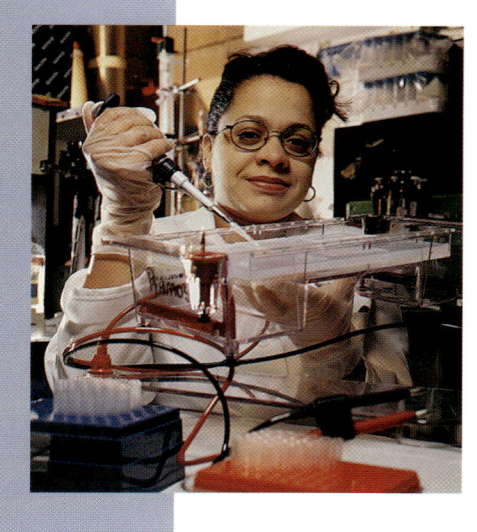

Researchers at UMDNJ's medical schools, dental school, and UMDNJ–Graduate School of Biomedical Sciences have been pathfinders in conducting research on AIDS, tuberculosis, cancer,

New Jersey residents have available one of the highest-caliber trauma care systems in the nation. UMDNJ–University Hospital in Newark is the core of the state's multimedical center trauma network. It also is the home base of NorthSTAR-Northern Shock Trauma Air Rescue, whose helicopter is shown above. Northstar's on-flight medical professionals are from UMDNJ–University Hospital. © Peter Byron

UMDNJ neuroscientists are conducting some of the leading research in the nation to increase understanding of the cellular mechanisms that control degenerative neurological diseases, such as multiple sclerosis, Parkinson's, and Alzheimer's. For example, while scientists know that an accumulation of amyloid plaque in the brain can lead to Alzheimer's, UMDNJ researchers are studying whether or not this buildup occurs because damaged brain cells lose the ability to repair themselves. © Peter Tenzer

multiple sclerosis, environmental illnesses, sickle cell disease, heart disease, and Alzheimer's and Parkinson's diseases. The university also has developed a reputation as a national leader in trauma care through UMDNJ–University Hospital in Newark.

The university has been sensitive to the specific health needs of New Jersey residents when establishing clinical programs. The UMDNJ–School of Osteopathic Medicine, for example, established the Center for Children's Support, which works with sexually abused children and their families. The UMDNJ–New Jersey Dental School established the first dental clinic in the state to treat HIV-infected patients and the only dental clinic in the state to specialize in the provision of care to physically and mentally disabled patients. University Behavioral HealthCare is nationally renowned for addiction treatment and grief-counseling programs. The UMDNJ–School of Nursing has established health care centers in Newark and Camden in medically underserved neighborhoods so that care is more accessible to families.

As the university has established new health care initiatives, accessible and affordable care has been an important consideration. Quality care is the guiding principle of the university's health maintenance organization, University Health Plans, the only HMO in New Jersey that is owned solely by a medical institution.

Perhaps the most significant impact UMDNJ has had on New Jersey's state of health has been through the number of health care professionals—more than 16,000—who have been educated by the university. One in eight physicians and one in four dentists practicing in New Jersey are UMDNJ graduates.

To meet the market challenges of a rapidly changing health care world, the university has developed innovative degree programs, many in collaboration with other institutions of higher education in New Jersey.

Technology has been harnessed to provide long-distance learning opportunities so that students can access programs no matter where in New Jersey they live. In fact, the UMDNJ–School of Health Related Professions and Thomas Edison College have established the first site on the World Wide Web where students can earn bachelor of science degrees in health professions.

THE UNIVERSITY OF MEDICINE AND DENTISTRY OF NEW JERSEY

SCHOOLS OF THE UNIVERSITY

UMDNJ–Graduate School of Biomedical Sciences
UMDNJ–New Jersey Dental School
UMDNJ–New Jersey Medical School
UMDNJ–Robert Wood Johnson Medical School
UMDNJ–School of Health-Related Professions
UMDNJ–School of Nursing
UMDNJ–School of Osteopathic Medicine
UMDNJ–School of Public Health

HEALTH CARE FACILITIES

UMDNJ–University Hospital
University Behavioral HealthCare

UMDNJ campuses are located in Newark, Camden, Piscataway/New Brunswick, Stratford, and Scotch Plains.

AFFILIATED INSTITUTE

Violence Institute of New Jersey at UMDNJ

PARTNERSHIP AFFILIATIONS

Center for Advanced Biotechnology and Medicine
Environmental and Occupational Health Sciences Institute
The Cancer Institute of New Jersey
University Heights Science Park

UMDNJ also is affiliated with more than 200 other health care and higher education institutions.

UMD NEW JERSEY
http://www.umdnj.edu

On the brink of a new millennium, the university's mission is as relevant as it was at the university's inception: to educate health professionals, discover and apply new knowledge, deliver health care, and serve communities throughout the state.

UMDNJ has harnessed information technology to provide long-distance learning, so students can take UMDNJ courses no matter where they live in New Jersey. The university is establishing an interactive video teleconferencing network that comprises not only its eight schools but also many of its satellite teaching sites at both higher education and health care institutions around the state. Medical residents at New Brunswick and Princeton clinical sites participate in weekly luncheon educational video conferences, such as the one at left, on topics ranging from hypertension to medical ethics. © Ken Gabrielsen

NEW JERSEY CITY UNIVERSITY

WITH RECENT UNIVERSITY STATUS AND ITS NEW NAME, NEW JERSEY CITY UNIVERSITY CONTINUES TO PROVIDE HIGH-QUALITY LIBERAL ARTS EDUCATION AND TO ENRICH ITS COMMUNITY SETTING

"New Jersey City University is a vibrant, active, and intellectually charged university," says Dr. Carlos Hernandez, president of the university. "We are invigorated and energized by our new university status and our new name."

New Jersey City University was originally founded as the Normal School in 1929; it became New Jersey State Teachers College in 1935, and then Jersey City State College in 1958. The programmatic focus was teacher education until 1968, when the institution expanded its mission and became a multipurpose liberal arts college. In 1998 the college received university designation and was renamed New Jersey City University.

Throughout its history the institution has evolved and grown in response to the changing needs of the community and the region. As New Jersey City University (NJCU) begins a new era with a new name and new status, the institution remains true to its original mission: to give a previously underserved urban population access to an excellent education.

The university is known for its extraordinary student support services and outreach programs. Small class size allows professors to interact closely with students. "There is a closeness, a sense of community, among faculty, students, and staff that creates an environment in which we nurture learning and build enduring relationships," says Dr. Hernandez. Students'

New Jersey City University's Hepburn Hall, an architectural gem constructed in 1929, is a replica of a fourteenth-century Norman cathedral. Its Gothic tower is a campus landmark. © Bill Wittkop

NJCU faculty members—some scholars, some practitioners—are outstanding professionals. They are devoted teachers who nurture students in an exceptional university environment that links academic exploration in the classroom with cooperative education experiences in all fields of study. © Steve Jordan

academic experience is further enhanced by the university's access to the wealth of culture and recreation available in New Jersey and New York.

New Jersey City University enrolls more than 10,000 students in its undergraduate, graduate, and continuing education programs. Although many students from the state's northern counties enroll at NJCU, the university also enrolls students from areas of the Garden State that are as distant as Atlantic, Cape May, and Sussex Counties. Out-of-state students are attracted to the university from fifteen states across the nation. In addition, students from fifty foreign countries enrich the multicultural atmosphere of the university.

CREATING THE FUTURE

"I am proudest of this institution when I look at the candidates receiving their degrees at commencement and see the diversity of the globe represented," Hernandez says. "When the graduates' names are announced, they are names from countries all around the world. This university population truly reflects the changing demographics of America."

The university is comprised of the College of Arts and Sciences, the College of Education, the College of Professional Studies, and the Division of Graduate Studies. Baccalaureate degrees are offered in twenty-five major fields. Graduate degrees are offered in such areas as education, accounting, criminal justice, health sciences, and the fine arts. The university offers a new master of arts in educational technology degree program to provide teachers with the academic tools required to meet the challenges of technology in education. Doctoral programs are under consideration.

New Jersey City University is the premier cooperative education university in the state of New Jersey. The Cooperative Education Program integrates employment in business and government with academic education in the classroom, allowing students to work while gaining professional experience in their fields of study.

The change to university status has affected not only academic programs but also facilities on the university's forty-seven-acre campus. The Forrest A. Irwin Library is being redesigned to support current and future information technology, giving students and faculty access to worldwide electronic resources. Fries Hall, built in 1954, will be transformed from an athletic facility into an arts center that will house the Media Arts department, a dance studio, and a small theater. Hepburn Hall's sixty-nine-year-old Margaret Williams Theatre, which seats 1,100, was renovated in 1998. The stenciled ceiling and sculpted-plaster proscenium arch were painstakingly restored to their original Gothic splendor.

The Electronic Learning Laboratory in the Professional Studies Building is one of many resource centers that are available to NJCU students. A number of academic computer labs and terminals are located at various sites across the campus. By August 1999, when the university's Irwin Library is completely renovated, the building will be a state-of-the-art information center designed for the technology age. © Bill Wittkop

Jersey City, the home of New Jersey City University, also is in the midst of a transformation. Corporations are investing in the city, the waterfront is under development, and the city is emerging as a new economic engine of New Jersey. As Jersey City grows culturally, socially, and economically, the university is growing with it.

"We have many new, top-quality jobs being created in Jersey City, but they require a higher level of skills. Our residents need the preparation for success that New Jersey City University provides," says Jersey City mayor Bret Schundler.

NJCU is playing a significant role in addressing urban issues and the dynamics of the metropolitan environment. The university established a Center for Public Policy and Urban Research in 1996 to promote and support issues related to teaching, research, and community partnerships.

"New Jersey City University is to be commended for its commitment to quality education and its positive impact on urban renewal and growth," says New Jersey governor Christine Todd Whitman. "As we near the new century, New Jersey City University will play an important role in the future of its students and in the future of our state."

Most students at New Jersey City University are commuters who work or have family responsibilities. Study lounges in the Gilligan Student Union provide NJCU's nonresidential students with a comfortable haven in the midst of campus activity. © Steve Jordan

EDUCATION 327

RUTGERS, THE STATE UNIVERSITY OF NEW JERSEY

Chartered in 1766, Rutgers, The State University of New Jersey, has grown to be one of the country's largest educational centers, with 100 major programs, outstanding opportunities, and a reputation few universities can match

Rutgers, The State University of New Jersey, is one of the leading public research universities in the United States. As New Jersey's land-grant institution and home to a host of centers, bureaus, and institutes, Rutgers has opportunities and a reputation that few universities can match: 100 major programs of study; 4,000 courses universitywide; 2,435 world-class faculty members; and a library system of more than 3 million volumes. Approximately 48,000 students attend classes on campuses in Camden, Newark, and New Brunswick.

Rutgers recently began implementing its strategic plan, which aims to place Rutgers among the very top public research universities in the nation by the year 2010. The university's core strategic planning priorities include excellence in instruction, research, and service; support for diversity; and encouragement of fostering a global perspective.

Rutgers offers continuing education programs; joint programs with other institutions; partnerships with K–12; partnerships with business, industry, and government; and a variety of other innovative programs. Students pursuing professional programs first affiliate with an undergraduate college, taking a variety of arts and sciences classes for two years before entering the professional school. Many undergraduate programs articulate directly into graduate programs, and interdisciplinary programs take full advantage of faculty resources in a number of departments. In addition, the Citizenship and Service Education program integrates public service and regular coursework.

In recent years faculty members have earned many coveted awards, including two Pulitzer Prizes, the National Medal of Science, the MacArthur Foundation Award, Guggenheim Fellowships, National Science Foundation Young Investigator awards, Sloan Fellowships, and the nation's highest teaching recognition, the U.S. Professor of the Year award.

First chartered in 1766 as Queen's College, Rutgers is the eighth-oldest institution of higher education in the United States. The university changed its name in 1825 to honor Colonel Henry Rutgers, a Revolutionary War veteran and former trustee of the college. From a colonial college with few students and a classic liberal arts curriculum, Rutgers has evolved into the state's only comprehensive public research university.

Through legislative acts in 1945 and 1956, all of the university's divisions were designated "The State University of New Jersey." Since that time, Rutgers has continued to expand its undergraduate, graduate, and professional offerings.

"Rutgers must respond to the continuing demand of our society for advanced knowledge. Rutgers is meeting this challenge by building a comprehensive, statewide network of outreach; educating a broader, more inclusive spectrum of our society; strengthening the learning community with additional supports for teaching and learning; taking the scholar-mentor as a model in the learning community; and building unity within its diversity," says President Francis L. Lawrence.

Old Queen's University Administration Building is just one example of the beautiful architecture found at Rutgers University in New Brunswick, New Jersey. © Rutgers/Alan Goldsmith

Ceramics graduate student Kate Bolen works on a Rigaku Rotaterflex X Ray Diffractometer at Rutgers University's facility in Piscataway, New Jersey. © Rutgers/Nick Romanenko

328 CREATING THE FUTURE

STEVENS INSTITUTE OF TECHNOLOGY

STEVENS INSTITUTE OF TECHNOLOGY IS ONE OF THE LEADING TECHNOLOGICAL UNIVERSITIES IN THE NATION

Stevens Institute of Technology is one of the leading technological universities in the nation. With its pioneering curriculum, and its education that is distinctly rooted in research, Stevens is helping to solve real-world problems in industry and government.

Founded in 1870, Stevens offers baccalaureate, master's, and doctoral degrees in engineering, science, computer science, technology management, and management, and a baccalaureate degree in the humanities and liberal arts. Located in Hoboken, New Jersey, it has an enrollment of 1,400 undergraduate and 2,000 graduate students.

The university is named for a distinguished family who perpetuated a tradition of applied research and engineering dating back to the early days of the Industrial Revolution. Colonel John Stevens, the patriarch and a treasurer during the Revolutionary War, was a pioneer in developing the steamboat. By 1825 he had designed the first American-built steam locomotive. The form of railroad track used today in much of the world, the T-rail, was invented by a son of Colonel Stevens, Robert Stevens. The first profitable United States commercial railroad was operated by Robert and another Stevens son, Edwin. The third son, John Cox Stevens, the first commodore of the New York Yacht Club, was joined by Edwin in building the yacht *America* that was the first winner, in 1851, of the trophy now known as the America's Cup.

So that students may pursue career aspirations while gaining a foundation for lifelong growth in a diverse, global society, the Stevens undergraduate curriculum is built on multidisciplinary core curricula in engineering and science with liberal arts study and a long-standing honors program. Its graduate programs educate professionals to advance in industries increasingly influenced by technology and enable scholars to explore the frontiers of their disciplines.

The Stevens Institute of Technology campus is in Hoboken, across the Hudson River from New York City. © G. Steve Jordan Photography

This breadth of the Stevens curriculum has allowed graduates to explore various careers ranging from engineering to the arts. Among the noted alumni of Stevens are: the "father" of scientific management, Frederick Winslow Taylor; artist Alexander Calder, inventor of the mobile and the machine-driven stabile; author and nationally syndicated columnist Richard Reeves; 1996 Nobel Prize co-winner in physics, Frederick Reines; inventor Louis Alan Hazeltine, creator of the neutrodyne radio receiver; founder and chairman emeritus of Texas Instruments, Eugene McDermont; and C. Stewart Mott, former president of General Motors. The first president of Stevens, Henry Morton, was the founding president of the American Society of Mechanical Engineers.

Stevens Institute of Technology is at the forefront of forging a new kind of working partnership among industry, government, and academe by establishing "steeples of research excellence" aimed at solving problems related to the industrial competitiveness of the United States in manufacturing, environmental cleanup, ecologically compatible industrial processes, rapidly expanding information networks, and increasing profitability through the effective management of technology. The "steeples" include the Design & Manufacturing Institute, Center for Environmental Engineering, and the Advanced Telecommunications Institute.

Dr. Harold J. Raveché is president of Stevens Institute of Technology.

For further information, contact Stevens Institute of Technology: Undergraduate admissions, (800) 458-5323; graduate school, (201) 4DEGREE; Web site: www.stevens-tech.edu

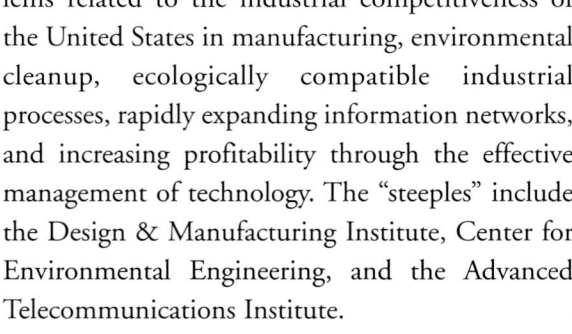

RIDER UNIVERSITY

WITH A TRADITION OF EXCELLENCE, A FINE FACULTY, AND SUPERIOR TECHNOLOGY, RIDER UNIVERSITY CHALLENGES ITS STUDENTS TO FORMULATE AND REALIZE THEIR PERSONAL AND PROFESSIONAL GOALS

As the Civil War was coming to an end, the city of Trenton was growing as an important center of business and industry. Recognizing that this development would create a demand for an educated workforce, local business-school operators Henry B. Bryant and Henry D. Stratton decided to found the Trenton Business College. This college was the forebear of Rider University; today Rider's mission is still shaped by the world around it.

"For more than 130 years Rider University has sustained a tradition of success and excellence," says its president, Dr. J. Barton Luedeke. "Over the years we have challenged individuals to formulate and realize their personal and professional goals in a learning environment that emphasizes career preparation and development. Today our graduates are successful business leaders and entrepreneurs, teachers and school administrators, doctors and lawyers, musicians, community leaders, and honored citizens."

Rider University is an independent, nonsectarian, coeducational institution of higher learning housed on two campuses, in Princeton and Lawrenceville, New Jersey. The university consists of four academic units—the College of Business Administration; the College of Liberal Arts, Education, and Sciences (composed of the School of Education and the School of Liberal Arts and Sciences); the College of Continuing Studies; and Westminster Choir College. Undergraduate programs are offered in fifty-eight areas and graduate programs in seventeen specialties.

The Lawrenceville campus, with thirty-eight buildings, is situated on 353 acres within easy reach of New York and Philadelphia. Westminster Choir College occupies the Princeton campus of twenty-three acres, offering undergraduate and graduate music leadership programs. Its choirs perform throughout the world.

Instructors are selected for their commitment to imparting the skills and knowledge of their disciplines. There is a thirteen-to-one student-faculty ratio, with 230 full-time faculty members of whom 93 percent hold doctoral or other advanced degrees. Full professors teach at all levels; there are no teaching assistants. *U.S. News & World Report* has consistently ranked Rider in the top tier of northern universities, based on the quality of its programs.

The university is dedicated to keeping pace with new technology. In 1995 Rider and Bell Atlantic announced a $5 million information technology infrastructure project that created a comprehensive communications network of voice, video, and data services for all students, faculty, and staff. It is designed to prepare for the year 2000 and beyond. The university also has recently expanded its Science and Technology Center.

"Relying on talented, dedicated faculty and technology-rich campuses," Dr. Luedeke says, "we are committed to building on our tradition of preparing students for the rapidly changing global workplace and the challenging opportunities of the twenty-first century."

The stately Franklin F. Moore Library, named for Rider's third president, overlooks the spring blossoms on the campus mall.

Anne Brossman Sweigart Hall, built in 1988, houses Rider's internationally accredited College of Business Administration.

NEW JERSEY INSTITUTE OF TECHNOLOGY

"A PLACE OF OPPORTUNITY," NEW JERSEY INSTITUTE OF TECHNOLOGY OFFERS SIXTY-SEVEN DEGREE PROGRAMS TO PREPARE GRADUATES TO TAKE ON POSITIONS OF LEADERSHIP AND TO MAKE A DIFFERENCE

As a leading public, urban research university, the New Jersey Institute of Technology (NJIT) is committed to the pursuit of excellence—in undergraduate, graduate, and continuing professional education. The institute was founded in 1882 in response to a growing need for a skilled workforce, a need that continues today. NJIT prepares its graduates for positions of leadership as professionals and as citizens.

NJIT enrollment includes more than 8,200 undergraduate, graduate, and doctoral students in its five colleges: Newark College of Engineering, School of Architecture, College of Science and Liberal Arts, School of Management, and Albert Dorman Honors College. The comprehensive array of seventy-nine degree programs offered includes engineering and engineering technology, computer science, architecture, applied sciences, mathematics, management, policy studies, and others.

"After more than twenty years of intensive development, NJIT has emerged as a public research university that enhances intellectual vitality, economic development, and the quality of life in New Jersey and the nation," says Saul K. Fenster, university president.

NJIT's leadership is nationally recognized. Not only did *Money* magazine rate NJIT as the sixth-best value among United States science and technology schools in its 1998 guide to "Your Best College Buys," NJIT also was ranked number two of the "100 Most-Wired Colleges" in the *Yahoo! Internet Life* magazine, second only to Dartmouth College. According to the magazine's editors, "The way that colleges use network technology—the way that they admit the Internet into their classrooms, dorm rooms, and offices—is already an important measure of success and will become increasingly vital in future years."

Ranked as the nation's second "most wired" university, NJIT is a national leader in computer-assisted design.

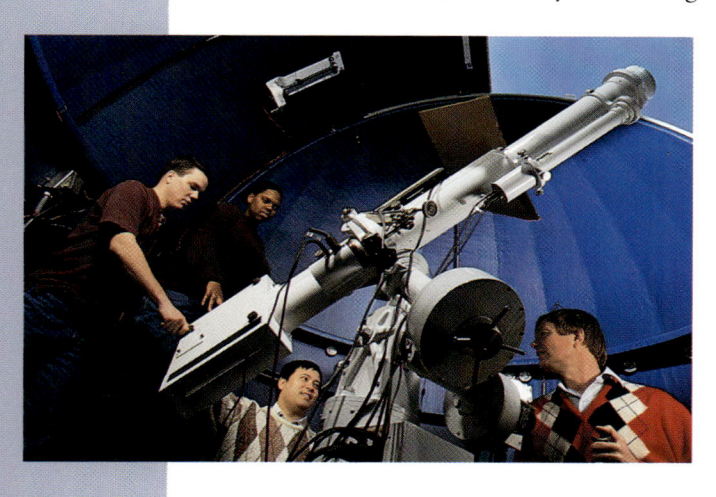

Through its Big Bear Solar Observatory in California, NJIT is nationally recognized for its research in solar physics.

As the new century approaches, a multiphase expansion of the NJIT campus is under way. To help support this new initiative, NJIT has launched a $120 million fund-raising campaign called "The Campaign for NJIT: Design for the Future," the largest and most ambitious fund-raising campaign in NJIT's history.

"NJIT is a 'place of opportunity' where students who have the fortitude to tackle rigorous course work in architecture, engineering, management, mathematics, computer science, and the sciences find the solid grounding they need to aim high, go far, and make a real difference," says New Jersey governor Christine Todd Whitman. "Time and again, when faced with complex policy issues, organizations throughout the state have turned to NJIT for objective, science-based analysis and advice."

EDUCATION 331

THOMAS EDISON STATE COLLEGE

A PREMIER NEW JERSEY COLLEGE FOR ADULTS, THOMAS EDISON STATE COLLEGE AFFORDS STUDENTS THE FLEXIBILITY TO RECEIVE THE EDUCATION THEY WANT AND THE OPPORTUNITY TO FOLLOW THEIR DREAMS

Named one of the "Top 20 Cyber-Universities" by *Forbes* magazine, Thomas Edison State College offers associate, bachelor's, and master's degrees exclusively to adults, wherever they live and work. With 120 areas of study and 12 degrees, the college offers adults many different ways to complete a quality degree. The college provides individual adults with a personalized path to a college degree and enables organizations to upgrade and enhance the educational stature of their employees.

Since its founding in 1972, Thomas Edison State College has partnered with state and national corporations to provide access to world-class learning. Companies such as AT&T and PSE&G have found in Thomas Edison a true partner in progress.

"AT&T and Thomas Edison State College have a strategic partnership," says Robert DeCarlo, general manager of middle markets for AT&T. "Thomas Edison State College is an institution with very talented, creative, innovative people who are cost-conscious in supporting employees pursuing either graduate or undergraduate degrees." Thomas Edison works in tandem with more than 100 companies to evaluate corporate courses and to provide a college education to employees without disrupting their personal or professional lives.

"Thomas Edison opened the doors of opportunity for me in a wide variety of areas," says Gregory Adkins, assistant commissioner for the New Jersey Department of Community Affairs and a Thomas Edison student. "Be it through portfolio assessment or independent study courses, the college offers a great variety of opportunities for individuals to demonstrate college-level proficiency they've acquired through their lives."

Paula Vaughan, a vice president at Prudential Insurance, earned her undergraduate degree from Thomas Edison State College after a two-decade absence from higher education. She recently graduated from the college's on-line Master of Science in Management program.

The $12.7 million expansion and renovation of the Thomas Edison State College campus will include interactive television classrooms, computer labs, and educational conference and training rooms. The five nineteenth-century town houses shown above will be restored to their original architectural style, doubling the college's existing space. © D. F. Gibson Architects, P. C. Architect; Clark Smith Rendering

Working with experienced educators, Thomas Edison students earn degrees by documenting college-level knowledge gained through life experience and by completing guided independent study courses. This accredited public college is a national leader in the assessment of adult learning and a pioneer in the use of educational technologies.

"I found Thomas Edison to be the perfect solution for my needs," says Paula Vaughan, vice president for change management with Prudential Insurance. Vaughan is president of the college's alumni association and recently graduated from Thomas Edison's on-line Master of Science in Management degree program. "I completed my undergraduate degree by taking independent study courses over a period of ten months. Even though I spent many hours at the office and had a long daily commute to work, Thomas Edison gave me the flexibility to study and take tests when I needed to. I feel very successful."

For information contact Thomas Edison State College: 101 West State Street, Trenton, NJ 08608-1176; telephone: (609) 984-1150; facsimile: (609) 984-8447; E-mail: Admissions@call.tesc.edu; Web site: www.tesc.edu

EDUCATION 333

NEW JERSEY FUN

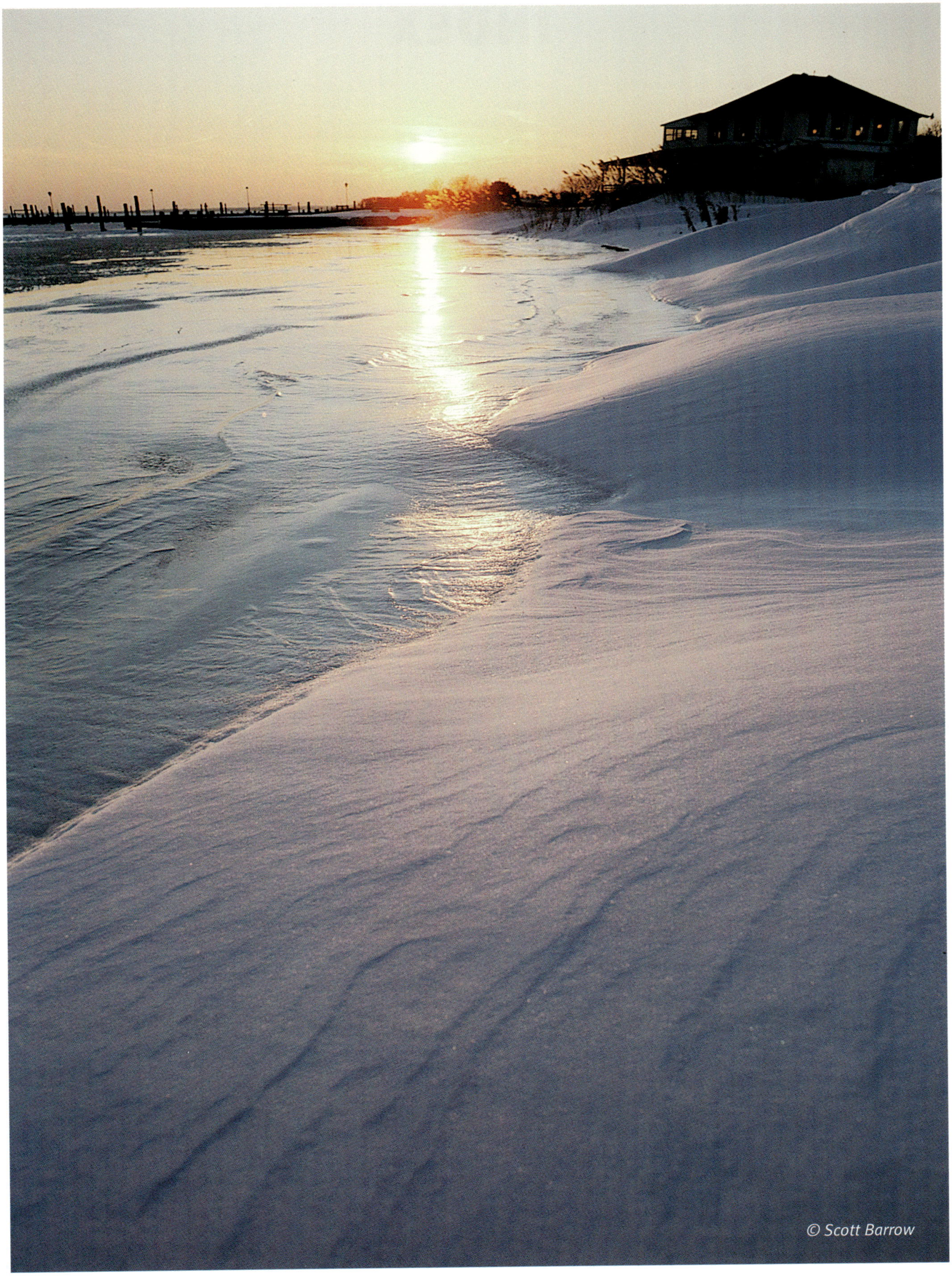
© Scott Barrow

INDEX

Abescon Lighthouse, 337
Academy Award, 350
Academy of Culinary Arts, 303
Accountants, 183, 184–85, 362–63
Accounting firms, 227
Acute-care hospitals, 113, 114
Advanced Biotechnology, center for, 159
Aerospace market, 262
Aetna, 243
Africa, 155, 240
African Americans, 348, 350
African American theater companies, 21
Agriculture, 48, 366
Agrylin, 156
AHP/Wyeth/Ayerst, 156
AIDS, 113, 158, 360, 361
Air compressors, 262, 263
Air conditioners, 261, 262, 348
Airlines, 86, 187
Air pollution policies, 89
Airport Circle, 348
Airports, 86–88, 89, 227
Airtemp, 264
Aldrin, Edwin "Buzz," 350
Alexander Hall, 305
"All-America" City, 38
AlliedSignal, 32, 262
Allopathic medical school, 113
All Star Cafe, 336
Allstate, 243
Alpharma, 154, 157
Alpine, 231
Alpine Lace Brands, 262
Alvin Ailey American Dance Theater, 24
Alzheimer's disease, 361
American Ballet Theatre, 21
American Cyanamid, 151, 265, 348
American Electronics Association, 61
American Home Products, 32, 152, 264. See also AHP/Wyeth/Ayerst
American Institute of Architects, 185
American Nurses Credentialing Center (ANCC), 114
American Public Transit Association, 85
American Red Cross, 158
American Revolution, 299, 351. See also Revolutionary War
American Standard Companies, 262, 264

American Water Works, 91
"America's Holly City," 48
Amper, Politziner and Mattia, 185
Ancora Psychiatric Hospital, 119
Anderson, C. Alfred, 348
Andover, 28
Angiography system, 113
Angioplasty, 120
Anheuser-Busch, 264
Animal health products, 264
Annadale, 158
Antibiotics, 156, 360
Anti-malarial drug, synthetic, 151
Anti-nausea, from chemotherapy, 156
Anzemet, 156
Apgar, Dr. Virginia, 349
Apgar Score, 349
Apollo 11, 350
Appalachian Trail, 22, 28, 29
Architects, 184, 185–86
Architecture and Urban Planning, 299
Armstrong, Major Edwin H., 348
Armstrong, Neil, 350
Arthroscopic procedures, 360
Arts, 38, 21, 36, 39, 52, 242, 305, 339, 340
Asbury Park, 12, 336
Asbury Park Press, 80
Asia, 5, 81, 365
Asian art, 22
Asparagus, 48
AT&T, 32, 62, 63–64, 66, 187, 229, 367
Atlantic and Pacific Tea Company (A&P), 189, 265
AtlantiCare, 122
Atlantic City, 21, 52, 55, 81, 114, 189, 267, 303, 335–37, 341, 351
Atlantic City Convention Center, 335
Atlantic City Expressway, 335
Atlantic City Monthly, 81
Atlantic coast, 15, 187
Atlantic Electric, 89
Atlantic flyway, 22
Atlantic Highlands, 339
Atlantic Ocean, 15, 57
Attorneys, 183–84
Audion tube, 348
Augusta, 341
Aurora, 115
Auto emissions, 6
Autoimmune disease, 158
Auto insurance, 82, 243–44
Automatic Data Processing (ADP), 188
Automotive products, 262

Autos, 88
Avapro, 156
Bacterial infections, 360
Ballantine House, 36
Ball bearings, 348
Ballooning, 33, 35, 341
Bally Fitness, 187
Bally's Park Place, 336
Baltusrol, 21
Banco Popular, 245
Band-Aid, 348
Banking, 241–42
 electronic, 65
Banking and Insurance, Department of, 241
Bank loans, 244–45
Bar code scanner, 66, 266
Bardeen, John, 349
Barnegat, 340
Barnegat Bay, 57
Barnegat Inlet, 15
Barnegat Light, 52, 339
Barnegat Light Township, 54
Baseball, 28, 230, 341, 348, 351
BASF Corporation, 354, 355
BASF North America, 232
Basking Ridge, 62, 63
Batets River, 15
Batoto Yetu African dance troupe, 8
Batsto, 23
Battle of Princeton, 11
Bauer Publishing Company, 81
Bayonne, 85, 231
Bayonne Hospital, 116
Beaches, 6, 15, 22, 25, 52, 337–39
Bears, 22, 33
Bed Bath and Beyond, 188
Bell Atlantic, 65
Bellcore, 367
Bell Laboratories, xi, 63, 64
Belmar, 53
Belmar Sand Castle Contest, 53
Beneficial Management Corporation, 186
Benjamin Moore & Co., 232, 264, 267
Bergen County, 5, 37, 40, 80, 85, 228, 351
Berrie, Russell, 116
Best Foods, 262
Bette Davis Lifetime Achievement Award, 350
Bicycling, 21, 25, 28, 33
Big Five accounting firms, 184–85
Biomedical informatics (also Bioinformatics), 306, 361
Biomedical technology, 65, 361, 366

Biotechnology Council of New Jersey, 155
Biotechnology industry, 43, 59, 63, 151, 155–59
Birds, 15, 22, 350
Birmingham, 157
Birth-control pills, 153
BISYS Group, 188
Black bears, 22
Black Experience, 82
Blackwood, 66
Blockbuster/Sony Music Entertainment Center, 48
Blood plasma, 151
Bloodless surgery, 114
Bloomberg Magazine, 81
Bloomberg News Service, 81
Bloomberg Personal, 81
Bloomfield College, 303
Blueberries, 348
Blue Cross and Blue Shield of New Jersey, 122
Boardwalk, Atlantic City, 52, 56, 335, 336–37
Boating, 22, 52
Bone cancer, 156
Bones, grafting of, 158
Boot camp, for juvenile offenders, 6
Bop, 350
Bordentown, 341
"Born in the U.S.A.," 13
Boston, 66, 88
Boston Red Sox, 42, 341
Bowman and Company, 185
Bowman's Accounting Report, 185
Bowne Theater, 305
Brain injuries, 117
Brain surgery, 114
Branch Brook, 37
Brattain, Walter, 349
Breast cancer, 114–15, 156, 360
Breen, Steve, 80
Bridges, 11, 87. See also George Washington Bridge
Bridgeton, 50
Bridgewater, 341
Bridgewater Commons Mall, 233
Bridgewater Courier News, 80
Brielle Antique Center, 340
Bristol-Myers Squibb Company, 152, 156, 367
British immigrants, 5
British Telecom, 63
Broadcast and entertainment technology, 63, 65
Broadcast media, 82–83
Brown bears, 15
Brownfields, 230, 231
Bubble Wrap, 349

Building materials, 261
Bulk cargo, 88
Burlington, 12, 48
Burlington County, 48
Burlington County Times, 81
Burn Center, 120–21
Burr, Aaron, 12, 351
Busch campus, 297, 301
Business communications systems, 64
Business Employment Incentive Program, 63
Businesses, minority-owned, 245
Business incubators, 367
Business investment, 244–45
Business loans, 244–45
Business News New Jersey, 81
Business services, 59
Bus services, 85, 88
Cable modems, 63
Cable television, 79, 81, 83
Cable Television Network of New Jersey, 83
Cablevision, 83
Cabling systems, 64
Caesars Atlantic City, 336, 337
Caldwell, 11
Caldwell College, 303
California, 66, 88
Campbell, Joseph, 262
Campbell Soup Company, 48, 260–62, 348
Cambridge University, 43
Camden, 21, 48, 50, 80, 82, 83, 261, 300, 341
 health care centers in, 113, 114
Camden and Amboy State, 350
Camden Courier Press, 80
Camden County College, 303
Canada, 189
Canals, 32
Cancer, treatment of, 156, 158, 360, 361
Cancer Institute of New Jersey, 113
Cape May, 15, 18, 25, 27, 52, 53, 337–38, 340
Cape May County, 3, 5
Cape May Music Festival, 52
Capital, state, 11, 42, 350
Capitol building, 42, 43
Cardiac clinic, 348
Carlin, George, 336
Carbon monoxide, 6
Cardiac clinic, 120
Cargo, 88–89, 364–65. See also Freight
Cargo containers, 88, 89, 364–65

372 NEW JERSEY: SETTING THE PACE FOR THE TWENTY-FIRST CENTURY

Caribbean Dance Party, 7
Caribbean grocery products, 262
Car rentals, 189
Carriage House, 340
Carriage Parade, 21
Carrier, Willis Haviland, 348
Carteret, Elizabeth, 230
Casino Career Institute, 303
Casino gambling market, 335
Casino-hotels, 56. *See also* Atlantic City
Casio, 64
Cataracts, 157
Catcher's mask, 348
Cathedral Healthcare System, 123
Catheterization suite, 116
Catholic colleges, 298
CAT scan, 115
Cendant Corporation, 183, 188
Center for Advanced Biotechnology and Medicine, 301
Center for the Analysis of Public Issues, 81–82
Center for Law and Justice, 306
Central nervous system research, 152
Central New Jersey, 42–47
Century 21, 188
Certified Public Accountants (CPAs), 362–63
Champale Brewery, 230
Charlotte, NC, 241
Charter schools, 302
Chase Manhattan, 241, 244
Chatham, 233
Chatsworth, 48, 49
Chavannes, Marc A., 349
Chemical Bank, 241, 244
Chemical industry, 354–355
Chemical manufacturing, 59, 156, 261, 262, 264, 265, 268
Chemotherapy, 156, 360
Cherry Hill, 48, 113, 233, 243, 265
Chester Village, 340
Chevron, 265
Chicago, 228
Children's Specialized Hospital, 117
China, 81
Chips Ahoy!, 262
Christians, 6
Christmas tree farm, 351
Chubb, Percy, 245
Chubb, Thomas Caldecott, 245
Chubb Computer Services, 63
Chubb Corporation, 66, 245
Ciccalese, Dr. Gerald, Sr., 119
Citibank, 228
City of Brotherly Love, 48

Clam State, 350
Clara Maass Medical Center, 119
Claridge, the, 336
Clark, 115
Classrooms, interactive video, 357
Clementon, 21
Cleveland, Grover, 11
Clinton Historical Museum Village, 33
Coastal marshes, 22
Coast-to-coast, first direct-dial telephone call, 349
College football, 298, 299, 351
College of New Jersey, The, 297, 298, 299, 303, 305
Colleges, 297–305, 358–59. *See also* Universities
Color TVs, 349
Colt, Samuel, 36, 348
Colts Neck, 52
Combinatorial chemistry, 361
Comcast, 83
Comcast Network Channel, 83
Commerce, State Department of, 61, 357
Commerce and Economic Development, Department of, 357
Commerce Bancorp, 243
Commerce National Insurance Services, 243
Commercial real estate market, 228–31
Commodores, 336
Communications satellite, 349
Community colleges, 303–05, 356–57, 358
Commuter rail system, 85–86
Comprehensive university, 302–03
Computer-aided design (CAD) systems, 297
Computer firms, 43
Computer Horizons, 66
Computers, 63, 64, 241, 366
Concept 2000, 189
Conectiv, 89
Congress, U.S., 184
Consolidated Edison, Inc., 89
Constitution, New Jersey, 350
Constitution, U.S., 11
Construction machinery, 262
Consumer electronics, 63, 64, 65
Consumer Health Network, 122
Continental Airlines, 86, 187
Continental Army, 42
Continental Congress, 300
Continuing education, 305
Cooper, James Fenimore, 12

Cooper Hospital and University Medical Center, 113
Coopers and Lybrand, 184
Corporate headquarters, 3, 59
Corporations, 32
Corrugated boxes, 265
Cosby, Bill, 52
County College Act of 1962, 256
Courier satellite, 349
Covered bridges, 87
CPAs, 184–85, 362–63
Craigmeur, 28
Cranberries, 18, 48, 49
Crane, Stephen, 350
Crane Pottery site, 230
Cranford, 228
Creeks, 15, 17, 22
Crime rate, 6
Crossroads Theatre Company, 21
Cruise ships, 88
Cuban immigrants, 5
CUC International, 188
Cumberland County, 5, 48, 267
Cunningham, John T., 27
Cytogen, 156
Cytoplasmic transfer, 123
Darrow, Charles, 267
Dartmouth, 301
David Sarnoff Research Center, 43
Declaration of Independence, 11, 299
Deep-water ports, 36. *See also* Ports
Defibrillator, 65, 349
DeForest, Lee, 348
Delaware and Raritan Canal, 42, 43
Delaware Bay, 15, 17
Delaware River, 11, 12, 15, 21, 25, 31, 42, 48–51, 187, 341
Delaware River Port Authority building, 185, 187
Delaware River Region, 341
Delaware Water Gap National Recreation Area, 28, 30, 341
Delmarva Power and Light, 89
Deloitte & Touche LLP, 184–85, 232
Deminski, Jeff, 82
Dempsey-Carpentier fight, 351
Dendrite International, 66
Denver, 266
Denville, 233
Depression, 360, 361
Diabetes, 360
Diabetic ulcers, 156
Diana Project, 349

Diesel-electric bus, 88
Digital camera, 65
Digital convergence, 63, 65
Digital signal processing software, 66
Digital Solutions, 188
Digital television receiver, 64
"Diner Capital of the World," 231
Dinosaurs, 300, 350
Dion, Celine, 336
Dirigibles, 351
Disabled adults and children, facility for, 117
Dissections, 115
Distance learning, 357
DNA, 159
Domestic cargo, 365
Dorrance, John, 261
Dow Jones, 81
Dow Jones Capital Markets and News Service, 81
Dow Jones Professional Investors Report, 81
Doyle, Bill, 82
Drew University, 298, 301, 305, 306
Driftwood, 23
Drills, 262, 265, 266
Drive-in movie theater, 348
Drugs, 6, 151, 156, 264, 348, 349, 360–61. *See also* Pharmaceuticals
Drug programs, 154
Drug Topics, 81
Dr. West's Miracle Tuft Toothbrush, 351
Dryden, John Fairfield, 242
Dugan Valva Contess, 187
Duke, Doris, 33
Dun & Bradstreet Corporation, 81
Du Pont, 265, 351
Duract, 156
Dutch immigrants, 5
Dylan, Bob, 36
Eagle Rock, 37
"Earth Smart Store," 189
East Coast ports, 365
Eastern Europe, 81
Eastern goldfinch, 350
East Hanover 151, 153
East Rutherford, 39, 81, 187, 340
Eastwind Airlines, 88
Easy Rider, 350
Economic Development Authority, 157
Economy, New Jersey, xi, 11, 59
Edgewater, 242
Edison, 65, 116, 185, 262, 266
Edison, Thomas, xi, 21, 37, 59, 61, 62, 64, 268, 348, 350, 351
Edison National Historic Site, 21, 340

Education, 5, 297–306, 363
Edwin B. Forsythe Wildlife Refuge, 337, 341
Einstein, Albert, xi, 299
Electric Dynamic Company, 348
Electric guitar, 348
Electric motors, 348
Electric utilities, 89–91
Electromagnetic telegraph, 66
Electronic Data Interchange (EDI), 365
Electronic media, 79, 82–83
Electronic microphone, 348
Electronics, 59, 261, 348
Electronics Design, 81
Electronic thieves, 363
Electron microscope, 348
Elizabeth, 41, 79, 189, 230, 350
Elizabeth Daily Journal, 79
Elizabeth-Port Authority Marine Terminal, 41
Elizabethtown Gas (NUI), 89, 91
Ellis Island, 36, 40, 351
Ellis Island Immigration Museum, 339
Elysian Fields, 351
E-mail, 64, 187
Emerson, 264
Emissions, auto, 6
Employment, 59, 61, 157, 261
Energy utilities, 89, 91
Engineering and Applied Science, 299
Engineering schools, 183
Englehard Corporation, 262
Englewood, 81
Englewood Cliffs, 228, 262
Englewood Hospital and Medical Center, 114, 116
English Channel tunnel, 263
Entertainment Publishing, 188
Entrepreneurs, course of study for, 306
Environmental protection, 6
Essential thromocythemia, 156
Essex Community College, 301–02
Essex County, 5, 37, 81
Essex County Courthouse, 229
Essex County Park Commission, 37
Essex Fox Hounds Race Meeting Association, 32
Ethnic festivals, 7, 8
Ethnic population, 5
Europe, 5, 151, 349
Ewing Township, 88
Exxon, 265, 367
Fairleigh Dickinson University, 305, 306

Fareston, 156
Far Hills, 32
Far Hills Race Meet, 21
Faxes, 64, 187
Fedders Corporation, 262, 264
Federal grants, 62
Feed additives, 157
Feedmill Plaza, 340
Femara, 156
Fencing, women's, 303
Fendell Housing Corporation, 231
Fenwick, Millicent, 184
Ferries, 41, 348
Festival of India, 8
Festival of the Sea, 52
Festivals, 7, 8, 33, 35, 52, 341
Fielding, Alfred W., 349
Fig Newtons, 262
Financial services, 241–45
Financing, mortgage, 233
First Data Corporation, 188
First Fidelity, 241
First for Women, 81
First Option Health Plan, 122
First Union Bank, 241
Fishing, 22, 52, 341
Fish vaccines, 157
Fitzhugh, Valerie, 303
Flanders, 267
Fleet Bank, 241
Flemington, 245
Florham-Madison campus, Fairleigh Dickinson University, 305
Florham Park, 228
Florida, 91
Florio, Jim, 82
Fluoroscope technology, 116
Fly fishing, 338
FM broadcast, first, 348
Food and Drug Administration, U.S., 153, 155, 156, 157
Food products, 261–62
Football, 21, 298, 299, 351
Footwear, 265
Ford mansion, 35
Forensic accountants, 362, 363
Forests, 15, 22
Forging supplier, 265
Forked River, 338
Forrestal Village, 45, 340
Forsythe, Dr. Albert E., 348
Fort Lee, 154, 157
Fort Monmouth, 64, 65, 348, 349
Fortune 500 companies, 3, 227, 229, 264
Foster Wheeler, 262
Foulke, W. Parker, 300, 350
Francois, Dontay, 117
Franklin, Benjamin, 11, 351
Franklin, William, 351

Franklin Lakes, 228
Freehold, 12
Freight, 36, 85. See also Cargo
French and Indian War, 341
French immigrants, 5
Frozen foods, 268, 348
Fruit orchards, 48
Funk, Casimir, 151, 348
Gale and Wentworth, LLC, 228
Gambling, 52, 56, 335, 336, 351
Gannett Company, 80
Garden State, xi, 3, 6, 11, 27, 48, 59, 63, 79, 83, 183, 242, 261, 350, 351, 355. See also New Jersey
  pharmaceutical industry in, 151, 153
  real estate in, 227, 231, 233
Garden State Matters, 82
Garden State Parkway, 42, 349
Gardner, John, 356
Garfunkle, Art, 336
Garibam, Donna, 119
Gateway National Park, 339
Gateway Region, 36–41, 339, 340
General Obligation rating, 233
Genes, 361
Genesis Direct, 244
Genetic engineering, 366
Genomics, 361
George Washington Bridge, 40, 268, 351
German immigrants, 5
Giants (NFL), 21
Giants Stadium, 22
GI Bill of Rights, 358
Gilbert, Cass, 229
Gladstone, 32
Glass, American, museum of, 339
Glass blowing, 303
Glassboro State College, 302
Glass producers, 267
Glen Rock, 6
Gloucester County, 48
Godiva Chocolates, 262
GOGO Worldwide Vacations, 189
Gold Coast, 36
Golden Island Shopping Center, 23
Golf courses, 21
Gordon stope drill, 265
Gore, Vice President Al, 230–31
Governor's Volunteer Award, 113
Goya Foods, 262, 263
GPU Energy, 89
Graf Zeppelin, 351
Grand Boulevard, 335

Grant, Ulysses S., 52
Graves, Michael, 185, 187
Graves Design Studio Store, 185
Great Atlantic and Pacific Tea Company (A and P), 189, 265
Great Depression, 151
Great Falls National Historic Site, 340
Great Falls of the Passaic River, 36, 228, 229, 26, 341, 348
Great Sergeant's Bridge, 87
Great Swamp, 32
Great Swamp National Wildlife Refuge, 35
Great Train Robbery, The, 351
Greenhouse facilities, 306
Greensboro, NC, 88
Greystone Park Psychiatric Hospital, 119
Griffin, Merv, 336
Griffith, D.W., 37
Grovers Mill, 80
Guitar, first solid-body electric, 348
Hackensack, 80, 114, 188, 242
Hackensack University Medical Center, 114, 115
Hacklebarney State Park, 33
Haddonfield, 300
Hadrosaurus, 300, 350
Hamilton, Alexander, 36, 261, 267, 348, 351
Hand tools, 265
Hard Rock Cafe, 336
Harlem, 8
Harness racing, 337
Harper's Weekly, 351
Harrah's Marina Hotel/Casino, 336, 351
Harrison, 15, 233
Hazardous substances, 268
Health care industry, 59, 113–23
HealthCare Institute of New Jersey, 151, 152–53, 156
Health law and policy, 306
Health maintenance organizations (HMOs), 121–23
Health sciences university, 298
Heart attack, 156
Heartbeat, regulation of, 65
Heart disease, treatment of, 360, 361
Heart transplants, 119–20
H-EASY 200, 233
Helicopter, 113
Heller Construction, 266–67
Hellman's, 262
Herbicides, 264
Heron sanctuary, 22
Hertz, 183, 189
Hess, 265

HFS, 188
Hidden Valley, 28
High-definition television (HDTV), 66, 82
Higher education, 5, 297–305, 356–59
Higher Education Act of 1965, 358
Higher Education Technology Infrastructure Act, 367
High Point, 27, 28
High Point Monument, 28
High Point State Park, 29, 341
High schools, 5
High technology, 60–68, 366–67
High throughput screening, 361
Highways, 22, 32, 42, 86, 227
Hiking, 25, 28, 341
Hillier, J. Robert, 186
Hillier Group, 186
Hilton, 336
Hindu, 6
HIP Health Plan of New Jersey, 121
Hip replacements, 114, 119
Hispanic grocery products, 262, 263
Hispanic Horizons, 82
Historic sites, 15
HIV, 349
Hoboken, 7, 12, 90, 229, 298, 348, 350, 351
Hoboken Ferry Terminal, 41
Hoboken Four, 350
Hockey, professional, 21, 339
Hoechst Celanese, 265
Hoechst Marion Roussel, 156
Hoffmann-LaRoche, 151, 152, 156, 349
Holland, Clifford M., 86, 348
Holland Tunnel, 11, 86, 348, 351
Holly trees, 48
Hollywood Golf Club, 336
Holmdel, 52
Home-improvement industry, 265
Homes, single-family, 231–33
Horseback riding, 28
Horse racing, 21, 39, 337
Hospital for Women and Children, 117, 118, 119
Hospitals, 113–123
Hot-air balloon festivals, 33, 35, 341
Household waste disposal, 6

Housing and Mortgage Finance Agency (HMFA), 233
Housing market, 231–33
Houston, Whitney, 12
Hubco, 241–42
Hudson, Henry, 37
Hudson and Manhattan Railroad, 86
Hudson-Bergen Light Rail System, 85
Hudson County, 5
Hudson River, 11, 15, 36, 37, 38, 88, 339
Humana Building, 185
Hunt, Richard Morris, 303
Hunterdon County, 32, 35, 87, 231, 341
Hydroelectric power, 90
Hydrofluoric acid, 262
Hypertension, 156
Hysterectomies, 114
IBM, 187, 228, 306
Ice boating, 28
Ice cream cone, 264
Ice fishing, 341
Ice skating, 28, 341
Image sensor, 65
Immigrants, 5
Income, per-capita, xi, 183
Income tax, 362
India, 375
Indian Arts Festival, 5
Indigent drug programs, 154
Industrial equipment, 262
Industrial sites, 6
Industrial Sites Recovery Act, 230
Industrial waste disposal, 6
Information age, 366
Infrastructure, 355
Ingersoll-Rand Company, 262, 263, 265, 266
IN Jersey, 83
Inner city, redevelopment of, 229–30
Inside PR magazine, 187
Insolvency, 363
Institute for Advanced Study, 299
Institute for Electrical and Electronics Engineers, 81
Insurance companies, 241, 242–44
Integrated circuits, 64
Interactive video classrooms, 357
Intercollegiate football game, first, 351
International Sports Summit, 351
International standard (ISO) container, 364
Internet, 63, 64, 83, 187, 306, 357
Internet TV, 64, 362, 363
Interstate 287, 42

Interstate Bank and Branching Act, 242
Interstate competition, 367
Intracoastal Waterway, 91
Investments, business, 244–45
Invirase, 349
IR camera, 64
Irish immigrants, 5
Ironbound, 5, 36
Iron making, 32
Iron ore, 23, 28
Island Beach State Park, 3, 17, 52, 57, 339
Italian immigrants, 5
Ivy League, 5, 43, 298
Jackhamer drills, 266
Jackson, 340
Jacobs, Walter L., 189
J and J Snack Foods, 262
Jarrett, Keith, 21
Jazz history, 306
Jenkinson's Aquarium, 24
Jersey Blue State, 350
Jersey Central Power and Light. See GPU
Jersey City, 11, 36, 38, 65, 114, 120, 228, 261, 339, 348, 351, 353
Jersey City Hospital, 348
Jersey City State College, 303
Jersey Devil, 49, 339
Jersey Journal, 79
Jersey Shore, 52–57, 80, 336, 337–39, 340
Jersey Shore Medical Center, 114
Jets (NFL), 21
Jet transport, 366
Jewish, 6
JFK Medical Center, 116, 117, 118
J. H. Cohn LLP, 185
Jobs, high-tech, 61
Jockey Hollow, 12. 15, 32, 35
Johnson, Robert W., 348
Johnson & Johnson, 43, 152, 156, 367
Johnson Rehabilitation Institute, 117
Johnstone, James Edward, 348
Joint Replacement Institute, 119
Juvenile offenders, 6
Kean University, 303
Kennedy family, 228
Kennedy Memorial Hospital and University Medical Center, 113
Kentucky, 185
Kessler Institute for Rehabilitation, 117
Kidney transplants, 117, 119

King Hassan II of Morocco, 228
Kittatinny Mountains, 28
Knee replacements, 119
Knoll Pharmaceutical, 156
Knorr soups and sauces, 262
Knowles, C. Harry, 66
Kohr Brothers, 56
Korea Commercial Bank, 242
KPMG Peat Marwick LLP, 184, 185
Kramer vs Kramer, 350
Labor, Department of, 357
Labor force, 59
Lafayette Mills Antique Center, 340
Lafferty, James, Jr., 335
Lake Hopatcong, 28
Lakehurst, 351
Lake Passaic, 32
Lakes, 15, 32, 338
Lambertville, 42, 340
Langston Corporation, 265
Laparoscopic procedures, 360
Laser technology, 66, 116
Las Vegas, 335
Latin America, 155
Latrobe, Benjamin, 303
Law, Harold B., 349
Law firms, 183–84, 227
Lawyers, 183–84
Lazor, Edward J., 184
League of Nations, 350
Leaves of Grass, 48
Lenni Lenape, 5, 90
Leyner, John George, 266
Liberty Corner, 262
Liberty Science Center, 36, 339
Liberty State Park, 7, 36, 339, 340
Liberty Travel, 188
Liberty Village, 340
Librium, 152
Light bulb, xi, 61, 268
Lighthouse, 15, 52, 337, 339
Light rail services, 85
Linden, 117
Liquid crystal display (LED) technology, 82
Little Falls, 188
Liver lesions, imaging of, 156
Liver resections, 114
Liver transplants, 119, 349
Livingston, 117, 119, 123
Loans, business, 244–45
Locomotive, 302
London, 364
London Symphony Orchestra, 21
Long Beach, CA, 88
Long Beach Island, 54, 338, 339
Long Branch, 52, 303
Los Angeles, 88, 348, 365

Lowenstein, Sandler, Kohl, Fisher and Boylan, P.A., 183
Lucent Technologies, 32, 63–64, 367
Lucy the Elephant, 335
Luxury yacht makers, 267
Maass, Clara Louise, 116
Ma Bell, 63. See also AT&T
Mack-Cali Realty, 228
Made in New Jersey Day, 264, 267
Madison, 264, 298
Magazines, 81–82
Magic of Alexandria Balloon Festival, 341
Magnet Hospital Recognition Status for Excellence in Nursing Service, 113, 114, 115
Magnetic Resonance Imaging (MRI), 154
Maher Terminals, 89
Mahwah, 241
Main-Bergen line, 86
Malls, shopping, 45, 189, 233, 340
Managed care, 121–23
Manasquan, 340
Manasquan River, 52, 91
Manhattan, 36, 38, 40, 52, 85, 86, 90, 233, 348
Manufacturing, 59, 261–68
Maplewood, 233, 262
Margate, 335
Marchiony, Italo, 264
Marino, William J., 122
Marketing and public relations firms, 186–87
Marriage of Figaro, 339
Marsalis, Wynton, 36
Marsh egrets, 341
Martians, 80
Mason, Jackie, 336
Maxwell House coffee plant, 229
Maxson, William, 268, 349
Mazola, 262
McCarter, Thomas, 91
McCarter and English, 184, 187
McCarter Theater, 21
McWilliams Forge Company, 265
Meadowlands Racetrack, 39, 337
Meadowlands Sports Complex, 21, 22, 37, 230, 340, 351
Mectizan, 153, 155
Medarex, 158
Medical Center of Ocean County, 114
Medical device companies, 151–54
Medical Economics, 81
Medical Economics Magazine, 81

Medical technology, 361
"Medicine Chest of the World," xi, 151, 361
Medicines, 261
Mediterranean, 365
Megan's Law, 6
Meistrich, Larry, 233
Menjou, Adolphe, 348
Menlo Park, 61, 348
Mercer County, 42, 88, 228, 232, 339
Mercer County Waterfront Park, 42, 227, 230
Merck & Co., Inc., 32, 151, 152, 155, 159, 367
Merck-Medco, 228
Mercury Theater, 80
Meridia, 156
MetLife, 243
Metromedia Company, 81
Michael Graves, Architect, 185
Michigan, 89
Microelectronic chip, 366
Microscope, electron, 348
Middlesex County, 8, 42, 88, 227, 232
Midtown Direct line, 85
Migrating birds, 22
Milford, 12
Millburn, 21
Millville, 48, 339
Minority enrollment, 297
Minority-owned businesses, 245
Miss America Pageant, 52, 351
Mississippi River, 89, 341
Molecular Medicine, center for, 159
"Money Guide: Best College Buys," 298
Money magazine, 298
Monmouth, 11, 303. See also Fort Monmouth
Monmouth County, 80, 88, 231, 338
Monopoly, 267
Monorail trains, 86–87
Montclair, 82, 341
Montclair State Teacher's College, 351
Montclair State University, 305
Montgomery, 81
Montvale, 184, 265
Moody's Investors Service, 81
Moon, 349, 350
Moorestown, 65
Moorland Farms, 32
Morey's Pier, 335
Morris and Essex line, 85
Morris Canal, 187
Morris County, 7, 12, 28, 32, 227, 231
Morristown, 11, 32, 35, 66, 114, 184, 227, 351

Morristown Daily Record, 80
Morristown Memorial Hospital, 117
Morristown National Historical Park, 12, 33
Morse, Samuel F.B., 59, 66, 348
Mortgage financing, 233
"Most Livable City," 38
Motion picture camera, xi
Motion picture capital, 351
Mountain bikers, 25
Mountain climbing, 22
Mountain Creek, 28
Mountainside, 117
Mount Rushmore, 262, 266
Mount Sinai School of Medicine, 114
Movie soundstage, 233
Mozambique, National Song and Dance Company of, 39
Mozart, 339
Multimedia products, 64
Multimedia workstations, 357
Murray Hill, 63, 81
Musculoskeletal Transplant Foundation, 158
Musgrave, G.W., 348
Muslim, 6
Mutual Benefit Life, 244
MWW Groups, 187
Myers, George H., Ph.D, 121
Nabisco Holdings Corporation, 32, 262
Nassau Hall, 299, 300
Nast, Thomas, 351
National Association of Industrial and Office Properties, New Jersey Chapter of, 227
National Basketball Association, 21
National Brownfields Showcase communities, 231
National Cancer Institute, 113
National Football League, 21
National Historic Park, first, 351
National Hockey League, 21
National Honor Award, 185
National Research Corporation, 115
National Reserve, 49
National Science Foundation, 61
National Science Foundation Industry/University Cooperative Research Center, 62
Native American population, 5
Natural gas, 89, 91

NatWest, 241
Navesink River, 52
NCAA varsity sports, 303
  See also Collegiate football
Neonatal intensive care unit, 119
Neptune, 12, 114
Networking systems, 64
Newark, 8, 12, 18, 21, 36, 38, 59, 184, 229, 242, 243, 245, 261, 298, 300, 302, 306, 340, 341
  shipping and, 88, 89
  health care in, 113, 114
Newark Banking and Insurance Company, 243
Newark Bay, 41
Newark Beth-Israel Medical Center, 119, 121, 349
Newark Daily Advertiser, 81
Newark-Elizabeth Rail Link, 87
Newark Heart Institute, 120
Newark International Airport, 36, 86, 89
Newark Museum, 21, 22, 36, 185, 340
Newark Star-Ledger, 79
Newark subway system, 87
New Brunswick, 21, 42, 300, 351
  health care centers in, 113, 114, 117
  pharmaceutical industry in, 151, 153
New-home market, 231
Newhouse Publications, 79
New Jersey, ix, 355
  arts and, 39, 52
  banking and, 241–42
  central region of, 42–47
  community colleges in, 303–05, 356
  economy of, 11, 59
  first and innovations in, 348–49
  Gateway Region of, 36–41
  health care in, 113–123, 361
  higher education in, 297–306
  historical highlights of, 350–51
  insurance industry and, 241–44
  manufacturing in, 261–68
  media in, 79–83
  northwest region of, 28–31
  pharmaceutical industry and, 151–54
  population of, 5, 11, 18, 350
  professional services in, 183–89
  real estate in, 227–33
  recreation in, 22, 25, 28, 341
  size of, 15, 27, 350

New Jersey *(continued)*
  spectator sports in, 21, 22, 28, 37, 230, 337, 339, 351
  technology and, 60–68, 367
  telecommunications and, 60–67
  transportation in, 38, 59, 85–89, 90, 91
  utilities in, 85, 89–91
  western counties of, 32–35
New Jersey Agricultural Experiment Station, 348
New Jersey Ballet, 52
New Jersey Bank, 241
New Jersey Board of Public Utilities, 89
New Jersey Business & Industry Association, 267
New Jersey Cable Industry, 83
New Jersey Cardinals, 28
New Jersey Center for Multimedia Research, 62
New Jersey Coastal Heritage Trail, 22
New Jersey Commission on Science and Technology, 61–63, 366
New Jersey Devils, 21
New Jersey Economic Development Authority, 63
New Jersey Ethnic Festival, 7
New Jersey Institute of Technology (NJIT), 61, 62, 159, 183, 184, 297, 298, 301, 305
New Jersey Law Journal, 183
New Jersey Legislature, 243
New Jersey Medical School Office Center, 113
New Jersey Monthly, 81
New Jersey Natural Gas, 91
New Jersey Nets, 21
New Jersey Network (NJN), 82
New Jersey Neuroscience Institute, 117, 118
New Jersey Normal School, 298
New Jersey 105.1, 79, 82
New Jersey Online, 83
New Jersey Performing Arts Center, 8, 21, 36, 39, 242, 340
New Jersey Seafood Festival, 53
New Jersey Shakespeare Festival, 305
New Jersey Society of Architects, 185
New Jersey Sports and Exposition Authority, 230
New Jersey State Aquarium, 21, 48, 50, 341, 351
New Jersey (NJ) Transit, 85–86, 87, 91

New Jersey Transit Passenger Rail System, 85
New Jersey Turnpike, 85, 266, 351
Newspaper Association of America, 83
Newspapers, 79–81
Newton, 187
New Wave Mall, 45
New York, 11, 36, 41, 42, 48, 79, 85, 86, 88, 114, 227, 229, 351, 364, 365
New York Bay, 15, 38, 41
New York Harbor, 36, 52, 364
New York Knickerbockers, 351
New York Medical College, 119
New York Nine, 351
New York Times, 79, 305
Nicholson, Jack, 12, 350
Nobel Prize, 151
Normiflow, 156
North Bergen, 245
North Brunswick, 62, 159
Northeast Corridor line, 86, 87
North New Jersey Newspapers Company, 81
Northwest New Jersey, 28–31
Norway, 154
Notebook PCs, 64
Novartis Pharmaceuticals Corporation, 152, 156, 367
Novo Nordisk, 156
Nuclear-powered pacemaker, 349
Nursing, 113, 114, 115
Nycomed Amersham Imaging, 154, 156
Nylon fibers, 262
Nylon toothbrush, 351
Obesity, 156, 360
Ocean Beach, 54
Ocean City, 52, 337
Ocean County, 52, 80, 88, 231, 338
Ocean Grove, 54
Ocean One Mall, 189
Ocean One Pier, 336–37
Oceanville, 337
Office space, 59
Ohl, Russell, 63
Oil refining, 156, 262
Oktoberfest, 7
"Old Barney," 52
Old Barracks Museum, 42, 45, 341
Old Gun Mill, 36
"Ol' Blue Eyes," 350
"Ol' Man River," 350
Omnicef, 156
Onassis, 228
One Flew Over the Cuckoo's Nest, 350

On-line banking, 241
"Open for Business," 227
Open-heart surgery, 120
Opera Festival of New Jersey, 339
Optical waveguide, 66
Orange and Rockland Utilities, 89
Oregon, 185
Oreo, 262
Organon, 157
Organ transplants, 360
Orlando, 88
Orthopedic procedures, 119
Ortho Pharmaceuticals, 153
Ospreys, 15
Osteotech, 158
Outpatient surgery, 116
Outsourcing services, 187–88
Outstanding Achievement Award, 85
Overlook Hospital, 116
Pacemaker, 65, 121, 349
Packaging, 264, 267
Paging system, 64, 81
Pain management, 116, 156
Palisades Interstate Park, 37, 339
Panama, 365
Panama Canal, 364, 365
Panasonic, 64
Paper Mill Playhouse, 21
Parks, 15, 21, 22
Parsippany, 188, 232, 262
Parsonnet, Victor, M.D., 121
Pascack Valley Hospital, 119
Pascack Valley line, 86
Passaic County, 5, 28, 80
Passaic County Community College, 303
Passaic Falls, 90
Passaic River, 36, 228
Paterson, 13, 36, 90, 114, 228, 229, 261, 267, 340, 348
PATH (Port Authority Trans-Hudson Corporation) system, 86, 90
Pathmark Stores, 189
Pathway of the Revolution, 350
Patterson Army Hospital, 65, 349
Paul, Les, 348
Peapack, 25
Pediatric AIDS, 113
Pediatric medicine, 117
Pelican Island, 23
Penicillin, 151
Penn, William, 48
Penton Publishers, 81
Per capita income, xi, 183
Perlman, Itzhak, 36
Peters, Tom, 357
Petrochemical center, 265
Petroleum processing, 265
Petroleum products, 88

Pharmaceutical companies, xi, 59, 151–54
Pharmaceuticals, 151–54, 360–61
Pharmacopeia, 158
Philadelphia, 11, 42, 48, 79, 85, 86, 227, 232
Philadelphia Inquirer, 79
Phones, 64
Phonograph, xi, 61, 62, 348
Picante sauce, 261
Pine Barrens, xi, 15, 23, 24, 48–50, 341
Pinelands, 338
Pine Valley, 21
Piscataway, 81, 113, 262
Pitcher, Molly, 351
Pittstown, 341
Pitney, Hardin, Kipp and Szuch, 184
Plastic packaging, 264, 268, 349
Plastics, 156
Planet Hollywood, 336
Plavix, 156
PNC Bank, 241
PNC Bank Arts Center, 52
Pneumonia, 360
Point Pleasant, 24, 114, 240
Point Pleasant Antique Emporium, 340
Point Pleasant Beach, 7, 52, 339
Polio vaccine, 360
Polish immigrants, 5
Polo, 32
Ponds, 15
Popcorn Park Zoo, 338
Pope Paul II, 22
Popular Electronics, 66
Population, 5, 11, 18, 350
Port Authority of New York and New Jersey, 86, 88
Port Elizabeth, 85, 88
Portland Building, 185
Port Newark, 88
Port of New York and New Jersey, 85, 88–89
Ports, 36, 41, 85, 88–89, 227, 364–65
Portugal, 8
Portugal Day, 5
Portuguese immigrants, 5
Posicor, 156
Powhatan tribe, 5
Power plants, 262
Power supply systems, 64
Prandin, 156
Preferred provider organizations (PPOs), 113, 121, 122
Pregnancies, high-risk, 117, 119
Prentice-Hall, 228
Prescription drugs, 264
Press, Asbury Park, 80
Press, Atlantic City, 81
Prestige Bank, 245

Price, Michael, 244
PricewaterhouseCoopers, 184
Princeton, 11, 21, 45, 64, 66, 158, 185, 186, 241, 340
Princeton, Battle of, 11
Princeton Battlefield State Park, 42
Princeton Packet, 81
Princeton Softech, 66
Princeton University, 5, 11, 42, 43, 45, 46, 62, 184, 185, 298–99, 303, 305, 306, 350, 351
Printed circuits, 349
Print media, 79–82
Professional services, 183–89
Promo magazine, 187
Prosperity New Jersey, 367
Pro sports teams, 21, 37
Prostate cancer, 360
Prudential Business Campus, 232
Prudential Insurance Company of America, 66, 242–43
Psychiatric facilities, 119
Public relations firms, 186–87
Public research university sector, 367
Public Service Coordinated Transport, 88
Public Service Corporation, 91
Public Service Electric & Gas Company (PSE&G), 89
Public Service Enterprise Group, 91
Public television network, 82
Publishing. *See* Magazines, Newspapers
Pulitzer Prize, 80, 350
Purple violet, 350
Pusan, Korea, 364
Quadremet, 156
Quality Leader Award, 115
Queen Anne cottages, 54
Queens College, 42, 300
Quick Chek New Jersey Festival of Ballooning, 33, 35, 341
Quick-frozen foods, 348
Radar, weather, 349
Radio, 79, 81
Radio broadcasting, 348
Railroads, xi, 32
Rail services, 85, 86, 90, 227, 364–65
Ralston General Store, 7
Ramada, 188
Ramapo Mountains, 28
Ramapo Ridge Psychiatric Hospital, 119
RAM Mobile Data, 64
Ramsey, 189
Raritan, 233
Raritan River, 42, 46, 338

RCA, 65, 83
RCA Laboratories, 348, 349
Readington, 33, 341
Real estate, 227–33
Real Estate Investment Trusts (REITs), 227, 228
Record, Hackensack, 80
Recreation, 15, 22, 25, 28, 341
Red Bank, 114, 340
Red Devil, 265
Regranex, 156
Rehabilitation, 116, 117
Rescued from an Eagle's Nest, 37
Research centers, 367
Respiratory Syncytial Virus, 117
Retail services, 45, 189
Revolutionary War, 11, 12, 23, 28, 32, 34, 350, 351
Revolver, 36
Richard Stockton College, 303
Ridgefield, 85
Riker, Danzig, Scherer, Hyland and Perretti, 184
Ringwood State Park, 31
Ripleys Believe It Or Not!, 336
Ritz, 262
River blindness, 155
Riverfront Plaza, 59
Rivers, 15. *See also* Delaware River, Hudson River
Riverview Medical Center, 114
Roadstown, 49
Roberts Pharmaceutical, 156
Robert Wood Johnson University Hospital, 113, 114, 117, 123
Robeson, Paul, 350
Robinson, Dr. William, 115
Rochester, NY, 88
"The Rock," 242
Rockaway Township, 28, 265
Rock drills, 262
Rockefeller, 228
Roseland, 184, 185, 188
Rothstein, Kass and Company, 185
Rotterdam, 364
Round Valley State Park, 33
Rouse Company, 233
Route 1, 42, 232
Rowan, Henry, 302
Rowan University, 302
Rumson, 339
Rumson River, 52
Rutgers, Colonel Henry, 300
Rutgers School of Criminal Justice, 306
Rutgers School of Law, 306

Rutgers, The State University of New Jersey, 42–43, 46, 151, 159, 297–98, 299, 300–01, 348, 349, 350, 351
Saddle Brook, 228, 264
Safe-deposit boxes, 241
Saint Ann's Italian Festival, 7
Saint Barnabas Health Care System, 123
Saint Barnabas Medical Center, 117, 119
Saint Michael's Medical Center, 119, 349
St. Peter's University Hospital & Health System, 114, 117, 118, 119
Salem Community College, 303, 351
Salem County, 5
Sales tax, 22
Sandoz Pharmaceuticals, 153
Sands, 336
Sandy Hook, 15
Sandy Hook Lighthouse, 52, 337, 339
Sandy Hook National Seashore, 52
Santa Claus, 351
Sapient Corporation, 65
Sarnoff Corporation, 64–65, 66, 82, 367
Satellite dishes, 79
Satellites, 349
SAT scores, 297
Savvy Living, 81
Saw Mill Pond, 29
Schatz, Albert, 349
Scherling-Plough, 152, 156, 367
SCORE, 349
Seabrook, Charles F., 348
Seabrook Farms, 348
Seabury, George, 348
Sea Girt, 339
Sea-Land Corporation, 349
Sealed Air Corporation, 264
Seaside Heights, 56, 57
Secaucus, 82, 244
Secaucus Shopping Outlet Center, 340
Secaucus Transfer station, 85–85
Securities and Exchange Commission, 362
Security Capital Industrial Trust, 266
Semiconductor, 61, 64
Sensar, Inc., 65
Sensors Unlimited, Inc., 64
Sergeantsville, 87
Serin Physics building, 297
Seton Hall University, 298, 305, 306
Sewage treatment, 6
Shad Festival, 42
Shaeffer Collection, 36
Shipping, 88–89, 364–65

Shockley, William, 349
Shooting Gallery, 233
Shoppers Advantage, 188
Shopping, 22, 45, 189, 233, 340
"ShopRite University" training program, 189
Showboat, 336
Showboat, 350
Shrewsbury River, 52
Signal Corps Laboratories, 349
Sikh temple, 6
Silicon, 63
Silicon Valley of the East, 65–66
Silk-making capital, 36, 261
Sills, Cummis, Zuckerman, Radin, Tischman Epstein and Gross, 184
Sinatra, Frank, 12, 350
Single-family homes, 231–33
Six Flags Great Adventure Theme Park and Safari, 340
Skiing, 22, 28, 340–41
Skippy peanut butter, 262
Skylands, 28, 29, 340, 341
Skylands Botanical Gardens, 31
Skylands Park, 28
Slack, 81
Small Business Administration (SBA), 244, 245
SnackWells, 262
Snowboarders, 28
Snowmobiling, 341
Soaps and cleaners manufacturers, 156, 261
Soccer, 21
Software services, 63, 64, 65, 66
Somerset, 7, 25, 88, 186, 233
Somerset County, 21, 32, 231, 341
Somerville, 33
Sonograms, 119
Sony Electronics, 64, 65
Sophie's Choice, 350
Sordoni Skanska, 229
Soups, 261–62, 348
South African Stope Drill Contest, 265
South Dakota, 266
South Jersey Gas, 91
South Mountain, 37
South Orange, 298
South Plainfield, 188, 265
Spanish-language newscasts, 82–83
Spectroscopy, tissue, 361
Spinal meningitis, 360
Sports medicine, 119
Springfield, 21
Springsteen, Bruce, 12, 13
Squibb, 151, 367

Squibb, Edward Robinson, 151
Stagecoach line, 11
Standard and Poors, 233
Stanley Cup, 339
Star-Class Regatta, 28
Star-Ledger, Newark, 79
State bird, 350
State capital, 350
State colleges, 297, 302–3
State flower, 350
State house, 46
State motto, 350
State nicknames, 350
State parks, 22
State Supreme Court, chief justice of, 242
Statue of Liberty, 36, 89, 339
Steamboats, xi
Steam-generating equipment, 262
Stern, Isaac, 21
Sternbach, Dr. Leo H., 152, 349
Stevens, John, 302
Stevens Institute of Technology, 298, 302
Stockton, 303
Stone Harbor, 22
Strait of Gibraltar, 365
Streep, Meryl, 350
"Streets of Philadelphia," 13
Streptomycin, 151, 349
Strokes, 360, 361
Submarines, xi
Subsidized public tuition, 359
Suez Canal, 365
Suffrage, for women, 185, 350
Sulfa drugs, 151, 348
Sulfathiazole, 151
Summit, 116, 243, 244, 350
Summit Bank, 241
Superfund, federal, 6
Supermarket chains, 189
Surgery, 114, 115, 116,117, 119, 120, 349, 360
Sussex County, 3, 5, 28, 29, 341
Switching systems, 64
Sybron Chemicals, 157–58
Syphilis, 360
Taj Mahal, 56, 336
Tall Pines Golf Club, 351
T'ang Dynasty, 22
Tavist-1 antihistamine, 153
Taxes, 362
Taylor, James, 52
Technology, 359, 361, 366–67
Technology Centre of New Jersey, 62–63, 159
"Technology Fast 500," 63
Technology transfer programs, 367

INDEX 377

Telecommunications, 59, 61, 63–65, 81, 366
Telecommunications, Inc., 63
Telegraph, xi, 66, 348
Telemundo, 82–83
Telephone, 63, 64, 349
Television, 43, 63, 65, 79, 82, 349
Television news coverage, 79
Tellium, Inc., 65
Telstar I, 349
Teslascan, 156
Teterboro, 82
Teterboro Airport, 88
Therapy, counseling and treatment facilities, long-term, 116
Thomas Edison State College, 305
Thomas' English muffins, 262
Thomas Paine home, 341
Thoroughbred racing, 337
Tibetan art, 21, 36
Tiffany glass, 339
Time magazine, 114
"*Time* Magazine's 100 Most Important People of the 20th Century," 350
Times, Trenton, 79
Tin, 90
Tingley Rubber Corporation
Tiros-1 satellite, 349
Tissue glue, 361
Tissue spectroscopy, 361
Titusville, 21, 341
Toll collection machine, automatic, 349
Tomatoes, 48
Toms River, 117, 339
Totowa, 90
Tourism, 52, 335
Tour of Somerville, 21
Toys "R" Us, 183, 189
Tranquilizers, 152
Transcontinental flight, 348
Transistor, xi, 61, 63, 349, 366
Transmission systems, 64
Transplant anti-rejection, 156
Transplants, organ, 117, 119–20, 349, 360
Transponders, 365
Transportation industry, 38, 85–89
Trauma system, 113–14
Traumatic Brain Injury Treatment and Cognitive Rehabilitation facility, 117
Travel and tourism industry, 335
Tremayne, William H., 152
Trenton, 11, 42, 43, 45, 46, 79, 82, 86, 88, 114, 230, 341, 350, 351
Trenton Bridge, 45

Trentonian, 81
Trenton-Mercer Airport, 88
Trenton Psychiatric Hospital, 119
Trenton State College, 297
Trenton Thunder, 42, 227, 230, 341
Tropicana, 336
Trout streams, 15
Truckers, 365
Trumbull, J., 11
Trump, Donald, 336
Trump Marina, 336
Trump Plaza, 336
Tuberculosis, 349
Tubing, 28
Tuition, subsidized public, 359
Turf grass, 348
Turkeys, wild, 15
TV dinners, 268, 349
Type 2 diabetes, 156
Ulcers, 156, 361
Ultrasound, 120, 154, 361
UMDNJ School of Osteopathic Medicine Primary and Specialty Care Centers, 113
UMDNJ University Behavioral Health Care, corporate offices of, 113
UMDNJ University Health Plans, 122
UMDNJ University Hospital, 113, 349
Underwater birth, 119
Union, 189, 265, 303
Union Camp Corporation, 268
Union County, 5, 81, 115
United Healthcare of New Jersey, 121–22
United Nations, 350
United Parcel Service (UPS), 188
United States Congress, 184
United States Custom House, 229
United States Equestrian Team, 32
United States Golf Association, 32
United Water Resources, 91
Universities, 297–306, 367. *See also* Princeton University, Rutgers, University of Medicine and Dentistry of New Jersey (UMDNJ).
University Heights, 36, 302
University Heights Science Park, 302
University of Medicine & Dentistry of New Jersey (UMDNJ), 113, 159, 298, 301–02, 351
Upper Saddle River, 231–32

Urban Home Ownership Recovery Program, 233
U.S. Army Electronics Command (ECOM), 65, 349
U.S. Constitution, 11
U.S. Food and Drug Administration, 153, 155, 156, 157, 361
U.S. News and World Report, 115, 298
U.S. Open, 21
U.S.S. Savannah, 349
U.S. Small Business Administration (SBA), 244, 245
U.S. Supreme Court, 40, 351
Utility industry, 85, 89–91
Vaccines, 360
Vacuum-tube computer, first, 349
Vail, Alfred, 66
Valium, 152, 349
Valley National Bank, 245
Vanderbilt, 228
Vaughan, Sarah, 350
Vegetable juice, 261
Vein thrombosis, 156
Venture capital, 244
Venturi, Robert, 303
Vernon, 28
Victorian homes, 18, 53
Video conferencing, 64
Video Audio Integration, 64
Viewpoint, 82
Vince Lombardi Park-and-Ride lot, 85
Vitamins, 151, 348
"Voice of the Garden State," 82
Voice processing systems, 64
Von Neumann, John, 349
Voorhees, 185
Vornado Realty Trust, 228
Voxware, 66
Wading River, xi
Wakefern Food Corporation, 189
Waksman, Selman, 151 349
Waksman Institute, 159
Walkie-talkie, 348
Wall Street Journal, 81
Walt Whitman Bridge, 351
Walt Whitman house, 21
Warehouses, 266–67
Warner-Lambert, 32, 156
War Memorial, 340
War of Independence, 11. *See also* Revolutionary War
War of the Worlds, The, 80
Warrall Community Newspapers, 81
Warren, 245
Warren County, 5, 341
Washington, D.C., 189

Washington, George, 11, 21, 28, 32, 35, 42, 351
Washington, Martha, 35
Washington Crossing State Park, 42, 43, 341
Washington State, 61
Washington Township, 113
Waterfowl, 22
Waterfront Park stadium, 42, 227, 230
Water supply, 6
Water utilities, 91
Waterloo Village, 21
Wayne, 245, 268, 303
Weather balloon, 348
Weather radar, 349
Weehawken, 36
Weequahic Park, 37
Welles, Orson, 80
Wells, H.G., 80
Westampton, 5
West Coast, shipping to, 265
Western counties, 32–35
Wetlands Institute, 22
West Orange, 157, 268, 340
Whalen, Jimmy, 79
Whale-watching, 338
Wharton, Joseph, 23
Wharton State Forest, xi
Wheaton Village, 21, 339
Wheeler Corporation, 262
White, Dr. Thomas J., 120, 348
White, Elizabeth Coleman, 348
Whitman, Governor Christie, 22, 63, 227, 243, 264, 357
Whitman, Walt, 48
Wholesale trade, 59
Wickecheoke Creek, 87
Wick House, 12, 15
Wife Beware, 348
Wild blueberries, 348
Wildlife preserve, 32
Wildlife restoration and management programs, 15
Wild turkeys, 15
Wildwood, 52, 335, 337
Wildwood Crest, 25
William Paterson, 303
Williams, William Carlos, 350
Wilmington, Delaware, 89
Wilson, Woodrow, 11, 52, 299, 350
Wind surfing, 338
Wine, 351
Wireless communications, 63, 64
Witherspoon, John, 299
Withum, Smith and Brown, 185
WJZ, 348
WKXW-FM, 82
Women's fencing, 303
Women's studies, 306

Women's World, 81
Woodbridge, 64, 189
Woodcliff Lake, 262
Woodrow Wilson School of Public International Affairs, 299
Woolworth Building, 229
Workers compensation, 244
Workforce, education of, 357
"Workshop of the Nation," 59, 261
Workstations, multimedia, 357
World Bank, 155
World Festival, 8
World Health Organization, 155
World Series, 348
World War II, 151
Worldwide Reservations Center, Hertz's, 189
World Wide Web, 61, 63, 83, 187. *See also* Internet
W.R. Grace, 264
WWOR TV Channel 9, 82
Wyeth-Ayerst Laboratories, 159
X rays, 113, 154
Yahoo! Internet Life, 61, 301
Yellow fever, 116
Yellow Pages, 65
Yemen, 155
Young People's Theater, 303
Zenapax, 156
Zworykin, Vladimir Kosma, 348